Logic

Studies in Continental Thought

Martin Heidegger

Logic
The Question of Truth

Translated by
Thomas Sheehan

Indiana University Press
Bloomington and Indianapolis

This book is a publication of

Indiana University Press
Office of Scholarly Publishing
Herman B Wells Library 350
1320 East 10th Street
Bloomington, Indiana 47405 USA

iupress.indiana.edu

First paprback edition 2016
Published in German as Martin Heidegger *Gesamtausgabe* 21: *Logik:
Die Frage nach der Wahrheit (WS 1925–26)*, ed. Walter Biemel
© 1976 German edition by Vittorio Klostermann, Frankfurt am Main
Second edition © 1995 by Vittorio Klostermann, Frankfurt am Main
English translation © 2010 by Indiana University Press

The paper used in this publication meets the minimum requirements of
the American National Standard for Information Sciences—Permanence
of Paper for Printed Library Materials, ANSI Z39.48-1992.

Manufactured in the United States of America

The Library of Congress has cataloged the original edition as follows:

Heidegger, Martin, 1889–1976.
[Logik. English]
Logic : the question of truth / Martin Heidegger ;
translated by Thomas Sheehan.
p. cm. — (Studies in Continental thought)
Fifty three lectures delivered Nov. 5, 1925–Feb. 26, 1926
at Philipps-Universität, Marburg, Germany.
ISBN 978-0-253-35466-2 (cloth : alk. paper)
1. Logic. 2. Truth. 3. Time. I. Title.
B3279.H48L6313 2010
160—dc22
2009039679

ISBN 978-0-253-35466-2 (cloth)
ISBN 978-0-253-00445-1 (ebk.)
ISBN 978-0-253-02165-6 (pbk.)

2 3 4 5 6   21 20 19 18 17 16

CONTENTS

Contents

PART II.
The radicalized question: What is truth? (A retrieval of the analysis of falsehood in terms of its ur-temporality)

Contents   vii

Translator's Foreword

Martin Heidegger delivered the fifty-three lectures titled "Logic: The Question of Truth," four days a week from Thursday, 5 November 1925, to Friday, 26 February 1926, at Philipps-Universität in Marburg. It was during the span of this lecture-course that the dean of the philosophy faculty walked into Heidegger's office and told him, "You must publish something now. Do you have an appropriate manuscript?"

Within a few months he would. As soon as the course ended, Heidegger went off to his cottage in Todtnauberg and started writing out *Being and Time* by hand. By the end of March he had finished much of Division One of the text, and by 20 April he and Husserl were reading page-proofs of those sections. In short, the lecture-course translated here is the last that Heidegger taught before rushing *Being and Time* to press. This lecture-course and Heidegger's 1927 text share many points in common, above all a strong focus on the questions of truth and of time.

Professor Walter Biemel's afterword to the present volume sketches a general outline of the course, and identifies the manuscripts and typescripts he used as the basis of his German edition. In this foreword, I will simply discuss some matters related to this translation of the course.

Professor Biemel based his German edition of the "Logic" course on three texts: Heidegger's handwritten lecture notes, Fritz Heidegger's typescript of those notes, and the word-for-word shorthand transcript that Simon Moser made during Heidegger's lectures and then typed up and submitted to Heidegger for corrections and additions.

Of these three textual records, Biemel relied most heavily on the handwritten notes that Heidegger drew up before the lectures. But this entails, for example, that all but two of the quite helpful daily summaries that Heidegger made of his previous lectures and delivered at the beginning of the following lecture—more than 68,000 words in all, equal to a small book—are omitted from GA 21 since they are not found in his lecture notes. Likewise, insofar as they do not appear in those same notes, the numerous and often lengthy asides which Heidegger made during the lectures and which are duly recorded by Moser, are entirely absent from GA 21. If one hopes to study the words that Heidegger *spoke* in this course, they will not be found so much in the notes he prepared before his lectures as in a transcript of his *viva voce* presentations, such as Simon Moser's faithful record. In sum, the German text of GA 21 is in no sense a critical edition of the lecture-course titled "Logic: The Question of Truth," but merely presents a reconstruction of the course by the editor of GA 21—and a fairly narrow reconstruction at that.

I frequently make use of the Simon Moser typescript, without giving notice, in translating GA 21. I have also consulted the handwritten notes of Helene Weiss, a student in the course (who eventually became a professor in Britain), and the typescript of those notes made by Ms. Weiss's nephew, Ernst Tugendhat. My thanks to Professor Tugendhat for making his aunt's notes available to me in 1974, and to the Stanford University Library Archives, which now holds the Weiss notes, for granting me renewed access to them. As Professor Biemel had also done, I have occasionally used these extra resources to clarify the published text.

In bringing into English such a long and dense text, one could certainly do worse than follow the example of Timaeus and the exhortation he made to himself toward the beginning of the eponymous Platonic dialogue. After invoking the gods and goddesses, he says, "And in addition I exhort myself to speak in a way that will be most intelligible to you, Socrates" (27d). In the interest of some such intelligibility I have freely followed common English usage, both rhetorical and syntactical, in translating the text. English rhetoric privileges the active voice over the passive and especially over such faux-reflexive constructions as *Etwas zeigt sich* and the like. In the present translation, I often render the passive voice by the active when it clarifies the sense of the passage, promotes the fluency of the prose, and does no harm to the meaning of the text. Likewise, I have broken down the frequently overlong paragraphs and sentences of GA 21 into shorter ones. (Extreme examples would include Heidegger's sixty-one-line paragraph at GA 21, pp. 50–52, or the seventy-nine-line paragraph at GA 21, pp. 191–193.) One is reminded of Mark Twain's quip that the German newspapers reported a brilliant operation in which a surgeon in Hamburg had removed a twelve (or was it seventeen?) syllable word from a German gentleman's stomach (see "The Awful German Language").

The glossaries indicate how I translate some of Heidegger's technical terms. Elsewhere I have made a case for always translating *Dasein* into English, but for *never* translating it as "being-there" or "being-here"—and least of all as "being t/here," as in the English edition of *Contributions to Philosophy* (p. xxxv). To render *Dasein* into English, I have chosen the most formally indicative English term—namely, "human existence." I do not expect that this will satisfy many or end the controversy over how to translate this key term. Rather, its advantage lies in saying so very little while formally indicating, in a direct way, the matter in question.

I frequently cite GA 21, the Moser transcript, and several other texts by page *and line*. Thus, for instance, "p. 1.14–15" refers to page 1, lines 14 and 15. The line-count does not include the "header" or any empty lines on the page, but does count the lines of section titles. Square brackets in the translation indicate my own (a) footnotes and (b) insertions into the text. Winged brackets indicate Heidegger's own insertions into the texts he is citing. Bracketed numbers indicate the beginning of the German pages of *Logik*.

I wish to thank the National Endowment for the Humanities for a grant to translate this text. Above all, I wish to thank Professor Corinne Painter, for her extraordinary help with this translation during the years of her graduate studies at Loyola University Chicago. Others who have supported this work are Professors William J. Richardson, S.J., John Sallis, Theodore Kisiel, and Reginald Lilly, as well as Professor David Schweickart, whose friendship and encouragement were of immense help during our days as colleagues at Loyola.

Thomas Sheehan
Stanford University

Logic

INTRODUCTION

§1. The first, most literal meaning of the word "logic"

We begin our treatment with a preliminary understanding of what the word "logic" means in its most direct and literal sense.

The terms "logic," "physics," and "ethics" come from the Greek words λογική, φυσική, ἠθική, to which ἐπιστήμη is always to be added. Ἐπιστήμη means roughly the same as the German term *Wissenschaft,* "science." *Wissenschaft,* like the German word *Landschaft,* refers to a region, and in this case a specific self-enclosed whole comprised of a manifold of grounded knowledge, that is, of cognitions drawn exclusively and judiciously from the very things the science seeks to know.

Ἐπιστήμη λογική is the science of λόγος or λέγειν (the science of speaking), ἐπιστήμη φυσική is the science of φύσις, and ἐπιστήμη ἠθική is the science of ἦθος.[1]

Ἐπιστήμη φυσική is the science of φύσις, that is, of "nature" understood in the broad sense of "world" or "cosmos." For the Greeks, φύσις takes in the entire realm of the world in the sense of what's out there—the totality of stars, earth, plants, animals, humans, and gods. Today "physics" is one particular discipline within the general science of the world: it is the science of the material, inanimate things of the world. More specifically, in contrast to inorganic chemistry, for instance, it is the science of matter in terms of its absolute laws of motion. As a modern science of nature, physics discloses only certain contexts of the being of those beings that we call "the world."

Ἐπιστήμη ἠθική is the science of ἦθος, the science of the behavior or comportment of human beings toward other people and toward

---

1. [The Simon Moser *Nachschrift* or transcript (hereafter cited as "Moser," followed by page and line) here corrects GA 21, p. 1.14-15. This is but one of the hundreds of disconnects between Moser's record of Heidegger's spoken words during the course and the text of GA 21.]

1

2 Introduction

themselves. It is the science of human being. Notice that we already mentioned human being when we spoke about ἐπιστήμη φυσική, the science of the world. But [2] now the subject matter is human being—not as a thing that just shows up in the world, with nothing ontologically special about it that would set it off from plants and animals, something that is just "out there" like the flora and fauna. Rather, in the present case human beings are understood as beings that, so to speak, take their very own being in hand.[2]

According to the divisions established by Hellenistic scholasticism, these three ἐπιστῆμαι make up philosophy, the science of the whole of beings as such in their wholeness. "Physics" and "ethics" we can understand; but how is a "science of speaking" supposed to fit in with those two? Physics and ethics are disciplines that deal with two distinctive, universal realms of beings: the world and human beings. But how does a science that deals with so specific a matter as speaking get lined up with them? Why exactly should "speaking" become the subject of a universal (i.e., a philosophical) reflection? We will understand why once we have a natural and unbiased understanding of what is meant by λόγος or "speech," just as we do of those other two realms of beings: the world and human beings.

We understand speaking not in the narrow and specialized sense of "giving a speech," but simply as "speaking to each other" for the sake of interacting and working with each other. Talking to each other in this way means speaking about what's going on, what could go on, and how to do things. It means discussing plans, projects, relationships, events, the ups and downs of life. To go back to what we said before: it means discussing how the world is and how human beings are. Speaking with each other is not something that goes on all the time, but speech itself—λόγος—is always operative—whether we're repeating what others have said, or telling stories, or even just silently speaking to ourselves or explaining things to ourselves or taking *re-sponsi*bility for ourselves. In this broad and natural sense, speech is a way that human beings behave, one that reveals to a natural, pre-scientific view what the difference is between human beings and other living things in the world. The specific being of humans is rendered conspicuous by speech. And [3] what is essential about speaking is that it is experienced as speaking *to* others *about* something.

Not only is speaking to others and to oneself the behavior that makes human beings stand out as human; speaking is also the way that hu-

2. [Moser (p. 2.30–3.5) records that Heidegger said at this point that human beings "are experienced insofar as they act, indeed act upon others and upon themselves." Here, in ἐπιστήμη ἠθική, "human beings are understood as beings that, so to speak, take their ownmost being in hand."]

mans direct and guide all their other kinds of behavior. It is in and through speaking that the modes and the objects of human action are disclosed, explained, and determined. Human behavior and human being first become conspicuous in and through speaking, and so in their early, pre-scientific characterization of human being, the Greeks defined human being as ζῷον λόγον ἔχον—the living being that can speak and that co-defines its being in and through such speaking.

It is clear, then, that speaking is not something incidental but an entirely distinctive and universal state of affairs, a form of behavior whereby humans give direction to their being and bring their world into discussion. Talking, therefore, is human being's distinctive, universal, and fundamental way of comporting itself toward the world and toward itself.

Λόγος, then, is what reveals an ontological connection between the other two universal regions we mentioned: human being (ἦθος) and world (φύσις). So the regions that these three words designate provide us with an essential (if rough) classification of beings. Correspondingly the three disciplines of physics, ethics, and logic do not come together by chance. Rather, this threefold division and articulation is essential, and by means of it the three disciplines deal with the entirety of all beings. The basic topic of philosophy is the whole of beings; and these three disciples present us with a division of philosophical labor that we must hold to as entirely natural.

In the development of the sciences, such divisions usually come later, after the original and basic investigations have first been carried out in each of the areas. The same goes for the names of these disciplines. Usually the names get set only when the divisions get established. [4]

According to Sextus Empiricus,[3, 4] Xenocrates was supposedly the first to make this division explicit. It had been already current among the Stoics, whence it passed over into Hellenistic school philosophy.

ἐντελέστερον δὲ . . . οἱ εἰπόντες τῆς φιλοσοφίας τὸ μέν τι εἶναι φυσικόν, τὸ δὲ ἠθικόν, τὸ δὲ λογικόν· ὧν δυνάμει μὲν Πλάτων ἐστὶν ἀρχηγός, περὶ πολλῶν μὲν φυσικῶν, περὶ πολλῶν δὲ ἠθικῶν, οὐκ ὀλίγων δὲ λογικῶν διαλεχθείς· ῥητότατα δὲ οἱ περὶ τὸν Ξενοκράτην καὶ οἱ ἀπὸ τοῦ Περιπάτου,

---

3. Sextus Empiricus, Πρὸς μαθηματικούς (Against the Mathematicians). The work deals with later skepticism, ca. 200 CE. Still valuable on skepticism is Paul Natorp, *Forschungen zur Geschichte des Erkenntnisproblems im Altertum. Protagoras, Demokrit, Epikur, und die Skepsis* (Berlin: W. Hertz, 1884).

4. [Of the eight books of Sextus Empiricus' Πρὸς μαθηματικούς, the last two, books 7 and 8, are sometimes treated as books 1 and 2 of Sextus' Πρὸς λογικούς (Against the Logicians). This is the case in R. G. Bury's bilingual edition, *Sextus Empiricus*. The translation above, as elsewhere in this volume, follows Heidegger's German translation of the Greek.]

ἔτι δὲ οἱ ἀπὸ τῆς στοᾶς ἔχονται τῆσδε τῆς διαιρέσεως. (*Adversus mathematicos* VII, 16)[5]

Those who have divided philosophy in a more complete way are those who say that one part of philosophy deals with φύσις, another part with ἦθος, and a third with λόγος. Plato first pointed the way to this possible division of philosophy insofar as in his philosophy he treats of many things that deal with the world, many things that concern human being, and quite a lot about what pertains to speaking. But it was the disciples of Xenocrates and the students of Aristotle who most explicitly divided philosophy this way. The Stoics, too, still hold to this division.[6]

Kant still liked to invoke this threefold division, the way he does in the Preface to his *Groundwork of the Metaphysics of Morals*:

Ancient Greek philosophy was divided into three sciences: *physics, ethics,* and *logic*. This division is perfectly suitable to the nature of the subject, and there is no need to improve upon it except, perhaps, to add its principle, partly so as to ensure its completeness [5] and partly so as to be able to determine correctly the necessary subdivisions.[7]

Note that Kant emphasizes the appropriateness of this division to the subject matter: i.e., it is a division that ultimately comes to the fore, more or less clearly, in every philosophical investigation. And when Kant says that one needs "only" to add the principle, we should bear in mind that the task of doing so continues to be one of philosophy's fundamental concerns, one that has not been answered to this day and, when you get right down to it, hasn't even been clearly posed either as a project or as a question.

The preliminary clarification of the meaning of the word "logic" led to a preliminary orientation to a fundamental division of the philosophical disciplines. It also provided a first view of the regions of being to which this division and indeed the whole of philosophy are directed.

5. Xenocrates (396–314 bce) was roughly a contemporary of Aristotle, and a follower of Speusippos, the first leader of the Academy after Plato. He catalogued and systematized Platonic philosophy in a scholastic way, taking studies that once were lived and putting them into the fixed form of a wisdom that could be taught.

6. Cf. Diogenes Laertius: τῆς φιλοσοφίας ὁ λόγος πρότερον μὲν ἦν μονοειδὴς ὡς ὁ φυσικός, δεύτερον δὲ Σωκράτης προσέθηκε τὸν ἠθικόν, τρίτον δὲ Πλάτων τὸν διαλεκτικόν, καὶ ἐτελεσιούργησε τὴν φιλοσοφίαν (III, 34). ["At first philosophical discourse was of one kind: the discussion of nature. In the second instance Socrates added the discussion of ethics, and thirdly Plato added dialectics, thereby completing (the contours of) philosophy."]

7. [*GM*, p. 387 / tr. 1.]

The division and the status attributed to logic as a discipline come about later than the issue they deal with—and the same goes for the emergence of the word λογική. For example, we find ή λογική in Cicero,[8] in Alexander of Aphrodisias[9] (ca. 200 c.e.), in Galen.[10] It does not yet show up in Aristotle, although the word λογικῶς does. By clarifying the meaning of the word λόγος, we have already indicated the arena that is the topic of logic: speech in the broadest sense. We will now pursue that indication so that as we move toward a concept of the word, we may also get an initial concept of the subject matter.

---

§2. A first indication of the concept of the subject matter of "logic"

If we desire a more vital concept of "logic," we have to ask a more penetrating question: What is the subject matter of the science of logic? In doing so, we leave aside any consideration of logic as one discipline among others—viz., the science of speaking and therefore of language— and focus instead on what it is *about*. [6] That might seem to imply that the proper science of λόγος would be linguistics or the study of grammar in the broad sense. In fact, even among the Greeks logic developed in connection with grammar understood as the study of language. More precisely, logic and grammar—the two disciplines that deal with λόγος— were not originally distinct. In fact, they were so *in*distinct that the Greeks lacked a word for what we call "language." That is, in the first stage of understanding λόγος, there was no distinction between λόγος as the act of speaking and λόγος as language. The word for "speaking" subsumed what we call "language." On the other hand, [speaking as] making verbal sounds was the most direct way that "language" was ex-

8. [Cicero uses λογική at *De finibus bonorum et malorum* I, 7, 22 ("iam in altera philosophiae parte quae est quaerendi ac disserendi, quae λογική dicitur"), and at *De fato* I, 1 ("Explicandaque vis est ratioque enuntiationum, quae Graeci ἀξιώματα [i.e., 'logical propositions'] vocant; totaque est λογική, quam 'rationem disserendi' voco"). See Cicero, *De Fato*, in *De Oratore*, trans. H. Rackham (London: William Heinemann / Cambridge, Mass.: Harvard University Press, 1960), vol. 2, p. 192. Also see Carl Prantl, *Geschichte der Logik im Abendlande*, 4 vols. (Leipzig, 1855–1870; reissued Leipzig: Gustav Fock, 1927 / Graz: Akademische Druck, 1955), vol. 1, pp. 535, 514 n. 27.]

9. [Alexander of Aphrodisias, *In Aristotelis Analyticorum Priorum Librum I Commentarium*, ed. Maximilian Wallies, *Commentaria in Aristotelem Graeca* (Berlin: Reimer, 1883), vol. 2, p. 1 (the opening sentence of his commentary): ή λογική τε συλλογιστικὴ πραγματεία ή νῦν προκειμένη: "Logic or syllogistics is the study that now lies before us."]

10. Cf. Carl Prantl, *Geschichte der Logik im Abendlande*, vol. 1, p. 533 n. 7.

perientially accessible to the Greeks. That is why they first came to understand "language" with regard to the differences between the various
forms of words and between the different possible ways words can be
brought together [in a sentence]. But the Greeks likewise, and just as
basically, understood that λόγος consists in speaking *about* something,
speaking *of* something. That is, they saw that the basic achievement of
speech consists in showing or revealing *what* one is speaking about, *what*
one is discussing. Indeed, making vocal sounds was quite secondary to
that.[11]

In such acts of revealing, whatever one is speaking about shows up,
becomes perceivable, and, as something perceived, gets *defined* in and by
the discussion about it. This revelatory defining of what is experienced
and perceived is the very same thing that we generally call "thought"
and "reflection."

In summary: in our primary, natural experience of how human
beings live together with each other, we understand speech as the revealing of something by speaking about it, and as a thinking that determines and orders it. Language, speaking, thinking: they coincide as
the human way of being. They are the way we reveal and illumine
(both for ourselves and for others) the world and our own human existence [*Dasein*], so that in this luminosity we gain sight: human insight into ourselves and an outlook on, and a practical insight into, the
world. Logic as the science of speaking, studies speech in terms of
what it properly is: the revealing of something. The subject matter of
logic is *speech* viewed with regard to its basic meaning, namely, allowing the world, human existence, and things in general to be seen. [7]

The fact that existence has and understands and strives for this
basic form of revealing implies that, for the most part, much of the
world stands in need of "revelation," of being un-covered and made
known. In other words, much of the world and much of human existence is by and large not un-covered. So beings can be drawn out of
their not-un-covered-ness, their hiddenness. They can be un-covered
or un-hidden. This uncoveredness or unhiddenness of beings is what
we call truth.[12]

*   *   *

Logic investigates speaking—the thinking that defines things—inasmuch as speaking uncovers things. The topic of logic is speech, specifically with regard to truth.

In other words, to the degree that we clarify the meaning of truth,
we will be in a position to properly understand speech, λόγος. The

11. [From Moser (p. 11), fleshing out GA 21, p. 6.17.]
12. [Here Heidegger ends his first lecture, Thursday, 5 November 1925.]

basic topic of the science of λόγος is truth in the quite general sense of the questions, "What is truth in general?" or "What constitutes the structure and make-up of truth?" and "What possibilities and forms does truth have?" and finally, "What is the basis on which rests what we properly call truth?"

Our definition of logic as the science of truth could be misunderstood. One might object that *every* science deals with truth, that truth is what all scientific knowledge is after. Yes, except that there is a misleading ambiguity here in how the word truth is being used. In a strict sense, no individual science other than logic deals with *truth*. The [natural] sciences, on the other hand, deal only and always with the true, i.e., *what*-is-true; and they do so within the arena of the knowledge of nature. Or outside of the [natural] sciences, one inquires into what-is-true for human action, or about the true that faith gives.

But logic does not ask about the what-is-true in just any sense. Rather, it inquires primarily and properly into the *truth* of [8] what-is-true. It asks: What makes this or that true thing *be* true in a given case? and what makes it be *this* true thing? The only way to make any grounded sense out of the truth of theoretical-scientific knowledge, practical reflection, or religious truth is to get to the foundation that lets us understand what truth means at all. Only from that foundation can we decide which kind of truth is most original, and whether the ideal of truth is to be found in theoretical-scientific truth or practical insight or religious faith. In other words, it is not easily decided which form of the true is primary and most basic. Even in today's philosophy, this question has not yet been settled.

Of course the philosophical tradition and philosophical research have, from their inception, always been oriented to a certain kind of knowledge and truth, namely, theoretical cognition. The truth of the theoretical proposition, the statement, has become the privileged paradigm for the true as regards its truth. One specific form of truth became the ideal, and whenever one reflected on the meaning of practical or religious truth, that reflection was always carried out in a framework that kept theoretical-scientific knowledge strictly separate from practical knowledge, which was thought to be a more limited and less rigorous form of cognition. In modern philosophy, the ideal of theoretical truth carried the day in a hyperbolic form inasmuch as the ideal of truth was not just theoretical truth in general but the truth-character of a very specific kind of theoretical cognition: mathematical knowledge. Mathematical knowledge was seen as the proper and most rigorous kind of knowledge. This ideal was so dominant that even until recently one was still trying to assimilate the science of history to the ideal of mathematical knowledge. Even when [9] one does not expressly articulate this ideal and adhere to it as such, nonetheless, thanks to the influence of modern philosophy, that ideal continues to have a strong impact on the question of the essence of truth.

Thus, among the various meanings of the word truth, the real priority goes to the sense of truth that is oriented to propositional statements. In order to first get some (in fact, very extrinsic) clarity on this ambiguous word "truth," let me mention some of its meanings by simply listing them at this point without going into the relevant explanations of what they mean.

In the first place, truth is understood to be a feature of statements about things. Truth is thus a property of propositions, by virtue of which they express something just as it is.

Secondly, however, truth is understood not simply as a property of propositions and statements. We also call the statement itself a truth, as when we say: "'Two plus two equals four' is a truth," or "There are many truths" (i.e., many [true] propositions and statements), or when we speak of eternal and temporal truths or of absolute and relative truths. In all these cases, truth is not just a property of propositions but is the propositions themselves.

Thirdly, truth means the same as *knowledge* of a truth, as when we say, "So-in-so cannot bear the truth." That means that so-in-so resists knowledge of the truth, hides from it.

Fourthly, we also use the word truth to mean an aggregate of true propositions about a state of affairs. When we say, "We want to learn the truth about this or that event," this refers to the collection of possible statements that must be made if we are to have access to the event just the way it happened, and, if we may say so, just the way it *is*. [10]

Fifthly, truth also has the sense of "the true," where "the true" means the real, just as it is. When we speak of "true gold," we mean real, genuine gold. The same goes for speaking of the "true God." In these cases, our statements are not focused on the mere *things* we are speaking about, so that the statement would be true by simply expressing how things are out there. It's quite the reverse. In these cases a thing is properly called "true" only when it is in such a way as to correspond to its "idea." When something *is* what it *should be* according to the idea of that thing, only then can we say, for example, it is "true gold" and not "sham gold," mere fool's gold.

Pulling these different senses of truth together, we see a formal structure that recurs in all of them. In the first four cases, the statement is true when it speaks of the thing *just as* the thing is. But in the fifth case—"true" in the sense of "real"—it is the reverse. The thing is true when it is *just as* it is according to its idea, the essence of the thing as apprehended by reason (νοῦς or even λόγος). In this latter case, *genuine* gold is what corresponds to the *idea* of gold. In both cases, however, truth has the formal structure of *just-as* or *as-so*.

The name we give this whole formal structure of just-as is "correspondence" or in Latin, *adaequatio*. For now let us be satisfied with this preliminary determination of the formal structure of the true. Later we will have to deal more deeply with the question of this remarkable structure of just-as: what its source is, how it is possible as such—in a word, the *ground* on which truth as such rests.

From what we have said, it is clear that from the very beginning, philosophical reflection took λόγος (speech) primarily as expressed speech; and within that, it took λόγος in what appeared to be its simplest manifestation: the statement, where "uttering" and speaking take the linguistic form of sentences in the form of statements such as, "The sky is blue." [11]

The more this form of speech obviously presents the most basic form of theoretical-scientific knowledge, the more it imposes itself on logical reflection. Any definitive study formulates its conclusions in propositions, especially insofar as they are statements about the world. Formulated as simple "propositions," statements about the world that reflect on and determine the world, came to be the simplest, most general, and likewise the most basic form of speech. Even the determination of truth now gets oriented, primarily and in principle, to this kind of speech, the propositional statement. The act of un-covering things in statements is what is true, and so the truth of theoretical-scientific knowledge has become the basic, original form of truth as such. The truth of [propositional] knowledge attains a universal primacy. To the degree that any other forms of truth enter the field of reflection, they are measured against the standard of the truth of [propositional] cognition and are understood as derived from it, as modifications of it.

It is far from evident, however, that theoretical-cognitive truth, or even the truth of statements, is the basic form of truth in general. Philosophy's first determination of truth, and the tradition of logic that follows from it, are oriented in terms of this idea of truth; but so too is linguistic usage, which is bound up with them in a certain way. So in its decisive origins logic was already oriented toward this truth of theoretical apprehension and cognitive determination. From that point until now, this orientation of logic and philosophy has remained fundamentally in place.

We will see that this primacy of theoretical truth within logical investigation is not accidental. But we must also make it clear that understanding the project of logic and questioning it more radically requires that we go back to this naïve beginning of logic and shake it to its roots. In other words, it is far from settled which kind of "true"—the theoretical or the practical—is original and authentic. Instead, the question about [12] the originally and authentically "true"—i.e., the question of the primary being of truth—is logic's most basic concern, but only when logic has the will to be a searching, scientific logic—a logic that philosophizes.

---

§3. A philosophizing logic and traditional scholastic logic

But if logic is, by definition, a discipline within philosophy, is there really any kind of logic other than philosophical logic? There certainly is. The kind of logic that is and was commonly taught in the universities of today and of yesteryear is a logic that has given up on any kind of philosophy, that is, any kind of serious questioning and investigation. This so-called "scholastic logic" is not philosophy, and it is not any one of the particular sciences. It is a form of sloth, kept alive by custom and by off-the-record academic arrangements and desires. It is also a fraud.

Scholastic logic is a form of sloth tailor-made for instructors. All they have to do, year after year, is parrot the same old stock of unchanging, shopworn propositions, formulas, rules, and definitions. Variations in how these logic courses are taught is confined to how the teacher packages it, how thorough he is, and what kind of examples he chooses. In this kind of "logic," the logician never runs a risk, never has to put up or shut up—which is the price that you have to pay to do real philosophy.

It is a fraud perpetrated on the students. They are trapped for a whole semester studying stuff of utterly dubious value. It would be easier and more expeditious for them—not to mention quicker and cheaper—to just read the stuff on their own in any logic manual.

This kind of scholastic logic can certainly appeal to a long tradition of teaching that reaches back through the Middle Ages [13] to the time when logic was originally established as a discipline (see above). But even the most ancient of traditions cannot claim its own legitimacy when it began as a result of a decline, or better, began *as* a decline.

Traditional scholastic logic comes from a period when philosophy had already lost its character as a productive force. The fact that later, creative philosophers have since taken this logic under their wings changes nothing basic. Traditional scholastic logic retains the content (but trivialized, uprooted, and mummified) of an original philosophical questioning that was alive in Plato and Aristotle but got completely stifled and rigidified by the schools.

The endless retailing of this over-the-counter stock of scholastic logic is an outrage to real philosophizing. It is beneath the dignity of the university as a place of questioning and searching.

Our decision for a philosophizing logic, our repudiation of the *collegium logicum* in its traditional form, is neither some rash rejection of the tradition, nor is it a supercilious disdain for solid learning, for getting an academic position, and even less so for the university. Quite the contrary, we should prepare ourselves to retrieve the genuine tradition from out of the ruins of the sham, to really appropriate the productive and living elements that lie under the rubble of scholastic logic. But we will engage in direct confrontation with that earlier philosophizing logic only if we ourselves do logic in a philosophizing manner. The result will be to see that Aristotle's logic, for example—or more precisely, his work on that area of research—is quite different from the scholastic logic that likes to appeal to him.

In his lecture course *Logic*, Kant says:

> Contemporary logic is a descendant of *Aristotle's Analytic*. This philosopher can be regarded as the father of logic. [14] He expounded it as an organon and divided it into *analytic* and *dialectic*. His manner of teaching is very scholastic and has to do with the development of the most universal concepts, which lie at the basis of logic, but no one has any use for it because almost everything amounts to mere subtleties, except that one [has] drawn from this the names for various acts of the understanding. From Aristotle's time on, logic has not gained much in *content*, by the way, nor can it by its nature do so.

Compare the Preface to the second edition of his *Critique of Pure Reason:*

> We can see that from the earliest times *logic* has traveled this secure course from the fact that since the time of Aristotle it has not had to go a single step backwards unless we count the abolishing of a few unnecessary subtleties or the more distinct determination of its presentations. These improvements pertain more to the elegance of that science than to its security. (B viii)

When Kant wrote or spoke those lines from the *Logic,* he knew nothing of Hegel and of the logic that he was already composing, which would eventually make Hegel what he became and will ever remain: the only-begotten and co-equal son of the Father of Logic. In philosophical terms this means that the philosophical logic founded by Aristotle and completed by Hegel will not be advanced by any further son-ship and uncle-hood. In order to advance philosophically, it needs a new lineage. When that will come about, no one knows. We of today are certainly not it. But the positive contribution to be made by those few who now understand what is at stake will consist in a work of transition: bringing to life again the productivity of the past and taking it into a future that we dimly see but are not yet up to. That's why it's all the more urgent that we carry through with questioning, and free ourselves from the chains of rigidity.

But is it in fact true that the cultivation of traditional scholastic logic really promotes only a cult of tradition and a dependence on custom?

Wasn't there some essential usefulness to it? I don't want to dodge the major reason people give for maintaining and encouraging this logic. People say and think and believe, in an agreement that goes without saying, that [15] studying scholastic logic teaches you how to think and helps you reach a higher level of learning and a greater exactitude in thinking. So it's something we should strive for right from the beginning of our scientific studies.

This is a basic misunderstanding. Thinking, and especially scientific thinking, can be learned only by getting involved with the subject matter. It would be the greatest mistake to think that a *collegium logicum* could make up for a lack of methodical, conceptual hard work in a science or the communication of that work through teaching.

The objectivity of scientific questioning and the precision of conceptual definition grow out of an increasing familiarity with the area of a given science's subject matter. What is more, such familiarity is possible in a positive sense only when an individual, at the core of his or her human existence, has gained a basic relationship to this subject matter, whether by an inner choice and decisive struggle or by an unexplainable inner calling.

This holds not only for theoretical scientific thinking but also for the field of practical undertakings and political power, where scholastic logic has nothing to say. It even misleads when it turns into mere drill and blind learning, and especially when it becomes a hair-splitting and empty form of arguing, cut off from the subject matter.

Conversely, understanding what scholastic logic has to offer presupposes a very comprehensive and well-developed philosophical thinking, especially when this logic is simply presumed, apparently naïvely, instead of going back into the vital origins of its settled formulae and theorems.

It's a fool's errand to expect that traditional logic will teach us how to think. But on the other hand we certainly can clarify scientific work and academic study—in a word, the whole form of existence that they encompass—but only by way of a philosophizing [16] logic, that is to say, only through a living and effective connection with the concrete practice of a given science.[13]

*   *   *

Transparency in one's scientific comportment and one's scientific life means having a relationship of understanding with the whole of a science and its basic components and their interconnections. For now let us simply note those components in a list:

13. [Here ends Heidegger's lecture of 6 November 1925.]

1. The subject matter of the science.
2. The world: generally speaking, the things from out of which the subject matter is selected.
3. The basic way in which the selection is made.
4. The relation to the world in which the science's subject matter is rooted.
5. The viewpoint that guides one's inquiry into the subject matter.
6. The kind of apodictic insight, expressible in propositions, that is to be attained.
7. The relevant ways of forming concepts. (There are structural differences between the *exact* concepts of physics, the *morphological* concepts of botany, and the *historical* concepts of philology.)
8. The manner in which proofs are communicated.
9. The sense of the validity of the binding "propositions" gained in the particular sciences.

All these components get modified according to the different sciences and groups of sciences.

Clarity in research is not attained simply by being aware that these basic components are present in a science. It is had, rather, when these elements spring to life, so to speak, in concrete occasions of our scientific work in such a way that the path of our work of research and assimilation is suddenly lit up and leads us forward or becomes problematic and unsure.

A science does not develop because some scholar discovers something new in a specific situation. Rather, in each case the sudden jolt by which any given science moves forward [17] consists of a revision of basic concepts. From then on, a science develops by taking the heretofore available stock of propositions and concepts and putting them on a new foundation. Einstein's revolution in contemporary physics was carried out in this way. It's not the case that he began to philosophize about basic concepts of physics. Rather, in working on specific problems he looked into the basic concepts contained in those problems and saw that if he was to remain at all committed to the goal of physics, a revision of those concepts was needed. It is hard to see it so clearly today, but an analogous revolution was Dilthey's achievement in the science of history, namely, the shift of historical research to what we now call the history of human spirit. Scholars up to the present, at least in their concrete work, still have not understood this achievement—which shows that a paradigm shift within this field is more difficult to carry out, whereas the siren song of dilettantism is easier to follow.

Understanding the nine points listed above is the source of transparency in the life of science. Those points are not just thrown together. They are understood from out of a primary pre-understanding

of the current whole of the sciences. The basic structure of that whole
is the possible "truth" within which any research activity operates. In
other words, the constitutive elements themselves are only necessary
structural moments of theoretical truth. Thus they can be understood
and are to be appropriated from out of the pre-understanding of theoretical truth and ultimately of truth in general. This means that clarity
in scientific research is possible only by way of a philosophizing logic.[14] Scholastic logic never delivers on its claim to teach us how to
think. On the other hand, what is basically meant by that claim—viz.,
of the transparency of scientific research—can be fulfilled only by a
philosophizing logic. To be sure, [18] that last sentence is spoken from
the viewpoint of the ideal. Trying to promise that the following "logic"
will concretely achieve anything like that would be not only presump-
tuous but also a misunderstanding of philosophy. Really very little can
be said about philosophy. Instead of giving an extended explanation of
its essence, I will merely allude to one thing that pertains to philosophy: the fact that the philosopher reserves to himself the possibility of
making mistakes. The courage to err does not mean just the courage
to put up with one's errors. It means much more: the courage to admit
one's errors. It is courage for the inner release of one's own self in
order to listen and learn, the courage for positive discussion.

*Not only in the realm of scientific research but in every possible kind of exis-
tence, individuals are only what they are able—and have the courage—to demand of themselves.*

The rejection of traditional scholastic logic can be easily combined
with true esteem for the tradition. To esteem the tradition does not
mean remaining blindly bound to what-has-been as such—the past as
such—or stubbornly refusing to go beyond the handed-down tradition
as handed down. True esteem for the tradition is grounded in the historicity of human existence itself, that is, in the original fidelity of
human existence to itself. Fidelity means getting close to and holding
on to that which is seized and won by struggle and that holds our existence in suspense.

Within the circle of tasks reserved to philosophizing logic, the central
concern—which will get clearer later on—is the question, "What is
truth?" We really have to ask this question. Philosophizing logic consists in the searching passage through this question. It is the only way
we gain the possibility of understanding *from the roots up* former attempts
to ask this question about truth. Only from those roots can we understand the process whereby this question dried up and died out in scholastic teaching. Consequently, the aforementioned rejection of traditional scholastic logic is nothing [19] other than the movement toward

14. Not to be confused with the theory of science [*Wissenschaftstheorie*].

the philosophical appropriation of the genuine philosophical content
that is locked up inside that logic.

---

§4. The possibility and the being of truth in general.
Skepticism

When we assign philosophizing logic the fundamental task of really
asking the question, "What is truth?" it might seem that we are giving
only a preliminary formulation of the problem and that logic is not yet
being put on the genuine road to originality.

The question to be asked before all others has to be: Does it make
any sense to ask about truth? Is not the very idea of truth an illusion?
"Is" there truth at all?—in other words, is there something whereby
things are given just as they are? And we could even ask the further
question: Are there things at all? And then we would end up with a
whole series of questions that the ancient skeptics have already
asked.

Compare Gorgias, as described by Sextus Empiricus:

ἐν γὰρ τῷ ἐπιγραφομένῳ περὶ τοῦ μὴ ὄντος ἢ περὶ φύσεως τρία κατὰ τὸ
ἑξῆς κεφάλαια κατασκευάζει, ἕν μὲν καὶ πρῶτον ὅτι οὐδὲν ἔστιν, δεύτερον
ὅτι εἰ καὶ ἔστιν, ἀκατάληπτον ἀνθρώπῳ, τρίτον ὅτι εἰ καὶ καταληπτόν,
ἀλλὰ τοί γε ἀνέξοιστον καὶ ἀνερμήνευτον τῷ πέλας. (*Adversus mathematicos* VII, 65)

In his book *On Non-being* or *On Nature*, Gorgias discusses three major theses
in succession: first, that there is nothing; second, that if there is something,
it cannot be apprehended by human beings; and third, that even if it can be
grasped, it still cannot be expressed and made intelligible to others.

Before the question of *what* truth is, there comes the question of
whether it is at all. Before sketching out what it is, we have to prove *that*
it is. Against this position, we may propose this formal argument: focusing on and discussing the question whether there is truth at all
implies that we already have some understanding of truth. We [20]
must somehow know what a thing is if we are to decide its being or
non-being.

So, even if it should turn out that there is no truth and that it cannot be understood and communicated, we still have to clarify what we
mean by "truth."

In fact, precisely because this thesis is supposed to be held as a fundamental proposition, the content of the thesis as well as the meaning
of "truth" must have the transparency of a principle. But that implies

that the explanation of what truth is comes before the question of whether it can be apprehended and communicated.

But with regard to the very question of whether there is truth, we would choose to say that the obvious answer is "yes." And then when we explain what truth is, we already presuppose that it is possible to make true statements about the essence of truth. The intention to discuss something presupposes the prospect and intention of clarifying it.

Basically, then, the question of whether there is any truth at all is already answered by the fact that we are discussing it. And (so one says) we answer the question ["Is there any truth?"] in the affirmative even when we deny that there is truth, insofar as the denial claims to be a true statement about the non-existence of truth. The denial of the existence of truth affirms the truth of the denial, and therefore the existence of truth. The positing of such a denial, which we usually call skepticism, contradicts itself and therefore is impossible.

So the outcome is: (a) The question that seems to be primary—whether there is truth at all—is not at all the first question. (b) In fact that question is not even the topic for a meaningful discussion insofar as it always presupposes the possibility of truth. At best, we can clarify in an explicit way the necessity of this presupposition. We might say that this task is the prolegomenon for any and all logic. [21]

There are no further grounds for asking an intelligent question that could get behind this basic presupposition that there is truth after all. Reflection has here reached a limit.

At this limit of reflection and discussion, the assurance that truth exists seems almost to be self-guaranteed. The possibility that skepticism could endanger the existence of truth is neutralized as soon as we realize that the skeptic refutes himself and cancels himself out, puts himself out of business as an alternative position.

But a refutation of skepticism is a refutation of every kind of relativism, every statement that there is no absolutely valid truth. For even the statement that there is only relative truth—if it is made in earnest—is self-contradictory. The statement says that it is absolutely the case that there is only relative truth. So there is at least *one* absolute truth. Consequently, the thesis itself is undermined, the position is untenable. So the situation is this: The question "What is truth?" is the basic question (1) because even the question of whether there is truth already presupposes the concept of truth, and (2) because likewise this question answers itself even before it is asked.

But the last reason we gave is ultimately not sustainable, because precisely when we formulate the question of a philosophizing logic, we have to doubt whether the problem of skepticism can be dismissed as cheaply and easily as that; whether it makes any sense to refute skepticism; and whether skepticism can be captured in such a simple formula.

Maybe skepticism is only a construction of its opponents who want to refute it in order to get a sense of security by refuting it.

On closer inspection, we see that both this skepticism and the refutation of it presuppose a very specific concept of truth; that this concept is not at all the original one; and therefore that this refutation is [22] not a radical consideration at all but only the semblance of a self-evident presupposition, only the mirage of a limit.

To be sure, the question "What is truth?" is the basic question—not, however, because it maintains that the problem of skepticism is already solved from the beginning. Rather, the problem of skepticism belongs in an essential way among the set of questions about the condition of the possibility of truth at all. But then there is a multitude of things to be discussed.[15]

* * *

1. One needs to demonstrate that this supposedly fundamental consideration—the refutation of skepticism—still does not and cannot deal with the real, genuine presuppositions. That is because both sides—the skeptic and his refuter—presume that the truth, whose being and non-being they are debating, is *propositional* truth. This is especially clear in the one who would refute skepticism. To confound the skeptic, he appeals to the principle of non-contradiction: there can be no truth where there is contradiction, especially the self-contradiction we find in the assertion of skepticism. But contra*diction* and non-contra*diction* make sense as a criterion only where this criterion is applied to "*diction*," to speaking back and forth, i.e., to λόγος, a statement in the sense of a proposition. Ultimately, the refutation is centered on the thesis that in every true statement, so one says, the existence of truth is co-affirmed. There the refutation rests its case.

It doesn't even go so far as at least to show *why* (i.e., on what basis) it must be the case that the existence of truth is co-affirmed in every true statement. It presumes the matter is self-evident. It never asks, much less answers, that question, and therefore this supposedly fundamental consideration that wants to get to ultimate presuppositions is not fundamental at all. [23]

2. This supposedly fundamental consideration makes an appeal to the principle of contradiction as a criterion, and therefore an appeal to fundamental proof and provability. But what does proof mean? What is the origin of the claim to prove? What is the condition of the possibility of proof at all? What is the origin of the "why?"—not to mention

15. [Here Heidegger ends his lecture of 9 November 1925.]

the "therefore"! And where does the necessity of unprovability find its basis?

3. The principle of contradiction and the principle of identity are presupposed to be self-evident, with no questions asked about whether they are actually ultimate. I don't mean to say these principles should be reducible to simpler ones. However, we should at least entertain the question of whether or not the "proposition" of contra*diction* is simply a specific and determinate "expression" for an original basic relation that does not primarily lie in the dimension of statements and propositions. Hence, appealing to this proposition—even apart from the fact that the appeal leads us into the dimension of the theoretical statement—does not as such touch on the real presuppositions of truth in general.[16]

4. In both the argumentation for and the refutation of skepticism, the issue is whether or not there is truth, whether or not it exists. But what goes unasked in all this is what the being of truth means, what the "there is . . ." refers to. There are automobiles, Negroes, Abelian functions, Bach's fugues. "Are there" truths, too? Or if not, what then?

5. This delineation of skepticism and of the refutation of skepticism claims to deal with the ultimate presuppositions of all philosophy—but without asking about the meaning and necessity and possibility of presupposing as such. After all, where is there such a thing as presupposing? And why must there be? What is the basis for the necessity of making *pre*-suppositions? The more noise one makes about "the self-evident," the more puzzles there are to solve. But to philosophize means to be entirely and constantly [24] troubled by and immediately sensitive to the complete enigma of things that common sense considers self-evident and unquestionable. Of course such philosophizing requires that we hunt down and look into these "immediately self-evident" things, and for that we need the right direction and the crucial light for finding our way.

This list of questions should make it clear that the supposedly basic reflection [on skepticism] is only a semblance of that. Later on, when we again take up and investigate these questions in their proper place, we will have to show how they are intimately connected with the question, "What is truth?" This will show us that the question about the essence of truth leads to a dimension that will remain completely closed to those who orient the basic concept of truth to truth as the validity of propositions.

Far from being a foundation-laying prolegomenon to philosophizing logic, the above discussion of skepticism and relativism is only an

---

16. Aristotle's principle of contradiction is also a relation of being and a law of being, something that has not been understood up to today.

indication of the fact that the basic question of logic has not yet reached the dimension of philosophical questioning.

Nowadays, however, that very discussion serves as a preparation for laying the foundations of logic. We find prolegomena to pure (philosophical) logic not in the realm of scholastic logic, but precisely in the one place where inquiry in logic is still alive in our day: in Edmund Husserl's *Logical Investigations*, published in 1900-1901, which, although little enough understood, was the first book to shake up present-day logic again and to advance its productive possibilities.[17] The first volume of these *Logical Investigations* is subtitled, "Prolegomena to Pure Logic," which means it deals with what first has to be clarified prior to any and all logic.

The first volume is a principled refutation of psychologism as a form of skepticism and of relativism, followed by the positive presentation of the idea of pure logic. If the questions we posed [25] about skepticism and especially about its refutation are correct, then it follows that even contemporary philosophical logic has not gotten down to the real foundations. In fact its questions have not even moved in that direction. Instead, it is constructed on something it presumes to be self-evident: truth as the truth of propositions, truth as the validity of statements.[18]

Given what we said about transparency and about skepticism, it is clear that the question "What is truth?" will force us into some fundamental reflections.

However, because this course is also supposed to be of an introductory nature, it does not start right off with a treatment of the question "What is truth?" Instead, in part I of the course we want to get acquainted with the crucial historical origins of the problem of truth in the Western philosophy in which we ourselves stand. In so doing, we will rely on the authentic documents of the origin of philosophical logic, and we will glean, as it were, a *collegium logicum* from Aristotle

17. [Edmund Husserl, *Logische Untersuchungen. Erster Theil: Prolegomena zur reinen Logik* (Logical Investigations, Part One: Prolegomena to Pure Logic) and *Zweiter Theil: Untersuchungen zur Phänomenologie und Theorie der Erkenntnis* (Part Two: Investigations into the Phenomenology and Theory of Knowledge) (Halle: Max Niemeyer, 1900-1901). All citations from this work will follow the pagination of the first edition, which is the one Heidegger cites in this course. Texts of the first and second editions have been reissued as *Husserliana* (The Hague: Martinus Nijhoff), vol. XVIII, ed. Elmar Holenstein (1975), and vols. XIX/1 and XIX/2, ed. Ursula Panzer (1984). For an English edition see *Logical Investigations*, trans. J. N. Findlay, 2 vols. (London: Routledge & Kegan Paul / New York: Humanities Press, 1970).]

18. [This is only one of the many critiques of Husserl that Heidegger articulated during the Marburg years.]

himself, the founder of such logic, but one freed of the incrustations and rigidifications of a bad tradition.

That should give us a preparatory basis for working out, in part II of the course, the question that radicalizes everything: "What is truth?"

Parts I and II are preceded by a prolegomenon in which we focus on the formulation of the questions that Husserl's *Logical Investigations* and phenomenology have introduced into contemporary logic. After that, we will steer the question back into the decisive beginnings. [26]

---

§5. Outline of the course.[19] Bibliography

What we said above indicates the basic plan of the course:

Prolegomenon. The current situation of philosophical logic. (Psychologism and the question of truth.)

Part I. The problem of truth in the decisive origin of philosophical logic, and the seedbed of traditional logic (focused on Aristotle).

   1. The theory of statement, proposition, judgment. (This in connection with Aristotle's treatise—which is more like a sketch of this problem—περὶ ἑρμηνείας, *De interpretatione, On Interpretation,* the second in the collection of Aristotle's so-called "logical writings." Later I'll say something about how we will carry this out.)
      a. The basic structure of λόγος and the phenomenon of meaning and sense: what do they both mean?
      b. The structure and the meaning of the "copula." (In the statement "This board is black," the "is" is designated as the copula. This particular "is" will concern us in great detail.)
      c. Negating, negation, the "not" and its origin.
      d. The so-called principles of identity and of contradiction.
   2. The doctrines of
      a. the definition or ὁρισμός, which is a specific kind of λόγος.
      b. essence, in Greek, the τί, "whatness": how and why we ask about the "what," whatness—thatness. (Our treatment will follow another Aristotelian text, ἀναλυτικὰ ὕστερα β (*Posterior Analytics* II).
      c. "proof" (the "why")—being—"the *a priori*"—the problem of "presupposition."

---

19. [Editor's note: The plan of the lectures was changed as the course unfolded.] [Translator's note: Nevertheless, in the present edition the table of contents and text follow Heidegger's outline of the course as it is presented here, on the conviction that its part-headings adequately represent the trajectory of his exposition.]

These questions make up part I, and by answering them we get an understanding of the ground from which ancient logic sprang and of what parts of it were treated in scholastic logic.

Part II. The radicalized question: What is truth?
  1. The foundations of truth in general.
  2. The authentic and original form of truth.
  3. The possibilities of truth that are grounded in the above—the inauthentic and the non-original essence of truth.[20]
  4. Philosophical truth and scientific truth. [27]

Aristotle lies at the basis of our treatment in part I. Our interpretation will stick close to the texts, but it is not meant to go into them in great detail. For now the point is simply to come to understand the issue. Therefore, I will give a direct translation of the passages we are to deal with.

The most important of the works on logic going back to the mid-nineteenth century are:

1. John Stuart Mill, *System of Logic, Ratiocinative and Inductive: Being a Connected View of the Principles of Evidence and the Methods of Scientific Investigation*, 1843.[21]
Mill's *Logic* had a very strong influence on Germany in the nineteenth century, but chiefly because of the opposition it provoked. It especially had an impact on Dilthey, who vigorously opposed what book 6 of this logic had to say about the humanities. Dilthey set his own position of the theory of the humanities against it. That is, in keeping with the entire orientation of his philosophy, Mill took it upon himself to interpret in a certain sense the humanities as a kind

20. [Here is a first hint at what Heidegger will call *Irre* and the *Un-wesen der Wahrheit* in his "Vom Wesen der Wahrheit" (GA 9, esp. pp. 193-198); see also *Pathmarks,* ed. William McNeill (Cambridge: Cambridge University Press, 1998), pp. 148-152. Heidegger's students heard him say, not *Wesen*—"essence"—but *Weisen*, "ways" or "modes" of truth (Moser, p. 60.9; Weiss, p. 17.32).]
21. [London: John W. Parker, 1843. Reissued in John Stuart Mill (1806-1873), *Collected Writings*, 33 vols., ed. John M. Robson (Toronto: University of Toronto Press / London: Routledge & Kegan Paul, 1981-1991); here, vols. 7 and 8 respectively. Heidegger cites the work according to its German translation by Theodor Gomperz, *System der deductiven und inductiven Logik. Eine Darlegung der Grundsätze der Beweislehre und der Methoden wissenschaftlicher Forschung*, in John Stuart Mill, *Gesammelte Werke,* ed. Theodor Gomperz (Leipzig: Fues (R. Reisland), 1872-1873), vols. 2-4. However, in both GA 21 (p. 27.8) and in Moser (p. 61.21), a comma is incorrectly added after *Grundsätze,* thereby changing the sense of the subtitle to: "the principles, the theory of evidence, and . . ." The Weiss transcript (p. 18.6) gets the title right.]

of natural science. This logic also influenced Husserl's teacher, Brentano. Even Husserl himself learned a good deal, both positively and negatively, from Mill.

2. Christoph Sigwart, *Logik,* 2 volumes, 1873ff.[22] A vast and important work on logic, recently published in its fifth edition edited by Hans Meier.
   In the traditional fashion, the first volume treats the theory of judgment, concept, and conclusion. The second volume treats the theory of method. Sigwart takes it upon himself to bring logic into close connection with the project of the sciences. In the second volume he specifically pursues an orientation to the philosophy of science. This logic has had its greatest influence on one of the contemporary schools of philosophy: the so-called value philosophy of Windelband and Rickert.

3. Hermann Lotze's *Logic,* published in 1874 as part 1 of his *System of Philosophy.*[23] It is equally as important as, and maybe even more essential and relevant than, Sigwart.
   It is in three books: "Of Thought," "Of Investigation," and "Of Knowledge." Philosophically speaking, the most important book is the third. It has exercised a strong influence on the modern logic that is usually called the logic of [28] validity, or validity logic, or value logic. It has had an influence on Windelband and Rickert, but likewise, in some essential elements, on Husserl. That is especially so as regards the peculiar interpretation of the Platonic idea in book 3 of the *Logic,* where Lotze tries to show that the Platonic idea is not a sensory thing but rather (to use his term) "has validity." Already in 1843, when he was a young teacher, he had written a logic that was a livelier and, in my opinion, a philosophically more acute work.[24] The large logic has recently been re-edited by Georg Misch

22. [Christoph Sigwart (1830–1904), *Logik* (Tübingen: H. Laupp, 1873–1878; 5th edition, 1924, ed. Hans Meier). See also Christoph Sigwart, *Logic,* 2nd rev. edition, 2 vols., trans. Helen Dendy (London: Swan Sonnenschein / New York: Macmillan, 1895); repr. in the series Phenomenology: Background, Foreground, and Influences (no. 12), 2 vols. (New York and London: Garland Publishing, 1980).]

23. [Hermann Lotze (1817–1881), *Logik. Drei Bücher vom Denken, vom Untersuchen und vom Erkennen: System der Philosophie* (Leipzig: S. Hirzel, 1874; 2nd edition, 1880), vol. 1. See also Hermann Lotze, *System of Philosophy, Part I. Logic, in Three Books: Of Thought, Of Investigation, and Of Knowledge,* 2 vols., ed. and trans. Bernard Bosanquet (Oxford: Clarendon Press, 1884). The second edition (1888) was reissued in the series Phenomenology: Background, Foreground, and Influences (no. 8), 2 vols. (New York and London: Garland Publishing, 1980).]

24. [Heidegger is referring to Lotze's *Logic* (Leipzig: Weidemann, 1843).]

in the series Philosophische Bibliothek, published by Felix Meiner Verlag.[25] Misch has written a valuable introduction to this logic, and within certain limits it is quite good on Lotze and on the whole development of logic.

4. Wilhelm Schuppe, *Erkenntnistheoretische Logik,* 1878.
Lastly a work that is mostly forgotten but that nonetheless is at a high philosophical level, Schuppe's so-called "epistemological" logic.[26]

Among the most recent works, I would mention:

5. Alexander Pfänder's *Logik.*[27]
This logic is influenced in an essential way by Husserl. It is elaborated phenomenologically, but in such a way that holds to the framework of traditional logic. It is, if I may put it this way, a traditional logic, phenomenologically purified. Very lucid, clearly written, and excellent for orienting the beginner. Published in 1920[28] both as a separate book and in the fourth volume of the *Jahrbuch für Philosophie und phänomenologische Forschung.*[29]

*   *   *

6. Heinrich Rickert.
Heinrich Rickert has been influenced in an essential way by *Logical Investigations,* and he first revealed the influence, reluctantly, in his article "Zwei Wege der Erkenntnistheorie" [Two Paths of Epistemology], *Kantstudien* XI (1909), which became important for his further development. Whatever Rickert has to offer that is new with regard to his earlier position, he essentially owes to Husserl's investigations.

7. Emil Lask.
Within this same school, Husserl has strongly influenced Lask— Rickert's student, who was killed in Galicia in 1915. In 1911, Lask

25. [Published in 1912, ed. Georg Misch, as a new printing of the second edition of 1880.]
26. [Wilhelm Schuppe (1839-1913), *Erkenntnistheoretische Logik* (Bonn: E. Weber, 1878).]
27. [Alexander Pfänder (1871-1941), *Logik,* in Husserl's *Jahrbuch für Philosophie und phänomenologische Forschung,* vol. 9 (Halle: Max Niemeyer, 1921; 2nd rev. edition, 1929).]
28. [The actual date of publication is 1921. See Edmund Husserl, *Aufsätze und Vorträge (1911-1921),* ed. Thomas Nenon and Hans Rainer Sepp = *Husserliana* XXV (Dordrecht and Boston: Martinus Nijhoff / Kluwer, 1987), p. 67.]
29. [Here Heidegger ends his lecture of 10 November 1925.]

published his *Logik der Philosophie und die Kategorienlehre,* which incorporates some of Husserl's crucial conclusions on the problem of categorial apprehension and categorial intuition. [29] See also his *Lehre vom Urteil,* 1912.[30]

8. Hans Driesch.
   Also essentially influenced by phenomenology is Dreisch, in his so-called *Ordnungslehre.*[31]

I will not go further into the effects of *Logical Investigations* now. Instead, I will describe, albeit very briefly, the genesis of this work.[32] [30]

30. [Both books were reprinted by the original publisher in Emil Lask, *Gesammelte Schriften,* ed. Eugen Herrigel (Tübingen: J. C. B. Mohr (Paul Siebeck), 1923).
    31. [Hans Driesch (1867–1941), *Ordnungslehre. Ein System des nicht-metaphysichen Teiles der Philosophie. Mit besonderer Berücksichtigung der Lehre vom Werden* (Jena: Diederichs, 1912; 2nd edition, 1923).]
    32. [GA 21, p. 30, is blank.]

PROLEGOMENON

The contemporary situation of philosophical logic. (Psychologism and the question of truth)

Logical Investigations grew out of efforts to provide philosophical clarity to pure mathematics. Husserl, who originally was a mathematician, was led to some principled considerations about the basic concepts and laws of mathematics, and as he said, he soon realized that logic in our day fell short of being an actual science and thus that the fundamental resources of logical reflection lagged behind the basic concepts of the sciences—especially in this case, of mathematics. He was faced with the question of the specific kind of conceptuality and ways of proof, and the significance of knowledge and truth in mathematical cognition. Finally, he came to reflect on the universal essence of mathematics, which had become all the more complicated insofar as Cantor's development of a pure theory of groups had shown that authentic mathematics was constituted not by the quantitative but by the formal and its law-giving character. So his reflections as a whole came to be focused on the question of the meaning of truth, and especially on the meaning of formal truth. In the beginning, around the 1890s, Husserl tried to carry out these philosophical reflections by means of the traditional philosophy of his day, that is, predominantly by way of so-called psychological reflections. Using a psychological analysis of mathematical thinking, he tried to get behind the specific structure of mathematical objectivity.

But he soon saw the principled difficulty contained in this analysis: Granted that mathematics does not attempt to understand empirical facts, is it even possible to establish [32] something fundamental about this science by using psychological ideas, that is, explanations ordered to the empirical sciences? By arguing out these basic questions, he finally came to realize that psychology has absolutely no qualification to be the science that can aid us in discussing questions like the structure of mathematics and of mathematical objects. Husserl's impartial pursuit of the guiding questions about mathematics and logic in the broadest sense, as well as his methodological reflection on the possibilities of a scientific solution to this question, finally led to the development of a new kind of research that Husserl called *phenomenology*. Husserl did not coin the term "phenomenology." Rather, it is older and originated at the time of the Enlightenment—even Kant used it now and again—and the term became widely known through Hegel's book, *Phenomenology of Spirit*. People commonly say that contemporary phenomenology has nothing to do with the Hegelian variety, but it is not that simple. With the proper precautions, we can say that contemporary phenomenology has a lot to do with Hegel—not with his *Phenomenology,* but with what he called logic. With certain reservations, we can identify that logic with contemporary phenomenological research.

I do not want to speak now about phenomenology itself, but only to clarify briefly what we mean by it. We do not mean "phenomenology" the way many of its disciples understand it—as a particular current in philosophy. Likewise, it is not essential that a so-called school of phenomenology exists. The crucial thing is the principle that guides the work, one that we call phenomenological. Taken as a whole, this principle is nothing new but is one of many issues in philosophy that go without saying. The principle is that we should inquire into and work upon the objects of philosophy just the way they show up. Thus, the tendency to press on to the real issues themselves, [33] to free them from presuppositions, overlays from the tradition, and hasty questions laden with presumptions. This is the proper thrust of phenomenology: to get to the real issues themselves. A "phenomenon" simply means a given object of philosophical research insofar as it is apprehended with the intention of understanding it as it is. So in a certain sense the word "phenomenon" always implies a task: negatively, protection against presuppositions and prejudgments; positively, to assure that the analysis of so-called phenomena must get clear with itself about which presuppositions it brings to the objects of philosophy. For ultimately we can show that no one can do without such presupposing, and therefore that the critique of the essential act of presupposing is an essential element of philosophical research. Right now I don't want to go into a long methodological explanation of this. Instead, we shall proceed phenomenologically throughout this course. So when I use the word "phenomenon," it should be understood in the sense I have just given. And we will be speak about the phenomenon of truth, the phenomenon of the proposition, the phenomenon of speaking, the phenomenon of time, and the like.

Husserl's *Logical Investigations* gave contemporary logic a push that, relatively speaking, impelled it deeper into the dimension of philosophical questioning. But on the other hand, people generally neglected the really positive suggestions and tendencies of the book, which also, in fact, were not so easy to understand since they were full of obscurities. Even today we are still caught up in the process of self-clarification, which can only occur in conjunction with concrete work. As long as the work is in progress, the process of clarification will remain open. In fact, it was not so much the positive work of Husserl's book that had an effect, but rather the *critical* work found in the first volume, titled "Prolegomena to Pure Logic." This critical work was more easily accessible to the understanding of problems at that time, [34] because as a critique, it had relevance to the predominant forms of inquiry into logic. From the critical perspective of his book, Husserl called those approaches "psychologism."

---

§6. Psychologism: the name and the concept

An "-ism" always means the emphasizing of something that legitimately or illegitimately takes priority. It could be a particular attention to something or a defense against something. "Psychologism" expresses the priority of psychology, particularly with regard to logic and its project.

How does psychology get its dominant position with regard to logic? How do these two disciplines come to be related? Logic deals with λόγος, the statement, whereas psychology deals with ψυχή, or in modern terminology, with "consciousness."

If you recall the threefold division of philosophical disciplines that we began with in our first meeting—logic, physics, ethics—you notice that psychology is not to be found there. Someone might say, "Well, the ancients did not yet have a psychology." True, they did not have a psychology in the sense of a particular discipline, but in those days psychology belonged in physics, the scientific study of the world or of nature in the broad sense. For the ancients psychology meant the science of living nature. In its ancient Greek sense, psychology meant roughly the same as what we today call biology, using the word in its literal sense: the science of life. Or more exactly we should say "zoology," because "life" as treated in ancient psychology had the connotations of ζωή. As Aristotle understood it, ζωή is the being of plants and animals. It is "life" in today's sense of "the biological," whereas for the Greeks βίος, taken in a quite extreme sense, means the same as human existence or personal being, as for instance the word "biography" shows. In Aristotle's *Ethics*, the word βίος refers to a possibility of existence. βίος θεωρητικός means [35] the existence of someone who does science.

The terms "biology" and "psychology" are interrelated. Biology would mean the science of human existence or of its foundations. It would be an inquiry into the foundations of "ethics." As the science of βίος, psychology belongs in ethics; as the science of ζωή, it belongs in physics. In fact, in ancient times psychology was worked out in both senses without a clear distinction. This confusion continues right up to today. If we are honest, nobody today can say what psychology is. Both as a concept and a project, this discipline is entirely ambiguous. The lack of clarity goes back to the beginnings of ancient philosophy and to its ways of posing the respective questions.

The very concept of psychology is ambiguous: on the one hand, it is the science of natural life; on the other hand, it is also the science of "psyche" in a narrow sense, the science of human existence. The ambiguity is heightened by the fact that the natural science of life has expanded whereas the study of life in the sense of human existence has gone deeper. And so people either try to unite the two sciences, or they give one of them priority over the other.

Today, for example, we speak of two psychologies. One of them specifically studies the causal interconnections of mind. Here we are thinking of a natural science; and insofar as it explains mind by means of the laws of causality, we call it an explanatory (*erklärende*) psychology. But at the same time, we realize that mental life—so-called "lived experience"—cannot be subsumed under the laws of nature as if we treated these experiences like mere things of nature. Instead, they can be *understood*. We can understand the interconnections of lived experience as interconnections of human motivations—and we see that mind is a field of interconnections that can be understood. So, for causal interconnections, an explanatory psychology; for human motivational interconnections, an understanding psychology. But if we ask what the whole of this psychology is—i.e., what holds both of them together not as a summation but as the underlying wholeness—we get no answer. In fact, the question has never really been posed.

But the problem [36] is even more complicated, inasmuch as in the course of its development in the modern epoch, the study of mind has concentrated on *conscious* mental processes. It has focused, in a word, on consciousness—"lived experience" in the narrow sense—so that since Descartes psychology is essentially the science of consciousness. Moreover, in the development of modern philosophy, this science of consciousness has fallen into a natural-scientific methodology with the result that even the network of objects that we call *understandable* has been characterized as a network of nature. Therefore from another viewpoint, we have to speak of the natural-scientific method's second breakthrough into the exploration of mind.

Nowadays, the project of psychology—if we can even delimit here a unified and self-clarified discipline—has an entirely chaotic form. Psychology is invaded by ethnology and research into the historical possibilities of the life of the primitives, by anthropology, by so-called parapsychology (the science of occult phenomena), by psychopathology (the science of mental illness)—so much so that we can no longer say what psychology is. It's everything and nothing. Of course, by characterizing things this way, I do not mean to cast doubts on the concrete, individual work of researchers in the specific fields, which always, within certain limits, brings to light relevant outcomes. Here we are speaking only of the philosophical idea of psychology and its foundations.

This particularly chaotic development of contemporary psychology is in fact only an indication of the process of inner self-dissolution that is going on in contemporary existence. The substance, so to speak, of to-day's existence is simply this business of the disintegration of one's own mind and soul. Finally this disintegration, out of disgust with itself, will hit bottom. So, if we speak of psychology in what follows, we have to be quite clear that we basically do not know what it is. Nonetheless, given the course objectives and the field [37] we are dealing with here, it will suffice to base our treatment on the concept of psychology that Husserl used in a quite traditional way.

We asked how logic and psychology get connected at all in such a way that psychology is able to play a special role within logic.

The connection of the two becomes clear as soon as we hold our-selves to the traditional understanding of the concept of logic. In that concept, logic is the doctrine of thinking, in fact of correct thinking. More precisely, it is the doctrine that teaches correct thinking, the "doctrine of reason"—the technique, or better, the technic of correct thinking.[1] But such thinking is correct if it follows the rules to which it is subject. Therefore, as such a technic, logic is the science of think-ing and its rules, the science of how we should think (even Kant gave it this definition), the science of the norms of correct thinking: a nor-mative discipline.

The correctness of thinking consists in the thinking's correspondence to rules. The rules are the formulations—"formulae"—of the laws that pertain to thought, the laws expressed and understood in propositions. Therefore, logic deals with thinking with regard to the laws that deter-mine it.

So, the basic theme of logic necessarily becomes the lawfulness of thinking—or (to put it more fully) it becomes that very thinking itself, in what it is and what it should be when measured against the laws of thinking.

Lawfulness is the theme. Where are these laws supposed to come from? If the determination of the laws is to be relevant to the material

---

1. [Heidegger uses three equivalent terms in this paragraph: *Technik, Technolo-gie,* and *Kunstlehre.* I render them all as either "technique," "art," or "technic": the theory, principles, or study of an art or process.]

in question, then the laws have to be taken from thinking itself. And not from just any kind of constructed thought, but from the actual acts and procedures of thought. In other words, the laws are to be sought in the living activity of the very processes of thought. Active thinking is the same as the mental occurrence, the mental reality, that must produce the laws. But mental reality is the theme of psychology. Therefore, [38] the basic project of logic—which is to get the laws of thought and to characterize the very act of thinking (which still remains a mental process)—belongs within the competence of psychology. So psychology is logic's foundational discipline.

Thus John Stuart Mill writes:

> [Logic] is not a Science distinct from, and coordinate with, Psychology. So far as it is a science at all, it is a part, or branch, of Psychology; differing from it, on the one hand as a part differs from the whole, and on the other, as an Art differs from a Science.[2] Its theoretic grounds are wholly borrowed from Psychology, and include as much of that science as is required to justify the rules of the art. (John Stuart Mill, *An Examination of S. W. Hamilton's Philosophy*.[3] Compare Husserl, *Logical Investigations*, vol. 1, "Prolegomena to Pure Logic," chap. 5, pp. 78 ff.)[4]

And Theodor Lipps:

> The very fact that logic is a special discipline within psychology distinguishes each from the other in a sufficiently clear way. (*Grundzüge der Logik*, 1893, §3)[5]

Compare further:

2. [Heidegger glosses: "That is, as a *Kunstlehre* or technique [differs] from a theoretical reflection."]

3. [Heidegger cites the German as it appears in the first edition of Husserl's *Logische Untersuchungen*, vol. 1, §17, p. 51 / tr. 90-91. Mill's text is from John Stuart Mill, *An Examination of Sir William Hamilton's Philosophy and of the Principal Philosophical Questions Discussed in his Writings*, 5th edition (London: Longmans, Green & Co., 1878), p. 461: Heidegger cites the text in Theodor Gomperz's translation. The work is reprinted as vol. 9 of John Stuart Mill, *Collected Writings*, 33 vols., ed. John M. Robson (Toronto: University of Toronto Press / London: Routledge & Kegan Paul, 1981-1991); here, vol. 9, p. 359.]

4. [In *LU*, vol. 1, §§25-26, pp. 78-84 / tr. 111-115, Husserl discusses Mill's position on the law of contradiction. Neither Weiss nor Moser provides this reference, which means that Heidegger did not read it out in class.]

5. [Theodor Lipps (1851-1914), *Grundzüge der Logik* (Hamburg and Leipzig: J. A. Barth, 1893; 2nd edition, 1911). Heidegger takes the citation from Husserl, *LU*, vol. 1, §18, p. 52 / tr. 91.]

Logic is a psychological discipline precisely because knowing occurs only in the mind, and because thinking, which reaches its completion in knowing, is a mental happening.[6]

Recall as well that in the nineteenth century the exact scientific method of modern natural science was carried over into psychology. According to its proponents, only in this way did psychology work itself up to the level of an exact science. That implies that, along with this psychology, there was also founded for the first time *the* exact and strict science that, by exact investigations into thinking and its laws, was also sure to create the exact and strict foundations of logic.[7]

*   *   *

In this view, the inclusion of logic within psychology is clear and self-evident, and the reasoning that argues for this connection is so consistent that scarcely an objection can be raised against it. And so [39] this interpretation of the meaning of logic and the project of psychology as regards logic gained widespread acceptance.

As the art of correct thinking, logic will primarily aim at the securing of correctness and at conformity to rules and laws. Its basic theme is the conformity of thought-processes to law, the lawfulness of thinking, which from time immemorial has been formulated as basic laws of thinking. If these laws are to rule all scientific thinking, they themselves cannot rest on insecure ground but must be proven and demonstrated with the highest degree of scientific certitude. They cannot be invented but must be gotten from the data of thought itself, and their universal validity must be demonstrated.

Psychologism reveals its characteristic way of asking questions in the very way it handles and interprets the principles of thought. As an illustration we choose its interpretation of the principle of contradiction and its way of proving the law-giving nature of this principle. We will do so in a general way, without going into the specific content of its structure and the full determination of its proper meaning. The principle: "The same proposition cannot at the same time be both true and false."
John Stuart Mill writes:

I consider it {the *principium contradictionis*} to be, like other axioms, one of our first and most familiar generalizations from experience. The original

---

6. [Lipps, op. cit.; cited in Husserl, *LU,* vol. 1, §18, p. 52 n. 2 / tr. 91 n. 1.]

7. [Here (Moser, p. 79) Heidegger ends his lecture of Wednesday, 11 November 1925 (also the seventh anniversary of the end of the Great War), to be followed by that of Thursday, 12 November, which opened with a 420-word summary that is omitted in GA 21.]

foundation of it I take to be, that Belief and Disbelief {by this Mill means taking something as true and taking something as false} are two different mental states, excluding one another. This we know by the simplest observation of our own minds. (*System of Logic*, bk. 2, chap. 7)[8]

Thus it is a matter of the ability of our mind to observe in an experiential way; and this shows that taking a proposition as true and taking the same proposition as false are two different states of mind. We meet up with this in observing our minds or our inner life. Continuing:

And if we carry our observation outwards {i.e., in words}, we also find that light and darkness, sound and silence, motion and quiescence, equality and inequality, preceding and following, succession and simultaneousness, any positive phenomenon whatever and its negative, are distinct phenomena, pointedly contrasted, and the one {namely, affirmation} [40] always absent where the other {negation} is present. I consider the maxim in question to be a generalization from all these facts. (John Stuart Mill, *Gesammelte Werke*, 1884, vol. 2, p. 326)[9]

The principle of contradiction is merely a generalization of matters of fact, both physical facts in the outer world and mental states of affairs. There are physical incompatibilities, things that cannot subsist together.[10] The same holds for facts of the mental world. States of belief and disbelief—i.e., holding something to be true and holding the same thing to be not true—these two acts are incompatible with each other. Affirming and denying the same proposition make it impossible for them to be co-present in one and the same mind.

The axiom [of non-contradiction] merely states these same facts in a general form when it speaks of propositions that can apply either to the physical or the mental.

Sigwart's logic has essentially defined the inquiry into logic since

8. [John Stuart Mill, *A System of Logic, Rationative and Inductive*, in *CW*, vol. 7, pp. 277–278. The glosses by Heidegger do not show up in GA 21 and are taken from Moser, pp. 82–83.]

9. [This reference, which does not appear in Moser or Weiss, is to John Stuart Mill, *Gesammelte Werke*, 2nd edition, ed. Theodor Gomperz (Leipzig: Fues, 1884). In the *Logische Untersuchungen*, Husserl used Gomperz's first edition (1872–1873), in which the cited text appears at vol. 1, p. 298, and where the reference is to §4 (§5 was added in the 1872 English edition of Mill's work, which is not reflected in Gomperz's first German edition). See *LU*, vol. 1, §25, p. 79 / tr. 111–112.]

10. [At this point in Heidegger's own manuscript (as published in GA 21, p. 40.7) there appears the following: "(cf. Leibniz's '*intra*'–the '*simul*')," i.e., "(compare Leibniz: 'between' and the 'at the same time')." There is no evidence in Moser or Weiss that he spoke these words during this lecture.]

the 1870s, and he agrees in principle with this derivation of the principle of contradiction (*Logik*, vol. 1, §45, p. 5 n.). He calls the principle of contradiction a law of nature that says, "it is impossible at any given moment to say, with conscious awareness, that A is B and that A is not B." Because it is a law of nature, it can also be understood as a standard law aimed at the practical regulation of thinking. In other words, it "applies to the whole range of constant concepts."[11]

It not only works as but also *is* a lawful demand, and it also presents itself as a norm for the procedure of thinking.

The validity of the principle rests "on the immediate awareness that, in negation, we always do and always will do the same thing—so certainly we are the same persons" (Sigwart, *Logik*, p. 402).[12]

In this way the lawfulness—and consequently, the validity—of thinking are reduced to the uniformity in the constitution of our nature [41] and of our way of thinking. Thus Sigwart:

> On the other hand, if we deny the possibility of knowing something as it is in itself, if the entity is only a thought that we produce {Sigwart thinks he is reporting the Kantian position here}, then it holds that we even attribute objectivity to such ideas that we produce with the consciousness of their necessity. And it holds that as soon as we posit something as existing, we consequently affirm that (even if taken hypothetically) all other thinking beings that have the same nature as ours have to produce the same thoughts with the same necessity. (*Logik*, §1, p. 8)

So even if we admit that, to put it roughly, we cannot know the outer world as it is but can only regulate and order our representations, nonetheless the necessity with which we connect certain representations with one another is the criterion for the objective validity of whatever we think by means of these representations. And we make the presupposition that other [thinking] beings are organized the way we are, and that they have to think what we think. Therefore, a communally held knowledge of the objective world is possible in spite of the fact that we do not get outside our own consciousness. In the same place Sigwart also says that this necessary and universally valid thinking is nothing else but the concept of what we call the essence of truth. Truth is nothing but the necessity and universal validity of the combination of representations, a necessity that is ultimately ruled by the principle of contradiction, the validity of which is founded on our mental nature.

Lipps says,

---

11. [H. Sigwert, *Logik*, 4th edition (1921), p. 401.]

12. Validity is reduced to the constancy of our behavior and our being; we are firmly predisposed in such a way that we cannot do otherwise.

... the rules that one must follow in order to think rightly are nothing
other than rules one must follow in order to think in the way demanded
by the proper nature of thinking, by its own particular set of laws. To put
it succinctly, they are identical with the natural laws of thinking itself.
Logic is a physics of thinking, or it is nothing at all. [42][13]

This reduction of the laws of thought—and therefore of the validity
of propositions, and therefore of truth itself—to the natural constitution of mental processes can now also be understood to say that mental organization is specific to human being. Human nature has this
organization; the laws of thought have a material, anthropological necessity; and psychologism is now, in a narrow sense, *anthropologism*.

Benno Erdmann has advocated this deteriorated form of psychologism in an extreme but consistent way in his *Logik* (cf. Husserl, *Logical
Investigations*, vol. 1, p. 155):

Since Aristotle, an overwhelming majority has held that the necessity of
these (logical) principles is unconditional and that their validity is, therefore, eternal. . . . People have tried to locate the decisive proof for this state
of affairs in the fact that it is impossible to think judgments that contradict
themselves. However, the only thing that follows from this {the impossibility of thinking A is B and A is not B at the same time} is that those principles mirror the essence of *our* way of representing and thinking. If they
reveal this, it will not be possible to carry out self-contradictory judgments,
since such judgments attempt to annul the very conditions to which all
our forms of representing, thinking, and judging are bound.[14]

Consequently, the validity of the laws of thought is only relative to our
human make-up. We cannot speak with reason about some uncondi-
tionedness of the validity of these laws.
Continuing:

The necessity of the principles thus established would be unconditioned
{i.e., absolutely valid} . . . only if our knowledge of those principles guar-
anteed that the essence of the thinking we find within ourselves and that
we express by means of those principles were itself unchangeable or indeed were the only possible essence of thinking; and {if we could show}
that those conditions of *our* thinking were at the same time the conditions

13. [Theodor Lipps, "Die Aufgabe der Erkenntnistheorie und die Wundt'sche
Logik (I)," *Philosophische Monatshefte* 16 (1880), here pp. 530–531; cited in Husserl,
LU, vol. 1, §19, p. 55 / tr. 93.]

14. Erdmann, *Logik*, §60, no. 369, p. 375. [Benno Erdmann (1851–1921), *Logik*,
vol. 1: *Logische Elementarlehre* (Halle, 1892; 2nd fully rev. edition, 1907). Cited in
Husserl, *LU*, vol. 1, §40, p. 137 / tr. 155. Heidegger adds the emphasis on "our."]

of *any* possible thinking. But we only know about *our* thinking. We are unable to construe some kind of thinking different from our own, and therefore, we cannot construe some thinking-in-general as a genus of such different kinds of thinking. . . . [43] Words that appear to describe such a kind of thinking have no sense we can work out that would satisfy the claim that this appearance allegedly raises. For every attempt {to produce} what they describe is bound to the conditions of our representing and thinking and moves within their orbit.[15]

The necessity of the logical propositions for thought is not an "absolute" necessity, but only a "hypothetical" one. They are valid on the presupposition that our thinking "remains the same."[16]

We cannot deduce the unchangeability of our mind and of its basic constitution as absolutely remaining the same. We are stuck with this fact, and therefore with the contingency and conditionedness of the factual. The possibility of a change in our make-up is not excluded: maybe in a hundred years people will have to think $2 \times 2 = 5$. Or maybe even now, on some other planets, living beings with a different make-up have a mental organization that gets along without these principles and that regulates thought with other principles.

---

§7. Husserl's critique of psychologism

Husserl's critique intends to be a fundamental one: it wants to get to the principles of the position that it criticizes. We can explain this critique from two points of view:

- a) as a demonstration of the contradiction that lies at the heart of psychologism's position;
- b) as a demonstration of the fundamental errors of this position when it tries to establish itself.

Concerning (a): Some preliminaries of the critique

The demonstration of the contradiction lying at the heart of the position takes as its goal to unmask psychologism as a skeptical relativism. For that, we have to establish a strictly formal concept of skepticism. [44] For that we have to begin with the positive—the idea of theory.

A "theory" in Husserl's sense is not some system of hypotheses, of principles posited conditionally for the sake of possibly explaining a

---

15. [Erdmann, *Logik*, vol. 1, §60, no. 370, p. 378; cited in Husserl, *LU*, vol. 1, §40, pp. 143–144 / tr. 155.]

16. [Ibid.; cited in Husserl, *LU*, vol. 1, §40, p. 147 / tr. 160.]

group of data. Rather, it is "theory" more in the Greek sense of θεωρία: the unity of a self-enclosed and grounding ensemble of true propositions—in the first instance, a deduction, e.g., a mathematical theory. For every theory—i.e., for theory as such—there are the conditions of the possibility of a rational justification of itself. One of these conditions, for example, is the principle of identity: the principle of the same universal validity of the theory's axioms as one proceeds through the grounded steps of the deduction.

Then there is the necessary validity of such axioms as such. If a given theory-and-science collides with these conditions, it collides with the very thing that makes the theory possible. That specific theory conflicts with the very meaning that it is supposed to have as a theory. It loses all rational (or, as Husserl would say, "consistent") meaning.

Now if the propositional content of a theory is such as to deny the conditions of the possibility of any theory at all, then that theory is absolutely absurd at its core, totally "inconsistent." And such inconsistency of meaning entails surrendering all rationality and abandoning every possibility of a justified statement and grounding. The distinguishing feature of any theory of skepticism is that the very content of its theory claims that the conditions of the possibility of any theory are at bottom false. (Compare *Logische Untersuchungen* vol. 1, 112.)[17]

When it comes to determining relativism, it may be said that all truth is valid only in relation to the subject who happens to make the judgment. This judging subject can be understood as the individual subject who is making the judgment here and now; or as the species: not this or that person but human being as such, [45] in contrast to, for example, the angels. That specific form of relativism that makes the validity of knowledge relative to the human species is also called "anthropologism."[18]

*   *   *

Having clarified the basic concepts employed in the critique, let us turn to the critique itself. Anthropologism as a specific form of relativism maintains that the true is what must hold true in relation to the mental make-up and law of thought of the species in question. This entails that the same proposition can be true for one species and false for another. But one and the same proposition cannot be both true and false. That would be nonsense. And it's equally absurd to talk about a truth that would hold only for this species or that.

17. [That is, *LU,* vol. 1, §32, p. 112 / tr. 136–137.]

18. [Here (Moser, p. 94) Heidegger ends his lecture of Thursday, 12 November 1925, to be followed by that of Monday, 16 November, which opened with a 400-word summary that is omitted in GA 21. Heidegger did not lecture on Friday, 13 November.]

What is true is absolutely true, true "in itself." Truth is one and identical, whether it be human beings or monsters, angels or gods who understand and judge it. Logical laws speak of truth in this ideal unity, as over against the *de facto* multiplicity of races, individuals, and experiences. And so do all of us, as long as we are not confused by relativism. (vol. 1, p. 117f.)[19]

Husserl varies this same line of reasoning in many different ways. From a formal viewpoint this argument about the contradiction in the theory of psychologism is the most basic. However, it's the second line of argument that packs a particularly incisive punch.

Concerning (b): Demonstration of the fundamental errors

To anticipate the heart of the matter at this point: Psychologism tries to demonstrate logical principles from facts, or (to put it in terms of Leibniz, whom Husserl has explicitly in mind) to shore up *vérités de raison*, "truths of reason" (truths [taken] from concepts), with *vérités de fait*, "truths of fact."[20]

α) This remarkable form of demonstration can be illustrated by the way logical principles are handled. Compare John Stuart Mill on the principle of contradiction: It is a generalization of facts, and as that kind of generalization, is always related to empirical facts.[21] [46] Now, however, it is not just restricted to physical facts but is broadened to the realm where it applies to mind—mental states. The principle: If there are two contradictory propositions, they cannot both be jointly true.

This inability-to-be-true is understood as a *de facto* relation between acts: their impossibility of subsisting alongside each other. Husserl now demonstrates that this interpretation of the principles of contradiction—the impossibility of the co-existence of mental states—turns the meaning of the principle upside down. The principle does not deal with the occurrence/co-occurrence of acts of judgment *qua* mental events. It deals with states of affairs that the judgments intend insofar as they cannot subsist together.[22]

So it is a not a question of a subjective, mental impossibility but of an objective, law-governed incompatibility of valid propositions. The direct meaning of what the principle says is that the two meanings intended by the two propositions cannot have joint validity. "A is b" and "A is not b"—the incompatibility of the intended "b-ness of A" with the "non-b-ness of A"—has nothing to do with mental occur-

19. [That is, *LU*, vol. 1, §36, pp. 117–118 / tr. 140.]

20. [The French phrases were not spoken in the lecture: Moser, p. 97.25–32.]

21. [Here and in what immediately follows, Heidegger contrasts the *real* and the *ideal*. To avoid misunderstanding, I translate these terms as "empirical" and "ideal."]

22. That is, not about the togetherness [*Zusammenvorhandensein*] or co-existence [*Ko-existenz*] of *mental states*, but about their con-sistency [*Kon-sistenz*]!

rences and states, and their co-existence. As regards the matter that is judged: The *meaning* of the judgment 2 × 2 = 4 is not something mental, not something that arises and transpires in a stream of mental occurrences along with such things as sense impressions and moods. The meaning does not go on for a period of time and then disappear. This content of the judgment, the content of the proposition—in a word, the proposition itself—is what is valid, what is the truth as such. At most, what is mental is the act of performing the judgment or performing the statement of the judgment. The judgment's adjudged content, that which is stated to be true, is not an empirical mental event. It is something non-empirical. It is *ideal being, validity.*

The basic error of psychologism is that it interprets the principle of contradiction as a statement about [47] empirical mental events and is blind to the real meaning of the principle. The principle asserts something about ideal being, about the possibility and impossibility of truths to have validity when taken together. It intends ideal relations between truths, and not relations of empirical facts and events in nature, be they mental or physical; it can simply never be a law of nature, a law of real being.

β) Psychologism misunderstands the fundamental distinction between the empirical being of the act of judging and the ideal validity of judged content. Corresponding to that, there is the misunderstanding of the kind of lawfulness that goes with each case. The lawfulness of the principle of contradiction is not an empirical lawfulness but an ideal one, and its necessity is not some empirical constraint but a normative regulation.

The law says nothing about the empirical, causal dependence of acts of thought upon each other (Wundt). The principle says nothing about the law-governed being of temporal, individual mental events running their course in the mind. It is not a law about empirical facts but says something about the intrinsically and eternally valid subsistence of truths, and the eternal impossibility of some of them being held together, be they actually performed or not. The laws not only *do not* govern mental events, they do not even presuppose them.

γ) Because the meaning of natural laws is that they pertain to empirical facts, they also can get their foundation only from these facts— that is, only by observing and surveying such facts—by way of induction. As regards their validity all these laws, even the most general ones like the law of gravity, are fundamentally only probable, even if this probability is of the highest order.

As empirical laws, their defining mark is to be *probable*. They never get free of this limitation which constantly and essentially goes with them and which says: "So far as we have observed and as long as [48] further experience does not contradict the probable law . . ." On the other hand, the principles that govern thinking are unconditioned laws and are able to be seen only by "ideation" or from pure concepts. They are not subject to the limiting condition, "if . . ." The principle of contradiction is intrinsically valid, and its validity is independent of how many people or what kind of people accept and enact it. It does not mean that the validities of two contradictions are incompatible *so long as* all individual minds think according to the same law, but the reverse. If thinking is to be lawful, it must be subject to this rule that is founded on the absolute state of mutual incompatibility between contradictory propositions and propositional meanings. The validity of the principle of contradiction is not and cannot be affected by the mental organization of human beings, because this very principle implies nothing about such organization. What can and do change are mental capacities for understanding, and the degree of the mental possibility of comprehension, and the degree of depth in understanding.[23]

δ) So we finally see that even the kind of certitude with which we understand and embrace the empirical laws of psychology and the ideal laws governing meaning and propositional content is different. Apprehending ideal laws is characterized by apodictic insight: the laws are absolutely free of doubt. The certitude of our knowledge of empirical laws is propositional: it yields only a *de facto* and probable "it's-this-way-and-not-otherwise." Apodictic certainty yields an unequivocal, absolute "cannot-be-otherwise."

But that lets us immediately see the fundamental error that psychologism lives off. It tries to establish something about the ideal being and ideal relations of valid statements by means of knowledge of empirical events in the mind, i.e., in temporally changing reality. As regards certitude, all knowledge of empirical facts has only the mark of probability. By their very nature and claim, the principles of thought, however, [49] are valid not for this or that case nor, as it were, for a while, but unconditionally and absolutely. Therefore the probable knowledge of facts can decide nothing about the unconditioned relations of validity. Likewise, the certitude of propositional knowledge of facts is inadequate for the vision that accompanies absolutely valid propositions: apodictic certitude.

Basic laws of thought, which do not intend empirical facts, cannot be *corroborated* or *refuted* by such empirical facts. For all its explanations, for all its claims to have the laws of thought for its subject matter, psychologism never operates in the arena where alone those judgments are made.

23. [The German *Ursprünglichkeit* here means "closeness to the origin" rather than "originality"; hence, "depth."]

With [Wilhelm] Erdmann, the extreme anthropologist, the only logical consistency is this: If psychologism is made the court of judgment on the nature and validity of the principles of thinking, then these principles are indeed only rules governing empirical facts. This means that the matter under investigation is determined according to the kind of science related to it, rather than vice versa. But then this procedure can be carried out only at the price of a complete misinterpretation of the principles of thought. These principles are not laws *qua* regulations of the course of mental processes. They are principles about "propositions"; and "propositions" are what is judged in a judgment. They are the adjudged state of affairs: the b-ness of A, the non-b-ness of A. Any incompatibility is an incompatibility of propositions. It is not an impossibility of thinking, but of what is thought as such. For example, someone mentally ill can very easily assert both propositions and unite them in one consciousness.

The meaning of the principle of contradiction is not at all related to the framework of mental events. That is, its validity is completely independent of a possible change in the mental nature of human beings.

Psychologism became possible only because of the domination of a naturalistic attitude over reason and spirit: the spiritual—namely, meaning—is accessible only as mental [50] reality. Thus, the guiding preconception of what is presumably to be treated gets inverted from what is thought as such to thinking as empirical and mental. This inversion of the meaning of logic's subject matter is the source of the absurdities.

The dominance of naturalism, whereby everything is experienced and interpreted as natural reality, is rooted in a blindness to the non-empirical, to propositional content as such—meaning—*ideal* being.

Psychologism's fundamental error is its failure to recognize the difference: a basic distinction in the being of beings. It becomes clear, then, that interpreting psychologism as the basic science of logic (the logic adequate to its subject matter) stands or falls with a correct recognition of this difference in being. We realize that, to the degree that logic is determined by this difference, logic is constructed on an ontological basis.

What kind of entity does logic study with regard to its being? In keeping with what we established earlier, the subject matter of logic is truth. What kind of being is something's being-true? And how is truth itself to be understood in relation to the idea of being in general? The following will have to suffice.

The discussion and criticism of psychologism makes it clear that in the background of the discussion lie basic concepts and distinctions taken from the fundamental, universal question about the meaning of being. [The critique distinguishes between] the empirical being of mind and the ideal being of the judged proposition, as well as between the temporal occurrence of the empirical and the supratemporal subsistence of the idea.

Today we can hardly conceive how such a fundamental mix-up was possible, and how anyone could believe that we could understand anything about the logical structure of what is thought as such—the "thought"—by way of a psychological study of thinking. But the fact is that only a very few [51] managed to stay free of this mess. Or, to put it another way: Thought and thinking got mixed up together for the most part; but when psychologism was attacked, it could always appeal to the fact that it did not deny the absolute validity of the laws of thought (which it understood in a natural sense) while empirical scientific inquiry pressed to the fore its attitude toward the mind. Only the Marburg School, and [Wilhelm] Schuppe with his *Erkenntnistheoretische Logik,* remained relatively untouched by these opinions.[24] The Marburg School, by means of a particular interpretation of Kant, protected itself against psychologism's invasion of the theory of consciousness, and therefore Natorp could legitimately say in a critique of Husserl's *Logical Investigations* (*Kantstudien,* 1901)[25] that the members of the Marburg School had been unable to learn very much from this critique of psychologism.

In fact, that is correct. But on the other hand, only Husserl's critique opened the way by largely exposing the contradiction, clarifying it, and tracing it to its roots. And in that regard, we have to say that the Marburg School, as counter-position, did not clarify everything. Within the School's position, the question about consciousness as distinct from the so-called mental has remained very questionable. That's bound up with the fact that the Marburg interpretation of Kant never clarified to what degree in Kant himself a specific psychology or even anthropology constitutes the essential foundations of his critique of reason.

Hermann Cohen, founder of the Marburg School, says in his *Logik*[26] that this proximity to psychology is a great danger for logic, but he believed that the emergence of so-called phenomenology (which he somewhat maliciously dubbed a new scholasticism) increased rather than removed the danger. And he was right. The phenomenological critique of psychologism in fact increased the danger. That is, philosophy will be forced to confront the question about what really is the case [52] with this "mental." Can we simply brush off the act of judging, its enactment, or the statement, as something empirical and mental, as contrasted with a so-called ideal sense? Or does an entirely different dimension of being

24. [Wilhelm Schuppe (1836–1913), *Erkenntnisstheoretische Logik* (Bonn: Eduard Weber, 1878).]

25. [Paul Natorp (1854–1924), "Zur Frage der logischen Methode. Mit Beziehung auf Edmund Husserls ‚Prolegomena zur reinen Logik'," *Kantstudien* 6 (1901): 270–283.]

26. [Hermann Cohen (1842–1918), *System der Philosophie,* vol. 1: *Logik der reinen Erkenntnis* (Berlin: B. Cassirer, 1902; 2nd edition, 1914; 3d edition, 1922).]

finally press to the fore here, one that can certainly be very dangerous once we glimpse it and expound it as something fundamental? Therefore we could say that although this critique of psychologism is from the outset utterly clear on the guiding distinction between empirical and ideal being, nonetheless the positive questions that now press forward from this distinction are quite difficult. These are questions that did not surface first of all in the nineteenth or twentieth centuries, but that already engaged Greek philosophy, especially Plato. This distinction is the same as the Platonic one between sensible being, the αἰσθητόν, and the being that is accessible through reason or νοῦς: the νοητόν. The inquiry today takes up again the question of the μέθεξις, the participation of the real in the ideal, and it is up for grabs whether or not we can get clear on the phenomenon of thinking, of the thought, and more broadly of truth, by stating the problem in these terms.[27]

*   *   *

I have already indicated that psychologism as a theory has not restricted itself to logic but has also played a role in ethics and aesthetics, insofar as people attempted to apprehend and understand the problems of ethics and aesthetics from psychology. Husserl's criticism was directed essentially to psychologism in logic, although his criticism occasionally touched in passing on basic questions in ethics. In that context, Husserl shows that every ethics claims to be a science of norms, a science of correct acting, analogous to logic as the science of the norms of correct thinking. But therefore it presupposes a theoretical discipline as the foundational discipline for a normative science of norms—and that science cannot be psychology. Rather, [53] just as logic deals with the pure content of propositions, so analogously ethics must deal with the pure content of norms, that is, with values. In other words, Husserl's critique of psychologism also opened the path to a critique of values. Scheler has taken up this question, and in the field of ethics or practical philosophy he has constructed an ethics of value.

We may say, then, that the essence of psychologism consists in a confusion of empirical mental being with the ideal being of laws. When I say "confusion," please do not take that in a superficial sense, as if psychologism somehow mixed up two available things, like red and blue. Obviously the theory did not begin that way. But I would say that the confusion is based on the fact that at that time philosophy was largely blocked off from various regions of being. It was blind to them, cut off from them and locked up in one specific area of being, that of

27. [Here (Moser, p. 112) Heidegger ends his lecture of Monday, 16 November 1925, to be followed by that of Tuesday, November 17, which opened with a brief 50-word summary that is omitted in GA 21.]

the empirical nature of the physical and mental, which were taken as if they were one. We can understand this confusion in terms of the destiny of philosophy toward the end of the nineteenth century. Every philosophy and science has its destiny, and it would be small-minded and bourgeois to think that we could exempt ourselves from these conditions imposed on questioning and seeing.

---

§8. The presuppositions of Husserl's critique: a specific concept of truth as the guiding idea

Every genuine critique has to speak from a positive position. In the present case, that means that Husserl could point out the error of psychologism and demonstrate it to be absurd, only insofar as he had already beforehand gotten a firm grip [54] on the basic distinction of being as empirical and as ideal. The content of the whole critique is basically nothing but the strict and relentless enforcement of this distinction with regard to thinking. The distinction is between thinking as an act of thinking and thinking as what-is-thought, the "thought."

The lawfulness of thinking, which has to be the subject matter of logic, is not the lawfulness of the *act* of thinking, but of *what-is-thought*. The legitimacy and correctness—the truth of thinking, the truth that originates from the adequation of things to laws—is also a feature of what-is-thought. With that we have a general direction for understanding the concept of truth that underlies the critique of psychologism and that is then explicitly carried through from the *Logical Investigations* onward—namely, validity.

Thus truth is not some kind of empirical property of a mental occurrence, like weariness or inhibition. Rather, it is a mark of the "content of thought." What is true in the primary instance is not the act of proposing or the connections of the proposing but what is proposed as such, the proposition. Truth has its home in the proposition in itself. The proposition itself , as such, and precisely as truth, is called a truth in itself: $2 \times 2 = 4$.

To exemplify this in terms of λόγος: In this view, what is true is not the λέγειν, the speaking and discussing, but the λεγόμενον, that which is said as such, that which is sayable and posited in each case and always in the same way: the λεκτόν [what can be expressed; the meaning].

οἱ μὲν ἐν τῷ σημαινομένῳ, τουτέστιν ἀσωμάτῳ λεκτῷ, τὸ ἀληθὲς καὶ τὸ ψεῦδος ὑποτίθενται, οἱ δ᾽ ἐν τῇ φωνῇ, οἱ δ᾽ ἐν τῷ κινήματι τῆς διανοίας. (Sextus Empiricus, *Adversus Mathematicos* VIII, 69)[28]

28. [See *SE,* vol. 2, pp. 270, 272.]

[Some assume that the true and the false is in the signified, i.e., in the incorporeal λεκτόν; others in the spoken sound; and still others, in the movement of the discursive intellect.][29]

Truth is thus a characteristic of ideal being.

At this point we should clarify the distinction between the real [i.e., the empirical] and the ideal, and determine how this distinction is relevant to the formulation of the concept of truth. To that end we begin with a statement, a proposition: "The board is black." The statement can be roughly characterized as a succession of positings. [55] The positing of the board as that-about-which the judgment is made; the positing of the black from out of the already given object (the board); and also positing as the positing-as-distinct (διαίρεσις) in the sense (and intent) of im-posing blackness upon the subject. What gets articulated, joined together, and intended in this succession of positings can be called the "judged" as such: that which is judged, the content of the positing, in short, the proposition of the blackness or being-black of the board. The content of this proposition can be asserted by each one of you—i.e., by different individuals in different circumstances, at different times, with different clarity, in different moods, in different propositional and judgmental contexts. But what is judged in this endless series of instances is always the same proposition. What is intended is always one identical propositional content.

Therefore, a proposition is always a self-identical thing that maintains its identity in face of the multiplicity of empirical acts of positing judgments with their empirical circumstances and properties. And this changing mental act is differentiated from the abiding propositional content not only as a matter of fact but also, at bottom, arbitrarily. What are differentiated are the identity and permanence of the proposition versus the variability and change of the positings; on the one hand, the temporal course of the mental act while the judgment is being performed; and on the other hand, the non-temporal subsistence of the ideal meaning that is judged.

But we also know this correlation from other regions of objects. We speak of "color" in contrast to a changing plurality of colors; and we speak of "red" in contrast to these or those red things, a limitless profusion of different shades of red, each one having this determination of "red." Or the "triangle" that is to be found in a series of different triangles, whether drawn, painted, thought of, or imagined. So we have the idea "triangle" as self-identical, just as we have the idea

29. [In Moser (pp. 130–132), Heidegger's opening remarks for the next lecture (19 November 1925) offered an extended commentary on this text from Sextus Empiricus; this commentary does not appear in GA 21.]

"color" as something that maintains identity in the plurality of its different presentations. [56]

Plato was the first to understand as a whole this relation and distinction of identity and difference, permanence and change. What is identical and abiding is what is present and visible in every triangle, in every color, what is always already there "in" them. It is, so to speak, what tells how the object in question *looks*. Triangle, color, house—this appearance, the real "looks" that make up the given thing and make it what it is, is called by the Greeks εἶδος—ἰδέα. In the first instance, ἰδέα means what we catch sight of: that which is seen. But it also means that in a thing which makes the thing be what it is.

It is not at first obvious or clear why what makes a thing be what it is gets called an "idea." But if we look at the *way* the thing in question is grasped, we can understand why the Greeks gave the name "idea" to the abiding essence of a thing, that which makes the thing be what it is. What makes a thing be what it is, is its permanence: that which is glimpsed in every individual instance. The act of seeing, in this very broad sense of "apprehending something in itself," was for the Greeks the highest way of apprehending any entity. And in this way of apprehending through seeing, we have access to what makes a thing be what it is. And since this content or essence of the thing becomes accessible through seeing, it is called an "idea." So the word "idea" is not a determination of *what* is meant. Instead, the term is derived from *how* the meant is *apprehended*. This determination grew out of the fact that, for the Greeks, looking and seeing—θεωρία, *intuitus*, intuition—was the primary form of apprehension. As Aristotle says at the beginning of the *Metaphysics* (I, 1, 980a20), seeing is really what human beings strive for in the field of knowledge.[30] The priority of seeing as the fundamental mode of apprehension ultimately has its roots in curiosity. Even in Kant and, generally speaking, in all of Western philosophy up to today—and today in an entirely new way[31]—[57] intuition, immediate seeing, has this remarkable priority in comprehending being.

And so this one identical something that is seen in the multiplicity of things is called the idea, and accordingly we now say that the being of this "what," of this self-identical something, is the idea-ness or ideal being of something. Ideal being can now be understood as the being of that something which makes an object be what it is, i.e., as the being of the identity that persists without change, in contrast to the variation of its concrete instantiations. And so for Plato the properties of

---

30. [Heidegger takes Aristotle's word εἰδέναι in its literal meaning of "to see" (compare ὀμμάτων, "eyes," at 980a24) rather than in its more usual meaning of "to know" (= "to have fully seen and therefore to know").]

31. [The implicit reference is to Husserl's *Wesenschau*, the "seeing" of essences.]

that identity that he calls the idea are as follows. First of all, these ideas or εἴδη, are ἀΐδια, i.e., eternal and ever the same, without change, in contrast to things that change. He explains that by saying they are ἀγένητα καὶ ἀνώλεθρα, i.e., what he calls an idea does not come into being or pass away, and is indestructible, free of change. The distinction between real and ideal being goes back to this basic ontological distinction in Greek philosophy, back to Plato.

Now we may characterize more precisely these two regions of being—the abiding, self-same ideal versus the changing real—in terms of the way we apprehend them. What is permanent about a sensible object is the element that is apprehended by [intuitive] reason, νοῦς. This means that the ideas or the idea is the νοητόν, the knowable. By contrast, the multiple things of the real world are accessible to sensibility—αἴσθησις—and so each is designated as the αἰσθητόν. Here again, ideal and real being are characterized in terms of the specific mode of access that we have to them, and not in terms of their being or modality of being. What is more, this distinction has continued up to our own day and above all, plays a major role in Kant's philosophy. So for example, a book of Kant's, his so-called dissertation of 1770 (which in fact is the real prelude to his *Critique of Pure Reason*), is titled *De mundi sensibilis atque intelligibilis forma et principiis.*[32] The *intelligibile* corresponds to the νοητόν, and the *sensibile* corresponds to the αἰσθητόν. Kant speaks of an intelligible and [58] a sensible world, and today as well we speak of sensible and non-sensible being and mean this distinction of the real and the ideal. This distinction still prevails today, and it dominates all inquiries, ontological as well as epistemological.

In refuting psychologism and, positively, in founding logic, there is a fundamental ontological difference that provides the proper orientation. To summarize a bit, the ideal is what always is. It is the permanent as against its changing instantiations. It stands in contrast to those ways in which it shows itself in any given instance and comes into appearance—i.e., in contrast to how it [sensibly] appears. The ideal is likewise the universal in contrast to the multiplicity of its individual instances. The idea "triangle" is the universal that is instantiated in each particular triangle. This concept of the ideal, specifically in its triple meaning of the *self-identical,* the *permanent,* and the *universal,* is the guiding thread of Husserl's critique of psychologism. At the same time it is the guiding thread for determining the being of truth

32. [In *Akademie-Ausgabe,* vol. 2, ed. Erich Adickes (Berlin: Walter de Gruyter, 1905; reissued, 1968), pp. 385–420; see also "On the Forms and Principles of the Sensible and the Intelligible World (1770)," in Immanuel Kant, *Theoretical Philosophy, 1755–1770,* trans. and ed. David Walford, with Ralf Meerbote (Cambridge: Cambridge University Press, 1992), pp. 373–416.]

as an ideal being. Accordingly Husserl says that just as the self-identity of the triangle (or better, the idea of triangle) is permanent in contrast to the real presentations of triangles, so too the self-identity of ad-judged propositions is permanent in contrast to the real multiplicity of the positings of those propositions. The adjudged proposition, i.e., the true proposition, is a truth. In cases regarding the ideal, what is as-serted in each individual proposition is a truth.

> Every truth presents an ideal unity in contrast to a potentially infinite, endless multiplicity of correct statements, each with the same form and matter.[33]
>
> Truth is something ideal [*eine Idee*] whose particular instance is actu-ally experienced in an evident judgment.[34]

The being-experienced of the content of the proposition in the judg-ment is the realization of the ideal in a given case, in the same way that, analogously, the idea "table" is manifest in a multiplicity of tables a carpenter produces. As we shall see later, this interpretation is wor-thy of note—both the interpretation of the judgment's content as ideal being, and the interpretation of its relation to acts of judgment as the realizations of that content. [59] In one regard, Husserl himself basi-cally overturned and quietly dropped this interpretation right after his *Logical Investigations*. But nonetheless, he continues to hold on to the determination of truth as ideal being. That will show up in the fact that there is an ambiguity in the concept of the ideal (which for him was the guiding concept) to which he himself fell victim. For one thing, he claimed that this distinction between truth as valid meaning and judgment as its realization held for individual truths and proposi-tions. But he also carried it through with regard to the connections of truths and the totality of propositions that we call a science.

> In the first instance science is an anthropological unity, i.e., a unity of acts and dispositions of thinking along with certain pertinent external arrangements.[35]

Here science is understood as something mentally empirical, as acts and arrangements of thought as a whole, as an anthropological unity. Science is realized in particular individuals and their processes of

---

33. [*LU*, vol. 1, §50, p. 187 / tr. 192. In the second edition, Husserl changed the verb *repräsentiert* ("presents") to *ist* ("is").]

34. [*LU*, vol. 1, §51, p. 190 (Husserl's emphasis) / tr. 194. The two prior sentences read: "Rather, evidence is nothing but the experience of truth. Of course truth is experienced only in the way that the ideal can be experienced in a real act."]

35. [*LU*, vol. 1, §62, p. 228 / tr. 225.]

thought; it is really present in people, in scholars. Science is present not only mentally but also physically in the form of writings, institutions, and the like. So in the first place, science is a real, physical-mental unity. And then Husserl says, "What makes this unified whole anthropological, and in particular what makes it psychological, is not our concern here." This does not refer to the empirical context but, to put it in very Platonic terms, to what "makes science into science." That is, the idea, the ideal context alone "provides [these acts of thinking] with a unified objective relation and, within this unity, an ideal validity as well." The unity of propositional content, the unity of the propositions themselves, is what makes a science be a science. In contrast to that, this anthropological physical-mental unity is only an accidental realization of science. [60]

> There is a *single* truth corresponding to the plurality of individual acts of knowledge that have the *same* content; and that single truth is simply the ideally identical content of those acts. Similarly the ideally identical content of a theory comes to be known as the *same* theory in a corresponding multitude of individual acts of synthetic knowledge, whether they occur now or at another time, whether they are performed by this subject or that. Therefore, the theory is constituted not by *acts* but by purely *ideal* elements: it is made up *of truths*.[36]

So too science, as an ideal network of propositions, is realized in a plurality of individuals and organizations. Within the network of truths, a set of concrete issues which operates within that network attains to "objective validity."[37] Or: The ideally existing (i.e., valid) propositional contents, as such, bring the issues in question to objective validity. The ideal being of the proposition—and this means truth—is valid, and as valid, holds true for the subject matter that it intends.

In contrast with the empirical reality of things, the ideal being of truth is called "validity." Truths themselves are validities, and therefore we speak of non-psychological logic as the *logic of validity*.

Thus, in its positive moment, Husserl's critique is focused on the ideal content of propositions, on the meaning that is valid, on validity. In the following sections, we will lay out the roots of this positive focus and of the determination of truth as *validity*.

Now we simply want to clarify how ideal being—the idea in Plato's sense—determines Husserl's positive orientation in such a broad and almost uncritical way that it led him into a fundamental error that he soon saw for himself and abandoned.

36. [*LU*, vol. 1, §66(b), p. 240 / tr. 234.]
37. [*LU*, vol. 1, §62, p. 228 / tr. 225.]

We have already dealt with this without being explicitly aware of it (cf. *Logische Untersuchungen,* vol. 2, Husserl's doctrine of meaning).[38]

In contrast with performances of judgments, the content of the judgment is the ideal or the idea, i.e., the universal that is seen by way of abstraction [61] or in Husserl's terms, "ideation" of the exemplary case as the thing's "whatness." It is seen from out of a plurality or (the plurality not being necessary) from out of one individual instantiation: from this table here, we see table in general.[39]

Thus Husserl:

> [Truth is] individualized in the lived experience of the evident judgment. If we reflect on this individualization, and if we perform an ideating abstraction, then instead of the object [of the mental act of judgment], the truth itself becomes the object of our apprehension. In so doing, we apprehend truth as the ideal correlate of the transient subjective act of knowing and as a *unity* over against the unlimited plurality of possible acts of knowing and of knowing individuals {and thus over against all its realizations}. (vol. 1, 229–230)[40]

In that regard we should say: The content of the judgment, insofar as it is ideal, is not at all empirical. Nonetheless, it is not ideal in the sense of a Platonic idea, as if it were the universal, the γένος, the genus of the acts of judgment. And yet Husserl says precisely that: As an idea, the content, the ideal meaning of the proposition is likewise the genus of the acts of judgment.[41]

The genus—e.g., "color"—applies only to kinds and particulars, to these and those colors. But the universal, as the content and meaning of the judgment, applies only to this and that meaning, but never to the acts [of judgment]. At best, the universal—the idea corresponding to real acts [of judgment] —is the universal essence of "act in general," but never the *content* [or *meaning*] of the act [of judgment]. To say that the *content* of the judgment is the γένος, the universal, the Platonic idea for the *acts* of (actual or possible) judgment, is as absurd as saying that the genus or concept "table in general" is the genus for a bunch of teacups. Husserl asserted that the *content* of the judgment was the genus of the *acts* of judgment by using the content of the judgment, the

---

38. [Heidegger refers to *Logische Untersuchungen,* vol. 2, First, Fourth, Fifth, and Sixth Investigations, as Husserl's "doctrine of meaning." See GA 2, p. 220 n. 1 / tr. 492 n. x.]

39. [With help from the Moser (p. 127) and the Weiss (p. 34) typescripts.]

40. [*LU,* vol. 1, §62, pp. 229–230 / tr. 226.]

41. [Here and in what follows, the translation is aided by the Moser typescript. For example, the crucial word «Platonic» comes from Moser, p. 128.7, and the critical reference to Husserl comes from p. 128.9-11.]

idea, in equivocal senses, both as non-sensible being and as "idea" in the Platonic sense—and then mixing them together. (This oversight is still operative in his doctrine of meaning.)[42]

No matter how widely you extend the content of the judgment (the idea), you will never get to the acts of judgment. Husserl's remarkable oversight was possible only because, fascinated as he was by the ideal and the Platonic idea, he synthesized the two meanings—propositional validity and the subsistence of the universal essence—into one meaning, and then spoke simply of the ideal in contrast to the empirical. This oversight merely illustrates what the critique of psychologism was really aiming at: to establish the ideal over against the empirical.

This very confusion, which is the basis here of the equivocity of "idea," both as non-sensible being and as [62] the universal, the genus—this confusion is already basically sketched out in the theory from which Husserl, within certain limits, took his essential orientation, namely, Lotze's doctrine of the world of ideas and his interpretation of Plato's doctrine of ideas in book 3 of his *Logik*.[43] It was from this context as well, that the term "validity" and the way of interpreting ideal being as validity came. Thanks to Lotze's logic, the term "validity" and what it refers to has become dominant today. Of course, only after Husserl's critique of psychologism and his elaboration of ideal being did the concept of validity achieve clarity. It was also subsumed into Windelband's and Rickert's value theory, so that in general we can say that logic today is this so-called logic of validity.[44]

*   *   *

§9. The roots of these presuppositions

Although our reflections bring us into an historical context, our goal is not to demonstrate how Husserl's critique depends on such a context. Rather, we are always guided by our specific interest in the issue, as signaled by the question: *How is truth understood both in psychologism and in the critique of psychologism?*

We now know that truth = true proposition = validity. So we ask: What does "to be valid" mean? What presuppositions let us acquire the concept "validity"? We can't say the ideal is an entity that has being if we use the word "being" in the narrow sense, with the result that "being" would be reserved for this very special entity. If "being" and

---

42. [The last sentence draws on the Weiss transcript (p. 34.27–28).]

43. [See «Bibliography,» above, p. 22.]

44. [Here (Moser, p. 130) Heidegger ends his lecture of Tuesday, 17 November 1925, to be followed by that of Thursday, 19 November, which opened with a 650-word summary that is omitted in GA 21.]

"entity" refer exclusively to empirical, sensible being, we cannot say that the ideal *is*. Lotze, who introduced the concept of validity into logic, used the term "being" in this narrow sense where "being" means the same as the empirical reality of things, so that "being" equals the empirical realness (out-there-ness) of something. [63] Therefore, if "being" means empirical reality, it cannot mean "ideality." In other words, we cannot say that [Platonic] ideas *are*. It is no surprise that, given the dominance of natural scientific research in the nineteenth century, the things of the world, the things of nature, came to be taken as true and proper beings. But it is remarkable that philosophy as well, and even Lotze—who spent his career fighting the predominance of naturalism and who did the real spadework for overcoming it—even Lotze had to pay tribute to naturalism by using the venerable term *being* in this narrow sense where it equals *empirical being, empirical reality.*

Now if somehow "there are" [*es gibt*] ideas,[45] and if ideas in some sense have (to use Lotze's terms) actuality, then the problem arises: Since we cannot use "being" in Lotze's sense of the term, what kind of actuality are we to attribute to the ideas? To avoid any confusion in what follows, let me note again: Lotze uses the word "being" as equivalent to "out-there-ness," and therefore he uses "being" for sensible beings, material beings in the widest sense. I have already stressed that the currently common term "sensible entity" does not characterize being [*Sein*], but only determines the way of apprehending being. I use the phrase here only as a concession. As an ontological term, it is absurd. So, how must we indicate and characterize the actuality of the idea?

Lotze used "actuality" in a very broad sense, such that being is a specific form of actuality, and that prompted the question: In contrast to empirically real being, what kind of actuality does the being of the ideas have? "Actuality" is the formal-universal concept, and "being" is a specific form of actuality. But in our terminology—and I say this to avoid confusion—I use "being" in the exact opposite sense, and in connection with the genuine tradition of Greek philosophy broadly speaking. There, "being" can mean both empirical reality *or* ideality *or* other possible modes of being. I use "actuality" (*Wirklichkeit*) in the opposite sense [to Lotze], as meaning [64] empirical reality.

In an earlier investigation of medieval ontology, I too followed Lotze's distinction and used the term "actuality" for "being."[46] But I no longer think that is correct. Hence our question: What kind of actual-

---

45. [By «ideas,» Heidegger means something like the «Platonic,» «separate» idealities or ideal meanings discussed in §8, and not empirical-real «thoughts in one's head.»]

46. [Heidegger is referring to his *Die Kategorien- und Bedeutungslehre des Duns Scotus* (1916), in GA 1, pp. 189–411.]

ity (in Lotze's sense) is to be ascribed to the ideas? Answer: The kind
of the actuality that applies to the ideas is *validity*. The ideal *is valid;* the
real *is*. Lotze asks: What kind of actuality do the ideas have? *We* would
ask: What kind of being do the ideas have? If we hope to grasp the
correct way of asking and answering the question, we must first clarify the context within which Lotze poses this question about the kind
of actuality that the ideas have.

Lotze took up this project in his *Logik,* book 3, chapter 2, "The World
of Ideas." To understand the way he interprets the being of ideas, of
"ideal being," and consequently of Plato's doctrine of ideas, it is important that we keep in mind the framework that led him to discuss the
world of ideas, its mode of actuality, and its form. The question comes
down to: What does the truth of knowledge consist of? Or more precisely: How are truth and is-true to be defined and specified? And so,
preceding the second chapter, where this question is broached, there
is a first chapter titled "On Skepticism."[47]

In the first chapter, Lotze tries to show that the notion underlying
the interpretation of truth as "the agreement of our forms of knowledge
with the way things are" (p. 490) is a prejudice. (Cf. chapter 3.)

The object of his investigation is not the issues and things themselves but

> always and only the connection of our ideas among themselves. (p. 491)

> The plurality of ideas in us, and where they may come from, constitute the
> only immediate datum from which our knowledge can begin. (p. 493)
> [65]

> We are convinced that the changing totality of our ideas is the only mate-
> rial given us to work upon; that truth and the knowledge of truth consist
> only in the universal laws of interconnection that are found to obtain
> without exception in a given majority of ideas as often as those ideas enter
> our consciousness. (p. 498)

Thus Lotze concludes this chapter:

> Let us leave entirely out of the question the opposition between our world
> of ideas and a world of things; let us look upon the former alone as the
> subject matter we have to deal with; and let us endeavor to ascertain
> where, within the world of ideas, the primary fixed points of certainty are
> to be found. (pp. 503–504)

47. [Hermann Lotze, *System of Philosophy, Part I. Logic, in Three Books: Of Thought,
Of Investigation, and Of Knowledge,* ed. and trans. Bernard Bosanquet (Oxford: Clarendon Press, 1884), vol. 2, pp. 166–199.]

His position is clear: it is Descartes's. What is given first and what alone is given with certitude is the manifold of ideas in us, in consciousness. I can never get outside them, but there is supposed to be knowledge of them, that is, an apprehension of their truth. But within this position (which is the only one possible), what is the one thing truth can mean? Not an agreement of ideas with things because (as says the argument so often repeated today), how am I supposed to measure the ideas within myself against things outside myself? How am I supposed to bring these into agreement? For things are always given to me only as ideas; so then I am measuring ideas against ideas. (Rickert also argues this way in his *Gegenstand der Erkenntnis*, and he attempts to show that ideas as such are not knowledge.)[48]

But from this it is already clear that truth is something that presents no exceptions, has no lacunae, and is never otherwise. It is the connection of ideas and the lawfulness of this connection. Truth is what keeps itself permanent, the firm point of certitude amid the changing world of presentations. The formal pre-conception of truth is: the true, the abiding, the stable. Truth = permanence = what always is.

Here emerges what we previously understood by "truth." The true is what remains permanent throughout the change of [66] presentations. In the flowing multitude of mental appearances and impressions, we effect a first formation of impressions by naming something. An example: When I have the sensation of red, I always sense a specific red (thing), here and now in the mental flow of experiences, a unique "*this* red," in this light, with this strength of color, etc. Now Lotze says that as soon as I recognize the sensed red as red, or think it as red, I have already transcended the sensation of *this* red and now apprehend it and in some way understand it from the universal content "red": this *individual* red as a particularizing of *red-in-general*.[49] "Red" is now raised up and thrown into relief, it is something objective which is no longer a condition we passively receive (in affection), but rather, is the content that we name "redness,"

> which in itself is what it is, and which means what it means, and which continues to be and mean this whether or not our consciousness is directed to it. (p. 15)

The affection is objectified into an autonomous content, which as an

---

48. [Cf. Heinrich Rickert (1863–1936), *Der Gegenstand der Erkenntnis. Einführung in die Transzendentalphilosophie* (Freiburg: Mohr, 1892; 6th, rev. edition, Tübingen: J.C.B. Mohr (Paul Siebeck), 1928). Heidegger read this sentence out in class (Moser, pp. 137–138), but GA 21 confines it to a footnote.]

49. [The two preceding sentences are aided by Moser, pp. 138–139.]

objectivized object is not some *thing* but rather something we intend with "redness," "blackness," "sweetness," "sourness," and so on. So we come to see that something black can become white, something red can become yellow, something sweet can become sour. But black*ness* never becomes white*ness*, sweet*ness* never becomes sour*ness*. Their respective content remains eternally equal to itself; and from out of these contents, and in terms of them, we name things as red, black, and the like. Sensible things flow and change constantly. They are "what they are" (p. 508) only with regard to the contents (redness, blackness, and the like). These are the determining concepts that we assert of things, predicates with which we determine things "as such and so."

We have already indicated that the formal pre-concept of truth is the permanent, the stable. And so Lotze says: These contents (the generic determinations of the sense qualities) form "the first adequate and solid object of an unchanging knowledge" (ibid.), "the truth of which is entirely independent of the skeptic's question about their agreement with some essence of things lying outside the knowledge" (ibid.). Seen within the sphere of consciousness, these contents are something that is "eternally and constantly equal to itself." (Descartes's *ideae!*) Here something is "stabilized as an abiding object of inner intuition" (p. 509). Accordingly, the changing whole is not "without a pervading truth" (p. 508). These contents are nothing other than what Plato designated as ideas [67] (i.e., permanent existence, ἀεὶ ὄν), the "first true object of certain knowledge" (p. 509).

Lotze calls Plato's doctrine of ideas "the first and most original attempt to make use of this truth that belongs to our world of ideas in itself quite apart from its agreement with some assumed essence of things outside those ideas" (pp. 506–507). Lotze imputed to Plato the idea of beginning, like Descartes, with our consciousness and its ideas and for finding in them what is permanent of itself, the qualitative content, as the being of the idea. We won't discuss whether Lotze in this case actually interpreted *Plato* and got the meaning of *Platonic* philosophy right. We are interested in how he understands the meaning of truth. The problems first begin when we ask: What is the status of these unchanging identical contents (blackness, sweetness, sourness, and the like) which, in contrast to their instantiations, are always there? Are colors as such and sound as such still something if no one sees or hears them? Does it make any sense at all to talk about a color in itself? Lotze poses two questions regarding this problem. First he asks: Are these contents something at all, or nothing? And secondly: Must not some kind of predicate of being and actuality belong to them?

Regarding the first question: Lotze says that they cannot be nothing at all, because we still intend these contents when we say, for example: "Color as such is different from sound as such." Here I am making a meaningful statement about something, not about nothing. We intend something when we distinguish it from something else. So they are something. But is "to-be-something" a form of being? And so we come to the second question: What does it mean to say that sound *is* when no one hears anything, or that blackness is, when no one sees something black? Lotze remarks: "We still suppose we know, dimly enough, what the being of things consists in, even when those things [68] are objects of no one's knowledge but are purely for themselves" (p. 510). But when it comes to these contents, we can no longer talk about "being." Yet in another case, when we *have* heard sounds, we distinguish these contents from others. And so the answer to the first question implies that these contents are in fact something and not nothing. As Lotze puts it, there is "a certain element of affirmation" (ibid.). If I distinguish color in general from sound in general, and if I say that they *are* different sense qualities, then I affirm something. I have something given, to which I say yes.

A certain element of affirmation belongs to these contents. They are not nothing, and yet they still are not things. In Lotze's sense of the term, they are not real. So how are we to understand the actuality of these somethings that are not nothing? There must be some kind of information about them. Lotze tried to introduce some clarity and find an answer, by moving into a fundamental consideration whose meaning is crucial for the genesis of the concept of *validity*, insofar as that concept was achieved within the horizon of this fundamental reflection.

As we saw earlier, Lotze already said that the contents are not nothing, and he formulated that as follows: They have a certain element of affirmation (or "affirmedness," as he put it more exactly in another passage) (p. 511). By "affirmation," he does not mean the act of affirming. He means what is affirmed, just as analogously the term "position" does not mean the act of positing but the posited as such, and a calculation is not the act of calculating but what is calculated and written down. Lotze's use of these general expressions and concepts is in obvious connection with Herbart's position, with which Lotze carried on a long and searching argument in his first *Metaphysik*.[50] Lotze says, "There is, to be sure, a very general concept of affirmedness or position" (ibid.). Our languages have no proper word for this concept of affirmedness, and Lotze says that even in the word "position" there is

---

50. [*Metaphysik; drei Bücher der Ontologie Kosmologie und Psychologie* (Leipzig, Hirzel, 1879); translated as *Metaphysics, in Three Books: Ontology, Cosmology, and Psychology*, ed. and trans. B. Bosanquet (Oxford: Clarendon Press, 1884). With regard to Johann Friedrich Herbart (1776–1841), see his *Allgemeine Metaphysik nebst den Anfängen der Philosophischen Naturlehre* (General Metaphysics, together with the First Principles of a Philosophical Theory of Nature), published in 1828–1829.]

a wholly inappropriate collateral idea of an [69] action that, when carried out, produces every kind of affirmedness we can indicate.

What the terms "affirmedness" and "position" refer to is not related to any kind of produced-ness, and therefore the term "affirmedness" is more adequate than "position," because "affirming" better expresses the fact that, as Lotze says, I recognize something that is already there, whereas the term "position" seems to say that I first of all produce something from out of myself. Affirmation is recognition of something which in some way already is, something which already has actuality. That is why Lotze says we do not have a proper German word for this general phenomenon of affirmedness, and given this problem, we would do much better to stick to an ordinary concept. And then he calls affirmedness as such "actuality," without even defining what affirmedness is. So in the general and formal term "actuality," we do not find at all *what* is affirmed or whether it is something real or ideal or some other kind of actuality. We find only affirmedness in general.

Then Lotze says that actuality or affirmedness (or he also simply says: "actuality or affirmation") can now be articulated in various forms, and he even says:

> We call a thing "actual" when it *is*, in contrast to another that is not; we call an event "actual" if it *occurs*, in contrast to another that does not occur; we call a relation "actual" if it obtains, as opposed to one that does not obtain; and lastly we call a proposition "actually true" if it *is valid*, as opposed to one whose validity is still in doubt. (ibid.)

Here different objects are named as actual, and actuality means

1. the being of things
2. the occurrence of events
3. the subsistence of relations
4. the validity of propositions.

Being, occurrence, subsistence, and *validity* are the four forms of being-actual, of actuality in general. And these four forms of actuality or affirmedness, according to Lotze, cannot be reduced to or derived from one another. [70] To put it in our own terms, with these four forms Lotze provides the basic forms of *being,* and among these four there now stands validity. In fact, in a certain sense validity is read off of the kind of actuality that pertains to *propositions*—something to be kept in mind. A proposition, Lotze says, has its actuality in the fact that it is valid. And in fact a proposition is understood insofar as it is taken in itself, apart from all the changes it can undergo.

Lotze now uses this differentiation of the forms of actuality to interpret the meaning of Plato's doctrine of ideas. He tries to show that Plato, with his doctrine of ideas and their being, wanted to teach nothing else than the "validity of truths" (p. 513). Validity is the form of actuality that Plato basically had in mind when he spoke of the being of the idea—but, according to Lotze, he had to speak of "being" because the Greeks had no word for validity and the kind of reality it refers to. In his interpretation Lotze is entirely caught in the spell of his narrowed-down concept of being (being = the actuality of sensible things); and he finds that "to ascribe [to Plato] the absurd opinion that the ideas have being" (*ibid.*), is irreconcilable with his admiration for Plato's profundity. In particular, Lotze tries to show that even in Plato's opinion the ideas have "the actuality of validity" (p. 514). For what we must assert of true propositions—their identity and their eternity/supratemporal nature—are determinations that belong to what Plato called ideas. The "content of a truth" in the proposition is "recognized" (i.e., it is not made) by us (p. 515). The truth already "has been valid" and will be valid, whether it is thought or not.[51] In its actuality, the content of a truth is independent of the minds in which it is thought. So too with the idea as a "form equal to itself." It is recognized as the same in various appearances (p. 514). The idea is what it is, independent of the things in which it can appear and independent of the minds that can give it the actuality [71] of a mental state. "Thus we think everything in terms of truth" (p. 515).[52]

*   *   *

Plato uses the expression ὄντως ὄν[53] when he wants to make the distinction between an "actually valid truth and an alleged truth" (p. 514). For Lotze, the fact that Plato designated the idea as οὐσία opened the door to a misunderstanding, because οὐσία means ὑπόστασις, the "out-there-ness" of an existing thing or substance. But ideas are not things. So, with the word οὐσία, Plato covered over what he really meant. But Lotze is speaking here on the presupposition that οὐσία

51. [By "has been valid," Heidegger means "is valid in its essence." This is what he calls elsewhere the ontological perfect as in Aristotle's phrase τὸ τί ἦν τίνι εἶναι, "what something always has been" in the sense of "what it *essentially* is [ἦν] to be something," "the essence (of something)." Cf. GA 2, p. 114 n. a.]

52. [Here (Moser, p. 146) Heidegger draws to a close his lecture of Thursday, 19 November 1925, to be followed by that of Friday, 20 November (Moser, pp. 147–164), which began with a 575-word summary (Moser, pp. 147–50) that is omitted in GA 21.]

53. ὄντως ὄν means that which is according to the [full] measure of being; that which is in the [full] sense of being; "is" such as only something that is properly in being can be; being in such a way as fully suffices for being and for the possibility of being. In Lotze's interpretation of Plato, this proper being points to truth.

means substance and even ὑπόστασις, whereas these are only later Greek distortions of the term, and they do not get at the meaning of the word at all. Οὐσία does not mean substance, thing, something "real" in Lotze's sense, or "entity." Οὐσία is what is present and/or its presentness, that which is always there. So the word is entirely and supremely adequate to what Plato meant. Plato is made to seem absurd only by his interpreters, and Lotze joins them even when he thinks he is refuting them.

But Lotze himself was in a certain sense compelled to retract his own interpretation of Plato's doctrine of ideas. Validity is the form of actuality that propositions have; but the ideas, Lotze himself admits, are not propositions but at most concepts. Lotze is forced to say: "This term [validity] can be applied to individual concepts only with some obscurity" (p. 521). And he grants that Plato in his doctrine of ideas only "rarely" deals with propositions. "But the fact that they had to be the most essential constituents of the ideal world still did not force itself upon Plato's mind" (ibid.). This means not only that Plato for his part did not [72] use the term "validity," but also that he did not mean what Lotze means by the term. Lotze understands the ideas not as propositions, but predominantly as "concepts" of which alone we can properly say: They are valid.

Of course, even this admission is fundamentally skewed. Lotze works with the distinction between *judgment* and *concept,* which Plato did not even know in that form. When he noticed this erroneous distinction, Lotze was able to find a foundation for his interpretation elsewhere, in λόγος—and in a certain sense he was right. Plato deals with neither propositions nor concepts, but only with λόγοι. But this is only an apparent foundation because Lotze overlooks the essential element of λόγος, namely, the factor of δηλοῦν [making accessible, making manifest] which λόγος always possesses, whether the λόγος be a judgment or a concept. What is essential for Plato is not the concept/judgment distinction, but λόγος insofar as it makes something manifest (λόγος as δηλοῦν), that is, lets it be seen. And what is sighted in λόγος is the idea.

In these constructive interpretations of Greek philosophers, especially of the ancient heroes of philosophical thought, it always turns out that so much of it remains obscure when we look at it through the eyes of the "scholars." On the other hand, it takes considerable insight and experience to really understand and explain the positive possibilities of this obscurity instead of trivializing it by way of allegedly "forward-looking" clarifications and distinctions. We always underestimate the necessity and the difficulty of the positive preparation we have to have in order to avoid violating the past. It makes you stop and think, when you notice that a thinker as distinguished and issue-focused as Lotze did not avoid this danger.

But Lotze's interpretation of Plato is not our theme, any more than criticizing that interpretation is our current project. What we are aiming at in our demonstration is something else: an understanding of the genesis of the concept of validity and of the doctrine of the ideal being of truth. By that I mean the question: What do we establish about truth when we say that the being of propositions is validity, and that validity is the form of actuality that Plato ascribed to the ideas, namely, ideal being? In answering that question we will come to learn something about the [73] roots (and about a major root) of the critique of psychologism. We get some insight into the basic orientation of the concept of validity by asking the question, "What is truth?"

In the first place, with regard to what we said earlier about the critique of psychologism, we can now see from Lotze's interpretation of the doctrine of ideas how Husserl really landed in that error of his that we noted above. Lotze says: Truth, as a true proposition, is valid; but validity is the form of actuality pertaining to ideas; and the idea also has the property of being universal in contrast to the sensible particulars. So in keeping with that, propositions—valid ones—are ideas; they are likewise the ideal in the sense of the universal for the particulars in the propositions—the "positions." So if we reduce Husserl's error to a syllogism, it consists simply in the fact that he proceeded as follows:

The major: *Idea = validity = proposition.*
The minor: *Idea = universal = form = genus.*
Conclusion: *Proposition = universal, identical with idea,* and thus: *Proposition = genus to the posited judgments.*[54]

But we now disregard Husserl's error and instead ask: When we characterize truth as validity, do we in fact gain anything toward clarifying the essence of truth? Let us not forget: Lotze makes the claim for validity that it is the form of the actuality of the true proposition. And we must keep firmly in mind how Lotze proceeds, to the point where he derives the four different forms of actuality.

Recall what he says at that point:

> We call a thing "actual" when it *is*, in contrast to another that is not; we call an event "actual" if it *occurs*, in contrast to another that does not occur; we call a relation "actual" if it *obtains*, as opposed to one that does not obtain; and lastly we call a proposition "actually true" if it *is valid*. (p. 511)

---

54. ["Posited judgments": the German is *Setzungen* (also in Moser, p. 154.14), which does not have the meaning of *Position* as affirmedness, that Heidegger discussed above. Here it refers to acts of judgment.]

In the last clause he does not simply say, as he does analogously in the first three cases, that a proposition is actual when it is valid, but when it is actually *true*. He claims that actuality is an additional determination of truth. That is: When this actuality of the true proposition gets identified with validity, and when validity is understood fundamentally as the affirmedness of a truth, then an additional determination ("true") is given to the true proposition [74] without anything being said about the *truth* that makes the true thing be true.

So already in the way we get to the expression "validity" within the distinct forms of actuality, we can see that Lotze establishes nothing at all about truth *as such*. Instead, something is said about what is true, i.e., about the possible form of its actuality. But when he says straightforwardly, but unclearly, that truth means validity, the statement conceals a seductive ambiguity—and modern logic, the logic of validity, has completely fallen victim to it. Appealing to Lotze, people say: "to be true" = "to be valid," and therefore, truth = validity. But the ambiguity lies in this expression "to be true." In Lotze's derivation, "being-true" means ambiguously the same as "the being *of* the true," i.e., the being of the true proposition; but one also understands this ambiguous "being-true" as what *truth* itself is, or the essence of truth. And then the two are taken as identical: being-true as *the actuality of true propositions,* and being-true as *the essence of truth.* And because the first of these two is defined as validity, one also says that the essence of truth is validity.

Lotze provides no answer to the question about what truth itself is, but merely tells us how true propositions are actual. He gets this form of the actuality of validity by differentiating it from things, events, and relations. Even propositions get fitted into this plurality of actualities. Here we cannot discuss further the correctness or incorrectness of this division into: things that are, events that happen, relations that subsist, and propositions that are valid. It is very problematic because propositions are already relations, and because the being of things that allegedly *are* mostly consists in the fact that something happens in and with them. All these distinctions that Lotze adduces intersect each other. To begin with, these distinctions between the forms of actuality, among which validity itself is found, are not clearly distinguished. Above all, what is not clarified is why the idea of actuality can and must be obtained by using affirmation as the key; [75] or why the correlate of affirmation, namely affirmedness, is what we are to call actuality; and therefore, exactly why being (or in Lotze's terminology, "actuality") in the widest sense must be interpreted with reference to affirmation. That is a pure assertion on the part of Lotze. He introduces it without a demonstration, and as a result his deduction of the various forms of actuality rests on an unspecified foundation.

Lotze might think that he has brought forth something new for clarifying the idea and its actuality, by operating (along with the entire tradition) within a fundamental obscurity about the question of being. In point of fact, affirmedness remains affirmedness whether we are investigating real *or* ideal being with regard to its actuality. "Sensible," "nonsensible," and "ideal" are not features of being. The affirmedness of the non-sensible says nothing about the kind of affirmedness as such.[55]

We emphasize that the genesis and possibility of these modes of actuality (being, happening, subsistence, validity) are not clarified, and that the legitimacy of the clue for getting actuality—viz., affirmedness—has been demonstrated. But Lotze could answer by saying that such demands are impossible. He writes:

> And one should not ask further what this validity means, along with the presupposition that what it intelligibly means could be derived from something else (p. 512) {in the sense of an increasing weakening in the form of actuality as we move from being to validity}. Just as no one can say how it happens that anything *is* or *occurs,* so neither can one say how it happens that a truth *is valid.* We must regard this latter concept, too, as a basic concept founded entirely upon itself alone, a concept which all of us can know what we mean by it, but which we cannot produce by constructing it out of components that do not already contain it. (p. 513)

Here Lotze is saying that if validity is a basic concept that cannot be further reduced, then it means something that we can comprehend. But at the same time [76] he emphasizes:

> And finally I have to add that, when we distinguish between the actuality of ideas and laws taken as *validity* and the actuality of things taken as *being,* we have first of all (thanks to the superior resources of German over Greek) merely discovered a convenient way of speaking that can warn us against interchanging [the two notions]. But the issue we designate by the word "validity" has thereby lost none of its wondrousness. (p. 519)

So it is more a matter of a convenient expression; but the issue itself remains wondrous.

But if wonder (namely, about the "obvious") is one element that motivates philosophical questioning, it can be only the occasion for asking a real question instead of getting thrown off by some prejudgment. For even here, Lotze is caught in a widespread prejudgment that remains just as dominant today, namely, that we must simply accept,

---

55. [At this point in the lecture Heidegger delivered a 225-word disquisition on being in Greek thought, followed by the next sentence (Moser, pp. 157.8-158.5).]

and leave untouched, these supposedly basic concepts—even in the case of the most general concept: "being" / actuality.

It is highly questionable that, as Lotze believes, the only way to clarify being is to tell how it is made. Here the prejudgment is that being is something that can be produced: a thing, i.e., a being—and the same goes for the alleged "validity." Certainly no one can tell us what being-produced is, because the question makes no sense. But granted we cannot treat being the way we treat beings, does that entail that a philosophical interpretation of being is impossible? Certainly not. It only says that the phenomena of philosophy are not things like tables and houses.

Lotze's idea that the so-called basic concepts cannot be clarified is the same as that of the tradition. It is usually said that being cannot be defined. Therefore, because a definition has to state what something is, we cannot ask what being "is." What is a definition about? It tells what a thing consists of, where it comes from, what its components are [77]—*homo: animal rationale.* A definition says something about the produced-ness of an entity, and thus is a way of determining beings and especially things. (The task of part two, section one, of the *Posterior Analytics* B is to point out exactly this τί.)

To discuss whether or not being and the like can be defined is in fact to understand being as a being. From the start, the whole discussion makes no sense. The statement "Being is undefinable" can indeed have a genuine sense, but one that has never been understood, namely, that because being is fundamentally different from beings, it requires a different point of departure from that of a definition. What I have just said entails the task and the challenge of questioning radically. It does not provide the comfortableness of the supposedly self-evident.

If, in saying that being is undefinable, we argue in the usual fashion, we would let it stand as something both self-evident and utterly confused. (Pascal!) From what we have said, that would make about as much sense as saying, "Since you can't play the piano on a bike, a bike is a useless implement," as if every implement had to have the property of "able-to-play-piano-on"—and as if everything we talk about had to be definable.

As inadequately as Lotze specifies the provenance of being or "actuality" as validity, the guiding thread he gives us is nonetheless on the mark—namely, that what Plato meant by the being of the ideas is what he, Lotze, understands as validity.

Whether or not Lotze's particular interpretation is correct, the upshot is that he understands validity (= the actuality or being of true propositions) as the kind of being that the Greeks called authentic being and that really means the same as the thereness or presence of φύσις in the broadest sense, although we cannot show this now.

Truths—as much as things, events or relations—"are." Regardless of whether propositions can be heard, [78] tasted, or touched, the essential thing about them (in our interpretation) is their thereness.

Validity has the ontological sense of the stable presence of something, and Lotze claimed that it determined the kind of being of true propositions. Propositions = truths. Thus, Lotze attributed to truths the being that the Greeks attributed to the world and that they understood as the only and authentic being (since they geared the question of the meaning of being to beings as world). With that we have for the first time gotten down to the roots whence the questions and the answers in the critique of psychologism get their determining power. Truth and the meaning of the true *qua* proposition—this "true" is directly identified with being as validity.

But with that, the meaning of being is not discussed any more than its provenance and limits are. The question of truth is certainly not posed, and it is not shown why exactly propositions are and must be the proper concretions of truth.

Therefore, to return to the question that guides our endeavors: What have we gained from the interpretation of truth as validity for the authentic question about the essence of truth? Answer: Nothing. In fact, just the opposite. The logic of validity begins by deceiving itself when it thinks that by identifying truth and validity, it has acquired a clear and firm foundation. In any case, this thesis does provide an answer to the question about the kind of being that images have, which in a certain derived way can be true, and as true can have a kind of being that may be called validity. Of course, it requires a further interpretation with a different focus (cf. below)[56] in order to show how that sort of thing is possible and to what degree truth can somehow have the kind of being of the φύσει ὄντα.

The logic of validity fails to show:

1. what truth is;
2. that propositions are the original and proper concretions [79] of truth, so that the being of truth could be determined primarily on the basis of true propositions;
3. why these propositions can have a kind of being based on the being of mere thereness;
4. that this meaning of being [viz., "thereness"] is the sole and primary meaning;
5. even less, why being must have such a meaning;
6. and why at all the question about truth is finally coupled with the question about being.

56. [Heidegger may be referring to his treatment of Kant's schematism, in §31, below.]

The questions we have asked here are not just some formal critical questions that we have pulled out of the blue and put to the logic of validity, to modern logic, and maybe to an entire tradition. No, they are concrete questions that we ourselves will have to ask in the course of these lectures in hopes of getting a preliminary answer.[57]

* * *

Precisely because of this link-up with the grand tradition of ancient philosophy, validity has almost become the magic word for contemporary logic—and not only for logic. People speak as well of ethical and aesthetic validity (non-logical validity) and claim to show, by analogy with the claims of psychology, the lawfulness, normativeness, and determinateness of all kinds of behavior: theoretical, practical, artistic, objective. But at bottom, this magic word "validity" is a tangle of confusion, perplexity, and dogmatism.

Why does "validity" cast such a spell? Answer: because the term is even more ambiguous than we have shown up to now, and this ambiguity allows the term to be very broadly applied according to the context. The reason is not that its referent has been unambiguously fixed as a universal phenomenon and that its universal relations have not been discovered. No, it's because the vagueness of the word and its referent allows such an unquestioned, broad application. Its broad employment is not because the function of its referent is clear and based on principles, but because of the concealed ambiguity of the term itself. [80]

We must again return to Lotze if we hope to show the essentially different meanings that "validity" has, along with those we've already mentioned. In sketching out Lotze's treatment of the doctrine of ideas, we showed how he rejects the traditional concept of truth and sets out from the flux of ideas as a whole and from the consciousness of ideas, i.e., from what is accessible to (in his words) "inner intuition." The result is that the true is what is permanent and stable, and can be apprehended by this intuition. What remains permanent and stable is the valid—invariable, ever recurring, without contingency, in a word, the necessary. At first, this permanent something is only in consciousness; but its material content consists of the determinations and law-governed togetherness of what we naïvely call external things. In the true and the stable, we find something given in our consciousness that asserts something about the outer world without needing or being able to be measured against it. The valid, taken as what is stable and necessary, now has the meaning of something that *qua* valid holds

---

57. [Here Heidegger closed his lecture of Friday, 20 November 1925, to be followed by his lecture of Monday, 23 November (Moser, pp. 164–181), which began with a 500-word summary (Moser, pp. 164–66) that is omitted in GA 21.]

true of things that exist independently of consciousness but that we do not attain with our ideas.

Validity as abiding content is now likewise the validity of given objects; it is objective validity: objectivity.[58]

Validity in this sense is valid not on the basis of a being measured against things, but on the basis of—and as—the stable, unchanging, lawful subsistence of consciousness. Hence we have a second sense of validity: "to be valid *of* something," i.e., as the objective validity of something.[59]

Now to the degree that something is valid in the first sense and therefore is valid in the second sense (as holding true of beings themselves), to that degree this [81] truth is likewise valid for all knowers. Now validity means neither the actuality of true propositions nor the validity of beings but, rather, validity for knowers. Being valid is now validity not as objectivity but as *universal* validity. Or more exactly, in this third sense validity is the state of being binding [upon all knowers]. Hence, in the word "validity," three fundamentally different meanings intertwine:

1. the actuality of true propositions;
2. the relation to the being that is asserted and meant in the statement; and
3. being binding for knowers.

Or:

1. truth in its actuality;
2. this truth as related to objects; and
3. truth as related to knowing subjects.

It is all called validity, and the term is meant sometimes in one sense, sometimes in another, sometimes in two of the senses or sometimes in all three.

Insofar as it is a statement, the valid (which also holds-true-*of*-something) provides information about something necessary, something that subsists of itself, which we recognize and understand, not something arbitrarily posited but what *demands* a "Yes!" and is binding for all.

It is necessary at this point to pay attention to an essential issue that

58. Cf. Lotze, p. 556: what is valid—as "objectively valid"; "real validity"; p. 557; general concept: "validity of beings," p. 561. And 569!!

59. [There is] a metaphysical presupposition of harmony. Here the problem of truth is turned upside-down: *verum* ["what is true," is understood] on the basis of *certum* ["what is certain"] and thereby [is understood] "critically."

Lotze's inquiry discussed in some detail, because his inquiry now becomes relevant to that issue. The primary instance of validity is the actuality of contents and propositions "in consciousness." That primary validity is the foundation on which objectivity is based; and bindingness is based on both of those two. A proposition is not valid because it holds true of objects—i.e., validity in the primary sense is not founded on validity as objectivity. Lotze obviates such a demand for measurement in the sense of a correspondence with something. We cannot say "truth *is* correspondence." It's the other way around. Because the proposition is valid, it holds true of something; and because there is something in consciousness that is stable, it agrees with something! But even this formulation is inadequate. Why is the proposition valid? Because it is something stable and permanent that must be affirmed in itself; because it is something we have to affirm in itself, something that we *must* acknowledge.

It is important to note that, as the earlier "derivation" indicated, validity remains primarily related to *affirmation*.[60] [82] The other two meanings of the word "validity" only corroborate the fundamental point we have already made: that Lotze does not investigate the phenomenon of truth at all. It is not the case that Lotze now broaches the question of truth for the first time. Rather, he presumes that the question is already answered in principle by the equation: to be valid = to be true. He builds validity as objectivity and validity as universal bindingness on the first concept of validity, and to that extent these concepts lead us even further away from the central question about the essence of truth.

The predominance of the concept of validity pushes the question of truth more and more into the background arena of secondary problems and ends up reducing it to the intrinsically unimportant question about the kind of relation [viz., "bindingness"] that truth has to the possible comportment of the "subjects" who acknowledge it. Sometimes this process of devaluation goes so far that the first meaning of validity is forgotten, and truth is even identified with universal bindingness. The true is what is valid for all, what everyone is bound to acknowledge.

The much-extolled "discovery" of validity is only the semblance of a genuine question about the essence of truth. But let me say one final thing: we have yet to reach the lowest point in the downfall of the question of truth.

Philosophers felt they had to get beyond Lotze. They wanted to radicalize him and for the first time get the final meaning of his doctrine of validity (and therefore true philosophy) by means of the following considerations.

---

60. Affirmation, *assensus,* agreement; *iudicium* [judgment] in the specific sense of recognition.

As one form of actuality, validity is related to affirmation in general. In validity, true propositions are affirmed, i.e., recognized and acknowledged. But on closer inspection, what gets acknowledged in such acknowledgment is not validity but *a value*. In other words, what the true proposition affirms—namely, truth as such—is a value. To acknowledge true propositions is to judge; but judging is the basic form of knowledge. In knowledge, a value is acknowledged. Thus, knowledge is directed to a value. The object of knowledge is a value. [83] Windelband and Rickert have followed the path of Lotze's theory of validity to the point of making it into a theory of knowledge. Not just practical and aesthetic behavior, but theoretical behavior as well is a comportment toward values. In general, therefore, that to which consciousness relates itself is always a value. And since we can concretely characterize human behavior in these various regions as culture, values are cultural values. Therefore, philosophy has to be the philosophy of value, and as such, it is a philosophy of culture. Its project is to work out a system of values.

That is why the journal *Logos,* which grew out of this philosophical circle, bears the subtitle "International Journal for a Philosophy of Culture."[61]

The above captures, in rough and ready fashion, the real meaning of value philosophy as worked out in connection with Lotze. In keeping with the prevailing winds of philosophy at the time, value philosophers linked Lotze's doctrine to Kant's philosophy.[62] In the process, people discovered that Kant had written three critiques: *The Critique of Pure Reason* (re., theoretical comportment), *The Critique of Practical Reason* (re., practical, moral comportment), and *The Critique of Judgment* (re., aesthetic comportment). Kant's three critiques are cut to order, to fit the three values of the true, the good, and the beautiful. So these three values are fundamental values.

But Kant also dealt with religion, although not in such a way that his treatment could be put on the same level as the "critiques." Yet religion has to be given a place in the system—and for that purpose, the value of "the holy" was invented. For Windelband, of course, the holy is not an independent value—I am speaking now of the period around 1900 and before the war. But since the war, the world has be-

---

61. [*Logos. Internationale Zeitschrift für Philosophie der Kultur,* ed. Richard Kroner and Georg Mehlis, with the collaboration of (among others) Edmund Husserl, Heinrich Rickert, Wilhelm Windelband, and Ernst Troeltsch (Tübingen: J. C. B. Mohr (Paul Siebeck)). This large annual—some three to four hundred pages per volume—was published in twenty-two editions between 1910 and 1933. Husserl published his "Philosophie als strenge Wissenschaft" (Philosophy as a Rigorous Science) in the first volume (1910-1911: pp. 289-341).]

62. Cf. Wilhelm Windelband, *Präludien. Aufsätze und Reden zur Einleitung in die Philosophie* (Strassburg, 1883; Tübingen: J. C. B. Mohr (Paul Siebeck), 1884).

come very religious—even world congresses are organized analogous to the International Union of Chemists or [84] of Meteorologists, so that today we can risk saying that religion, too, is a value. And we don't stop there. The insights presumably get more profound: *God* is a value, indeed the highest value. This proposition is a blasphemy, and it is not made less blasphemous by the fact that theologians propound it as ultimate wisdom. This would all be very funny if it were not so depressing. It shows that philosophers no longer philosophize from the issues but only from the books of their colleagues. In all of this the only thing of import for science is to understand the direction of this philosophy and theology, and to get an insight into the source of this utterly radical distortion.

Windelband and Rickert have taken the path of devaluing Lotze's doctrine of validity into a philosophy of values. We may briefly mention the major steps in this devaluation as well as some evidence.

The most important essay on the connection of value philosophy with Lotze is Windelband's "Beiträge zur Lehre von negativen Urteil" [Contributions to a Theory of Negative Judgments].[63] There he connects up with Brentano's doctrine of judgment, which maintains that judgment is acknowledgment. Windelband shows the connection with Lotze's doctrine of validity. (Brentano's doctrine is mentioned, but not really in keeping with the significance it has for Windelband.)

Rickert got a fundamental grip on the idea that judgment acknowledges values in his *Der Gegenstand der Erkenntnis,* in 1892 (his inaugural dissertation at Freiburg).[64] In keeping with the then-dominant view that judgment is the basic and authentic form of knowledge, Rickert broadens Windelband's thesis: Judgment is acknowledgment of values; judgment is knowledge; truth is a value. To this day, Rickert has not retracted one of these fundamental theses. His ideas today are merely less clear, because he has subsumed into his theory of knowledge both phenomenology and some essential suggestions of his student, Lask.

As evidence, some propositions from Rickert: [85]

All knowledge begins with judgments, advances in judgments, and can consist only in judgments. . . . Knowledge is affirmation or denial. We want to try to learn the consequences of that. (First edition, pp. 55–56)

Judging is a mental process. It does not belong to those processes in which we examine things with an indifferent attitude, but only to the processes of judgment: affirmation and denial {or approval and disap-

63. [The essay was published in the *Strasburger Abhandlungen zur Philosophie* (1884), as part of a festschrift honoring Eduard Zeller on his seventieth birthday.]

64. [Heinrich Rickert, *Der Gegenstand der Erkenntnis; Einführung in die tranzendentale Philosophie* (Tubingen: Mohr, 1892).]

proval, acknowledgment or disavowal—for Rickert they are all the same},
in which we take an interest in the content of our consciousness as something of value to us. (p. 56)[65]

So in affirming and denying, I take an interest in a content of consciousness as a value.

> Now because what is valid for the judgment must also be valid for knowl-
> edge, the affinity of judgment to willing and feeling entails that pure theo-
> retical knowledge is a matter of comportment toward a value. The alterna-
> tive comportment of approving or disapproving makes sense only in
> contrast to valuing. (p. 57)
>
> In each judgment, I know—at the very moment I judge—that I am ac-
> knowledging something timelessly valid. Thus evidence, treated psycho-
> logically, is a feeling of pleasure, combined with the peculiarity that the
> evidence lends a timeless validity to a judgment and consequently gives it
> a value that no feeling of pleasure otherwise yields.
>
> Because it is timeless, the value is independent of any content of con-
> sciousness. (p. 61)

Thus, because it subsists in timeless independence—in other words,
because it is a validity—value is the object of all cognition.

Criticism of this position is unnecessary and fruitless. What interests
us is only its connection with Lotze and its interpretation of Lotze's
ideas. As insignificant as value philosophy is in itself, it nonetheless did
have a certain function in the last century, especially between 1880 and
1900: to fight against rationalism and against the predominance of natural science in philosophical thought. To be sure, Dilthey had already
been long at work during this period with very different insights. But,
hard pressed by the issues, driven onward by a genuine search, and
guided by a noble sense of caution, he had to forego, basically for his
whole life, putting his investigations into convenient [86] propositions
and systems for easy consumption in the marketplace. Dilthey also had
an essential effect on the other vein mined by value philosophy: concern for the humanities. The well-known distinction between general-
izing and individualizing concept-formation and between the natural
sciences and the humanities goes back, in this form, to Dilthey. However, now the distinction is linked up with the concept of value.

Demonstrating the ambiguity of the concept of value gave us the
opportunity to show how contemporary value philosophy could origi-

---

65. [Moser (p. 177) prints this paragraph as a quote from Rickert. GA 21 puts
quotation marks around only the last sixteen words (". . . we take an interest,"
etc.).]

nate from it. But what is important for us is the reverse connection, the connection backwards with the grand tradition of philosophy. Taken in its first sense—that of the being of the ideas—validity is connected with Greek ontology. Secondly, inasmuch as validity is also understood as objectivity and holding-true-of-something, Lotze's doctrine of validity gets linked up with Kant. And thirdly, Lotze's doctrine, with Kant's, also leads back to Descartes, to the degree that holding-true-of-something is likewise understood as certitude in the sense of absolute certitude and universal holding-true, and to the degree that this whole inquiry into objectivity and holding-true is geared to the doctrine of the immanence of consciousness. So, in the background of this whole theory of validity, with all its ambiguity, there stands Greek philosophy, Descartes's *cogito ergo sum*, and Kant when he is interpreted in a certain way. With this, the origins of the logic of validity are exposed for the first time.

In examining the roots of the presuppositions at work in the critique of psychologism, I have limited myself to the connection with Lotze. But just as important as this line to Lotze, is the line to Bolzano, the Austrian philosopher of the beginning of the last century, who published the four volumes of his *Wissenschaftslehre* in 1837.[66] There, free from any kind of psychologism, he states in the most extreme form his doctrine of propositions-in-themselves and truths-in-themselves. [87] Bolzano had been entirely forgotten in the course of the nineteenth century, but in the 1890s Twardowski, who came from the school of Brentano, went back to Bolzano the logician. In 1896 Twardowski published his treatise *Zur Lehre von Inhalt und Gegenstand der Vorstellungen*, which has become very important for contemporary logic.[67] In the context of this small monograph, reference was made for the first time to Bolzano. However, he came into the public eye only by the fact that Husserl's *Logical Investigations* (vol. 1, §61, 224ff.) awakened a special interest in him and, I am convinced, overestimated him philosophically.

Because of this new attention to Bolzano which was stimulated by Husserl, an interest in him grew up, but his works were very difficult to find; thus a new edition of his *Wissenschaftslehre* began to be published in 1914, when two volumes, the most important, were released. But it is a complete misunderstanding of the proper sense of Husserl's

66. [Bernard Bolzano, *Wissenschaftslehre*, 4 vols. (Sulzbach: Seidel, 1837; 2nd edition, 1914–1931; repr. Aalen: Scientia Verlag, 1970). The text appears in *Bernard-Bolzano Gesamtausgabe*, vol. 1 (Stuttgart-Bad Cannstatt: Fromann-Holzboog, 1969).]

67. [Kazimierz (Kasimir) Twardowski (1866–1938), *Zur Lehre vom Inhalt und Gegenstand der Vorstellung* (Vienna, 1894); translated as *On the Content and Object of Presentations: A Psychological Investigation*, trans. R. Grossmann (The Hague: Martinus Nijhoff, 1977). The text was Twardowski's *Habilitationsschrift*.]

Logical Investigations to simply say—as is common with Rickert, and with contemporary logic generally—that what Husserl provides in his *Logical Investigations* is an emendation of Bolzano.[68]

*   *   *

Bolzano himself was determined in an essential way by Leibniz; Husserl was as well, and directly—not only via a detour through Bolzano. The connections with Leibniz that Husserl expressed himself on (*Logical Investigations* vol. 1, §60), concern less the doctrine of truths-in-themselves than another essential element of contemporary philosophy.

With the above, we have shown the roots of the distinction between real and ideal being in thinking, as well as the doctrine of the true proposition as validity. We also looked at the consequences the doctrine of validity has for the development of value philosophy. Moreover, we have already anticipated certain questions of the critique, which according to the arrangement of this course, were reserved for §10. But it only seems that way, for in fact we are not yet prepared to make a critique of—and hence, to take a fundamental stance on—the critique of psychologism. The reason for this is that we have not yet clarified Husserl's critique of psychologism in [88] its positive core. Rather, we have *intentionally* sketched out psychologism and Husserl's critique of it only in the form and to the degree that Husserl laid it out in the first volume of the *Logical Investigations* and that his contemporaries understood it then and still understand it today. That is, we sketched it out in the form that this critique has taken positively, e.g., in the logic of validity and value.

But we have by no means gone to the core, to the sense in which Husserl wanted these critical affirmations to be understood. Husserl's critique of psychologism is a critique of psychology—and it intrinsically must be that, if it is to become something positive and not merely an identification and demonstration of errors. It is a critique of psychology in the sense that in place of the function and role that psychology ascribes to itself, a new kind of research is introduced: *phenomenology.* The fact that the critique of psychologism is really a critique of psychology also shows that, yes, the problems that psychologism claims to answer are conceded and affirmed to be legitimate—but with the proviso that psychology, in both its former and present conditions, is shown to be incapable of solving these questions, or even of asking them in a meaningful way.

This meaning of the critique of psychology is no more understood

---

68. [Here (Moser, p. 181) Heidegger ends his lecture of Monday, 23 November 1925, to be followed by that of Tuesday, 24 November, which opened with a 1000-word summary that is omitted in GA 21.]

now than it was then. Philosophy saw the opposition of ideal to real being as the only essential thing, so much so that, when the second volume [of the *Logical Investigations*] was published right after the first volume—which had four times the pages and positive content of the first volume, and which contained the phenomenology—some said that in the second volume Husserl was still continuing to do psychology. Or, as Sigwart says at the end of the introduction to the third edition [of his *Logik*] in 1904: "Husserl may be battling against psychologism, but he is guilty of the very same heresy." So, we will be able to take a position on Husserl's critique of psychologism only when we have understood this critique in its proper sense. [89]

---

§10. Anti-critical questions. The need to take the question of the essence of truth back to Aristotle

We now pose three questions:

a) What is the core of the critique of psychologism, and why must the critique of psychologism be a critique of psychology?
b) What positive element does this critique of psychologism offer with regard to the guiding question about understanding and interpreting the phenomenon of truth?
c) What is the connection between this interpretation of truth (= b) and the one we distinguished in the first place, that of propositional truth (validity)? And do the two formulations satisfy the demand for a radical exposition and interpretation of the phenomenon?

a) Why must the critique of psychologism be a critique of psychology?

The separation of the real mental being of thinking and the ideal content of what is thought is so obvious that you might think that you only have to maintain this separation firmly and consistently in order (a) to thwart any complicating influence from psychology (which deals with the real mental), and (b) to have a univocal, delimited arena for logic. The logic of validity, and especially Rickert's concept of psychology, is of this opinion. It is most clearly seen in Rickert's concept of psychology, which sees psychology as quite analogous to mechanics. Psychology deals with real being and therefore is a pure natural science. On the other hand, logic deals with the ideal being of validity (*Die Grenzen der naturwissenschaftlich Begriffsbildung*).[69]

---

69. [The reference is to Heinrich Rickert, *Die Grenze der naturwissenschaftlichen Begriffsbildung. Eine logische Einleitung in die historischen Wissenschaften* (Tübingen:

So we have an apparently inviolable separation between two disciplines, one of which deals with the being of thinking and the other with validity. What could be more plausible? And yet this is the way to exempt ourselves from really understanding and investigating the issues. [90] For in the final analysis we have to ask whether the thinking-of-what-is-thought is what is really actual. In the final analysis, *neither* real mental thinking in and for itself *nor*, quite separate from the former, the ideal being of thought (where what-is-thought = the valid) —neither one of the two—ever really touches on what we mean by the concrete thinking-of-what-is-thought, which is the most vital actuality in which thinking and thought "are."[70]

Then what about this thinking-of-what-is-thought, i.e., this thinking that, as long as it is thinking something, actually *is* "real" thinking? Given the distinction that has already been made, in this thinking-of-what-is-thought, a "relation" is actual between real thinking and the ideal thought as long as there is actual, living thinking going on. And when thinking is actual thinking, it obviously is not thought-*less*, or better, thought-*free*, for even so-called thoughtless thinking is always thinking about something, only without being disciplined and methodically focused on the issue. But in that separation, thinking is something psychologically real—and then next to it, or over it, or behind it, or who knows where, there is the ideal. If the ideal is what is thought about and conceptualized, then it also must be *at hand* along with the ideal. What kind of relation does the ideal have to the real? Do they border on each other like two regions of things—like the land and the sea? Is there a real mental thing, and then glued on to it (or, as Rickert used to say, "adhering" to it), there is the ideal? Seriously now, has anyone ever seen or found something like that?

Is the relation of the ideal to the real a real relation? How does validity, so to speak, become being in Lotze's sense, entirely against Lotze's thesis that each region is absolutely irreducible to the other? Or maybe it's the other way around: Does the thinking-of-what-is-thought, as real, become the ideal? Even that will be impossible as long as one maintains the total distinction and non-interchangeability of the two. And yet "between the two" there is precisely a real act of thinking as a thinking-of-what-is-thought, a realness of the ideal! And yet the tenor of the whole critique of psychologism as we have sketched it up to now is that the timeless is diametrically opposed to the temporal. [91]

J. C. B. Mohr (Paul Siebeck), 1896; 5th edition, 1929); translated as *The Limits of Concept Formation in Natural Science: A Logical Introduction to the Historical Sciences*, ed. and trans. Guy Oakes (Cambridge and New York: Cambridge University Press, 1986).]
    70. [With help from Moser, p. 189.9-16.]

What about this "reciprocal relation"?[71] Isn't there a gap here, and don't we need to build a bridge across it? An old question seems to emerge here in new form, the question about the participation or μέθεξις of the real (the sensible) in the ideal (the non-sensible). The thinking-of-what-is-thought *is;* but what kind of being is that? Is it the being of this existent unity of the real-ideal? Let us resist being overawed by the obvious separation of the real and the ideal. Above all, we must maintain that living thinking is the thinking-of-what-is-thought and that this is the only reason we inquire into it and seek its rules. If we do that, we will see that behind the seemingly obvious separation of the real and the ideal there lurks a difficulty, in fact the heart of the problem. In the final analysis, this separation not only contributes nothing to solving the problem but in fact radically inverts the formulation of the problem, and thereby condemns the discussion to futility. But the central problem here is how we can throw a bridge over this gap. As Spranger[72] says:

All of us—Rickert, the phenomenologists, the movement connected with Dilthey—we all find ourselves in the great struggle {imagine: the great struggle!} for the timeless in the historical, for the realm of sense and of its historical expression in a developed, concrete culture, for a theory of values that leads beyond the subjective to the objective and valid.[73]

That is correct except for one thing: Dilthey would have repudiated this association in horror.

But philosophers were able to get almost sentimental about this deep and ponderous thought. But maybe it is time to say thoughtfully for once that in more than two millennia this problem has not made any progress. [92]

Maybe it is time to ask ourselves whether it is a real question at all, or whether there is something fundamentally wrong with it or with our understanding of it, or even whether Plato really meant anything like that. Perhaps this seemingly profound question about bridging the gap between the real and the ideal, the sensible and the non-sensible, the temporal and the timeless, the historical and the suprahistorical, is only

---

71. An empty determination! For an extreme case, cf. Richard Hönigswald, *Die Grundlagen der Denkpsychologie.* [*Studien und Analysen,* 2nd unchanged edition (Leipzig: B. G. Teubner,] 1925), 39–40: "The basic mental function of the temporal/non-temporal determinedness. Just as 'thought' can be experienced, just as it must be able to be realized temporally in [the act of] being experienced, so too meaning 'becomes' word in precisely the same way."

72. [Eduard Spranger (1882–1963), a student of Dilthey's (and briefly arrested by the Nazis in 1944). His works are published in his *Gesammelte Schriften,* 11 vols., ed. H. W. Bahr et al. (Heidelberg: Quelle & Meyer, 1960–1980).]

73. *Logos* 12 [1923]. Festschrift for Rickert. On Rickert's system, cf. p. 198.

a foolish undertaking that doesn't even care to ask whether one actually thinks these "opposing pairs" as simply and easily as such lists make it seem: real and ideal, sensible and non-sensible, being and validity, historical and transhistorical, temporal and timeless. Nonetheless, this foolishness gets the semblance of a justification as follows. First you invent these two regions, then you put a gap between them, and then you go looking for the bridge. "Take the gap and build the bridge"—that's about as clever as the old instruction: "To make a gun barrel, you take an empty space and put some steel around it." Intelligent psychologism has yet to concede that it has been refuted, and perhaps the reason for that lies in this meaningless way of stating the problem. For psychologism can rightly appeal to the fact that this almost chemical separation of thinking from knowledge has provided nothing essential toward understanding what is the most actual of all: lived thinking itself, lived life as knowing.

I will say further that this position, which thinks itself *so* philosophical in contrast to psychologism, and which believes itself to have surpassed naturalism, in fact harbors an even grosser and more basic form of naturalism, one that is much harder to get a grip on. Basically we are in a situation where we have to see these two separate orders or fields or spheres or regions as coming together in unity: that which has being and that which has validity, the sensible and the non-sensible, the real and the ideal, the historical and the transhistorical. We have not yet apprehended an original kind of being in terms of which we could understand these two fields as possible and as belonging *to* that of being. [93] Philosophers don't even ask about such being. Instead they flaunt the "fundamental uniqueness" of this separation and see themselves as constrained to bridge or link the two together so that they can adhere to each other and become a whole. Even contemporary physics does not present the structure of the atom in such a primitively atomistic and mechanistic way. Such patching together might make sense as regards atoms, as material beings—but no, not even there! So obviously it's absurd to use such a linking-up of opposites when it comes to beings like the mental and the ideal, which have absolutely no character of material thingness.

But what about the entity that does not, as it were, cast a bridge over the gap between these two regions, but instead (if one has to understand it in this way) renders possible these two regions of being in their original unity? Husserl has not asked the question. Rather, within the framework of psychologism and in a manner that derives from psychologism, he asks what the mental as such must be if it is able to stand as the real in relation to the ideal.[74] From the beginning, therefore, Hus-

---

74. [With help from Moser, p. 195.15-17.]

serl also held to that distinction and then asked about the basic structure of the mental, especially as regards what we call presentation,
judgment, acknowledgment, taking positions, positing, insight, and
thinking. Are these phenomena—which we are so quick to call processes and events—actually inside us in the way that the circulation of
the blood and the function of gastric juices are, with the simple difference that they are not sensible and cannot be treated in a direct chemical and physical way? Or does what we mean by thinking, judging, and
so forth—this "mental," as such—have its own structure and its own
kind of being? We should have asked about the structure of one of the
two regions in order to understand in it the μέθεξις. To put it more exactly: Husserl did not really need to ask for a directive regarding the
basic character and elements of the mental question, insofar as he already had received such an orientation from his teacher, Franz Brentano.[75, 76] [94]

*   *   *

Brentano had already explained these basic determinations of the
mental in his *Psychologie vom empirischen Standpunkt,* of which only the
first volume was published.[77] This *Psychology from an Empirical Standpoint* is divided into two books: book 1, "Psychology as a Science"; and
book 2, "Mental Phenomena in General," the real heart of Brentano's
investigations. The point is to determine what the mental really is, in
order to go on from there to the various ways in which mental being
can comport itself. The basic determination of the mental is *intentionality.* Understood very roughly, intentionality is self-directedness-to-
something. All mental comportments, as mental, are determined by
the fact that they are directed toward something. Now, there are various ways to be directed toward something: presenting, judging, taking
a position, willing—i.e., the ways we understand the usual divisions of

75. [Editor's note: Cf. Heidegger's lecture course, Summer Semester 1925, *Geschichte des Zeitbegriffs.*] [Translator's note: Published in English as Martin Heidegger, *History of the Concept of Time: Prolegomena,* trans. Theodore Kisiel (Bloomington: Indiana University Press, 1985).]

76. [Here (Moser, p. 198) Heidegger ends his lecture of Tuesday, 24 November
1925, to be followed by that of Thursday, 26 November, which opened with a 230-
word summary that is omitted in GA 21.]

77. New edition in the series Philosophische Bibliothek, published by Felix
Meiner. The introduction that precedes this edition is entirely worthless. [*Psychologie vom empirischen Standpunkt,* 2 vols., ed. Oskar Kraus (Hamburg: Felix
Meiner, 1955; repr. from the 1924–1925 edition: Philosophische Bibliotek, no.
193); translated as *Psychology from an Empirical Standpoint,* ed. Linda L. McAllister,
trans. Antos C. Rancurello, D. B. Terrell, and Linda L. McAllister (New York: Humanities Press, 1973).]

the so-called mental faculties. In Brentano's words, mental phenomena are distinguished by the way in which something is objective for them. In presentation, what is presented is objective in one way; in willing, what is willed is objective in another. The differences between these ways of being objective or, as Brentano says, of the intentional inexistence [i.e., mental presence] of the object—these different ways are the clue to a first classification of the mental. Brentano distinguished three ways of mental comportment or intentionality: *presentation*—simply having something present; *judgment*—as acknowledging or rejecting what is presented; and the phenomenon of *taking interest* in something—i.e., phenomena that Brentano also collected under the heading of the behaviors of love and hate. And to this basic division he added a fundamental [95] determination wherein he grasped a structural connection within such intentional comportments: "Every mental phenomenon is either itself a presentation or is founded on one." This means that all acts of judgment, along with all acts of taking-interest in something, are possible only because there is given beforehand a "presented something" in which we take interest or on which we pass judgment. Consequently presentations, in the sense of presenting something, acquire a distinctive significance. Let that suffice for Brentano. It should be enough to orient us on the question of what Husserl used as the foundations for his *Logical Investigations*.

With intentionality we highlight a structure of the mental that had already been noted earlier, in the Middle Ages and even among the Greeks, but without its structure being understood in the clear sense it has in Brentano. But it is obvious that even Brentano merely emphasizes a structure of the mental; he is far from understanding it in its real meaning. On the one hand, the fact that Brentano emphasized intentionality is something essential; but on the other, it reveals an equally essential shortcoming that was critically demonstrated by Husserl in his *Logical Investigations,* both in the Fifth Investigation and in an appendix at the end of the whole work, where he dealt with external and internal perception and with physical and mental phenomena.

Husserl had already received from Brentano a direction for determining thinking insofar as it is something mental. Thinking is the thinking-of-what-is-thought, because thinking, as mental, already necessarily has the structure of self-directedness-to-something. In its essence, thinking as something mental is already from the start related to something. It is not first of all something real only, as it were, within consciousness, and then afterwards, by some kind of mechanism, related to something outside. We must guard against the usual misunderstandings. [96] Even those who talk about intentionality have mostly misunderstood it, as if intentionality meant that first of all the mental is real inside of consciousness, and then an indicative direction forward is applied to the mental so as to help it point outward into the external world. No—the mental is first and only this very self-directedness, and as such it is "real."

The project, then, was to understand thinking within the horizon of this structure of the mind and, along with that, to understand what-is-thought in its thought-ness. But out of this project grew another one: not just to point out and preserve intentionality by concretely pursuing and investigating specifically logical behaviors—naming, designating, presenting, meaning, intuiting, judging—but also, and for the first time, to properly understand the meaning of intentionality and thereby to secure the field of mind in its basic constitution. With this *phenomenological* project, Brentano was really striving to secure the ground on which logic, as phenomenological, could make some actual progress in research by taking its directives from the issues themselves.

The project was to antecedently determine the structure of the field of the subject matter, and it first of all had to be adequately dealt with if psychologism's basic goal was to be possible. Thus, a critique of psychologism has to be a critique of psychology. But as we now see, this critique of psychology is not about correcting its results or improving its methods by inventing new instruments or broadening the arena and the field of investigation by, e.g., making use of child psychology.— Yes, child psychology is of the greatest importance. Perhaps at a later date the psychology of the elderly will also be of great import. All of these are possible and legitimate projects, but they are not the arena in which the real work of research is to be played out.

No matter how much psychological knowledge we accumulate, it will never help us clarify fundamental principles unless we pose the question of those principles right from the start. The accumulation [97] of such knowledge can go on *ad infinitum*, but it will never get an answer to the question of what the mind is, and yet this question is *the* concrete, essential question of the science itself. Of course, the path of science—of any science—mostly proceeds by first taking a naïve running jump into a seemingly limitless field, in which it establishes some fixed points of relative value. But then it requires some basic philosophical investigation and clarification of that field it wants to investigate. Only then is the science really put on its path—but it stays on that path only by always understanding how to make the philosophical move, i.e., to continually question its field and revise its basic concepts. People have completely misunderstood the critique of psychologism—and Husserl's in particular—when they have read out of it an animosity toward experimental psychology. Those kinds of investigations have their own legitimacy and projects, but they have nothing to do with philosophy—any more than physics does. So what is needed is a fundamental reflection on the thematic field of psychology.

Some years ago, in 1916, in his inaugural lecture as Rickert's succes-
sor at Freiburg, Husserl compared the philosopher's tasks with those of
Galileo in the natural sciences.[78] Naturally, the philosophically un-
washed understood these reflections simply as Husserl comparing himself with Galileo and presenting himself as someone greater. Now, we
intellectuals are certainly conceited—some more than others, and philosophers above all. They often make this impression because they don't
talk about the despair that haunts them. But in that lecture (which, like
many others, is not published), it was certainly not Husserl's intention
to compare himself with Galileo. His purpose, rather, was to show that
people had already experimented with nature long before Galileo, but
that Galileo was the founder of modern natural science only because, as
a physicist, he was a philosopher. The discovery that movement is the
fundamental determination of nature had already been made by Aristotle, whom Galileo studied assiduously. [98] Long before Galileo, people had employed numerical calculation. What mattered, however, was
not that, but the fact that Galileo asked: How must physical processes be
defined if adequate scientific knowledge of them is to be possible?

Comparing philosophy to Galileo's project means: As regards
"mind" or "consciousness" (which is indeed the subject of experimental, numerical calculations), we have to ask what makes mind be mind
and what kind of determination must mind have if we are to be able
to gain an adequate knowledge of it.

Applied to the critique of psychologism, that means: Psychologism is
to be rejected not because psychology wants to force its way into a place
where it does not belong, but because it is the application of a psychology that does not understand its own subject matter; not because psychologism merely transgresses a boundary, but because it transgresses
into what is not *psychology,* and for that reason is confused.

Because of this insight, and guided essentially by it alone, even
Husserl in the beginning titled his phenomenological investigations a
"descriptive psychology," where "descriptive" did not have the sense of
a narrative versus experimental psychology, or a psychology without
instruments versus one that uses them, or of "desk psychology" versus
laboratory psychology. In Husserl, "descriptive" entails leaving all of
these [supposed contraries] behind and getting back to exhibiting the
issue itself, its field and its structure.

The basic feature of mind is intentionality. This means that the
mind in and of itself is (if we may use this formulation just once) a

78. [This is now published as "Husserl's Inaugural Lecture at Freiburg im Breis-
gau (1917)," trans. Robert W. Jordan, in Peter McCormick and Frederick A. Elliston,
eds., *Husserl: Shorter Works* (Notre Dame: University of Notre Dame Press, 1981), pp.
9–17.]

relation of the real to the ideal. Husserl doesn't deal with this question in itself. It surfaces only now and then. His interests are focused above all on concrete research into the intentional structure itself.

By now it should be clear what the [99] sole authentic meaning of the critique of psychologism is, and why such a critique must necessarily be a critique of psychology.

b) What positive contribution does the phenomenological investigation of psychologism make to the question of the concept and interpretation of the phenomenon of truth?

In the present context, we need not develop what phenomenology is, in what investigations it first emerged, and what essential discoveries we owe to it. Instead, from the start we will limit ourselves to the question: What was established about the phenomenon of truth as a result of this phenomenological inquiry? In what context does the phenomenon of truth now emerge? Answering this question will also make it possible for us to characterize intentionality more precisely.

Up to now, we have met truth as a determination or "property" of statements. A true statement, a statement to which truth accrues, has validity and is a truth. This characteristic belongs to the field of validity and ideal being. But now we ask about the connection of the real and the ideal—or more exactly, we ask about the phenomenon in which such a connection is supposedly possible. In our earlier treatment, truth was geared to the statement, and the statement to λόγος in a specific, narrow sense. From now on we will simply call it "λόγος-truth." We will not ask what this λόγος-truth is in itself, although in a certain sense we have already determined its location. Instead, we now look into the phenomenon of the statement, within which λόγος-truth supposedly has its proper home.

I now aim the investigation not primarily at the spoken statement and its meaning—that which is thought and known as such—but at the act of thinking-what-is-thought, the act of knowing the thing. I mean this not according to the context or method of Lotze, who proceeds from what is "in consciousness" as something constantly and stably given, and goes on from there to the question of objective validity. Rather, our treatment prescinds entirely from validity and non-validity, [100] and aims at determining *what knowing is at all.*

Knowing, as a phenomenological relation, is intentional. This is part of the definition of its essence. The question is: What does knowing direct itself to, and what property does this self-directing have *qua* cognitive?

The first question: What does knowing direct itself to? In answering the "to what?" we neither wish to put a limit on the objects that are knowable, nor recount that knowing directs itself to houses, streets, baby buggies, people, the sky, geometric relations. Rather, our question is: What characterizes each of those things insofar as it is and can be a "toward-which" [*Worauf*] of knowing? We are asking about the toward-which of knowing as such—its (if you will allow the phrase) toward-which-ness [*Woraufheit*], so as to pin down what is intended. In order to answer this question from the phenomenon itself, let us follow the lead of a concrete act of knowing something ordinary that is close to us and familiar.

I follow the lead of my present looking around and about.[79] To put it naïvely, I find that my knowledge is directed to you the audience as well as the window, the walls, the chalkboard. These very things are what my cognitive self-directedness intends. My act of knowing does not intend them as "contents of consciousness." When I look at the bench over there, I certainly do not participate in a content of consciousness to which I attribute value, as Rickert puts it. When I see this lamp, I do not apprehend sense-impressions but the lamp itself and the light; even less do I apprehend sense-impressions of red and gold. No, I apprehend the grey wall itself. Nor am I related to concepts. Even less so do I see something like an image in my consciousness—an image of the wall, which I then relate to the wall itself in order thereby to slip out of my consciousness, in which I am allegedly imprisoned. No, it is the wall itself that my looking intends. This does not seem to be a particularly deep insight, and in fact it is not. But it becomes a crucial insight in the face of the erroneous constructions of epistemology. Epistemology snaps to the ready, armed with a theory, and though blind to the phenomenon of knowledge, goes ahead and explains knowledge—instead of leaving its theory at home [101] and for once starting by examining what underlies its "explanation."

As regards currently circulating theories, the crucial thing is, first, to establish inchoatively the toward-which, the entity itself, and then above all to hold on to it. Even the unbiased, when asked what it is they see, are inclined to think they have to say something learned. And since everyone seems to know that what is first given intention-

79. [Moser (p. 211) records Heidegger as saying in place of the next few lines: "To put it naïvely, I find that my perception, in which I am now living, is directed to you the audience as well as to the wall and the window over there. My act of knowing does not intend them as 'contents of consciousness.' When I look at the bench over there, I certainly do not participate in a value-laden content of consciousness, as Rickert puts it. When I see this lamp, I do not apprehend sense-impressions but the lamp itself and the light that burns here in this auditorium. Even less so am I related to concepts, and least of all do I first know an image [of light] in my consciousness, with the help of which and with the help of the image of the wall, I somehow slip out to the wall out there. No, what I know is the audience, the wall, the window, and the chalkboard themselves."]

ally are only ideas, they say they see not the wall but a "representation" of it. It is not only an inability to take what they directly saw as what they saw. Rather, it is a matter of not wanting to say what one has seen, an attitude that is nourished by the dominant prejudices.

If right now, while I am speaking to you about knowledge, I ask someone to erase the chalkboard, I am speaking about the chalkboard behind me. At the moment, I don't see it—I don't perceive it. Usually people say I have only an idea of the chalkboard. What does that mean? Maybe it means that I am presently directed to my idea of the chalkboard, and would someone please erase that idea. But obviously not. Even in "having an idea of," what I mean is the chalkboard itself—the one behind me here in the classroom. When I turn around, I see it bodily. Even the first time I spoke about it, although I did not see it bodily, I intended the chalkboard itself.

I may say I have an idea of the chalkboard or only an idea, but that does not mean that what I am intending is my idea. No, I intend the chalkboard itself, but now in the mode of merely an idea.[80] So we ask what the difference is between this mere idea of the chalkboard behind me and my perception of the wall in front of me. At first one might say that the chalkboard that I'm now speaking about is itself the one that I intend—that chalkboard itself—but that it is given to me indeterminately insofar as I currently cannot provide the measurements of the chalkboard, the relation between its height and its breadth, or how its frame looks, or even whether it [102] has a frame. And therefore, whatever is intended in a mere-idea is indeterminate as regards its content, whereas what is bodily given is determinate, or in any case *can* be determined by having a perception of the bodily given.[81]

* * *

This distinction does hold, but it is not an essential distinction that would phenomenologically distinguish an idea from a perception in terms of their respective intentionalities. That becomes immediately clear if we consider the following case. It quite possible for me to have an entirely definite idea of the chalkboard, so definite that I could describe it very exactly and by heart. On the other hand, that wall over there can be given bodily and yet indeterminately. To use the chalkboard as an example: When I see the chalkboard while writing on it, it is given to me in a bodily way. I feel the pressure and resistance

80. [That is, I intend the chalkboard itself—of which, until I turn around, I *directly* have only an idea.]

81. [Here (Moser, p. 213) Heidegger ends his lecture of Thursday, 26 November 1925, to be followed by that of Friday, 27 November, which opened with a 750-word summary that is omitted in GA 21.]

of the chalkboard, but it is not given to me in a definite way. When writing on it, I do not see the chalkboard in its full extension but only a certain section of it. So, the difference of degree or content is not the essential distinction that draws the line between an idea and a perception. The definiteness and clarity of the intended content are not crucial. What *is* crucial is the fact that in perception the intended thing is itself bodily there, whether definitely or not, whereas when I have an idea of it, the thing is certainly intended but is not bodily present.

Now obviously this is only a preliminary description, and we will not go into it further at this point. But we want to keep this distinction in the back of our minds in order to understand something essential about it. We have two cases: having an idea of the chalkboard, and seeing the wall. One is an idea, the other is a perception. Let's remember that what is meant in both cases is the thing itself. We designate perception— where we have the thing not only "itself" but also "bodily"—as proper knowledge in the strict sense. Thus knowledge is apprehending and having the thing itself [103] in its bodiliness. In phenomenology, that is called *intuition*: "Apprehending and having the thing itself in its bodiliness" is the phenomenological definition of intuition. And intuition is not limited to the ways of apprehending something by sight in the narrow sense of seeing with the eyes. Hearing a piece of music, so long as the music itself is heard, is also characterized phenomenologically as intuition, insofar as the apprehending is an apprehension of the entity itself in its bodiliness. Likewise, pronouncing the judgment "2 × 2 = 4" is an intuition, so long as in carrying out the proposition explicitly in its individual positions, we understand what is being said in itself: "Two, taken twice, is four." In that case the statement is an intuitive statement as well as an intuiting statement: it renders present the very thing intended. In this case, of course, the thing intended is not perceptible by the senses and cannot be seen with the eyes or heard with the ears. Nonetheless the thing intended is itself to be apprehended and understood in what it is. Here we take the concept of intuition in a very broad sense, but one that, despite its breadth, is well defined. There is intuition wherever the thing that is intended in this comportment is bodily present. Perception is only one mode of intuition, namely, the mode that is constitutive for sensibility.

Why is intuition in the sense we have defined it—the immediate having of something as bodily there—authentic knowledge? Because intuition delivers the thing itself, and as such it alone properly has the capability of proving and verifying opinions, cognitions, things said, propositions. But why is there and why must there be proof at all?

Our knowledge and understanding, which is first and always directed to the world, lives in and draws upon "sense experience." Although our knowledge remains (within certain limits) constantly related to its firsthand lived world,[82] we mostly do not have things present "bodily" (in the sense we defined), [104] not even—and especially not—when we are involved with these things. In the precise moment that I write on the chalkboard something I am saying, I certainly do sense the resistance of the board, and the board is bodily given to me. However, in a strict sense, the board is not bodily present to me as I write. Rather, I am present to the words I am writing and their meaning. On the other hand, of course, (and I just throw this out in passing without going into it) someone could say that in (another) sense the chalkboard most certainly is bodily present, precisely in fact when I do not see it, when I just stand here and occasionally during the lecture write on it. At that moment, someone might say, the chalkboard is bodily present in a real and proper sense, in fact in its most proper actuality, when it is used for what it is. In this way, the chalkboard is disclosed in its proper sense, whereas when someone who has absolutely nothing to do with the room walks in and sees it there, the board is not present to him as what it is. I mention this distinction so as to indicate that the concept of the bodily present is geared to theoretical apprehension and knowledge. We are speaking exclusively about the theoretical in the present context.

It is not only our firsthand lived world that is by and large not given bodily, directly, and explicitly. Even less so is the world that lies just beyond the firsthand world. We have some understanding and some knowledge of it. We can speak of it and communicate something about it to others by way of reports and instructions, but only within certain limits. The limits are not those of memory, which does not apprehend and hold on to everything. Rather, this knowledge and understanding of . . . , this ability to speak about . . . , has a limit in itself, even if everything experienced remains stored up in it in the form of a memory. The limits of knowledge and speech come to light when they have to prove themselves as the "knowledge of . . ." and "speech about . . ." that they claim to be in their very being as knowledge and speech. We see their limits when they have to show themselves for what [105] they are instead of being taken simply as something that might occasionally be of value to others, such as a normative opinion, or an authority figure's judgment and pronouncement, or the dictum of an expert.

Thus, although knowledge and speaking communicate something, or mean something without communicating it, nonetheless they are what they properly are only because of that whereby they show and prove their legitimacy: the fact that what they say, they say legitimately—i.e., when they say *just how* things are. However, the subject

---

82. ["Seine nächste Umwelt," where the noun *Umwelt* does not mean the world that is physically around one, but rather the lived world of one's interests and concerns.]

matter that I know and speak about need not be constantly and immediately present, and I myself need not be present to it. To that extent our knowledge and speaking to a large degree finally always requires proof. Or let me put it positively. Even though the subject matter
is, in a strict sense, always in need of proof, nonetheless for the most
part it is "step by step" brought to light, passed on, and accepted on the
basis of trust and belief. Thus, proof requires that the thing itself become present and that knowledge of and speaking about it be brought
face-to-face with it. Knowledge of and speaking about must, so to
speak, show their cards to the thing of and about which they make the
claim that it has been "revealed" in the broad sense—i.e., *logos,* as previously defined.[83] They must let themselves be checked out by the
thing itself.

But intuition delivers the thing itself. For the most part, knowledge
and speaking that do not stem from the immediate presence of the thing
are largely indeterminate, or "one-sided," or frequently such that, yes,
the thing is intended, but intended in a completely empty way. In contrast with such indeterminate or empty ideas, intuition gives the full
store of the determinations of the thing, or the possibility of having that.
Intuition gives the fullness as distinct from the emptiness of a mere idea
and generally a mere intention. Intuition is the fulfillment—in the sense
of the filling up—of the emptiness of the idea.

But we just heard that there is no essential distinction between the
idea and intuition, only a distinction in the manner of intentional relation and function. Consequently, the term "fulfillment" has yet another
[106] sense, the primary one, with which it is conjoined. Intuition fulfills not simply by giving fullness but also by redeeming the expectation
that in a certain way can be found in the empty idea. In speaking, I
intend something and intend it in this sense: that it can be confirmed at
every moment by a concrete intuition of the thing and the state of affairs I am talking about—for example, in the lecture itself, by pointing
to the thing in question. Fulfillment now means: a confirmation that
redeems [an expectation], and it indicates an intentional characteristic
that has an essential relation to that of the empty idea.

Now there are various modes, grades, and levels of fulfillment in
intuitions, specifically according to the twofold sense of fulfillment: as
providing fullness in the sense of *the full;* and as *providing* fullness in
the sense of confirmation.

We run up against the phenomenon of proof when we realize that
a broad swath of our knowledge and speech is dominated by empty
ideas, and that not even adequate cognition counts as knowing. Rather,

---

83. [Heidegger is referring to λόγος / λέγειν as δηλοῦν, "bringing to light, rendering manifest."]

this knowing passes over into the mode of empty intention, and the empty idea is itself in need of fulfillment. It also has an explicit tendency toward proof, but not in some indeterminate way. Rather, the content of this knowing has an intrinsic directedness toward the field that provides intuitive fulfillment.

Now, what does proof mean? It means that what is intended in the empty idea is brought, just as it is intended, before the very thing that is intended. But why so? We have put all our emphasis on seeing that the empty idea intends the thing itself—yes, but in the mode of emptiness. This mode is modified when confronted with the bodily presence of the thing itself.

The [legitimacy of the] empty idea is proven by the thing itself that is given in intuition and is seen to be identical with what the idea intended. The empty idea proves its legitimacy by way of the thing itself: by identifying what it intended with the thing, and by seeing the thing and the intention as identical. [107] This empty [idea] now sees that what it intended is identical with the thing that is present in intuition.[84]

In proof, what is emptily intended in the idea and what is intuited are seen as coinciding. But we must understand this figurative way of speaking correctly, i.e., in terms of the structure of the phenomena in question. The coming-to-coincide of the empty idea and the intuited thing is a matter of intentionality. It is not some sort of mental process in which, as it were, (a) two disks—idea and intuition—are superimposed one on top of the other and coincide; and then (b) some later reflection establishes that coincidence has taken place, which is taken as a sign that the empty idea has been proven. No, this proof happens intentionally, as a matter of directedness-toward-something. That is, the empty intentional idea itself, in its tendency to fulfillment, *lives in* the act of identification, i.e., its nature is to identify itself with something. It is not simply that unreflected proof precedes reflective proof.[85] Rather, as intentional, the empty idea that proves itself knows itself as proving itself. In enacting the identification as an intentional act, that very enactment sees the proof and sees that it is the proof of the enactment itself. Proof is not something that gets attached to the empty idea. Rather, it is a mode of the enactment itself.

When I live in the intuition of a thing as a proving intuition, the act of intuiting does not lose itself in the thing and its content. Rather, this content is intuited as bodily present and explicitly as fulfilling, as identifying-itself-with the empty idea. But this implies that knowing lives not only in the thing but also with itself insofar as, in performing the

84. [GA 21 (p. 107.1) mistakes *sieht* ("it sees") for *sucht* ("it seeks"); cf. Moser, p. 224.22.]

85. [Literally, "The proof does not simply go before itself."]

identification, the act of knowing knows how things stand with regard to its own legitimacy. But the legitimacy of knowing is its ability to be proven, or its proven-ness in and with the thing. Identification or proof is an intentional matter. It is carried out; and thereby, without any reflection on its part, it attains to a clarification of itself. If this moment of unreflected self-understanding, which lies in the intentional performance of identification, [108] is specially apprehended of and by itself, then it is to be taken as what we call evidence.

Evidence is the self-understanding act of identification. This self-understanding is given with the act itself, since the intentional sense of the act intends something identical *qua* identical; and thereby, in and with its intending, it *eo ipso* clarifies itself.

The essential thing about this apparently primitive (but from a phenomenological viewpoint extraordinarily important) analysis is this: Evidence is not an act that accompanies proof and attaches itself to it. Evidence is the very enactment of, or a special mode of, proof.

But insofar as legitimacy makes its appearance in such proof, what we have said about evidence also means the following. The legitimacy of knowing is not established after the fact, as it were, in a new act of knowledge whose content would be that the first act of knowledge (the one proven in the first place) is legitimate. Rather, the legitimacy of knowledge becomes visible in, through, and for the intentional enactment of identification. If we do not grasp the phenomenological situation in this way, that is, if we do not see the phenomenological structure, we will be inevitably thrown into an absurd conclusion, namely, that the legitimacy of an act of knowledge is established only when it is known in a second act of knowledge, which in turn would need another demonstration of *its* legitimacy, and so on *in infinitum*. The first act of knowledge, the true and proper knowledge of the thing, would never gain legitimacy because *a priori* and unto infinity it would always be necessary to know the legitimacy of the knowledge of the legitimacy of knowledge, and *this* knowing, in turn . . . , and so on and on.

The legitimacy of an act of knowledge or of speech is its ability to be proven or its actually having been proven. (The state of having-been-proven is the identity of the intended and the intuited, an identity that is seen in the proof.) As an act of knowledge whose legitimacy can be provided at any time by an intuition of the thing it intends, it is [109] true. Truth is the identity of the meant and the intuited.

Truth is identity or sameness, although obviously not in a universal sense, for not every form of identity is truth. But in this case, truth is interpreted in terms of identity, and specifically as the identity of the intended and the intuited.

With this we have now determined truth itself. To put it formally: Identity is a relation. And truth as an identity is a relation between the meant and the intuited. Therefore, truth is the specific relation (of identity) of a certain "just-as": something is meant *just as* it is intuited.

"True-ness" now means the identity of the two parts of the relation. In this case, true-ness does not mean the actuality and kind of truth [that pertains to propositions]. Rather, it means what truth itself *is:* a recognized identity.

To be sure, we will leave open the question whether this is the final answer. In any case, this is the determination of truth that we have been looking for, namely, the interpretation that Husserl provides through his investigations into knowing as intentional comportment, or more precisely, knowing as intuition.[86]

c) The connection between propositional and intuitional truth. The need to return to Aristotle

Let us hold on the point that truth is now determined not primarily in relation to the proposition, but rather in relation to [110] knowledge as intuition. We established the first determination of truth as validity, where truth characterizes the actuality of a true proposition, as λόγος-truth, that is, the truth of speech insofar as we take speech in the sense of the statement. Now we have made a statement not only about the actuality of what-is-true, but also about the structure of truth itself—namely, identity.

We essentially arrived at this second determination of truth by focusing on the act of knowing and specifically on knowing as intuition. This refers to intuition in the very broad sense that coincides with the Greek νοεῖν and which is also often indicated as αἴσθησις. When we take this second determination of truth also back to a Greek word, we see that now this second and authentic concept of truth constitutes the truth of νοῦς and the truth of intuition, or νοῦς-truth. I have already remarked that when I use this perhaps comic juxtaposition of Greek and German it is to show how these two questions about truth are geared to λόγος

---

86. An inherent consequence of the concept of intuition and of the understanding of truth in relation to intuition is that it is not merely "the synthesis of [true] representations" (according to Kant in his *Logic:* the representation of a representation). No, a manifold of intuitions plus their connections is not the only kind of truth. There is truth even where there is an isolated intuition: the intuition can be proven (or not) by what it intends. "Strict adequation can bring non-relating intentions as much as relating intentions into union with their complete fulfillments. If we now consider in particular the field of expressions, we need not concern ourselves only with judgments (i.e., the intentions and the fulfillments of statements). Rather, even acts of naming {"single-rayed" ideas} can also achieve their adequation." Cf. *LU,* vol. 2, Sixth Investigation, §39, p. 768 (1913 ed., p. 125). [Husserl treats "single-rayed" ideas at, for example, ibid., vol. 2, §38, no. 2.]

and νοῦς, two basic starting points of that ancient philosophy in whose tradition we stand today.[87]

*   *   *

The question comes up: How is νοῦς related to λόγος? From the phenomenological distinction we made between the intentional structures of knowing and its outcome, i.e., the determination of truth [as identity], what have we gained toward understanding the kind of truth that we mentioned first, the truth of the proposition?

A proposition has the property of truth. It is true; it is "a truth." Why is the proposition the "place" of truth? How can it be the locus of truth, in fact the first and only authentic locus? Using what was just said about truth itself, can we shed some light on this issue?

The proposition, taken as a simple statement—"This board is black"— gives expression to an intuition. I do not mean [111] a spoken expression, a voiced utterance. I mean, rather, that the structure of the proposition as such, whether it is spoken or not, consists of one or more words. And the structure of the proposition as such articulates the simple content of what is intuited, namely, the chalkboard. So, the content of the proposition is the intuited *qua* articulated, and this content, as articulated, is elevated to a new dimension of "understanding." We will not go into this any further. Instead we take up another issue:

The proposition, which gives expression to the intuited by articulating it, can be spoken out loud, and as such can be spoken over and over again. In all this, the proposition is indeed related, as regards its *content,* to the same thing. However, that thing is not given bodily in the statement.

The intuition is, so to speak, pulled out from under the statement. Of course, the statement still intends the same thing, and it is true insofar as what it intends in the manner of empty idea or spoken words can be proved by reference to the very thing that is meant, insofar as the thing is bodily present in intuition. At this point the proposition is nothing but an empty idea or something said. Its content is a merely-intended. But that means that the proposition, as intended, is one member of the relation that we determined as truth; it is one *relatum* in the relation of identity. It is a member of this specific relation of identity—in fact it's the member that can be proven, the one to which provability accrues.

Therefore, the proposition is true because it is one relational member of the relation of truth. If this relation of identity between the intuited

87. [Here (Moser, p. 230) Heidegger ends his lecture of Friday, 27 November 1925, to be followed by that of Monday, 30 November, which opened with a 900-word summary that is omitted in GA 21.]

and the intended holds, then *eo ipso* the *relatum* also holds in the sense that what is intended can itself now be designated as true. Now we have a situation that is the very opposite of the situation with Lotze. His treatment took off from the proposition and said: The proposition is valid, is true, and because the proposition is valid, therefore it is objectively valid of the thing. But in our treatment, because the proposition is provable in and by the thing—that is, because it belongs, as a *relatum*, to the subsisting relation of identity—therefore it subsists and holds, therefore it is valid. But now we take validity in the sense of the true-ness of propositions back to authentic truth in the sense of identity. From that, it follows that the truth of propositions, in the sense of validity, is a derived [112] phenomenon that is founded on the truth of intuition. Because truth in the sense of identity *subsists,* therefore the proposition *is valid.* When we speak here of "subsisting," we mean the term precisely in Lotze's sense, for Lotze says: "When relations subsist, we say they are actual." Therefore, according to Lotze, relations have *their* kind of being as subsistence. But truth is a relation of identity between the intuited and the meant. Identity as truth subsists, and because it subsists, it is valid for a member of the relation, a member that can and should be proven.

Now the question comes up about what "subsisting" is supposed to mean here, that is, the subsistence of identity as such. This is the subsistence of the relation of intended and intuited or, as we formulated it above, the subsistence of the *"just-as"* relation. What is the status of this subsisting? In any case, when we talk about truth as identity, we are talking about a relation,[88] and specifically one that does *not* subsist between the thing and its determinations. So it is not the relation that subsists between, say, the chalkboard and its blackness. The relation we have in mind belongs to the content of both the intended and the intuited. We are talking about the relation of the intended propositional content ["This board is black"] *to* what is intuited [this chalkboard]. So there are two issues: (A) In the proposition as such, there is the so-called propositional relation in which the thing is intended according to its content; and equally, the content is also present in the thing that is intuited. (B) But further, in identity taken as truth, there is also a relation, that of the intended with regard to the intuited. We call this the "truth-relation" [*Wahrverhalt*], because it is a special relation, a relation of truth.

Now Husserl himself called this relation between the intended and the intuited a "content-relation" [*Sachverhalt*], and therefore, in accordance with its own structure, he brought it into line with the other content-relation, $S = P$, "This board is black" (the relation of black and

---

88. [Heidegger identifies *Verhalt* and *Verhältnis* at Moser, p. 236.21–22: "und zwar einem Verhalt, einem Verhältnis."]

board), but with the following difference. In the $S = P$ content-relation, the members of the relation are the thing and the thing's determination, whereas in Case B, the relation is between the intended as such and the intuited as such. Now [113] if you take this truth-relation of Case B in the very broadest sense, it has the same kind of being as the proposition—ideal being—and so the identity of the intended and the intuited can be understood as ideal being! And so, by a remarkable path, we have come back to where we started.

In the one case, the proposition as one member of the relation is founded on the intuition-truth of identity, whereas in the other case, identity itself as a state of affairs has the same kind of being as a proposition or a propositional state of affairs: ideal being. And in all this, the treatment remains within the bounds of phenomenology. We will want to keep in mind this connection between propositional content and truth-content for when, later on, we take up these connections in more positive analyses.

Now the question comes up: Why is propositional truth connected in a special way with intuitional truth, as a *relatum,* a member of a relation? And regarding Case B, why does intuitional truth take its truth—insofar as it is understood as identity—back to propositional truth?[89] Does there finally exist between the two determinations of truth a more basic connection than the one we showed above, a connection where propositional truth is founded in intuitional truth? In any case, it follows from our demonstration that the truth of intuition has priority; and if a more basic connection does exist between the two, then our inquiry has to reach back behind both of them.

First of all, how is the priority of intuitional truth to be understood? The answer is that truth is so originally a determination of knowledge that we can say that true knowledge is a tautology, because knowledge is knowledge only if it is true knowledge. (False knowledge is like a square circle. If I understand something wrongly, I do not have knowledge of it.) Knowledge was defined as intuition; but not every act of knowledge is an intuition. Nonetheless, true and proper knowledge is intuition, and every other kind of knowledge aims at intuition and has intuition as its "idea," i.e., its ideal.

Husserl held to this typically broad and principled understanding of intuition as the giving and the having of an entity in its concrete presence. Such an understanding of intuition is not limited to any particular field or any particular faculty, [114] but rather formulates the intentional sense of intuition. With this unique and radical understanding of the concept of intuition, Husserl thought through a great tradition of Western philosophy right to its end.

89. [Following here Moser, p. 238.3–6.]

Now we must briefly indicate, first, how it happened that this apparently obvious fact—that truth is patterned on knowledge *qua* intuition—is connected with some specific and very basic issues, and, second, how the outcome of our discussion of intuition-truth and the related problems leads us to a central question of philosophy and indeed of the whole philosophical tradition.

First of all, let us document the importance of Husserl's basic understanding of the concept of intuition by citing his formulation of "the principle of all principles" (formulated for knowledge in general and for research). Husserl says:

> No conceivable theory can mislead us regarding the principle of all principles: that every originarily presentative intuition [*Anschauung*] is a legitimating source of cognition, that everything that is offered originarily (in its reality "in person," so to speak) in "intuition" [»*Intuition*«] is to be simply accepted as that as which it is given, but also only within the limits in which it is given there. (*Ideas I,* 1913, §24)[90]

Thus the origin of any research at all and of all knowledge is intuition as the primary source of legitimacy. It was in reference to intuition that Husserl formulated the "principle of all principles" of research. At §136 of *Ideas I,* Husserl says that "The First Fundamental Form of Rational Consciousness [is] Originarily Presentative 'Seeing',"[91] i.e., intuition that presents the subject matter "in person." Husserl puts the word "seeing" in quotes here because he meant the word in a fundamentally broad sense, and not as limited to visual sight.

Likewise, we can understand Kant's *Critique of Pure Reason*—or better, all of his philosophizing—only when we see and hold firm to the fact that for Kant authentic knowledge is intuition. [115] In a certain sense, Kant formulates the idea of intuition (*intuitus*) in even more extreme terms [than Husserl,] and his formulation brings to light the connection with the Greeks.

In his famous letter of 21 February 1772, to Marcus Herz, in which he established the problem of the *Critique of Pure Reason*—or better, of his whole philosophy—Kant poses the question: "What is the basis on which rests the relation of what in us we call representation [*Vorstel-*

---

90. [Edmund Husserl, *Ideen zu einer reinen Phänomenologie und phänomenologischen Philosophie, I. Buch: Allgemeine Einführung in die reine Phänomenologie* (Halle: Max Niemeyer, 1913), §24, p. 43; corrected edition in *Husserliana* III/1, ed. Karl Schuhmann (The Hague: Martinus Nijhoff, 1976). The translation here is adapted from Edmund Husserl, *Ideas Pertaining to a Pure Phenomenology and to a Phenomenological Philosophy. First Book: General Introduction to a Pure Phenomenology,* trans. Fred Kersten (The Hague: Martinus Nijhoff, 1982), p. 44.]

91. [Heidegger here cites the title of §136 of *Ideen I* (1913), p. 282 / tr. 326.]

lung], to the object?" (*Akademische Ausgabe,* vol. 10, p. 124).[92] "Representing" in Kant means, as he himself says, "having an object." And in
this context, Kant goes on: This representing—having-an-object—is
understandable,

> if what in us is called representation were active with respect to the object,
> that is, if the object itself were produced by the representation, in the same
> way as we imagine divine knowledge as the prototype of things, the con-
> formity of the representation to its object would be intelligible.[93]

Thus the *intellectus divinus,* the divine act of knowing, is the highest kind
of representing, of having-an-object. However, God's intellect is not first
of all brought face-to-face with objects as bodily out there. Rather, it
brings the object face-to-face with *it* in a way that first brings the entity
into being. It goes out ahead of it in such a way that it produces it in the
first place. That is why Kant calls this *intellectus* the *intellectus archetypus*
(ibid.) or the *intuitus originarius* (*Critique of Pure Reason,* B 72). We might
compare this with Husserl's "originary intuition," except that Kant now
understands the *intuitus originarius* in a much more extreme way. It is
called "originary" because it originally gives being to what is intuited in
the intuition. Therefore, divine intellect is the origin (ἀρχή) whereby
things come into being. It makes the intuited be immediately there insofar as this *intuitus originarius,* this intellect, originally thinks the possibilities of things as such and, in and with these possibilities, gives things
the basis on which they can be actual. This intellect does not come after
the entity and then seek it out. Rather, as intellect it really produces it,
makes it possible, in the first place. The divine intellect renders it a possibility because only if things are possible can they become actual.[94] Kant
emphasizes the relation between the representation in us and the object.
God is the *substantia infinita.* The *intellectus divinus* is the intellect of an
[116] infinite being, whereas a cognitive entity such as the human subject, because it is created, is finite.[95]

92. [Kant, *Akademie-Ausgabe,* vol. 10, pp. 123–130; translated as Immanuel
Kant, *Selected Pre-Critical Writings and Correspondence with Beck,* ed. and trans. G. B.
Kerferd and D. W. Walford (Manchester: Manchester University Press / New York:
Barnes & Noble, 1968), pp. 111–118, here p. 112. The German *Vorstellung* can be
translated either as "presentation" or as "representation"; in both cases, as Heidegger points out, it means the mental *having*-of-an-object.
93. Conformity. Thomas [Aquinas] always characterizes truth as *conformitas,* in
fact in the very same context as Kant does here, namely, God's knowledge.
94. [Cf. Moser, p. 241.8–242.1.]
95. In the Neo-Kantians, the subject is neither human beings nor God. No one
knows who it is. And if we ask, "What is this consciousness in which the world is
constituted?" Rickert answers: "A concept."

This merely preliminary determination of the finitude of human reason shows up in Kant only in passing and usually in a phrase that he repeats from time to time: ". . . for us human beings, at least." But nonetheless, Kant's entire problematic is contained in this determination, and we will understand nothing about Kant's philosophy unless we keep in mind its crucial effects. As a finite being—*substantia finita (creata)*—the human subject has not produced the world that is out there. Rather, the human subject has been produced along with the other things and has been placed into the world with them. To the degree that these things have a relation to intellect, they have it primarily only because they have been created. They have such a relation of essence only to the *intellectus archetypus,* since they did not bring themselves before that intellect but just the opposite. As finite, these beings cannot, in the primary sense of intuition, produce and therefore know each other, but insofar as they are *created,* whether as material or spiritual substances, the path of intuition in the radical sense is denied to them. Instead they have to announce themselves to each other. The *commercium* between these worldly things is based on this announcing of one for the other. As having been created, they can merely act upon one another, and they must do so if there is to be any exchange between them. This acting-upon, when it is done by an entity that can represent things through ideas, is a matter of giving information about something. With a material entity this announcement regards their kind of being, and it must be addressed to an entity that is capable of receiving such an announcement. It must be related to a receptivity, a capability of being given objects that are material. This ability-to-be-given-something (i.e., intuition) is sensibility [*Sinnlichkeit*]. The basic element of sensibility is sensing, i.e., sensation [*Empfindung*]. That's the basis on which the *commercium* is possible; it is that whereby one sensibility can be present to another. According to Kant, sensations are representations (ways of having objects) "that are *caused* by the presence of a thing" (*Reflexionen,* vol. 2, no. 315). By way of interpretation, we have to [117] say the reverse: In sensing, sensibility as intuition is [*a priori*] *open to* the presence of things.

Knowing necessarily entails that the things themselves are present in some way and that they announce their presence. This means that knowledge is necessarily intuition. And for that reason a finite subject's knowledge is necessarily founded on sensibility, that whereby the finite knower can first be "open-to-the-world" at all.

If it is to know at all, the finite being (the human being) must have an *intuitus*. But as finite, this entity is denied the *intuitus originarius* and has only an *intuitus derivativus*. For a "true Kantian" who is concerned only with validities and categories, this fact is a ghastly state of affairs—and interpreting Kant in this way is finally even more ghastly.

But Kant was not a Kantian. The current, inchoate discovery of meta-physics in Kant can be a useful contribution to an objective inventory of what really is [to be found] in Kant as contrasted with the lopsided-ness of the Kantians. But even with that, we still have not reached what is philosophically relevant in Kant. We now have two Kants, and depending on how they evaluate the metaphysics and the epistemol-ogy, philosophers will take him one way or the other and will treat the other side as an unpleasant appendage. But what will then be needed is not to create some external synthesis of these two "sides," but rather to ask why there is this apparent doubling, and where the necessity, and thus the fundamental limits, of Kant's philosophy lie.[96]

So solidly does intuition remain the sense and core of knowledge, that even thinking gets the meaning of its function from intuition. [118] Its function is to be simply a means for bringing our knowing face-to-face with the thing itself. Proof of this is the first sentence that opens the investigation proper of the *Critique of Pure Reason:* "In what-ever manner and by whatever means knowledge may relate to objects, that by which it is immediately related to them, and to which all thinking as a means is directed, is *intuition*" (§1, B 33).[97]

* * *

For Kant the one who most exactly and decisively formulated this concept of knowledge is Leibniz, and I mention Leibniz because he was of crucial significance both indirectly for Kant and directly for Husserl. Earlier I mentioned Leibniz when I was characterizing Hus-serl's critique of psychologism, at the point where it was a matter of showing that Husserl, in his critique, maintained the validity of truths-in-themselves *à la* Bolzano, whose position relies directly on Leibniz. A characteristic treatise of Leibniz is his *De cognitione, veritate, et ideis,* "On Knowledge, Truth, and Ideas," 1684 (in Gerhardt's edition of Leibniz, vol. 4, pp. 422–426).[98] He gives four determinations of knowl-

96. In *Critique of Pure Reason* (B 51), Kant speaks of the "sensibility of our intu-ition" as "that kind of presentation that is peculiar to us." It is not a productive intuition but a "sensible intuition" that is able to be given something, an intuition "that therefore is called sensible because it is *not original.* It is not an intuition through which the very existence of the object of intuition would be given (some-thing which, as far as we can see, can belong only to the Original Being). Instead, our intuition is dependent on the existence of the object and therefore is possible only insofar as the presentational capacity of the subject is affected by that exis-tence" (B 72).

97. [Here (Moser, p. 246) Heidegger ends his lecture of Monday, 30 November 1925, to be followed by that of Tuesday, 1 December, which opened with a 620-word summary that is omitted in GA 21.]

98. [G. W. F. Leibniz, "Meditationes de Cognitione, Veritate et Ideis" (Novem-

edge: *Cognitio* is *clara, distincta, adaequata,* and *intuitiva* [clear, distinct, adequate, and intuitive]. Leibniz emphasizes that if an act of knowledge is *simul adaequata et intuitiva* [at one and the same time adequate and intuitive], then it is *perfectissima* [most perfect]. Thus, intuitive knowledge is the most perfect. In order to formulate this characteristic of knowledge as Leibniz understands it, I will list in rough fashion, the four properties he mentions without going into any special interpretation at this point.

1. According to Leibniz, an act of knowledge is *clear* when I have the thing to be known in a certain way, that is: *cum habeo unde rem repraesentatam agnoscere possim:* when I have the thing that is mentally intended,[99] in such a way that I can recognize the what-is-intended in and of itself, i.e., when I bring-present to myself the thing that I meant, in such a way that I can identity what-I-meant with that thing. Therefore, what constitutes the character of clarity and what makes knowledge clear is the possibility of re-cognition of the thing, the possibility of [the] identity [of what-I-intend] with the thing itself. And [119] if I want to prove that an act of knowledge is clear, I must take that act of knowledge, and *duco in rem praesentem,* "I lead it to the thing that is present." In other words, I must make present to myself the very thing I intend.

2. An act of knowledge is *distinct* when, briefly put, I have a nominal definition of it—in Leibniz' words, a *definitio nominalis.* By that Leibniz means the *enumeratio notarum sufficientium,* the enumeration of the determinations of the thing that are sufficient to distinguish it from other things and to determine it as this thing—thus, the enumerability of adequate characteristics. And then Leibniz says there is also distinct, clear knowledge of things that are undefinable, that have no nominal definition—namely concepts, which are *notiones primitivae* [primitive notions]—there is also clear knowledge of a simple concept. That is, the simple concept is *nota sui ipsius:* it is the distinguishing mark of itself; it simply presents itself. It is not reducible to other determinations, *caret requisitis:* it lacks determination by means of another. It is given by means of itself.

3. Leibniz characterizes knowledge as *adequate—cum vero id omne quod notitiam distinctam ingreditur, rursus distincte cognitum est.* An act of

ber 1684), in *Die philosophische Schriften von G. W. Leibniz,* 7 vols., ed. C. J. Gerhardt (Berlin, 1875-1890), vol. 4, pp. 422-426; translated as "Reflections on Knowledge, Truths and Ideas (1684)," in G. W. F. Leibniz, *Selections,* ed. Philip P. Wiener (New York: Scribner, 1951), pp. 283-290.]
    99. [Misread in GA 21 (p. 118.29) as *representatem;* cf. Moser, p. 250.6-7.]

knowledge is adequate when, after we have recognized clearly everything pertaining to the things, we now apprehend it in its wholeness,
i.e., we clearly apprehend all of its intelligible features as a whole.

Or again: *cum analysis ad finem usque producta habetur:* "when the
analysis of a thing's determinateness has been carried out to the
full," such that the whole structure of the thing is clear in one
stroke. To be sure, he adds: *cuius* (that is: *cognitionis*) *exemplum per-
fectum nescio an homines dare possint:* "I do not know whether human
knowledge can offer a case of such adequate knowledge." Here we
have a hint that such knowledge clearly transcends human capa-
bilities. He says that for the most part human knowledge is a *cognitio
caeca*, knowledge that is blind and not a *visio*—not a seeing but [120]
nonetheless an intending. Or he calls it [*cognitio*] *symbolica*, which is
nothing but what we have characterized as an empty representation. I intend something without clearly or adequately possessing
the intended thing itself.

4. And finally:

*et certe cum notio valde composita est, non possumus omnes ingredientes eam no-
tiones simul cogitare.*

Because concepts are certainly and in the strong sense composites, it is
impossible to adequately grasp the whole of its determinations at once.

Ubi tamen hoc licet, vel saltem in quantum licet, cognitionem voco intuitivam.

But where that is feasible, or at least insofar as it feasible, I call such knowledge {i.e., knowledge given adequately in one stroke} intuitive knowledge.

You must keep in mind that the first three determinations he mentions are always preserved and taken up into the final class, that of
intuitive knowledge. If I can have a knowledge in which the object
is itself present—that is, where the knowledge is identified with the
thing itself and where the totality of determinations is present,
worked out, and understood as such—then that knowledge is *intuitive*. So again, intuition, the concrete having of the thing, is true
and proper knowledge.

I note in this regard that in the *Ideas*, when Husserl himself worked
out and determined the idea of this kind of knowledge—especially in
the context of the various basic kinds of evidence—he did so with an
eye to, and under the essential influence of, these Leibnizian determinations. On the other hand, Leibniz formulated this idea of *cognitio
clara, distincta, adaequata*, and *intuitiva* with help from Descartes. What

Leibniz provides us is merely a more precise determination of the Cartesian criterion of all knowledge, namely: *clara et distinctio perceptio.*

In Descartes, *perceptio* means the same as the German *Wahrnehmung* in the sense of the *animadvertere, comprehendere,* or grasping the thing itself. Descartes further distinguishes between two *actiones intellectus* [acts of intellect], two different ways our knowing can comport itself: *intuitus* and *deductio,* intuition and deduction. He says that intuition is more certain than deduction because it is more simple [121] and because it does not have the thing merely indirectly, by way of the individual steps of the proof. Rather, it is with the thing itself. Characteristic of intuition is *evidentia praesens* [present evidence]. In intuition the thing itself is seen, and at the same time one's seeing of the thing is itself co-seen and co-known: This is the peculiar self-certitude that intuition has and that Husserl formulated in his principle of all principles. And this Cartesian understanding of the concept of knowledge (which I will not go into further) goes back in turn to *Scholasticism.* I want you to see that this idea—that *knowledge properly speaking is intuition*—has an even greater importance than came out with Kant, and to do so I have to talk about it in some other contexts.

The notion that knowledge is intuition or direct seeing is found in the Middle Ages, not only in the context of what we call mystical, philosophical, or theological speculation, but precisely in those thinkers who understood problems in an essentially Aristotelian way. These gave great importance to argumentation and to indirect, syllogistic proof—in Descartes's terminology, to deduction. For a thinker like Thomas Aquinas, the primacy of intuition shows up precisely in that context, and in fact intuition is not only the authentic and highest comportment within knowing but is also the highest possible way of being human, since in intuition, to the degree the human truly and properly intuits, he or she is in the presence of the highest entity—the one that most properly *is,* namely, God. God is the *ens perfectissimum,* the most-perfect entity; and insofar as God is intuited, this intuition of God is the highest kind of human being, one that humans do not have on earth but will attain only in heavenly bliss. Which means that the determination of *beatitudo,* happiness, is given by intuition. And why is this intuition—this pure *visio Dei* or pure intuition of God, this unadulterated having-God-present—why is it the highest kind of being that humans can have? Answer: Because this intuitional comportment [122] no longer looks beyond itself but is fulfilled in itself, whereas by contrast the second basic faculty of human beings as rational beings, the will, precisely as willing *something,* is by its very nature still unfulfilled. Willing as such is still directed toward something that it does not yet possess and that it is not yet. But in the intuition of the being itself—namely, God—there is complete fulfillment.

As proof, a brief text from Thomas Aquinas—chosen almost at random, since you can quite easily pile up similar proof-texts. The following is from *Summa Theologica* I-II, question 3, article 5, body of the text:[100]

> Si quidem beatitudo in hominis est operatio, oportet quod sit optima operatio hominis. Optima autem operatio hominis est, quae est optimae potentiae respectu optimi objecti. Optima autem potentia est intellectus, cuius optimum obiectum est bonum divinum, quod quidem non est obiectum practici intellectus, sed speculativi. Unde in tali operatione, scilicet in contemplatione divinorum, maxime consistit beatitudo.

> If human happiness is an activity, then it is necessary that it be the best human activity. But the best human activity is the activity of the best human faculty in relation to its best object. {In this passage, Thomas determines what the *optima operatio*, the best human activity, is. It is the *operatio* of the *optima potentia*, the operation of the best and highest human capability, and it is directed to the *optimum obiectum;* and *optimum est divinum:* the best is the divine.}

> But the best activity is the intellect {that is completely Greek}, whose best object is the divine good. But this divine good is not the object of practical thought, but of speculative thought. {In Scholasticism, *speculativus intellectus* is also used for *theoretice,*[101] i.e., it is the Greek θεωρεῖν.}

> Therefore, it is in such activity {of the theoretical intellect, that is, of pure intuiting in relation to the *bonum divinum*}—namely, in the pure intuition or contemplation of the divine—that there is true and proper happiness {i.e., the very highest way of being that human beings as such can have}.

Thomas determines this *intelligere*—the highest capability human beings as such have—as follows: *intelligere nihil aliud est quam praesentia quocumque modo:* "[intellect is nothing but] the [123] presence of the knowable to the knowing." This last understanding of the concept of knowledge comes from Augustine (who in fact is cited in Thomas's

---

100. [(1) GA 21, 122.10 incorrectly cites this text as "III" instead of "I-II," that is, as "Tertia pars" instead of "Prima secundae partis." Cf. Moser, p. 255.12, and Weiss typescript, p. 61.16. (2) The *corpus* referred to by Heidegger (rendered here, "body of the text") is the division of the article in which Thomas presents his own position. (3) Heidegger places his German translation at the end of each complete Latin clause. I gather it, in English after the Latin, and place Heidegger's running glosses within the English translation.]

101. [*Theoretice* (gen., *theoretices*) is a rare Latin noun that translates the Greek (ἐπιστήμη) θεωρητική. It refers here to the theoretical or speculative intellect.]

text),[102] *De utilitate credendi,* chapter 11. The upshot is again that knowledge is intuition of a here-and-now present thing. And with these concepts of intuition and of knowledge, which determined Augustine as well as the Middle Ages, we come up against the concept of knowledge as the Greeks understood it. True and proper knowledge is θεωρεῖν—pure, visual relatedness to the thing itself. And for the Greeks, the highest form of knowing is that which is related to the being that truly and properly is. You can see that in trying to determine the Greek view, I am simply repeating what Thomas said, except that for Thomas the *objectum optimum* for the intellect was precisely *Deus* as he could be apprehended through biblical revelation, whereas for Aristotle the proper object of knowledge was that-which-is-eternal—the heavens and the νοῦς—and this object of knowledge does not have the least to do with Thomas's God.

You can see the significance of the concept of intuition for the interpretation of knowing. But perhaps it has struck you that in the course of this characterization, I have not mentioned one perhaps essential figure: Hegel. Hegel's logic and dialectic seems to break out of this idea of knowledge—but it only seems to, for far from breaking out of it, his logic and dialectic is nothing other than the *intuitus originarius* raised to a higher power,[103] the intuition of the act of thinking and of its self-intuition, νόησις νοήσεως. Dialectics is authentically and radically *speculative* philosophy (cf. Thomas and Aristotle).

Even from a rough consideration of these connections, it is not surprising that knowledge was and is interpreted as intuition and with reference to intuition.[104] In traditional logic it was presupposed as obvious that [124] truth as a characteristic of knowledge is intuition-truth.[105] But the task of a philosophizing logic in the sense that we characterized it is to ask questions like these: Is this preliminary determination of truth, which goes unquestioned, in fact ultimate and self-grounded, or not? Is it not finally a prejudgment, even if a necessary one? And why it is a necessary prejudgment? In contrast to this preliminary determination of truth, what is the more radical question about truth that has to be asked? And what kind of investigations will

---

102. [In the *sed contra* that precedes the *corpus* of I-II, quest. 3, art. 5, Thomas cites Augustine at *De trinitate* I, 8: "contemplatio promittitur nobis, actionum omnium finis, atque aeterna perfectio gaudiorum" (Migne, *Patrologia Latina* XLII, p. 831): "We are promised contemplation, which is the fulfillment of all our actions and the everlasting perfection of all our joys."]

103. [In class, Heidegger said *potenzierte* (Moser, p. 257.18) rather than *erzwungene* (GA 21, p. 123.21).]

104. [The following sentence renders Moser, pp. 257–258.]

105. Cf. what we said above (§4) about how logic today is built on something that is supposedly obvious.

be necessary in order to answer that question? This preliminary foundation does not hold as a foundation; rather, it is a starting point for an inquiry that undermines this foundation.

And now, with regard to the way of determining truth, as we have shown it to be rooted in the tradition, we inquire into the "why." Why is truth intuition-truth? Why is intuition the basic kind of knowing, and why must truth, understood in this way, be understood as sameness (identity)? Why is this truth the truth of propositions, and why does the actuality of propositional truth have the kind of being that Plato attributed to the ideas?

Briefly: Why is truth identity? How is it that the being of the true is timeless validity? We are not posing these questions casually, over against the treatment of the problem of truth in philosophy heretofore. Rather, we are asking about the concrete roots of this interpretation of truth, and about its impact, by going back to its historical origins. That is, we are going to concern ourselves with history, not out of some interest in antiquity—say, to know what Aristotle thought, to know what his view of truth was. No, the historical questions that we ask should confront us with ourselves and force us to enter our own history. [125]

In order to put ourselves into question, we are critically questioning back [into history], and in that regard we can clarify the project as follows. In a radical critique that starts with the whole and goes back to the whole, we actually have to make the adversary put forth his most crucial points. But the remarkable thing is always this: In philosophizing, you first have to "acquire" great and creative adversaries by waking them up. Then you can grow and mature by arguing with them and establishing the simple outlines of elemental issues, where "elemental" means both "simple" and "explosive" at the same time.

These questions are elemental in their historical origin. They are "simple" not just because they are still clumsy questions and haven't quite been understood, but "simple" because you don't need elaborate contraptions to investigate them.

So once again, the two questions:

1. Why is truth interpreted as identity?
2. Why does the true have its being as validity?

We must ask these questions in an elementary way. Therefore, let us seek help from a place where these questions necessarily became elementary. And so we come to the first part of our treatment.[106]

---

106. [Here (Moser, p. 262) Heidegger ends his lecture of 1 December 1925, to be followed by that of Thursday, 3 December, which opened with an 870-word summary that is omitted in GA 21.]

PART I

Part I

The problem of truth in the decisive origins of philosophical logic, and the seedbed of traditional logic (focused on Aristotle)

Prefatory remark

[127] As we now discuss this question with a glance back to some texts of Aristotle, it does not mean that we are trying to give a complete interpretation of those texts. Let's presuppose such an interpretation as having already been carried out. Then, using our guiding question, let us simply focus on some individual theses of Aristotle. Our investigation aims at an original understanding of the problem of truth and a radical way of solving it, one in which our investigation of the problem up to now will gain its legitimacy, and in which its positive content will come to light.

We begin our concrete investigation of the current determinations of truth by characterizing the truth of propositions. This is hardly accidental or arbitrary. We do so because according to the traditional report, the proposition or judgment is the proper place of truth. What is the connection here?

In §11, we will deal with the place of truth and with the proposition (λόγος). Out of those preliminary discussions will come the need to discuss the basic structure of λόγος and, in connection with that, to clarify the phenomenon of meaning.[1]

§11. The place of truth, and λόγος (proposition)

The thesis that the proper place of truth is the proposition or judgment must be understood as an image insofar as "place" is a spatial term,

---

1. [Here GA 21 omits Heidegger's presentation of and commentary on the outline of §§11–15. Cf. Moser, pp. 261–262.]

whereas λόγος is not extended in space. [128] What the expression means is: the proposition is where truth originally and properly belongs. The proposition is what makes truth possible as such. When this thesis is asserted and taken unquestioningly as the basis of every explanation of truth, it is most often accompanied by a second thesis, one concerned with content—namely, that the thesis about the proposition as the place of truth was first enunciated by Aristotle. And usually this second thesis is connected with a third, namely, that Aristotle was the one who first determined the concept of truth—as the correspondence of thought with things. However (so this thesis usually affirms), since this concept of truth cannot stand up against critical reflection, Aristotle is the originator of this naïve concept of truth.[2]

To put it another way, we have three theses:

1. The place of truth is the proposition.
2. Truth is the correspondence of thought with beings.
3. These two statements originate with Aristotle.

These three theses, which are widespread today and have been for a long time, are so many prejudices. It is not the case that Aristotle enunciated the first two theses, nor does he directly or indirectly teach what these theses assert. He originates theses (1) and (2) only in the sense that these came into circulation through an appeal to Aristotle that was based on an inadequate interpretation of him; and it continues unabatedly, even today, to determine the conception of the problem.

What does Aristotle say about *truth* and its relation to λόγος as proposition?

In the first place, we must keep in mind the basic point: Aristotle never determined "truth" as such by going back to the proposition. Rather, if he ever makes any connection between λόγος (proposition) and truth, he does so in such a way that he determines the proposition through [129] truth, or more precisely, through the ability-to-be-true. But even this way of putting it is inadequate. The propositional statement is determined by Aristotle as speech that can be true or false.

ἔστι δὲ λόγος ἅπας μὲν σημαντικός . . . ἀποφαντικὸς δὲ οὐ πᾶς, ἀλλ' ἐν ᾧ τὸ ἀληθεύειν ἢ ψεύδεσθαι ὑπάρχει. (*De interpretatione* 4, 17a1–3)

All speech is about something {i.e., in general terms, it means something} . . . but not all speech is indicative {i.e., lets something be seen}, but only

2. See H. Maier, *Die Syllogistik des Aristoteles* (1896), vol. 1, pp. 13–14. The "concept of truth" has its "proper field of action" in the judgment—this [concept of truth] is the "original" one. The truth of perception and representation is a "derived" and "altered" concept of truth.

speech in which being-true or being-false is present {as the ways of speaking}.[3]

This makes it clear in principle that being-true is the distinguishing feature of a certain kind of speech, the kind that states or asserts something. The proposition is determined by its reference to truth—not vice versa, as if truth were derived from the proposition. When Aristotle emphasizes that the statement is a special kind of speech because of its reference to truth, we need to understand this correctly. The statement has a reference to the ability to be true or false. Being-true *simpliciter* and being true *or* false, are entirely different phenomena.

According to Aristotle this "either/or," this "either-true-or-false," is intrinsic to the proposition. Therefore, for him the proposition certainly does *not* have to be there in order for truth to be what it is; and if a proposition is true, it is true as something that also can be false.

Of course, we have not yet established what this either/or really means or why the proposition can be characterized in terms of it. We have not even shown what it is about the proposition that requires that it be caught in this alternative.

This either/or is what distinguishes speech *qua* statement and delimits it from other kinds of speech. [130] What other kinds? Aristotle gives a brief indication of those other kinds when he continues the sentence previously cited:

οὐκ ἐν ἅπασι δὲ ὑπάρχει, οἷον ἡ εὐχὴ λόγος μέν, ἀλλ' οὔτ' ἀληθὴς οὔτε ψευδής. (ibid., chap. 4, 17a4)

But being-true-and-false is not present in every kind of speech. A request, for example, is a form of speech, but it is neither true nor false.

Here Aristotle envisions (although he does not name) a rich variety of other forms of speech, including wishes, commands, and questions. Aristotle merely mentions in passing that the proper disciplines for studying them are ῥητορικὴ ἢ ποιητική, rhetoric or poetics.[4] Sentences like "Please pass me the scissors" or "Get off this land!" or "Was there another storm today?" are not statements, because they are neither true nor false. This division that Aristotle makes within the various forms of

---

3. "Enuntiativa vero non omnis [oratio], sed in qua verum et falsum inest"; Boethius, *Commentarium in librum Aristotelis Peri hermeneias,* vol. 2, chap. 4, p. 95 (ed. Besarrion, p. 324); i.e., "in which there is truth or error," Eugen Rolfes (p. 4). The ἀποφαίνεσθαι is emphasized in *Poetics* 6, 1450b10–12.

4. ὁ δὲ ἀποφαντικὸς τῆς νῦν θεωρίας (chap. 4, 17a6): "However, the object or theme of the investigation we are now conducting is the indicative-declarative [*aussagende*] λόγος."

speech has not always been maintained. In fact, it has been strongly challenged—by Bolzano, for example,[5] and in a certain sense even by Husserl—to the effect that even sentences expressing wishes, commands, and questions are thought to have the property of statements.

The question is still debated, and yet anyone can see that getting a clear resolution of the question is a basic presupposition [131] for any scientific grammar.[6] Here we will not pursue the question as a matter of controversy. Instead, we will try to see whether discussing the phenomenon of truth can lead us to a foundation on which we can at least correctly pose (if not resolve) the much-debated question about the expression of objectivizing and non-objectivizing acts. Let us simply get a bit clearer on the distinction Aristotle established.

What does it mean to say that being-true and being-false are not present in an εὐχή, a request? If I say, "Please give me the scissors that are on the table," when in fact there are no scissors on the table, what I say does not correspond with what is the case. My speech is objectively false. I am deceived, and my utterance expresses that deception. That act of speech says something false—but is my *request* false? Obviously not. Is it true? No, not that either. Why is it neither one nor the other? That becomes clear as soon as we really translate—i.e., interpret and express in our own language—the two Greek sentences we have quoted, in which Aristotle delineates speech *qua* propositional statement. Let us translate [*De interpretatione,* chap. 4,] 17a1.

Not all speech is indicative, i.e., shows something, but only speech in which being-true or being-false is present.

That translation fails to convey the degree of understanding that the Greeks had of that Greek sentence, due to the indeterminateness of the words "being-true" and "being-false." When understood correctly and literally (in the strict sense of that word), the Greek word for "being-true"—ἀληθεύειν—means *to uncover* in the sense of unveiling something, removing the hiddenness from something. An adequate word for that is "to un-cover"—not in the strong sense of bringing something to light for the very first time, but in the more general sense of unveiling something that is still veiled or of again unveiling that which has again become veiled-over. In short, it means to uncover what has been covered until now, or that has become covered again. Likewise the opposite concept, ψεύδεσθαι, [132] does not meaning "being-false." If we translate it that way, the meaning of the sentence remains obscure. Ψεύδεσθαι

5. See his *Wissenschaftslehre,* vol. 1, §22, pp. 87ff.

6. For example, unless this question is clarified, the optative and the imperative cannot be conceptually understood in contrast to the indicative.

means: "to deceive," for example, to deceive another person by giving him not what he expects to see but something else that looks like it. In deceptive speech, therefore, I put into words not what I have in mind but something different. The person expects to hear what I have in mind, but I say something else. So speech can either uncover or misrepresent what I am speaking about. To show that the concept of ψεύδεσθαι is the opposite of "to uncover," we translate it as "to cover-over." This translation is all the more justified by the fact that a false sentence need not be uttered by a "false person," someone who is insincere and intent on deception. The other side of the coin is that every false statement uttered, even if uttered without the intent to deceive, is objectively misleading, a misrepresentation, because as a statement *about* something, it automatically gives the appearance of saying something about that thing, whereas in fact it covers it over and deceives.

Let us try to understand the issue more adequately by translating the sentence as follows:

> The only speech that indicatively shows something, {and thus is a statement,} is speech in which uncovering or covering-over is present.

The Greek word that we translate as "is present," is ὑπάρχειν, "to be there." But in this case it does not have the meaning it often can, namely, "occurring" in the quite broad sense of "there is something," as if Aristotle meant to say: "Only such speech is indicative in which uncovering and covering-over occurs"—as if covering and uncovering could sometimes occur, and sometimes not. Here, instead, ὑπάρχειν has the weighty sense of the philosophical concept that is used by Aristotle: ὑπάρχειν means "being there *a priori*," "underlying something in such a way that everything else is sustained by this thing that is there *a priori*." For that reason Boethius translates the Greek ὑπάρχειν in an entirely correct way as "*in-esse*," "being-within-[something]," in this case: "belonging to the very essence of speaking." [133] Therefore we have to translate it as follows:

> Only that speaking in which uncovering or covering-over sustains and determines the authentic intention of the speaking is an indicative {statement} that shows something.

Now the second part of the text (17a1) becomes clearer, and we can understand the distinction Aristotle has made.

> Not all ways of speaking are primarily oriented to uncovering and covering-over. For example, a request is speech, but as a request, it neither uncovers nor covers-over.

A request does not have the sense of uncovering or covering-over.[7]

*   *   *

So uncovering and covering-over are what determine the λόγος as indicative showing-something-as.[8] A sentence gets its determination as a statement by uncovering and covering-over. The essence of a proposition is ἀποφαίνεσθαι—showing a thing ἀπό: in terms of itself. The meaning of an assertion as a form of speech is to show (δηλοῦν) something as. That λόγος is ἀποφαντικός whose distinctive possibility as an act of speech is to show something as, whose mode of expression can bring something into view—that is, only if it is an ἀπόφανσις, a "statement," or more exactly, an "indicating . . . as." However, we will stick with the more normal word "statement," but will give it the meaning that is contained in the phenomenon of this kind of λόγος. What a statement says about something is drawn from that thing itself, so that in this kind of speech, what the speech is about comes into the clear, becomes available for comprehension. In the expressed statement, therefore, the very thing it indicates has become accessible and, as it were, preserved [verwahrt]. This sense of statement must be kept in mind in the future as the primary sense.

In our understanding, what is asserted in a statement is: "the chalkboard in its being-black." But in addition and above all, a "statement" is understood only as "predication," that is, asserting that a "predicate" belongs to a subject. A subject is that to which we give a determination. In this instance, therefore, "statement" has the meaning of "an act of determining." A statement in this sense has an essential relation to statement in the first sense: an act of determining is always an act of showing something as, and it is possible only as such. Whether every statement as such also determines, is a question that we shall have to leave open. It is a question that we will [134] explain in the following paragraphs, when we investigate the full structure of ἀπόφανσις. So we have what is asserted and the act of asserting as "predicating," e.g., "being-black." The statement as determination is a bit restricted with respect to statement in the first sense.

In the third place, a "statement" can mean the same as a "communication," i.e., the expression of something. This is connected with the first meaning and consequently with the second. But unlike the first, this one means not so much indicating something as, showing it

7. [Here (Moser, p. 274) Heidegger ends his lecture of Thursday, 3 December 1925, to be followed by that of Friday, 4 December, which opened with a 680-word summary that is omitted in GA 21.]

8. [A declarative sentence (λόγος) never simply "shows something," but always "shows something as something." I occasionally indicate this by putting "as" in brackets after "shows."]

as such, as it does communicating a state of affairs *as* one that has been indicated. The *expression* of the statement or indication (i.e., what is stated) is now not only "the chalkboard in its blackness" (i.e., what was indicated and brought into view), nor is it merely "black-ness" (i.e., the predicate *qua* predicated). Rather, it is the blackness of the chalkboard as *expressed*, the spoken-forth-ness of what has been indicated, and indicated in the matter of predication. In living speech, an ἀπόφανσις is a statement in all three senses of the word at one and the same time. These three meanings are not just empty or invented distinctions within the meaning of "statement." No, each of them refers to a specific structural moment of λόγος. The various determinations of "statement"—1. showing, 2. determining, and 3. communicating—are issue-oriented directives for studying the phenomenon itself.

In laying out the three meanings we have also indicated (although only roughly) their interrelation. The first one makes the other two possible. The basic movement is not from language to speaking but from speaking to language.[9] In fact, language and speaking are not distinguished at the start; and the first explorative questioning of that started from both sides at once, that of language and that of speaking, and oscillated between the two with no fixed point of reference.

That point of reference is "truth" understood as uncovering, as indicative showing-as. In order to be understood as ἀπόφανσις, speech needs to be brought back to the act of uncovering. [135] The proposition is not the place where truth first becomes possible, but the reverse. The proposition is possible only within truth. However, that requires that we understand the phenomenon which the Greeks meant by "truth" and which Aristotle was the first one to capture in a clear concept. "The proposition is not the place of truth; truth is the place of the proposition." At first glance this formulation may seem forced and dogmatic. But later we will show its complete legitimacy.

In this regard, we must keep in mind that the proposition has a peculiar relation to truth since, as propositional truth, it is necessarily caught in an either/or. It is the kind of speech that is neither true as such nor false as such, but can be *either* true *or* false.

Our question now is: What makes this either/or accrue *of necessity* to the proposition as a statement? What exactly is the structure of a statement, and why is that structure necessarily qualified by this either/or?

---

9. This is important because all of Greek logic, and consequently our own logic right up to today, takes its orientation from this, the spoken sentence.

§12. The basic structure of λόγος and
the phenomenon of making sense

The question we have just formulated could also be put this way: What makes λόγος able to be false, i.e., able to cover-over at all? The indirect outcome of our explanation thus far is that λόγος is not through-and-through true, i.e., uncovering. Rather, it uncovers only insofar as it can also cover-over. In a somewhat exaggerated formulation: The statement can be true (can uncover) at all, only because it can also cover-over—only because, as a statement, it operates *a priori* in the "as." The statement's uncovering is an uncovering that does not cover-over. That is, what structures the truth of statements is in principle the same as what structures falsehood. To state the matter as a whole: The possibility of being true *or* false—which is the essential feature of any statement—is as such necessarily grounded in one and the same structure of λόγος. [136]

Let us now pose the question in an extreme form: What is the structural condition in λόγος that accounts for the fact that it can be false? The answer will shed light as well on the condition of the possibility of the truth of statements, i.e., on the kind of uncovering that goes with λόγος. Aristotle says:

τὸ γὰρ ψεῦδος ἐν συνθέσει ἀεί. (*De Anima* III, 6, 430b1)

Covering-over is {as such} always a "synthesis."

He likewise says:

ὁ δὲ ψευδὴς λόγος οὐθενός ἐστιν ἁπλῶς λόγος. (*Metaphysics* V, 29, 1024b31)

Whenever speech covers-over, it is never non-synthesizing speech about something.

Or,

Wherever there is covering-over, there is necessarily a "synthesizing" within the structure of the statement.

What that means only seems to be clear. But what we said earlier immediately allows us say further that where there is uncovering—"truth"—there is also necessarily a "synthesizing," because the statement's uncovering is an uncovering that does not cover-over. But that does not mean it is a non-synthetic statement, supposedly because synthesizing is found, necessarily and structurally, in covering-over. It only says: Every covering-over is necessarily synthetic—but not every synthetic act of speech is necessarily one that covers-over. It *can* also uncover. But not every un-covering is synthetic, only the uncovering in statements:

ἐν οἷς δὲ καὶ τὸ ψεῦδος καὶ τὸ ἀληθές, σύνθεσίς τις ἤδη νοημάτων ὥσπερ ἕν ὄντων. (*De anima* III, 6, 430a27–28)

Nonetheless, where covering-over as well as uncovering is possible, there is already some kind of synthesis of the things intended, of what is repre-sented in representations, as if they were one.

Accordingly, synthesis is the foundation of falsehood and truth. That is, here we have the kind of truth in place of which there could also be falsehood. In other words, here we have the truth of statements. Now:

ἐνδέχεται δὲ καὶ διαίρεσιν φάναι πάντα. (*De anima* III, 6, 430b3)

But all of these can also be called a "taking-apart."

That is: every σύνθεσις [act of synthesizing] is likewise a διαίρεσις [act of separating], and vice versa. All synthesizing is separating, and all separating is synthesizing. Therefore, in the crucial passage where his theme is λόγος as *statement,* Aristotle can summarize the determi-nations given up to this point [137]:

περὶ γὰρ σύνθεσιν καὶ διαίρεσίν ἐστι τὸ ψεῦδός τε καὶ τὸ ἀληθές. (*De inter-pretatione*, chap. 1, 16a12)

In the sphere of synthesizing and separating, covering-over and uncover-ing are [always] found together.[10]

* * *

Clearly, with putting-together and taking-apart we have found some-thing that constitutes (or at least co-constitutes) the basic structure of λόγος as statement. But how are we now to understand this putting-to-gether and taking-apart (σύνθεσις-διαίρεσις), and how might we apply it to the entire phenomenon of a statement? It is certainly not hard to find examples. Take the statement, "This chalkboard is black." Here we have an uncovering statement and a synthetic statement. Therefore, ac-cording to our explanation, we can say the statement is true—i.e., it con-tains within itself the very thing, now uncovered, that it intends. It shows the thing about which it makes a judgment just as that thing is in itself.

10. [Here the lecture of Friday, 4 December 1925 draws to a close, to be fol-lowed by Heidegger's nineteenth lecture on Monday, 7 December.]

Again, according to what we said, this statement, in order to be capable of being-true or uncovering, must somehow share *a priori* in the structure of σύνθεσις-διαίρεσις. The statement is a synthetic one: that's obvious from the linguistic form of the sentence. In this statement "black," or "is-black," is synthesized with "chalkboard," and because it *does* synthesize the two, the proposition is itself true. However, precisely because it enacts a synthesis, this proposition runs the risk of being either true *or* false.

The opposite statement, "This chalkboard is not black," covers-over and misrepresents the thing to which it refers with the words, "This chalkboard." It does not allow the intended thing to be seen as what it is. The statement is false; and it has the structure of separation. With the word "not" it separates blackness from the chalkboard, and precisely because of that separation, the statement is false.

The upshot of this first example is as follows: σύνθεσις (linking together) is the condition of the possibility of uncovering (truth), and διαίρεσις (separating) is the condition of the possibility of covering-over (falsehood). Synthesizing and separating: these are what make possible the distinguishing property of the proposition, namely its ability to be true or to be false. And at the same time, this lets us indicate some structural relations in the proposition that have not been noted up to this point. [138]

The first statement is a matter of synthesis: it attributes blackness to the chalkboard. Aristotle calls such an attribution κατάφασις, which gets interpreted and translated as "affirmation." The second statement says that something does not pertain to the chalkboard; it is called ἀπόφασις, "denial" or "negation." So it is not simply that synthesizing and separating are the condition of possibility of trueness and falsehood. In addition, by focusing on synthesis we came up with affirmation. And by focusing on separation, we came up with negation. In fact, earlier we saw that attribution and denial are the two forms into which simple, original statements are divided:

> ἔστι δὲ εἷς πρῶτος λόγος ἀποφαντικὸς κατάφασις, εἶτα ἀπόφασις. (*De interpretatione* 5, 17a8)

> The kind of speech that indicates something {i.e., the kind of speech that is a statement} is, first and foremost, affirmation, and then denial.

That seems to generate the following simple chart, where sentences fall into one of two types:

either	*or*
σύνθεσις (synthesizing)	διαίρεσις (separating)
ἀληθές (uncovering)	ψεῦδος (covering-over)
κατάφασις (affirming)	ἀπόφασις (denying)

But this schema is altogether too neat to capture the interrelations of these phenomena. We can see that the chart misses the mark once we stop focusing on what Aristotle said about σύνθεσις and διαίρεσις, and instead simply look at a couple of statements that we ourselves might make.

Leave aside for a moment the structural features of σύνθεσις-διαίρεσις, and consider just the other two pairs, ἀληθές-ψεῦδος (uncovering, covering-over) and κατάφασις-ἀπόφασις (affirming, denying). The chart says that affirmative statements uncover (i.e., are true) whereas statements that deny cover-over (i.e., are false). But no one can seriously hold this position, namely that in order to always speak the truth, one would simply have to avoid negative statements. No, there are negative statements that are also true (uncovering), just as there are affirmative statements that cover-over. For example, the statement "This chalkboard is gray" is an affirmation—it attributes "gray" to "this chalkboard"—and yet it covers-over. On the other hand, the statement "This chalkboard is not gray" is a denial or negation, and yet it is true: it uncovers. That gives rise to problems and second thoughts. [139] Does the second statement *show* the chalkboard? Yes it does. However, it shows the chalkboard as what it is *not*. Then can we uncover and see something by showing it as what it is not?

At any rate, the second statement doesn't simply assert *nothing* about the thing it names—as would be the case if we claimed that "The chalkboard is not ambitious." The statement, "The chalkboard is not gray," in fact does assert something, because the chalkboard could very well be gray. Our uncertainty about statements like these comes from the fact that the statements are artificially stripped of any real context in which they might be made. They are put forward in a form in which we hardly recognize them. (This is a problem that as a matter of principle should be explained in logic.)

As a matter of fact, the determinations in the above chart overlap. An uncovering statement can be either affirmative *or* negative, in just the way that a statement that covers-over can be. Likewise, an affirmative statement can either cover-over or uncover, just as a negative statement can do.

But what does this mean for σύνθεσις and διαίρεσις, which are our primary concern? Affirmation is not co-extensive with uncovering, and denial is not co-extensive with covering-over. Then is affirmation (attribution of the predicate to the subject) co-extensive with synthesis? And is negation (denying that the predicate fits the subject) co-extensive with separation? But let us remember what Aristotle says at *De anima* III, 6, 430b3: "All this {every σύνθεσις} can also be called a διαίρεσις." That is, attribution as linking-together is also separation; and denial, as separation, is also a linking-together. Therefore: (1)

Every affirmative statement is never simply synthetic. (2) When it comes to true and false, it is not a matter of either/or (i.e., either synthesizing or separating). Rather, every affirmative statement both synthesizes and separates, and every negative statement both synthesizes and separates. And there is a further consequence: (3) Since every affirmative statement can be either true *or* false, it is not the case that uncovering = synthesizing and covering-over = separating. Rather, every uncovering statement and every covering-over statement *both* synthesize *and* separate. In other words, a structure of every statement *qua* statement is that it synthetic-*and*-separating. Therefore, this structure obtains in every statement, and it obtains *prior to* affirmation and negation, attribution and denial—and it does so absolutely. This is the case [140] not, as one might allege, because attributing-to is primarily synthesis and only secondarily separation, or that denying-of is primarily separation and only secondarily synthesis. No—attribution is no more a matter of synthesis than it is of separation, and denial is no more a matter of separation than it is of synthesis. What all of this means is that synthesis and separation are found at a level that is prior to attribution and denial, and are the condition of the possibility of attributing-to and denying-of, just as they are the condition of the possibility of covering-over and uncovering.

What have we gained by this discussion of the various forms of simple statements with regard to σύνθεσις and διαίρεσις? As concerns an insight into their very structure, it has achieved nothing. On the contrary, that structure has gotten even more obscure and puzzling. The reason, as we have seen, is that synthesizing and separating are not two possible forms of statement, so that statements would be divided into one or the other. Rather, they belong to every statement as such and therefore go together essentially and therefore are a matter of a unified phenomenon that originally constitutes the unity of a statement as such. So even though the structure itself is not yet entirely clear, nonetheless the result is not merely negative. It is also positive insofar as we have gained a reference point and a direction for understanding this linking-together that is a separation and this separation that is a linking-together *as* a unified phenomenon. The phenomenon is not something cobbled together from these two forms, something that leads, at best, to a merely extrinsic understanding of the unity.

But there was a further result: What really led us in the first place to that simple chart that ordered σύνθεσις, ἀληθές, κατάφασις, and their opposites? We said that synthesis is already manifest in the linguistic form of the sentence *qua* unified sequence of words and in its true enactment. Words are not just strung along, but are also synthesized into the whole of a verbal manifold. We focused on the expressed sentence, (although here, too, in a less than precise way). But on a closer look it already became clear that even in the linguistic form the σύνθεσις-διαίρεσις schema could not be carried through.

"The chalkboard is not black," is indeed a separation. [141] But are the words in this sentence any more separated or any less synthesized than in "The chalkboard is black"? The "not" that separates and denies does not leave the sentence in pieces. Rather, as a moment in the statement, the "not" itself is possible *only* because "blackness" has been related to and synthesized with "chalkboard." As easy and seductive as it is to focus on the expressed sentence and its linguistic form, we must avoid that. Or whenever it enters the field of logic, we should treat it merely as proof of how speaking *qua* statement can become an expressed statement (and *this* particular expression), and of how much linguistic formation is determined by specifically logical moments concerning speech as the showing of something as.

But we must be just as careful with "attribution" and "denial," as if these forms of expression were almost abbreviations of "synthesis" and "separation." We now know that synthesis and separation cannot be divided and lined up with affirmation and denial. Rather, they are themselves inseparable in every affirmation and every denial.

In short, it is a matter of understanding a phenomenon that in itself is both synthesis and separation, one that is prior to linguistic relations of expression and to their attributions and denials, a phenomenon that, on the other hand is what makes it possible that λόγος can be true or false, revelatory or covering-over.

But again, where can we get some guidance for understanding what constitutes the basic structure of λόγος *qua* statement? Aristotle himself, apart from an important indication (which is, again, all too vague) fails to provide the information. He and the Greeks, as well as the later tradition, neglected to really inquire into this structural phenomenon. Linking-together and separating are the structures that basically clarify what the statement or judgment is. Unfortunately the question of analytic and synthetic judgments has gotten mixed in with this interpretation so that the confusion is huge [142]—and in the apparently perfected and secure science of logic basically nothing has been clarified.

To stay with Aristotle for a moment: he never got away from his orientation to speech. For the Greeks that would be impossible. And yet, as we will soon see, his work on the structures of σύνθεσις and διαίρεσις, and on their relations to the true and the false and to κατάφασις and ἀπόφασις, are certainly not as clear as the way we worked them out above. Of course, once we get clear on the σύνθεσις-διαίρεσις structure and understand it in its origin, we can understand certain indications that Aristotle gives for clarifying this structure.

The problem has been posed here and elsewhere in a less than explicit way. Nonetheless we should not allow an essential indication, as obvious at it seems, to slip away from our understanding. The usual interpretation fails to exploit Aristotle's hint that the basic function of λόγος is ἀπόφανσις—indicative speech that shows something. This merely says more pointedly what Plato had already nailed down and what was part of the Greeks' basic understanding of λόγος. The function of speaking is δηλοῦν, making things manifest.

Have we gotten anywhere with this, especially regarding the question about the unified phenomenon of σύνθεσις-διαίρεσις, which presumably makes statement possible in the first place?

In the *Sophist*, Plato asks: What makes a plurality of words that follow one after the other form a κοινωνία, an ensemble in which the words are present to each other? The answer, he says, consists in the fact that λόγος is λόγος τινός: speaking is speaking of and about something. The unity is constituted and becomes intelligible from what is being spoken about.

The question we now pose is that of the unity of a succession of words. We have not yet arrived at the statement as something expressed. [143]

a) The as-structure of our primary way of understanding: the hermeneutical "as"

We now inquire into a structure of λόγος that first makes λόγος as such possible. Will Plato's indication help us along here, or that of Aristotle? Λόγος is the act of indicatively showing the thing being spoken about, which earlier, when we were clarifying the concept of statement, we characterized as the statement's subject matter [*das Worüber*]—as contrasted with what the statement predicates [*das Wovon*] about that subject matter. In actually showing and determining something, we grasp the subject matter. Or more precisely: the subject matter is already present, and from that present thing the statement—the blackness of the chalkboard—is lifted out and highlighted, as it were, not as a new object but at first only in the sense of making the subject matter more accessible as what it is.

But in order for something like a predicative highlighting and determining to be possible, the subject matter must have already become accessible. In the case we have been discussing, the usable thing in front of us must be already familiar, already accessible. For example, it might be familiar in terms of the service it can render, what it can be used for, the use for which we meet up with it at all—in a word, its "for-writing-on." This end-for-which [Wozu] is itself already comprehensible and known, as is the thing itself that is there for this purpose and as this: the chalkboard. (We restrict our investigation to statements about things in the lived world, postponing discussion about whether this is proper or not. Later it will become clear that this limitation is not a limitation at all.)

When the chalkboard is perceived in its character as the subject matter of the statement, our having-it-present includes an experiential knowledge of its current suitability-for. The thing's suitability-for is uncovered insofar as we already live in a disclosure of it.

As regards its basic meaning for us as a concerned being-unto-the-world, use is only a more accessible form of meaning. Existence is, in itself and by its very nature, world-open, open for the world; and corresponding to that, the world is dis-closed, opened-up. The primary form of that disclosedness is the opening up of whatever thing is being questioned. [144] Every form of speaking about things is, as an ontological comportment of existence, already grounded in existence as world-open. That is, all speech speaks about something that is somehow already disclosed.

Speaking indicatively about something—"this table here," "that window over there," "the chalk," "the door"—already entails [their prior] disclosure. What does this disclosure consist in? Answer: the thing we encounter is uncovered in terms of the end-for-which of its serviceability. It is already posited in meaning—it already makes sense [be-deutet]. Do not understand this to mean that we were first given a something that is free of meaning, and then a meaning gets attached to it. Rather, what is first of all "given"—and we still have to determine what that word means—is the "for-writing," the "for-entering-and-exiting," the "for-illuminating," the "for-sitting." That is, writing, entering-exiting, sitting, and the like are what we are *a priori* involved with. What we know and learn when we "know our way around" are these uses-for-which we understand it.[11]

Every act of having things before our eyes, every act of perceiving them, is held within this [prior] disclosure of those things, a disclosure that things get from a primary making-sense-of-things in terms of their what-they're-for. Every act of having something before our eyes and perceiving it, is in and of itself a matter of "having" something *as* something.[12] Our directional being-unto-things-and-people functions within this structure of "something as something." In short, it has the *as-structure.* However, this as-structure is not necessarily re-

---

11. A chalkboard, if it were unintelligible, would, as such, not be present here. Unless it were understood as for-writing-on, it would be hidden. The same with a door unless it is understood as for-entering-and-existing. These things are intelligible because we ourselves move among and operate with them, although we do so in such a taken-for-granted way that we forget this state of affairs in its basic structure as constituting these things. [GA 21 takes this footnote from Heidegger's twentieth lecture on Tuesday, 8 December 1925 (cf. Moser, p. 307.19), and inserts it at this point in the nineteenth lecture of Monday, 7 December.]

12. This "having" is not a matter of merely observing. It is meant entirely in the sense of our everyday *dealing* with things.

lated to predication. In dealing with something, I make no thematic, predicative statements about the thing.[13]

* * *

Therefore, we must explicitly emphasize the pre-predicative nature of the as-structure, because otherwise we might rely on the readily available linguistic expression and think that this as-structure is primarily and properly given in the form of a simple propositional statement such as "This chalkboard is black"—that is, in a thematic discussion [145] of this chalkboard as black.

Yes, we certainly can interpret the sentence that way, but in doing so we have to understand that, in the first and authentic instance, this "as" is not the "as" of predication *qua* predication but is prior to it in such a way that it makes possible the very structure of predication at all. Predication has the as-structure, but in a derived way, and it has it only because the as-structure is predication within a [wider] experience.

But why is it that this as-structure is already present in a direct act of dealing with something? The most immediate state of affairs is, in fact, that we simply see and take things as they are: board, bench, house, policeman. Yes, of course. However, this taking is always a taking within the context of dealing-with something, and therefore is always a taking-as, but in such a way that the as-character does not become explicit in the act. The non-explicitness of this "as" is precisely what constitutes the act's so-called directness. Yes, the thing that is understood can be apprehended directly as it is in itself. But this directness regarding the thing apprehended does not inhibit the act from having a developed structure. Moreover, what is structural and necessary in the act of [direct] understanding need not be found, or co-apprehended, or expressly named in the thing understood. I repeat: The [primary] as-structure does not belong to something thematically understood. It certainly can be understood, but not directly in the process of focally understanding a table, a chair, or the like.

Acts of directly taking something, having something, dealing with it "as something," are so original that trying to understand anything without employing the "as" requires (if it's possible at all) a peculiar inversion of the natural order. Understanding something without the "as"—in a pure sensation, for example—can be carried out only "reductively," by "pulling back" from an as-structured experience. And we must say: far from being primordial, we have to designate it as an artificially worked-up act. Most important, such an experience is *per se* pos-

13. [Here (Moser, p. 304) Heidegger ends his lecture of Monday, 7 December 1925, to be followed by that of Tuesday, 8 December, which opened with a 1,030-word summary that is omitted in GA 21.]

sible only as the privation of an as-structured experience. It occurs only *within* an as-structured experience and by prescinding from the "as"—which is the same as admitting that as-structured experience is primary, since it is what one must first of all prescind from. [146]

The as-structure belongs, roughly put, to our "comportment," which is not to say, however, that it is something subjective. Therefore, we must keep in mind that, while we certainly do attribute this as-structure to human comportment, we do not mean that such as-structured comportment—i.e., the act of making-sense-of—is somehow a subjective way of forming and understanding what's out there.

So making sense of something is an act that always has the as-structure, but this as-structure is primarily enacted in dealing with something. What we are mainly asking now is whether and to what degree the act of sense-making is the basis of any statement *qua* statement. Using Aristotle, we have already indicated that σύνθεσις and διαίρεσις make up the basic structure of the statement. The question now is (1) whether what σύνθεσις and διαίρεσις (linking-together and separating) refer to is ultimately this phenomenon of the "as," and (2) to what degree this unified phenomenon of the "as"—which sense-making and understanding always have—*can*, and first of all *must*, be understood through σύνθεσις and διαίρεσις.

When we analyze this as-structured comportment of sense-making, we see that, in it, something is always already understood. What is understood therein is the thing's "what-as," i.e., that in terms of which I understand whatever object or thing I meet—say, this door here. This what-as is already understood from the outset, and only in terms of it does the thing that I encounter and deal with become understandable as such. This what-as, in the light of which I understand and which I already have from the outset (although unthematically) is, nonetheless, not understood thematically in this "having-from-the-outset." Rather, I *live* in the understanding of writing, illuminating, entering-and-exiting, and the like. More precisely, as existing—whether in speaking, entering/exiting, or understanding—I am an act of intelligently dealing-with. My being in the world *is* nothing but this already-operating-with-understanding in those various way of existing.

If we now look at matters more closely, we see that the so-called *direct* having-something-present and understanding it—for example, this chalk, this chalkboard, this door—is, when viewed structurally, [147] not at all a "direct" understanding of something. Taken structurally, I do not have direct access to the immediately understood thing. Instead, I understand it in such a way that from the outset, as it were, I already have had something to do with it, i.e., I already understand it in terms of what it serves-for.

So in this apparently direct understanding of the things closest to me in the lived world, when I apprehend and understand something, I have *always already* gone *further ahead*[14] than the thing that is given (in an extreme sense) "directly" to me. I am always already further ahead by understanding the end-for-which and the what-as in terms of which I am taking the thing that is given and encountered at the moment. And only *from* the what-as and end-for-which (in terms of which the thing in question can serve)—only *from* this end-for-which, where in fact I always already am—do I return to the thing that I encounter.

Thus the direct understanding of something that is given in the lived world in the most natural way *is* constantly a *returning* to what I encounter, a constant return that is necessary because my own authentic being, as concernful-dealing-with-things-in-the-world, has the property of always-already-being-ahead-with-something [*Immer-schon-vorweg-sein-bei-etwas*]. Because my being is such that I am out ahead of myself, I must, in order to understand something I encounter, come back *from* this being-out-ahead *to* the thing I encounter.

Here we can already see an immanent structure of direct understanding *qua* as-structured comportment, and on closer analysis it turns out to be *time*. And this being-ahead-of-myself as a returning is a peculiar kind of movement that time itself constantly makes, if I may put it this way.[15] So when I simply understand the most natural things that I deal with without thematically understanding them, I do not see, for example, a white thing that, by a some kind of manipulations I then figure out is chalk. Instead, from the outset I already live in connections that are related to the end-for-which, I am held out into a specific lived world that is oriented to specific kinds of behavior and concern, and from these behaviors and concerns [148] I understand this thing as chalk.

Even if my sense organs and sense perception possessed the most highly developed and refined sensibility, so that I had a greatly enhanced sense for receiving such things; and even if my understanding had the richest store of concepts for such data, it would remain forever incomprehensible how I might happen to see, simply and directly, a piece of chalk. That is, it would be incomprehensible until I include this basic behavior of existence (dealing-with as a form of concern-about) in my interpretation, along with the as-structure we just discussed.

Therefore we see that the as-structure is bound up with a primary human comportment, and we see that this sense-making behavior is a way of being that we may briefly characterize as: "Always already

14. In principle, I meet usable things in terms of a *world*.

15. [GA 21 (p. 147.24–25) has "eine eigentümliche Bewegung, wenn ich so sagen darf, die das Dasein selbst ständig macht," whereas Moser (p. 315.15) reads "die Zeit" instead of "Dasein": "die die Zeit ständig macht." Weiss (p. 76.10) confirms Moser's record here.]

abiding with the source of meaning and understanding, *while* return-ing to whatever we encounter." This "abiding" is a matter of (1) stay-ing with the what-as I take the encountered object, and (2) staying with the returning from there, i.e., from the source that is the basis for understanding the object. This *returning* is precisely what *discloses* whatever we encounter, for example, *as* a door or *as* chalk. Therefore this returning from the whence-and-whereby with which I already am present is precisely what has the special function of disclosing. This is the first level in our interpretation of such as-structured behav-ior. Later, in clarifying the statement even further, we will need to track its structure (as interpreted thus far) further back. Then you will see that truly understanding a phenomenon as simple as the state-ment, "This chalkboard is black," requires that you have already un-dertaken a good deal of preparation and study.

Now as regards the structure we have been characterizing, which has the as-structure—the "already-ahead-of-oneself that returns to something and by returning discloses it"—we could also determine this making-sense-of-something (as I put it briefly) in this way: That in terms of which one makes sense of something must be brought to-gether and taken together with what is being made sense of. This is the σύνθεσις part. At the same time this bringing together and taking together [149] entails that both of them—the whence of the sense-making and the thing to be made sense of—are separated and must be kept separate in the act of sense-making. This bringing together and taking together is possible only by keeping them separate. And vice versa: keeping them separate is possible—as this specific act of keeping separate—only in an encompassing act of keeping them together.

So we see that the act of sense-making, owing to its as-structure, can in fact be understood with the help of these formal determinations of σύνθεσις and διαίρεσις. But then at the same time you can see that this as-structure can be characterized, with demonstrable legitimacy, as the unity of σύνθεσις and διαίρεσις only if beforehand the phenomenon of sense-making has already been laid out and seen as such, since this phenomenon of sense-making cannot be construed in a purely formal way by means of the structures of a synthesizing separation and a sepa-rating synthesizing. In other words, the formal structure of σύνθεσις and διαίρεσις does not get to the authentic sense of the comportment itself. Of itself, the mere structure of a separating synthesis does not explain why a comportment that has this structure is a sense-making and intelligent comportment of the kind we indicated earlier. Σύνθεσις and διαίρεσις are merely empty, formal determinations, and they are not intrinsically and exclusively adapted to making-sense—even though *their* own ultimate origin may have to be understood in terms of sense-making.

This as-structure—or more precisely, the act of dealing-with as a direct having and taking, insofar as it is determined by the as-structure—determines our being unto the world and in large measure even our being unto ourselves. For its part, sense-making is possible as a basic form of our being only because our existence itself is capable of understanding. Even if one's existence is thick and dull, that dullness is merely one mode of the understanding that necessarily belongs to every existence that is being in the world. Obviously the mode of understanding can vary widely. [150]

The act of making-sense or understanding is directed primarily not to individual things and to general concepts. Instead, it is alive in one's firsthand lived world and in one's world as a whole. In this act of sense-making, the world is opened up for existence. This disclosure is the uncovering of the current form of a being's suitability-for, whereby it is present as a being. Whatever gets opened up this way can be held on to, even when the worldly thing in question is not itself present. That is, the opening-up of the world—which unfolds in the act of understanding or sense-making—can be possessed and preserved as meaning, i.e., as a world of understanding in which existence operates.[16]

*   *   *

In the preceding lecture hour, we delineated the structure of the "as" more precisely. It is important in analyses like this to remember the context we are working in. Briefly: Our topic is truth, specifically the truth of λόγος and more precisely yet, the question "What makes λόγος as such able to be true or false?" Aristotle's answer is: λόγος can be true or false because it has the structure of σύνθεσις. So we asked how much λόγος has to do with σύνθεσις. Further study showed that σύνθεσις is only *one* structural moment of λόγος, and it is necessarily accompanied by διαίρεσις. That led to a further question: Which phenomenon possesses these two properties in a unified way?

That phenomenon is the "as," the structure that belongs to understanding as such. Here understanding must be understood as a basic form of being of our existence. This form of being is defined as one which always already lives ahead in the source of sense-making (in

16. [Here the lecture of Tuesday, 8 December 1925, draws to a close, to be followed by the twenty-first lecture on Thursday, 10 December (Moser, p. 319). Whereas up to this point GA 21 has omitted all summaries of the previous lecture, here (GA 21, pp. 150–151 n. 6) the text provides part of the summary that Heidegger read out at the beginning of his 12 December lecture, but confines it to a long footnote. For the complete summary that Heidegger read in class and that I draw on, cf. Moser, pp. 319–324. I put the summary in its proper place at the beginning of the lecture.]

the what-as) and which comes back to a present thing and, in thus coming back, discloses this thing as being this or that.

This way of being—always already living ahead in the end-for-which *as* returning-to and disclosing—is an original, unified, fundamental comportment whose structure expresses the "as." The "as" has the function of uncovering something in terms of something, of uncover something *as*—i.e., as this or that. The "as" *is* the structure of understanding. The understood is a ἑρμηνεία, that-which-is-understood in an understanding. We said that understanding is a basic comportment of existence. Therefore, the structure of the "as" is the fundamental hermeneutical structure of the being of that being which we call existence (human life). This fundamental hermeneutical structure can be apprehended in a relatively (and I emphasize *relatively*) original form of what we called "direct dealing-with-something."

This basic, unified structure that is expressed in the "as" cannot be further broken down into pieces but is simply to be interpreted more originally as a whole in its wholeness. Later we shall see that where this structure is not yet adequately clarified, it is understood extrinsically in an indirect and formal way—determinations that are, in any case, possible.

In the primary understanding that goes with dealing-with-something, the thing that is understood or made sense of is disclosed. In this way understanding is able to take for itself the disclosure—the "result," as it were, [of the sense-making]—and preserve it. The result of an act of sense-making is precisely *sense* or *meaning*—not what we usually call the "meaning of a word" but the primary meaning, to which words can then accrue.[17] [151]

Only insofar as this capacity to understand—to make sense of—already belongs to existence, can existence express itself in sounds, such that these vocal sounds are words that now have meaning. Because existence, in its very being, is sense-making, it lives in meanings and can express itself in and as meanings. Only because there are such vocal sounds (i.e., words) that accrue to meanings, can there be individual words [*Wörter*],[18] i.e., the linguistic forms that are stamped by meaning and can be detached from that meaning. We call such a whole of sounds in which existence's capacity to understand has somehow evolved and become existential, *language;* and when I speak here of a whole of existence I do not mean an individual act of existence, but being-with-each-other *qua* historical.

The kind of being that pertains to the phenomenon we call language

---

17. [The abbreviated summary ends here.]

18. [That is, φωναί (Latin, *voces*), sounds uttered by the human voice, as contrasted with ψόφοι, the inarticulate sounds of an animal.]

is even today still fundamentally obscure. Language—which every day grows and every day dissolves, which changes from generation to generation or lies dead for centuries—is still entirely unexplained, as is the peculiar being of language itself. In other words, basically the kind of being that pertains to this phenomenon which is the topic of all philology and linguistics is, in the final analysis, ontologically obscure. Nonetheless we are able to say something about the being of language, insofar as language is possible, only because of the human capacity to understand—that is, existence itself, to which the structure of understanding belongs. And because existence, as understanding and sense-making, is intrinsically historical, so too the particular kind of being [152] of that manifold of words that we call our vocabulary as a whole, or language, is also historical.

Of course, this determination is still quite empty, but even so, it indicates that the phenomenon of language—taken now in the narrow sense of its linguistic *form*, separated somehow from the *content* of the meaning—this whole structural interrelation of linguistic forms can itself be understood only in terms of the historicity of existence.

At this point we shall not go into the phenomenon of language as such. We will mention the phenomenon only in terms of our focus on meaning, in which language is grounded. In keeping with this founding matrix of linguistic and verbal sounds bound up with understanding and sense-making, we must also keep separate some questions that one asks (usually in an erroneous way) about language. The question about how language began is fundamentally different from the question about the origin of meaning. The question about how a particular language (or language as such) began or developed—if it is a possible line of questioning and investigating—presupposes that one has already cleared up the question about the origin of meaning as such. So we begin to see the depths we are being led into by the task of understanding, in all its basic dimensions, something as simple as the spoken sentence: "This chalkboard is black."

We now limit our specific investigation to a broad analysis of the as-structure and its function as the foundation of the statement. The question about the basic structure of λόγος has led us beyond the phenomenon of the "as" and further down the path to the phenomenon of meaning, which is mentioned in the title of this section (§12). Our understanding of the as-structure itself stands or falls with the possibility of a more penetrating interpretation of *sense-making* and *understanding*. Our question now is not first of all about the origin of meaning. It is, rather: "What function does meaning or the [153] as-structure have as regards the possibility of those statements that have the distinguishing characteristic of being able to be true or false?"

b) The modification of the as-structure in the act of determining: the apophantic "as"

The statement, as indicatively showing-something-as, is possible only on the basis of our already-being-with the subject-matter-to-be-shown, specifically in such a way that the subject matter is somehow disclosed. To a linguistic orientation, a statement can be understood as an interconnection of meanings of words. To that degree, it entails that the plurality of meanings in the unity of a sentence is possible only on the basis of and in the medium of meaning. Whatever specific structure it may also have as an act of predication, the act of indicatively showing-something-as operates in the act of having and understanding the subject matter of the speech. This act of having and understanding (i.e., our underlying familiarity with the subject matter) has the structure of "as." Thus all the ways of showing-as—i.e., the particular forms in which such showing-as is carried out—cannot as such renounce the as-structure. The "as" is the basic structure whereby we understand and have access to anything. The possible subject matter of any applicable determination is understood first of all and *a priori;* and in accessing and appropriating that subject matter, the "as" necessarily preserves it.

These ways of asserting, i.e., determining something about something, get modified in accordance with the possible ways of showing-as and with the thing that is to be shown-as. Regardless of how they are modified, these ways of asserting something about something are essentially assigned to the as-structure and at the same time help to modify it.

In carrying out a statement in the form of predication, specifically in the sense of a categorial statement, the *"as"* of the primary understanding is simultaneously flattened out into the pure and simple determination of a thing. The showing takes on the sense of letting us see the presence of something with and near something else. [154] We see something—and as co-present with it, we see something else. We must now show this flattening-out in the phenomenon in order to show the context of the "as" that does the primary uncovering, along with the leveled-down "as" that enacts a determination.

In a direct act of understanding and dealing with something, the thing is understood in terms of what it is *for.* In such cases the end-for-which (or, seen in terms of [predicative] understanding, the what-it-is) is not thematically considered, much less thematically understood. Rather, we already live *in* it in some form of concern-about. Questions about which kinds of "end-for-which" actually and genetically come first (even a vegetable lives its not-too-bright life in terms of an end-for-which) are entirely of secondary importance in comparison with the question of the essential structure of the end-for-which.

Concern-about can diversify itself as this or that kind of concern-about enacted in this or that particular way *only* if that which underlies such a factual "development" is itself, by its nature, already concern-about. Managing and dealing with things does not first occur when I begin to handle something. Rather, I can start to handle something only because my existence is already determined in the first place as concern-about and dealing-with. Existence as such "is" concern-about; and all I can do is develop certain degrees of it and directions that give expression to concern-about and fulfill it.

So, insofar as we are at all, we live existentially in concern-about, which is to say, in the understanding of an end-for-which. But in such dealings we never thematically understand or even thematically think about this end-for-which that makes understanding possible in the form of the "what-as." Rather, in our direct dealings it is the *means-whereby* that is thematic. The means-whereby or means, is what gets understood *as* this-or-that thematically in the "as." But while it is thematic, it is not thematic for theoretical understanding.

Now what about the statement? In the statement, the means-*whereby* of our dealings becomes the thing-*about-which* of an act of showing-as. Taken ontologically, such showing-as is also a dealing-with. We will have to interpret this more precisely, but in any case showing-as is a dealing-with, in which the means-whereby (which is already uncovered and understood in understanding) has to come to light. [155] And along with that, what is already uncovered must be further uncovered. So a dealing-with whose concern-about brings about an uncovering is itself an act of uncovering. The statement is an act of understanding in dealing-with, whose concern [*Sorge*] is the act of uncovering, which therefore necessarily has the as-structure in an emphatic sense.

If, in an act of dealing directly with something, we encounter the means-whereby in such a way that we make a statement about it, the means-*whereby* becomes that-*about-which*. The thematizing of the about-which at first does not change anything in the means-whereby—i.e., it does not change its intelligibility. We encounter the means-whereby as something that from the start was already understood in the structure of the primary "as."

But what happens when we thematize in the form of making a statement and thematically speaking *about* the means-whereby? The thematizing performed by the statement works within the statement's function, which is to show-something-as. In other words, the statement is purely concerned with ἀποφαίνεσθαι, uncovering-something-as. In a statement, the uncovering understands the means-whereby in terms of what-it-is, but it does not draw that "what-it-is" from anything else—from some practical function, for example—but only *from the thing it is speaking about.*

This is the first peculiarity: the what-it-is is now *not* taken from the thing's *end-for-which* but from the very thing about which the statement is made. The proper sense of a statement, is to express something *as* something, to take the that-in-terms-of-which a thing is to be determined expressly from the thing spoken about.

So we find that the statement has a double aspect: In the first case, what-the-thing-is corresponds to the task to be performed and thus to the kind of concern that is expressed in the statement about the thing. Second, the what-it-is is *not* taken from any practical function or from any orientation to another thing. Instead, it is taken from the very thing that is spoken about.

Here we find the third characteristic of the statement: [156] the particular kind of showing and uncovering that pertains to the statement is to a certain degree *concentrated* on *what* the speaking is about. In dealing with and understanding the chalk, we do not think about the chalk thematically. We don't even enact our understanding of the chalk thematically and explicitly in terms of its function.

The statement, however, concentrates on the chalk itself as something present. In the statement, "This chalk is white," the declaration consists in bringing into view something that is already there in the subject matter that the speech is about, and this subject-matter-about-which is likewise already there. This form of indicating and uncovering something that is just there (e.g., the chalk), bringing it closer and into focus in terms of what it is as just being there (its whiteness), is what we call *determining*. Determining is thus a mode of indicating and uncovering, and as such it has a specific structure to its "as." The difference between the as-structure of a determining statement and the as-structure of a direct understanding is manifest in the three factors we mentioned above.[19]

Now our question is: "To what degree must we see the determination of things by statements as a leveling-down of the primary form of understanding, namely, dealing-with?" We saw that in determining by way of statements, the as-what-it-is (the whiteness) whence comes the determination is drawn from the given subject-matter-about-which itself. So the statement, a concernful comportment of existence, is broadly speaking also an act of dealing-with—but not in the way a worker deals with things, but simply as an act of speaking about something. To a certain

---

19. There are various levels between a functional involvement with something, on the one hand, and a pure determining on the other. However, our analysis deals chiefly with the two "extremes."

   1. A statement in and for a practical function;
   2. a determining that describes one's specific lived world;
   3. a determining as a statement about what is just there, what merely occurs.

degree such an act of dealing-with something by speaking about it some-how *solidifies* itself in such a way that the chalk is now simply *there*.

With the statement, the act of dealing-with something has now been [157] *withdrawn* from the primary function of, for example, writing. This means that, after this withdrawal from an immediate task, the understanding no longer really lives in a practical function, no longer lives into the task for which the given implement can be used. Concern-about and dealing-with are now restricted to the status of "there": the chalk is just *there*. And regarding the focus of its way of showing things, the statement is now tied, so to speak, to what-is-there as just-being-there. Its sole orientation is to *bring closer* what-is-there as being-there, for the purpose of understanding it.

This entails that, in and through this process of thematization, the subject-matter-about-which (which we have already determined as the thematic *means-whereby*) gets covered-over to a certain extent as regards that-as-which it was properly understood. So now when I say "This chalk is white," this statement about something that I might deal with is no longer a statement that, as such and in its very form, is primarily related to dealing-with. If I were to say as I am writing, "This chalk is too hard"—or "too scratchy," or whatever—I would be making a statement *within* a practical function, namely that of writing. I would be making a statement that I simply could not interpret as:

> This statement, "This chalk is too scratchy," is an act of defining the chalk *as well as* spelling out my relation to the chalk—and inability to relate to it—i.e., my inability to write "properly" with it.

No, when I make the statement, "This chalk is too scratchy," I do not mean to determine the thing I have in my hand as something possessed of the property of grittiness or scratchiness. Rather, what I mean to say with my statement is that it is an *obstacle* to my writing. The statement is interpretatively related to my writing activity, my primary concern to write. That is, the statement is a spelling-out of my being-in [the world] as a being-with [the chalk]. In a practical function, the means-whereby is necessarily co-understood: I live by being immersed in it. We must keep this in mind in order to understand the kinds of contradictions that run through traditional logic when the usual example of a determination comes up: "The roses are in bloom." One then says that these things, the roses, have the property [158] or condition of blooming.

That is not what anyone means when he or she says, "The roses are in bloom." The example is a pure construction taken from a statement that is simply oriented to giving a flat determination of something just-there. When a thing gets thematized in such a way that the means-whereby of firsthand dealings-with-things gets transformed into the about-which of a statement that determines the thing, at that point the genuine ontological property of the thing (the chalk, for example) withdraws. The chalk gets flattened out into a mere thing, "This white thing here"—whether this piece of paper or that lamp—is no different from any other thing, since I understand them all as just things on hand.

The chalk's particular, original way of being—as an implement—is now leveled down to this average state of mere thereness, where it is no different from any other thing. This way of showing something— this determination performed in the declarative-determining form of "The chalk is white"—is possible only on the basis of a *re-concealing* of the chalk as a means whereby we deal with things. Admittedly, it is not necessarily a concealing: in this statement too, we can still hold on to the original implement. However, we come to understand this kind of statement when we in some way clarify the two *limit-cases:* that of a direct, unexpressed, unthematic dealing with something, and that of the thematizing determination of a something that is just there. This latter way of uncovering and showing-something-as by means of a statement is itself a modification of the structure of the "as."[20]

*   *   *

We have defined *determining* as the act of indicating and bringing into view something just-there in its state of being just-there in this way or that. Such determining, as a declaration, is a way of uncovering, and therefore it necessarily has the structure of the "as." Insofar as it is a way of uncovering, the original hermeneutical as-structure has been modified. This modifying, which I explained by contrasting three different forms [of the statement], now signifies *in se* to a flattening out [159] of the original structure. In fact, insofar as the statement is now directed thematically toward something (the chalk) with which I have original functional dealings, the thing about which I make the statement becomes merely something-there. It is now simply something to be understood, a statement's subject matter in its mere thereness.

When something that was originally used as an implement gets thematized into something just-there, the original ontological character of the object (the chalk) is at the same time covered-over insofar as the chalk is now no longer immediately there as an implement, but rather as a mere present-thing in which I find a *property* that I attribute to the thing and, by so doing, determine the thing. The statement as indicating and determining hovers over, as it were, the objects that are given

20. [Here (Moser, p. 319) Heidegger ends his lecture of Thursday, 10 December 1925, to be followed by that of Friday, 11 December, which opened with a 340-word summary that is omitted in GA 21.]

firsthand in one's lived world and that are primarily oriented to use. Because of that the things of the lived world—things of use or in general anything oriented to concern-about as a non-theoretical comportment—are leveled down to things that are merely present, so that they are no longer differentiated as being implements adapted to certain functions.

However, the statement's modification of the as-structure always presupposes the original as-structure, the underlying understanding of the thing that gets flattened out in and through the statement. Thus, determination-via-statement is never a primary act of uncovering. It never determines a primary and original comportment toward beings, and as a result this form of λόγος can never become our guide to the question of what beings are.

In the logic and doctrine of being of the Greeks, and in the tradition up to Husserl,[21] λόγος as determination-via-statements has in fact been the guide for pursuing the inquiry into being. [160] That is to say, beings are there as objects of a possible determination or determinability. But once we recognize that this very determining, along with its entire structure, is a derived phenomenon, we also see that the phenomenon of determination cannot be the starting point for the question of being—if, that is, this question is supposed to understand the phenomenon of being in its roots.

We have shown the extent to which the as-structure of primary understanding—i.e., the "as" of the basic hermeneutical structure of existence—can be characterized formally and extrinsically as σύνθεσις and διαίρεσις. We also emphasized that when Aristotle speaks of σύνθεσις and διαίρεσις, he does not and cannot mean the structure of this primary "as." Rather he is referring to another structure, that of the derived, flattened-out and flattening "as." Now, on the basis of our interpretation of the "as" used in determining thereness, we need to explain why the formal structure of synthesis is used to characterize this "as."

In the first place, why did the as-structure necessarily come to the fore at this point? We answer: Here the "as" structures a concernful comportment that highlights an as-what and thereby highlights the determination of something *as* something in terms of that as-what. The statement, when performed explicitly, thematically highlights an as-what, and it does so explicitly in terms of the subject matter itself that is to be determined in light of this as-what. What is more, in this case the "as" is flattened out into a determination. Formally speaking, determination is a relation and specifically a synthetic relation. In any

21. On being and truth in correlation with the ideas of statement, judgment, "doxa" *qua* determination, see Husserl, *Ideen I*, §§103ff., especially §142, "Rational Positing and Being," which concerns the essential correlation between the idea of true being and truth, reason, consciousness.

case, in this relation the synthetic factor [that flattens out the "as"] presses to the fore ahead of the "analytic" moment. This synthetic relation can be isolated over against the primary function of λόγος, which is to show-something-*as*. Then, when λόγος gets cut loose, so to speak, from the specific relation of the subject matter (the about-which) and the predicate (the as-what), it gets passed off as the relation of anything to anything, equivalent to formal synthesizing as such.

In a certain sense, Aristotle uses the term λόγος formally. But at the same time he endows it with the sense of the "apophantic," i.e., [161] the showing-of-beings-as. Aristotle also sees in ἀπόφανσις the primary and essential relatedness of the λόγος (taken as λόγος τινός, speech about something) to beings, and this λόγος has to indicatively show-something-as *only* via determining them [in statements]. As regards structure, this view of λόγος is obviously quite close to that of an empty "relating and synthesizing." What is more, the determining statement, taken as something uttered (a series of words related to each other and to a context), itself becomes just "something there."

These observations make one thing very clear: we have not understood the phenomena of making a statement—*qua* showing-as, determining-as, etc.—as long as we simply characterize them as synthesis, and let it go at that. To do only that is to grope around and latch on to the first thing we come up with, no matter how irrelevant. But there is something even more fatal. If we think that synthesis, taken formally, is the structural meaning of λόγος in general, we preclude any possibility of understanding sense-making, understanding, explication, and, more generally, even language. Of course, for the sake of shorthand characterizations, we can make use of these formal determinations, but only after we have first understood the complete structure of the phenomenon. Making an indicative statement has the sense of determining something in its mere thereness, and it characterizes the "as" in this way. To understand synthesis, when it is not taken formally, we have to begin with this.[22] [162]

---

22. Nonetheless, taking the as-structure in its formal character has yet another consequence, not just for the interpretation of λόγος and for the concept of the "logical" (i.e., determining and determinedness), but also for the interpretation of being. The ontic is conceptualized in terms of logical structures ("logical" understood in the sense we have indicated). How does that come about? When we indicate something as something by way of what we have characterized as a statement, the thing comes to be seen. The subject matter (= what is simply there) gets shown *as* something, while the "as-what" gets shown as the "as-what" of what is simply there. This being has been synthesized as the synthetic being it is. The thing itself, as something that [*de facto*] *is* there-together, now gets [explicitly] *brought* together. It gets understood as simply out-there-together. It is apprehended

§13. The conditions of the possibility of λόγος being false.
The question of truth

With this examination of λόγος as an apophantic determination of what's there in its thereness we are sufficiently prepared to answer the question, *What makes the λόγος that has this structure able to be false?* From the start, we have intentionally formulated the question in this pointed way. In its complete form the question is: "What makes λόγος able to be true *or* false?" As we shall show, the way in which the λόγος can be true is co-determined by the kind of falsehood that pertains to λόγος. The false, says Aristotle, is always and only where there is σύνθεσις. Now, on the basis of σύνθεσις as originally understood, how are we to clarify the degree to which λόγος, which is structured by such σύνθεσις, can be true or false? We know what the structure of λόγος is, but we certainly do not yet know what "true" and "false" mean, nor, therefore, what kind of determinations can pertain to λόγος.

If you recall the chart that we began with earlier, you will remember that, in characterizing the chart, we said that our expressions "true" and "false," "truth" and "falsehood," are not adequate to what the Greeks meant by the corresponding expressions ἀληθές and ψεῦδος. By these terms, the Greeks understood that truth = the act of uncovering or uncoveredness, and ψεῦδος or falsehood = covering-over or dissembling. Further, in discussing truth and falsehood we have already said that it would be a prejudice to think that Aristotle championed a theory of truth as a copy-theory [*Abbildtheorie*], as if truth consisted in the fact that representations within the soul reproduce things outside. Aristotle's concept of truth and the Greek concept of truth generally are neither oriented to images nor to be understood in terms of this kind of correspondence. [163] Rather, our understanding of them should be oriented to uncovering and covering-over.

a) Preparatory interpretation. *Metaphysics* IV 7 and VI 4, and *De interpretatione* 1

Now we first attempt to provide a very general characterization of truth and falsehood as Aristotle understands them. That will serve as the necessary basis for asking how σύνθεσις makes truth and falsehood possible. I will discuss somewhat briefly only two citations that can provide you with a rough idea of what kind of interpretation of truth one finds in Aristotle:

(logically) in terms of the statement defined as synthesis. This becomes clear from Aristotle's definitions of true and false.

τὸ μὲν γὰρ λέγειν τὸ ὂν μὴ εἶναι ἢ τὸ μὴ ὂν εἶναι ψεῦδος, τὸ δὲ τὸ ὂν εἶναι καὶ τὸ μὴ ὂν μὴ εἶναι ἀληθές. (*Metaphysics* IV 7, 1011b26)

To say-and-show that what-is is not, or that what-is-not is, is to cover-over. But to show that what-is is, and what-is-not is not, is to uncover.

And if we read this determination of truth in our role as twentieth-century Europeans, we think it is really quite trivial. But we need to consider that this determination is the result of the greatest philosophical effort that Plato and Aristotle ever made. You can hardly conceive of what it means to press forward into such a "triviality." So: truth and falsehood are taken in connection with λέγειν, speaking.

The essential element in this text is that speaking is understood here not as judgment but, as the translation indicates, as the showing of a being, ἀποφαίνεσθαι. Once this basic structure of λέγειν is understood, this determination of being-true and being-false can offer no support to the notion that truth is a matter of verifying the correspondence between beings and the images or copies of them formed in consciousness.

By its very meaning, to indicate a being is to be already present with that being, even [164] when the subject matter that the speech indicates is not bodily present but only intended. Even when absent, the very sense of the statement entails that the being itself is intended, not some representation or image that "corresponds" to the absent being.

Truth is not a relation that is "just there" between two beings that themselves are "just there"—one mental, the other physical. Nor is it a coordination, as philosophers like to say these days. If it is a relation at all, it is one that has no analogies with any other relation between beings. If I may put it this way, it is the relation of existence as such to its very world. It is the world-openness of existence that is itself uncovered—existence whose very being unto the world gets disclosed/uncovered in and with its being unto the world.

Aristotle certainly did not really see this phenomenon, in any case not in the ontological structure that is proper to it. But even less did he invent anything like a copy-theory of truth. Rather, he stuck to the phenomena and understood them as broadly as possible. That is, he avoided a fundamental error in seeing, and thus kept the road open—only, of course, to have it thoroughly blocked again.

The second text from which we can understand truth and falsehood in Aristotle's sense comes from *Metaphysics* VI 4. I emphasize that these *explications de texte* do not yet constitute an authentic interpretation but are only preparatory. Only later will we come to understand the phenomena on the basis of σύνθεσις.

τὸ μὲν γὰρ ἀληθὲς τὴν κατάφασιν ἐπὶ τῷ συγκειμένῳ ἔχει, τὴν δ᾽ ἀπόφασιν ἐπὶ τῷ διῃρημένῳ, τὸ δὲ ψεῦδος τούτου τοῦ μερισμοῦ τὴν ἀντίφασιν. (*Metaphysics* VI 4, 1027b20–22)

In a translation, with explanations in brackets:

> Uncovering {as a form of enactment} entails attribution {of something to something} regarding things already-present-together, and denial {of something to something} with regard to what is taken apart; {or more precisely, with regard to what is already present but not together-with}. [165] But covering-over consists in saying the opposite {about what is already together-with or already separated from something else}.

So, covering-over consists in attributing something to something when they actually are apart in the given thing, and in denying something of something when in fact they are together in the thing.

This second text gives us something new in relation to the first text, but the new element is already familiar to us. When, in what we have characterized as a statement, we indicate and determine something as something, the being does indeed come to light. What is present is indicated as something, in such a way that the *what* as-which the being is shown "lies" there in that being (cf. κείμενον—κεῖται ["lying there—to lie there"]). That is, the *thing*, the statement's subject matter, is brought together as something that lies together. The being is understood as something lying-there-together. But that means that the being is characterized on the basis of the σύν- of σύνθεσις. With explanations in brackets:

> τοῦτο δὲ {τὸ ἀληθὲς καὶ τὸ ψεῦδος} ἐπὶ τῶν πραγμάτων ἐστὶ τῷ συγκεῖσθαι ἢ διῃρῆσθαι, ὥστε ἀληθεύει μὲν ὁ τὸ διῃρημένον οἰόμενος διῃρῆσθαι καὶ τὸ συγκείμενον συγκεῖσθαι, ἔψευσται δὲ ὁ ἐναντίως ἔχων ἢ τὰ πράγματα. (*Metaphysics* IX 10, 1051b2–5)

In a translation, with explanations in brackets:

> With regard to existent things, this {uncovering and covering-over} is about their {already} lying-together or taken-apart-ness. Therefore, whoever takes the taken-apart in its taken-apart-ness, and the lying-together in its lying-together-ness, uncovers. But when someone {in taking beings, i.e., discussing and thus showing them} relates to them in the opposite way, that person covers-over.

Insofar as synthesis is the structure of λόγος as indicative comportment, the ὄν and its structure is interpreted on the basis of the λόγος and its structure. The structure of being has the character of being "logical" in the strict sense of the word: not an ontology of beings, but a logic of beings.

Catchword determinations like this are always dangerous, and for the most part are usually false. What we have said should simply make us notice the fact that σύνθεσις [166] emerges when we characterize truth with regard to the thing itself that is to be shown-as.

Σύνθεσις is the structure not only of the λόγος but of the subject matter *qua* that-about-which, insofar as the subject matter after all is and must be a being in the sense of something true. Thus, from the first characteristic of truth and falsehood we see that there is no basis or possibility for interpreting this definition in the sense of a copying. From the second characteristic we see that the thing itself, which is correlative to the indicative statement, is understood by way of synthesis. To be sure, we may expect an objection that might be drawn from *De interpretatione* (chap. 1), the treatise in which λόγος itself is Aristotle's theme. The second sentence of chapter 1 starts right off with a brief explanation that might actually tempt us to prove that Aristotle's concept of truth does indeed intend something like the copying-of-things through mental processes. In fact, this passage is also the classical one that philosophers appeal to (usually in a variety of roundabout ways and always in ignorance of the context) in an effort to point out and prove that Aristotle introduced into philosophy this naïve concept of truth, as it is usually dubbed. I will discuss this passage very briefly. It is also important for our later discussions about the copula and negation.

> ἔστι μὲν οὖν τὰ ἐν τῇ φωνῇ
>   τῶν ἐν τῇ ψυχῇ παθημάτων σύμβολα,
>   καὶ τὰ γραφόμενα τῶν ἐν τῇ φωνῇ.
> καὶ ὥσπερ οὐδὲ γράμματα πᾶσι τὰ αὐτά,
>   οὐδὲ φωναὶ αἱ αὐταί·
> ὧν μέντοι ταῦτα σημεῖα πρώτων,
>   ταὐτὰ πᾶσι παθήματα τῆς ψυχῆς,
> καὶ ὧν ταῦτα ὁμοιώματα πράγματα ἤδη ταὐτά. (*De interpretatione* 1, 16a3–8)

In a translation, with explanations in brackets:

> There are linguistic utterances {words} in which something that is found in
>   our mental comportment {perception, reflection} is made known.
> And what is written makes known the words. {So Aristotle begins with the
>   spoken word wherein—to put it briefly—the meaning is made known.
>   And the spoken word can express itself in the written word.}
> And just as written signs are not the same for all peoples {the Egyptians

[167] have different ones from the Greeks}, so too the sounds {the forms of the utterances} are not the same.

However, the things of which these uttered words are first {and properly} signs {i.e., what the words give utterance to, what they are words for}— these {the things intended, the apprehended as such} are identically the same for everyone.

And the things {the πράγματα that we deal with} of which they {the intended and perceived, the meanings} are similitudes, they too are the same, already {from the outset} and of themselves.[23]

*   *   *

From that last sentence people derive the "copy-theory." Yes, ὁμοίωμα can in fact mean an image or a copy. But on an equally original footing it means "that which has been assimilated to, become similar to," that which is *just the same as.*[24] If we translate παθήματα as "representations" and understand that as "mental states," then it is easy to come up with a copy-theory interpretation. That is: In the mind there are "states of mind," mental states as images of things that are not in the mind itself.

But the word in the text is not πάθη (which can indeed mean such states) but παθήματα—something that we meet, something that, when met, is taken up—an *affectio* in the broadest sense. And ὁμοιώματα means the assimilated, that which ὁμοίως ἔχει, that which, as encountering, is just the same as the thing itself. Our apprehending comports itself in the same way as what is to be apprehended. The παθήματα is the apprehended of an apprehending. The apprehending gives the thing itself, lets us meet the thing just the way it is.

What is at stake here is not just any kind of assimilation. It is not, for example, the assimilation of a mental state to a physical thing (which is nonsensical). The assimilation we are taking about here concurs very easily with the determination of truth in the text from *Metaphysics* IX 10 that we cited earlier.[25] [168]

The text from *Metaphysics* VI 4 is particularly clear about the meaning that σύνθεσις has when it comes to clarifying not only the true and the false of λόγος but also truth as the uncovering of things, i.e., as the

23. [Here (Moser, p. 351) Heidegger ends his lecture of Friday, 11 December 1925, to be followed by that of Monday, 14 December , which opened with a 430-word summary that is omitted in GA 21.]

24. Therefore Aristotle can also say in *De interpretatione* 9, 19a33: ὁμοίως ὁι λόγοι ἀληθεῖς ὥσπερ τὰ πράγματα. "Λόγοι {i.e., the indicative showing of beings} uncover just as much as the being itself does {insofar as it is uncovered}."

25. We are talking about ὁμοίωσις in terms of ἀποφαίνεσθαι. The act of showing something assimilates itself to that thing in the only way that makes any sense in such a comportment, viz., in the νόημα.

structure of those things themselves. That is why we said earlier that Aristotle uses σύνθεσις not in a purely formal sense but in an apophantic sense, as related to and with regard to the things themselves.

Σύνθεσις, as the condition of possibility of being false and especially of being true, is a chameleon-like concept, sometimes logical, sometimes ontological—or more precisely, usually both at the same time. More precisely yet: neither the one nor the other. That is the characteristic stage of both Aristotle's and Plato's philosophy. We only imagine we understand the problems when we jump into this murky business armed with our seemingly beautiful distinctions and concepts of a modern system instead of guarding this authentically productive lack of clarity. The supposed clarity of the moderns consists merely in the fact that they have killed off the problems beforehand. It is now a matter of clearing out this thicket of relations within the concept of σύνθεσις so that we can understand how σύνθεσις is the condition of the possibility of falsehood and truth.

For Plato, the false—and in connection with it, deception, deceit, and error—were special phenomena that first of all had to be, so to speak, battled with in a particular demonstration that there are in fact such things and that they thus have a certain kind of being. Under the weighty pressure of Parmenides' proposition, "Beings are, non-beings are not," it seemed absolutely to be the case that deception, falsehood, and error—as negative, as nothing—were not and could not be.

It remains one of Plato's undying achievements to have shown that even error and falsehood exist. This was possible for him only because he posed anew the problem of being. Of course, he also did not answer the question of how the being of the false is possible and what it means, [169] any more than Aristotle did, even though by building on Plato's work, Aristotle pressed further ahead. Aristotle showed how a condition of the possibility of falsehood lies within beings themselves and the possible ways they can be. This is a discovery that later fell into absolute oblivion (where it remains today), because the problem of truth was no longer understood. We think that error and deception are something subjective and have their origin in one's thinking when it violates its own laws and the like.

If we understand the phenomenon of truth (as uncovering) more radically—from existence itself and what we characterized as its basic hermeneutical structure—then we can understand from the beginning that falsehood necessarily depends on the very beings about which statements are possible.

We have to clarify this briefly and in outline form. Truth is the uncovering of beings. If λόγος is presumably able to be this possibility in a specific form of performance, then, as λόγος, it must already have a relation to beings. It is one of existence's ways of being unto the world

and unto itself (as existence)—in short, being unto beings. If falsehood is supposed to pertain to λόγος, then it must have something to
do with the structure of λόγος. Therefore, falsehood is determined:

1. from the being itself and its being, in connection with which λόγος
   is what it is;
2. from existential comportment itself.

According to Aristotle, the condition of the possibility of falsehood
is synthesis and therefore synthesis in this double aspect: in beings
(whatever is there) as subject-matter-about-which; and in the very
comportment of making a statement.

With regard to its structure as the uncovering of beings, truth can
be divided in a corresponding way.

1. On the one hand, as uncoveredness it is a characteristic of beings
   themselves (and in a special way a characteristic of the world);
2. on the other hand, as uncovering, it is a characteristic of the comportment of existence.

But this comportment itself, and existence as such, is uncovered in
and for itself. The phenomenon of [170] uncovering has several essential "sides." But understanding must aim at seeing the original whole
out of which and for which these "sides" (to use this superficial name)
are what they are.[26]

According to the structure of truth itself, synthesis is oriented both
to human comportment and to the subject matter that a statement
might uncover.[27] The problems now are: How do falsehood and truth
in Aristotle become intelligible on the basis of synthesis? And what
can we understand in the Greek concept of truth that is more fundamental than the traditional concept? And granted this broadening [of
the concept of truth], how far will we get in understanding not just
the fact that but also the reason why truth must be understood as the
truth of intuition?

It is possible there are many ways to gain an understanding of the
concept of truth and falsehood in Aristotle and in the Greeks generally. We wish to choose one way that will spare us a long drawn-out
interpretation and instead will take us directly to the basic question

26. For "sides" in the phenomenon of uncovering, see ὂν ὡς ἀληθές ἔν διανοίᾳ
["beings as uncovered in the discursive mind" (*Metaphysics* XI 8, 1065a22)].

27. [This appears to be the sense of the passage. Moser (p. 359.4–6) records
Heidegger as saying, "Synthesis is thus oriented to the comportment of existence
and at the same time to the subject matter of the statement"—that is, (1) to
ἀπόφανσις, and (2) to τὸ ὄν.]

about the structure of truth-and-falsehood, and about truth in general. This will clarify how synthesis constitutes the framework and the clue for understanding truth and falsehood conceptually. Simultaneously our discussion should find an explanation that had decisive significance (although in a rather implicit way) for the history of the problem of truth and of logic.

b) Truth and being. Interpretation of *Metaphysics* IX 10

To reach these goals we have chosen *Metaphysics* IX 10 as the basis of our interpretation of the problem of truth. This text is the basis from which we must develop the problem of truth historically, both backward [171] to Parmenides and forward to the Stoics, Boethius, the Middle Ages, Descartes, and modern philosophy right up to Hegel.

We limit ourselves to these guiding questions. The first is: To what degree is synthesis the condition of the possibility of falsehood and truth? In pursuing an explanation we will keep in mind our promise to explain how the question of truth in the Greeks is primarily oriented to knowledge as intuition, a fact that determines all succeeding epochs. Moreover, we will demonstrate more concretely than heretofore that the *problem of truth is inextricably linked with the question about being.*

Metaphysics IX 10 is the concluding chapter of a book (or treatise) that is one of the most difficult of the treatises gathered under this title of *Metaphysics.* This treatise Θ (or book IX) itself belongs together with the two that precede it, Z and H (books VII and VIII), in such a way that in IX 10, which deals with truth as such and with truth and falsehood, we reach as it were the highest pinnacle of the fundamental investigation of ontology. But this seems contradictory and impossible to traditional philosophy, where truth is a characteristic of judgment and thinking—ἐν διανοίᾳ, as even Aristotle himself says. Exactly for that reason truth is not, in the tradition, a determination of the being of beings—and least of all the "most proper" determination. This explains all the embarrassment, uncertainty, and wavering on the question of whether this chapter even belongs to book IX of the *Metaphysics.*

In his first book, *Studien zur Entstehungsgeschichte der Metaphysik des Aristoteles,*[28] Werner Jaeger drew the final consequences of the earlier work of Hermann Bonitz and others regarding the literary character of the treatise. He forcefully demonstrated that book IX is a collection of individual treatises, parts of lectures, and introductions all of which deal with ontology but which do not belong together in any obvious fashion as regards their content and method. Jaeger emphasized the coherence of Z, H, and Θ [books VII, VIII, and IX]. [172] He likewise

---

28. [Werner Jaeger, *Studien zur Entstehungsgeschichte der Metaphysik des Aristoteles* (Berlin: Weidmann, 1912).]

took Z, H, and Θ to be the most positive as regards ontology; but precisely for that reason, he found it doubtful that IX 10 belonged to book IX. Jaeger writes: "We can be brief in discussing this chapter because Schwegler and Christ have already noted that it does not fit into the context and the progression of the thinking" (ibid., p. 49). And in italics: "*We are not talking about a gradual increase in ontological content regarding the objects that are successively treated*" (p. 52). The series substance–possibility–actuality–truth does not in itself constitute an increasing development of being. That is to say, being as uncoveredness is not a more radical understanding of the concept of being [than the others], such that the explanation of uncoveredness would possibly elevate the ontological discussion to its apex.—"So the fact remains that this chapter is there without any connection" and as "an appendage" (p. 52).

But on the contrary, Hermann Bonitz (whom Jaeger refutes, but inadequately, on p. 52) maintains in his *Commentarius* (1849)[29] that on the basis of its content, this chapter belongs to the book as a whole. Bonitz says:

> Propterea non assentior Schweglero, qui hoc caput exterminari iubet e Metaphysica. (*Commentarius,* p. 409)

> Therefore I do not agree with Schwegler, who decrees that this chapter is to be excised from the *Metaphysics.*

The reasons Bonitz gives for why the chapter belongs here are admittedly just as inadequate as Jaeger's contrary reasons, because, as regards the issue, neither of them understands the problematic that runs through the chapter and indeed through all of book IX. But here as generally throughout his *Commentarius,* Bonitz shows that he has much better instincts than Jaeger. Moreover, in his idea that IX 10 belongs to book IX, Bonitz completely agrees with Thomas Aquinas; see *In XII libros Metaphysicorum,* ed. Parma, vol. 20, p. 549. Suarez included Thomas's notion in his *Disputationes Metaphysicae.*[30] These literary filiations might seem to be of little import, [173] but we note their fundamental impact when we observe that the metaphysics of Descartes, Spinoza, Leibniz, Wolff, Kant, and Hegel grow out of Suarez's *Disputationes Metaphysicae.* Through these reflections, the ontological

---

29. [Hermann Bonitz, *Aristotelis Metaphysica. Commentarius* (repr. Hildesheim: G. Olms, 1960; originally published in 1849, as vol. 2 of his *Aristotelis Metaphysica*).]

30. [*Opera omnia* (Paris, 1866), vol. 25, introduction, p. liii.] This *Disputationes Metaphysicae* in two volumes is not a running commentary on Aristotle's *Metaphysics* but an ontology in its own right, although of course closely connected with the outline of the inquiry in Thomas. [Heidegger provides the above reference in his lecture of Tuesday, 15 December (Moser, p. 370.23-25).]

problematic and conceptuality of Suarez himself, Thomas, and therefore Aristotle, entered the modern era. In the most recent edition of Aristotle's *Metaphysics* (Oxford, 1923), W. D. Ross says that chapter 10 "has little to do with the rest of book IX,"[31] the theme of which is potency and act. And Ross says it is hard to decide between Bonitz and Jaeger. That is generally characteristic for Ross's edition.

Jaeger himself, in his great book *Aristoteles. Grundlegung einer Geschichte seiner Entwicklung* (1923),[32] has fundamentally, if quietly, given up his early thesis and shifted to that of Bonitz, although without providing any reasons. Now the situation has gotten even more obscure, because at the same time Jaeger explicitly appeals to his own earlier book. Now he no longer talks about an appendage or a passage out of context. Rather, with Bonitz he says that Aristotle puts this chapter about truth "at a fitting place, namely between the end of the doctrine of potentiality and at the beginning of doctrine of the actuality of the supersensible, which was intended to follow immediately"; and "[this insertion, which likewise must have been made on the occasion of the introduction of Z-H-Θ,] clearly shows once again Aristotle's attempt to arrange a gradual ascent up the scale of being to immaterial essence."[33] Earlier he had brusquely dismissed the idea of a gradual increase in ontological content. The turn-about is explained by the fact that Jaeger is now attempting to reconstruct Aristotle's basic development. Why truth is a "level of being" and even of "act" is just as unclear here as it was in his earlier work, when he claimed there was no gradual increase in ontological content.

So Jaeger's clarification of the question has not gotten any further than did Bonitz or Thomas Aquinas. The uncertainty about whether this chapter can be assigned to the ensemble of the other chapters, and the obscurity of justification, [174] are merely an index of the fact that the problematic of *being* and its elementary connection with the phenomenon of *truth* are basically not understood. Before advancing vague philological conjectures about how these texts belong together on the basis of their content, it is requisite that we first understand phenomenally the inner connection between the interpretations of being and truth. That is, we must philosophically master the relevant content of these problematic texts. I have intentionally introduced these discussions so as to make it clear, first, that the understanding of

31. [Aristotle, *Metaphysica*, ed. W. D. Ross (Oxford: Clarendon Press, 1924; 2nd edition, 1963), vol. 2, p. 274.]
32. [Werner Jaeger, *Aristoteles. Grundlegung einer Geschichte seiner Entwicklung* (Berlin: Weidmann, 1923), pp. 211ff.; translated as *Aristotle: Fundamentals of the History of His Development*, trans. Richard Robinson (London: Oxford University Press, 1934; 2nd edition, 1948), pp. 204ff.]
33. [Ibid., p. 212 / tr. 205. The bracketed words appear in Jaeger's text.]

Greek ontology and the problem of truth depends on our ability to get inside this chapter; and second, to show the kind of basic questions that can be hidden behind seemingly insignificant questions like whether a chapter belongs to a book.

To facilitate our interpretation of the chapter, we preface it with a translation that has already grown up within that interpretation. I must emphasize that all the textual difficulties of the passage have not been eliminated from the following translation and interpretation. Here I cannot go into individual explanations of, or even possible disagreements with, other efforts at interpreting the text on the part of Bonitz, Schwegler, or Ross.[34]

*   *   *

Translation of the text[35]

I. The problem: Being and uncoveredness in synthetic beings.

1051a34–b2, 6: *Viewpoints for studying being. Uncoveredness.*

"Beings" and "non-beings" are understood {in their being} in one instance in terms of the forms of the categories, in another instance in terms of possibility {i.e., not-being-there as *not-yet*-being-there} and actuality {thereness *simpliciter*} of the being or non-being {i.e., its opposite} intended in those categories.

But when a being is understood in the most proper sense of all—in its uncoveredness and coveredness—{we now skip to b5}, the question arises: When is there, and when is there not, [175] that which we are calling "uncovered" and "covered-over"? We have to investigate what we mean by these terms. {Now back to the lines we skipped above.}

b2–5: *Preliminary determination: uncovering in λόγος.*

As regards [composite] beings themselves, their most proper being is grounded in their state of being-together and/or being-apart.

Therefore, one uncovers when one takes {"has" present} what-is-apart in its apartness, and what-is-together in its togetherness.

34. [Here the lecture of Monday, 14 December 1925, draws to a close, to be followed by Heidegger's lecture of Tuesday, 15 December, which opens with an 800-word summary (Moser, pp. 368–71) that is omitted in GA 21. At the end of his 14 December lecture (Moser, pp. 367–368), Heidegger notes that *Metaphysics* IX 10 is divided into two parts, "I. The exposition of the problem" and "II. The answer to the question about the being of beings insofar as it is interpreted in terms of truth or uncovering."]

35. In this translation, [writes Heidegger,] I place clarifications and paraphrases in wing-brackets. The translation does not aim at being linguistically polished but aims at precision in expressing the meaning that belongs to an issue-oriented discussion of its content. In that regard, compare and contrast *Aristoteles Metaphysik*, trans. Adolf Lasson (Jena: E. Diederichs, 1924).

On the other hand, one covers them over when, in taking them as this or that, one relates to them in a way opposite to how they are.

b6–9: *The foundation of uncoveredness in beings themselves.*

You are white not because we {by uncovering} take you in your presence-there as white. Rather, you are white because of your presence-there as white.

That is, only if our speech shows what-is-there do we uncover.

b9–13: *The being of composite beings as their uncoveredness. Being as synthesis and unity.*[36]

Now some beings are always-together and {in their being} have no possibility of being taken-apart; other beings are equally always-apart and have no possibility of being taken-together; and finally, there are other beings that admit of both of these opposed states {i.e., they can be-together as well as not-together}.

Granted the above, {we may deduce that} being means being-present-with {one being present with the other} and unity, and non-being means not-being-present-with {one not being present with the other} and multiplicity.

b13–17: *Two kinds of λόγος and their respective trueness and falseness.*

Now, in the cases where {and for the very reason that} beings can be together *as well as* apart, the same opinion about something as something and the same declarative indication of something as something may at one time uncover and at another time cover-over.

The [same] statement itself can uncover at one moment and misrepresent at another.[37] But in the case of beings that are incapable [176] of being other than what they are, the statement does not uncover at one moment and cover-over at another.

Instead, the same statement is always uncovering or misrepresenting.

II. The answer to the problem. Uncoveredness and the being of beings in its most proper form (1051b17–1052a11).

b17–22: *The being and uncoveredness of non-synthetic beings.*

Now regarding being and non-being, and being-uncovered and being-covered-over, what do these mean in the case the ἀσύνθετα—

---

36. [During his lecture (Moser, p. 373.16), Heidegger glossed this paragraph with: "Here Aristotle determines 'being'."]

37. It is so due to the thing being uncovered as well as to its kind of being, which is μεταβολή [change]. That is why the same statement can uncover at one moment and misrepresent at the next, even while remaining the same statement. The identical statement is true now but false later.

things that lack any synthesis {as well as the unification that comes from synthesis}?

There is nothing to be synthesized {in these cases}, and so we cannot speak of "being" [Sein] when something-is-together-with versus "non-being" [Nichtsein] when something-is-not-together-with—the way we can say, for instance, that being-together-with pertains to white in relation to a piece of wood, or incommensurability pertains to the diagonal of a square.

Similarly uncovering and covering-over occur differently in the present case [of the non-synthetic] than in the previous case [of the synthetic].

b22–33: *Uncoveredness and coveredness in non-synthetic beings. The crux of the chapter.*[38]

Just as "uncoveredness" is different {in ἀσύνθετα}, so too is being. In the case of non-synthetic beings, "uncoveredness" {"and covered-over-ness"—this phrase makes absolutely no sense in the text, and I am convinced it was not written by Aristotle but inserted by a scribe} entails just touching and addressing oneself to[39] the unhidden.

{Affirmation—attribution of something to something—is not the same as purely and simply addressing oneself to it.}

In these cases {of non-synthetics}, not-apprehending is the same as not-touching.

Being-deceived is not possible in uncovering a pure "whatness" in itself {Being-deceived does not pertain to "whatness." It can occur only if one's gaze falls} on something that is just incidentally present {with the "whatness"}.

It is the same with whatever is there in-and-of-itself without any synthesis. In that case, too, it is impossible to be deceived.

Moreover, all these things are just there in the manner of simple, constant already-there-ness, without any "not yet" or "a moment ago," for if that were ever the case, things that are simply there would necessarily come to be and pass away.

But being[40] does not come to be or pass away; because if it did, it would have to come to be from something {i.e., being would be derived from a being}.

---

38. [Heidegger provides this note in Moser (p. 375.20–21), and in the Weiss typescript (p. 92.26).]

39. [Addressing oneself to it in a simple "utterance." Aristotle contrasts κατάφασις ("affirmation," attributing something to something) and φάσις (from φημί, a simple "utterance"), which can be taken as equivalent to the Latin *dictio*. Heidegger translates the latter as *Ansprechen*, "straightforwardly addressing oneself to something" or "simply referring to it."]

40. [Here Heidegger uses *Sein* to translate Aristotle's τὸ ὄν.]

Clearly whatever is being [*Sein*] in and of itself and whatever is al-ways-already-there[41]—of such things there is no deception but only apprehension or non-apprehension. [177]

In this realm of {simple} beings, one looks for *what* something al-ways is and not whether it is this way or that {or is this kind of thing or that}.

b33–35: *Again, the being and uncoveredness of synthetic beings.*

Therefore, being [*Sein*] in the sense of uncoveredness, and non-be-ing [*Nichtsein*] in the sense of covered-over-ness are one—[each is] a unity of synthesis.

In the first case, the unity {of the being} is a matter of synthesis. If {one synthesizes} what is together, there is uncoveredness.

If one synthesizes what is not together, there is covering-over. {But such unifying can uncover only if the being of the entity is that way itself, namely, determined by σύνθεσις.}

1052a1–4: *The being of non-synthetic beings.*

In the second case, where that is not so {i.e., where the being of the entity is not determined by σύνθεσις}, uncoveredness does not entail the unity of synthesis {it is not a matter of διανοεῖν nor of the "as" that is proper to an act of determining}.

Instead, here uncoveredness is simply a matter of apprehending being.

There is no covered-over-ness at all, not even deception.

There is only not-apprehending {ἄγνοια}.

But that is not to be understood as a form of blindness, because in the arena of apprehension {acts of understanding and determining in thought}, what would correspond to blindness would be an utter in-ability to apprehend at all. {That is only one kind of ἄγνοια or not-apprehending, one that remains on the level of νοεῖν as διανοεῖν.}

a4–11: *Applying the above to possible kinds of statements. Essential and factual truths.*

It is also obvious that in the field of what cannot be otherwise, there is no possibility of being deceived about the "when" {of time}, if from the start one already understands and means the unchangeable.

For example, if we assume that by its very nature a triangle does not change, then we will not think that the sum of the angles is oc-casionally equal to the sum of two right angles and occasionally not, because that means the triangle would have to change. Such a state-ment could only mean that a thing can be this way for one person but not for another.

41. [Aristotle: εἶναί τι καὶ ἐνέργειαι.]

For example, no even number is a prime number. Some numbers are prime numbers, and some are not.

But there is no possibility of stating anything similar about what makes a number be only one {in the sense of being always identical to what it is}.

One cannot maintain that some numbers admit of a certain whatness and others do not [178] {in fact there is no "some"}.

Rather, one will either directly uncover or cover-over insofar as the being does not change but always comports itself the way it is.[42]

*   *   *

Interpretation of the text.

The preceding translation has already introduced some divisions into this passage. In order to facilitate an overview of the whole, let us, prior to interpreting the text, briefly lay out the divisions according to their content.

The chapter falls into two major divisions:

I. 1051a34-b17

The first division provides an exposition of the problem: getting the proper being of beings from an interpretation of uncoveredness, and doing so while also invoking and taking up the previous interpretation of being as οὐσία (presence) and δύναμις-ἐνέργεια (not-thereness and pure and simple thereness).

II. 1051b17-1052a11

The second division provides the answer: it determines the kind of uncoveredness of beings within those two modes of being—οὐσία and ἐνέργεια—and consequently determines the most proper being of beings. Likewise there is the application of this to "truths" in the sense of uncovering statements about always-existing beings.

We will now look at some particular points.

Outline of the text
  I. **The problem: Being and uncoveredness (1051a34-b17).**
    1051a34-b2, 6:
      Possible viewpoints in studying being, the most proper of
      which deals with uncoveredness.
    b2-5:
      In a parenthetical sentence, uncoveredness is determined in
      a preliminary way in terms of the uncovering performed by
      λόγος.

---

42. [Here Heidegger draws to a close his lecture of Tuesday, 15 December 1925, to be followed by his lecture on Thursday, 17 December.]

b6–9:
> The essential foundation of uncovering in beings themselves:
> here uncovering is what it properly is.

b9–13:
> The structure of beings themselves is understood in terms of
> uncoveredness. Being: synthesis and unity.

b13–17:
> This text provides a sharper characterization of the possible
> trueness and falseness of λόγος. Statements are divided into
> (a) those that can be true as well as false (sometimes they
> are one way, sometimes the other); and (b) those that are ei-
> ther true or false (always one or the other).

II. **The answer: Uncoveredness and the being of beings in its
most proper form (1051b17–1052a11).**
> Up to this point, being and uncoveredness have been consid-
> ered with regard to those beings whose being is determined by
> "synthesis" and "unity." Now, however: [179]

b17–22:
> The question of the being and uncoveredness of things that
> cannot be understood, in themselves, by way of a synthesis
> of something with something else.

b22–33:
> First of all, determining the possible uncoveredness of [non-
> synthetic] being. Here the opposite of uncoveredness is not
> coveredness, but lack of access for direct apprehension.

b33–35:
> Then again, the being and uncoveredness of beings determined
> by synthesis: a further characterization (cf. 1051b9–13, above).

a1–4:
> The being of things that are not determined by synthesis.

a4–11:
> Applying the above to possible kinds of statement. Essential
> truth and factual truth.[43]

Our thematic interpretation of this chapter in connection with the
preceding chapters and books [of the *Metaphysics*] must show (a) how
being first attains its full and proper determination by being characterized in terms of the ἀληθές, and (b) to what extent the pinnacle of
the investigation of being is thereby reached, such that this chapter
constitutes the necessary conclusion about that issue.

If this concluding clarification of being is also to be the most proper
one, then it must also take for its theme the being [*Seiende*] that is con-

---

43. This is important for the critique of historicity.

stitutive for all beings in their being. This being [*Seiende*] that, in every being, *is* the being [*Seiende*], or is its being [*Sein*] (this oscillation of terms is characteristic)—this being [*Seiendes*] that makes every being be what it is, is the *essence,* the *what,* from which everything that is has its origin. That which from the outset always already is in every being that is there (and which therefore is there in an entirely special way) must be investigated as and in terms of being [*Sein*], if being is to be understood in its most proper sense. The question about being must be finally directed to essence and its being. In effect, it is the question about the being of beings.

How are we to determine the being of essences (εἴδη) [180] using the ἀληθές as our guiding thread? That entails the prior question: In general how, on the basis of the ἀληθές, are beings to be understood in terms of their being?

With this prior and introductory question, Aristotle first focuses on the ἀληθές of the λόγος, and his answer is: Being means "synthesis" and the unity (of this synthesis). Non-being means non-synthesis and multiplicity. Specifically, this is the character of the being of those beings that always are what and how they are, the ἀδύνατα ἀλλώς ἔχειν— those which, by the very meaning of their being, cannot be otherwise.

Then against the background of the ἀεὶ ὄν, Aristotle determines the ἐνδεχόμενον ἀλλώς—that which sometimes is composed and sometimes not, that which sometimes has the unity of synthesis, and sometimes the multiplicity of the not-composed.

This understanding of things with an eye to the ἀεὶ ὄντα is adequate to the task insofar as essence itself is also an ἀεὶ ὄν. At the same time, however, this characteristic of being is inadequate from the viewpoint of the ἀληθές, because essence is something that lacks any synthesis. In principle, therefore, its being cannot be understood by way of synthesis and its unity.

How then are we to conduct an interpretation on the basis of the ἀληθές? If a being in and of itself cannot possibly be synthetic (i.e., synthetically unified), then the corresponding act of uncovering that points out the being, likewise cannot be synthetic. In order to understand, on the basis of the ἀληθές, a being that excludes all synthesis, we first have to establish what can be said about its state of ἀληθές. The uncovering of, the unhiddenness of a being that in and of itself is not composed offers no possibility of seeing anything else in the being other than that being's own self. Such uncovering offers no possibility of focusing on something else in the being, or of showing the being in terms of something else. The being is present simply in and of itself and "as" itself.

With regard to such a being, the only possible kind of uncovering is θιγεῖν and φάναι, the act of simply touching it and addressing oneself to it. Aristotle chooses these words to express the pure and simple *having* of something in itself (neither derived from nor veering off toward some other thing). That which we encounter in such a having is pre-eminently "near" with a nearness that [181] contains no distance. The nearness contains only the thing we meet in its own self and nothing else; in a radical sense there is nothing else but it, purely in itself.

Aristotle stays with the kind of access and uncovering that characterizes the act of touching, and he uses it to clarify the unique way in which the ἀσύνθετα are encountered. In doing so, of course, he does not at all mean that uncovering is an act of actual touching, as is shown by the word that follows, φάναι, which has the sense of δηλοῦν, showing. At 1052a1 Aristotle paraphrases it as νοεῖν, the act of intellectual apprehension. Correspondingly, 1051b25 paraphrases μὴ θιγγάνειν [not touching it] as ἀγνοεῖν [not knowing it]. And at 1052a2, the opposite of [intellectual] apprehension is ἄγνοια [not knowing], as contrasted with νοητικόν [knowable] at a3.

In *De anima* II 2, we find the words ἀφή . . . αἴσθησις, "touch" as one form of "sense perception."[44] Moreover, at *De anima* II 424a1, we read that τὸ γὰρ αἰσθάνεσθαι πάσχειν τι ἐστίν ["Sense perception is some kind of receptivity."] But here in *Metaphysics* V, νοεῖν, which is pure ἐνέργεια, is also called a πάσχειν.

Aristotle occasionally designates νοεῖν as an αἴσθησις, even though the senses play no role in it. The decisive point is that whatever is uncovered in αἴσθησις is had *directly* in itself. For that, Aristotle uses the flexible expression θιγγάνων [touching] for the ways [in which the] intellect functions. At *Metaphysics* XII 7, 1072b21 we find θιγγάνων καὶ νοῶν [touching and knowing].[45]

If we want to determine the being of these beings by using uncovering as our clue, we can do so only by looking at how these beings are manifested of and by themselves in this uncovering which opens up entirely the beings it encounters. Our gaze is now directed exclusively to the thing to be understood, and not to any other thing that might make the determination possible. Rather, the gaze itself is pure uncovering in such a way that not only does it require no determining [of its

---

44. [GA 21 (p. 181.13) misreads "B 2" as "B 11," and accents ἀφή incorrectly. The Greek text is found at 413b5: "The primary kind of perception, common to all [animals], is touch."]

45. At *Metaphysics* XII 7, 1072b13, Aristotle also uses this expression "touch" for the way intellect functions in another very important context, a clarification that Hegel put at the end of his *Encyclopaedia* in order to document in a certain way that he was saying nothing different from what Aristotle says in that text. [See G. W. F. Hegel, *Enzyklopädie der philosophischen Wissenschaften im Grundrisse (1830)*, ed. Friedhelm Nicolin and Otto Pöggeler (Hamburg: Felix Meiner), p. 463.]

object], [182] but it also cannot require one, because viewing things in *that* way would already be tantamount to blocking our access. And at 1052a1, where Aristotle, using the clue of θιγεῖν and simple νοεῖν, poses the question about being, he gives the same answer as he does to the question about the kinds of an uncovering access to these beings. So the answer to the question about truth (uncovering) stands in for the answer to the question about being—all of this in a discussion that asks about being in the proper sense. Roughly put: Being is determined "by means of" thinking, both of them posited as identical.

This formulation, as it might be understood in modern philosophy, is certainly inadequate, but it is nonetheless noteworthy that it was precisely Schwegler who wanted to throw this whole chapter out of the *Metaphysics*, the very Schwegler, who as a Hegelian should have had some understanding for the fact that in a certain sense Aristotle here identifies thinking and being.

Therefore, we have now found a mode of uncovering that distances itself from the others, insofar as this truth has no possible opposite in the sense of falsehood. Or more exactly, it is an uncovering for which there is no covering-over.

c) The three conditions for the possibility of a statement being false, taken in their interconnection

But what have we gained for the question that now concerns us exclusively: To what extent is σύνθεσις the condition of the possibility of falsehood? What help have we gotten from discussing a kind of truth that allows no falsehood as its opposite? With that kind of an issue, haven't we strayed from the ground of our topic? No, not at all. In fact, only now do we have the basis for deciding the question. Now we can take away from the uncovering that allows no covering-over (falsehood) [183] all that pertains to the possibility of falsehood to the degree that it does.

The uncovering of something that is not a composite in and of itself has no covering-over as its opposite. As Aristotle says: Being deceived is not possible. There can only be a not-apprehending (ἀγνοεῖν), a not-acceding, a lack of access to the being in question. But this means first of all that being deceived entails some access to the being, that is, the tendency and intention to understand and possess it. In order to be deceived, I must in general live in the comportment of uncovering. In a certain sense, I must already have the subject matter if I am to make a mistake about it. The first condition of the possibility of deception is the prior having of something.

I cannot be deceived when it comes to uncovering those "simple" beings which are always there, because here the only possible uncovering is a direct having of those beings. By the very nature of the case, the uncovering comportment toward beings that is required if I am to be deceived is the uncovering and having of the being itself. But why cannot covering-over and falsehood get the better of this having of the being? As will be shown later, it is quite possible for me to live in an act of uncovering and to have pointed out a being, to know about that very being on the basis of having pointed it out—it is possible to live in the knowledge about and truth of the thing and yet be able to fall victim to deception about the very being that I intend in the act of truth (i.e., uncovering).

So why isn't that possible in the case under discussion?

The answer is: πᾶσαι εἰσὶν ἐνεργείᾳ—δυνάμει [all these are either in ἐνέργεια—or in δύναμις]. These simple beings, the ultimate beings on the basis of which all beings are determined, are simply and directly present and never "not-yet-present" and thus never not-present. Their being excludes every possibility of non-presence regarding what and how they are. These beings are never not-present just as they are. [184]

No deception is possible because there is no possibility of dissembling. How so? For a being to be disguised, and for the disguising to result in a mistake (a wrong understanding of the being in question), the being must be intended at some point. There must be a tendency to uncover, a specific tendency directed toward the being. But a being can be disguised only insofar as something can be synthesized with the being *as* something. Given that "something," the being can be seen and determined-as, and deception means alleging and pretending that something *is* something. But nothing can be synthesized with a simple being because, as simple, the being stands in no need of synthesis with anything. In fact, here we have an absolute exclusion of the possibility of synthesis.

The being lacks not only everything that could be put in front of it to help pass off the disguised being as something that it is not, i.e., to dissemble it. What's more, this simple being excludes the very possibility of synthesis with something else. Because it is completely lacking in synthesis, the being cannot be taken as something else. Rather, when the being is understood, it itself is present there. If you intend this simple being as itself from the start, and then try to determine it on the basis of something else, you have already misunderstood the thing you intended. If you try to determine a simple being in terms of what it is not, at the very least you cover it over it in what it is.

Let's take some examples from the field of sense perception, wherein Aristotle recognizes an analogy with direct [intellectual] perception—for example, the direct seeing of qualities such as colors. Now if I were to lay out, in the most extravagant dialectic that you can imagine, the relations that colors happen to have among themselves, that would never get me to an understanding of color. So, for example, the relations and differences of all colors except red would never result in an understanding of red. I understand red only when I [185] dispose myself to see it, and all the relations that red might have to other colors are of no help. Red is the kind of being that is understood only insofar as it is taken purely in itself. It's the same with [modes of being such as] essence, movement, time, and the like. For these reasons, the opposite of understanding a simple being is not-apprehending. Not-apprehending can never be the same as covering something over in an act of taking-something-*for* and supposing it to be this or that, because that would always already entail already *having* the thing.

But this not-apprehending does not mean having no apprehension at all. Ἄγνοια does not mean simply the non-presence of νοῦς as such. Rather, this ἄγνοια is founded on the predominance of νοεῖν *qua* διανοεῖν. It is founded on the disposition to have and grasp the apprehended as apprehended only by grasping it as taken apart—διά—[i.e., taking] something in terms of something else, as defined in the proposition: Something *is* only when it is determined. Something appears only when λέγειν functions as διαλέγεσθαι, and not just as φάναι.

If dissembling and covering-over are to be possible at all, the being itself must have an ontological structure such that, on the basis of its being [*Sein*] and as the being [*Seiende*] that it is, the thing offers the possibility of synthesis, indeed demands synthesis with another being. That is, the thing must be what it is only within the unity of such a synthesis.

When the being of a being consists in such a synthesis, there is a twofold possibility of dissemblance:

1. The being can be synthesized with another being in such a way that it is always synthesized with one specific thing—and always not synthesized with another.[46] The act of showing something by synthesizing it with something with which it is always not-synthesized must necessarily cover-over, because in an act of determinate indication it shows something as something when the thing is never able to be that way. In this instance, dissemblance is necessarily based on a possible synthesis, but one that entails the impossibility of composing that which is always not-composed. [186]

   The impossibility of synthesizing what is always divided must be sharply distinguished from what we mentioned earlier: the absolute exclusion of any synthesis at all within a simple being. In the present case there certainly is the possibility of synthesis. It is just

46. [In Moser (p. 389), Heidegger offers the example of the incommensurability of the diagonal and the side of a square.]

that this specific synthesis is not possible. In the case of a simple
being the very possibility of synthesizing is excluded, along with
this specific synthesis.

2. In the case of a being that is determined by synthesis with another,
   the being can be synthesized with another being that can attach to
   it but need not always do so. This is a being that can be this way or
   that, and thus different from the way it now is. When it comes to
   such a being that can be different from the way it is now, covering-
   over is based either in the being itself or in the covering-over comportment (ontically or delotically).
   (a) A statement about such a being can be false/covering-over as
       a result of a change in the subject matter of the statement.
       This is an *ontic* covering-over. The statement itself can remain
       the same as regards its content and yet cover-over [because
       the thing has changed]. That is, while remaining the state-
       ment it is, it can become false.
   (b) But the statement can also cover-over by speaking about a
       being in terms of what *can* attach to the being but happens not
       to be synthesized with it "at the moment" of the statement.
       This is a *delotic* covering over.[47, 48]

*   *   *

Now it has become clear how σύνθεσις is the condition of the possibility
of falsehood or covering-over. In the one case, as the [ontic] togetherness of something with something; and in the other case, as an act of
showing which, along with this to-be-indicated subject matter, co-sees
something that can be synthesized with this subject matter.

This synthetic showing is a showing on the basis of, and is performed within, a focus on something else. The act of showing something by focusing on something else that has the feature of "can be
together-with," is what we have already characterized as the determining act of speaking about [187] something as something—λόγος
as a statement that determines something. This brings to light an inner
connection between the ontological structure of synthesis and of the

47. ["Delotic" translates Heidegger's neologism *delotisch*, which is related to the
Greek δηλοῦν, "to show."]

48. [Here the lecture of Thursday, 17 December 1925, draws to a close, to be
followed by Heidegger's lecture on Friday, 18 December. At the very end of the 17
December lecture, Heidegger said: "[Tomorrow] we will lay out two [more] conditions of the possibility of falsehood and then bring them together with the first
one. Then we will ask about the unitary root of these three conditions of the possibility. With that, we will actually encounter the possibility of truth and the understanding of being" (Moser, p. 390.15-22).]

as-structure, which we earlier characterized as the basic hermeneutical structure.

We may now summarize the three structural conditions of falsehood.

1. The orientation to the uncovering of things—the prior intending and having of the subject matter.
2. Within this basic comportment of uncovering—in fact, dominated and guided by it—there is the showing of the subject matter in terms of something else. Only on the basis of this structure is there any possibility of passing something off as something *else*.
3. At the same time, such showing-something-as-something-*else* is based on the possibility of synthesizing something with something.

Before going on with our discussion, let's take some examples of deception and the covering-over of beings. Say I am walking in a dark woods and see something coming toward me through the fir trees. "It's a deer," I say. The statement need not be explicit. As I get nearer to it, I see it's just a bush that I'm approaching. In understanding, addressing, and being concerned with this thing, I have acted as one who covers-over: the unexpressed statement shows the being as something other than it is.

We can point out how the three conditions are present in this deception:

1. It is necessary that beforehand I already have something given to me, something coming toward me. If something did not already encounter me from the outset, there would be no occasion to regard it *as* . . . Always already there is *a priori* disclosure of world.
2. It is also necessary that, as I approach the thing, I take it *as something*. In other words, in the field of everyday experience, I don't just stand there, as it were, in the woods and have something simply and immediately in front of me. A situation like that is pure fiction. Rather, in an unexpressed way, I encounter something that I already understand, something that is already articulated *as something* and, as such, is expected and accepted in my way of dealing with the world. [188] Only because I let whatever encounters me encounter me *on the basis of* the act of envisioning something (say, a deer), can that thing appear as a deer.
3. And the encountering-being can show itself to my act of envisioning "as this thing" and "in this way" only because, along with the encountering-being and the other things present in this world (particularly in the lived world of "forest"), something like "a deer" can indeed be present among the trees. This

is so insofar as the encountering-being entails the general possibility of synthesis, a possibility which, with regard to concrete deception, is always oriented objectively, i.e., includes within itself a range of indications. To take the above example, I would not, in fact, think that what was approaching me was the Shah of Iran, even though something like that is intrinsically possible. The Shah is a being that *could* appear among the trees in a German forest at night, whereas there is not a chance that I would see anything like the cubed root of sixty-nine coming toward me.

These three conditions of the possibility of falsehood are obviously interconnected. The decisive question is: How? If we find the answer, then we have to position our investigation to be able to clarify the origin of falsehood more radically in terms of the unified root of the conditions of the possibility of falsehood. What is required for that? Answer: an understanding of the three conditions as a unity in their common root; a clearer exposition of the connection of the three conditions; and likewise a concept of that which makes the connection fundamentally possible.

Regarding the connection itself, it is clear that the second condition is founded on the third. Envisioning a "that as which" is possible only when there is a possible "other." But the second condition is founded equally on the first. The envisioning of a "that as which" is performed within and for a prior act of already having something, something that should be able to stand in the "as." Therefore, the third condition will also be connected with the first.

To be sure, this is only a formalistic argument; empty deductions like this, made with an acumen that is finally blind, [189] only give the illusion that they mean something when in fact they get us basically nowhere. It may be indisputable that the second condition is founded on the third and on the first, and therefore that the first is connected with the third. But is the founding of the second condition on the third the same as the founding of the second on the first? Is the connectedness of the first and the third the same as a founding? Or does "founding" mean something else—and if so, what? We want an understanding that comes from seeing for ourselves, not formal deductions from empty propositions! We are asking phenomenologically, and not syllogistically, whether (a) the second condition is connected with the first and (b) the third is connected with the first, and what that means.

(a) The connection between the second and first conditions:

The envisioning of an other is carried out within the tendency to intend and uncover something that is supposed to be determined via the envisioning of an other—this other that appears to me: a deer. The revelatory tendency of an act of showing already has in view, from the outset, the subject matter of the determination; indeed, this persists throughout. But this act of persisting-in-having-present the about-which is, of itself, not yet an act of determining. Rather, it is a simple and direct having, and in a certain sense a θιγεῖν. For in the first place, all simple beings are, as such, accessible in a θιγεῖν; but θιγεῖν itself is a mode of access not just to simple beings, but to anything that can be had in the manner of a simple being, namely, as something whose determinations have not yet been made explicit. From the beginning, the about-which is the focus of attention precisely in the mode of not yet having its determinations made explicit—and as such, it is held onto as the basis upon which the act of having-by-determining becomes explicit.

Thus the that-about-which appears as something that encounters me within a persisting θιγεῖν, as something that is already uncovered from the outset, as something approaching in the woods. Envisioning an "as" operates within an uncovering and a holding-uncovered that already dominates such envisioning. The second condition of falsehood operates within the first.

(b) What may we say about the third condition, the ontological structure of the composite and its relation to the first condition? The ontological structure of being-composed does not pertain to beings that encounter us in a θιγεῖν, and yet at the same time, [190] Aristotle understands it as ἕν. What does ἕν mean here? It is the unity of something present *and* of something present-together-with-it. Compositeness is the state of being-together-with, which is possible only within the unity of a more fundamental, underlying presence. The differentiation between what is present and that as-which we encounter it (a deer) is such only within the unity of a presence that encompasses and precedes the differentiation and that lets the present being appear as differentiated. The ἕν indicates a prior presence within which alone presence-together-with is possible as a mode of presence. The third condition of falsehood is therefore founded on an original phenomenon, a primary presence.

Now, do these two phenomena[49]—the one to which the second condition is to be traced (prior uncoveredness) and the one to which the third condition goes back (prior presence)—themselves have a primary connection? The prior presence of a simple being, of the *being* of whatever encounters us, is related to that thing's prior *disclosedness*, which sustains the act of envisioning. Aristotle says: being "is" uncoveredness. He lets "being" be substituted for the primary uncoveredness found in θιγεῖν. At b24, he determines the ἀληθές of a simple being via θιγεῖν,

---

49. [Here I correct GA 21 (p. 190.13) in light of the Moser transcript (p. 403.20–23) and the Weiss typescript (p. 101).]

and at 1052a1, where he asks about the being of simple beings, Aristotle again has recourse to direct νοεῖν—θιγεῖν. Thus uncoveredness takes over answering the question about being. One of the characteristics of the being of beings, and especially of the being of the most proper beings, the simple, is determined by means of uncoveredness.

Thus, the second and the third conditions of the possibility of falsehood are both founded on the unified togetherness of being and uncoveredness. How is this togetherness itself to be understood? What must being itself mean, and how does that let us understand uncoveredness as a characteristic of being, indeed as the most proper characteristic? And does it explain why beings must finally be interpreted, as regards their being, in terms of uncoveredness? [191]

---

§14. The presupposition for Aristotle's interpretation of truth as the authentic determination of being

If we have understood what presupposition must be made, and what meaning of being must be presumed, so that uncoveredness or truth can signify a mode of being, then we have also understood the unifying bond to which the conditions of possibility of falsehood lead back. Aristotle did not ask why uncoveredness or truth is and can be the determination of being—in fact, the most proper determination. He simply enacted this determination. But if we want to understand the issue, if we want to interpret and appropriate it in an authentically philosophical manner, we have to get behind Aristotle's enactment and explain it in terms of the unexpressed presuppositions—the unexpressed, implicit understanding of being—in Aristotle and the Greeks. Whenever thinkers like Aristotle and Plato uttered the proposition (or at least operated within the interpretation) that *truth equals being* or is the most authentic mode of being, we may safely assume that, in doing so, what they saw and had in mind was a certain phenomenal context. The only question is whether this connection was explicit for them and whether they were methodically conscious of the hidden presuppositions that this connection entails.

We ask: What does *being* mean such that *truth* can be understood *as a characteristic of being?* As we have pointed out, Aristotle in *Metaphysics* IX 10 introduced the idea that the being of a synthetic being means presence-unto: the presence-together of something with something in the *unity* of a present being. This unity, this primary presence that precedes and grounds presence-together, must be understood as *presence, presenting* [Anwesenheit, Präsenz]. Why? If being means and (mostly implicitly) is understood as [192] presenting or presence, then the genuine and corresponding act of relating to beings as beings is one that, *qua* relating, also has a pres-ential character. But an act of relating is pres-ential not insofar as it is merely present the way a mental event is, of which (it is commonly held) I am immediately aware. Likewise it is not presentative insofar as the presentative character of an act of relating is basically no different from the presentative character of a thing. Rather, the act of relating to something must have its presentative character *as* an act of relating. An act of relating, taken as such, is presentative insofar it means "rendering present" or, as we say in German, *Gegenwärtigen:* "making-something-present." By making-present, the act of relating lets a present thing encounter us.

Corresponding to the act of making-present or rendering present there is the presence of the thing that underlies and fulfills the making-present, the thing that gets uncovered and disclosed in the very act of making-present. In the case of deception, as we have said, the supporting structure and primary condition of the deception is the act of constantly letting the already-given encounter me. This constant letting-something-encounter-me is nothing but the simple and direct making-present of something in its immediate presence, specifically something that is already there prior to its representation. This act of making-present *in which I constantly live*—and making-present specifically in the mode of awaiting—offers the possibility that something can encounter me; that is, it offers the possibility that a present being is uncovered and can be present.

"Making-present" means the very same as "letting a present being encounter us in a now-moment [*Gegenwart*]." What gets disclosed in the act of making-present is thereby understood as something we encounter in a now-moment, something that, in this now-moment, can appear in its presence. But the presence of the thing we encounter need not be already and completely present-now, that is, it need not be completely uncovered. The only thing that is completely present is something that we encounter in an act of pure making-present, therefore something that, in itself and in its presence, can offer nothing except that as which it is present. *Pure* making-present or presenting is of such a nature that, [193] in it there is nothing about the thing-to-be-uncovered that is not now-present. The thing to be uncovered is brought into pure, direct nearness. In other words, the *pure* uncoveredness of beings—as Aristotle understood it with regard to simple beings—means nothing other than the pure unchanged and unchangeable presence-now [*Gegenwart*] of what is present. Uncoveredness—in this case, pure presence-now—is as such the highest mode of presence. But presence is the fundamental determination of being. Therefore, uncoveredness—which, as presence-now, is the highest mode of presence—is a mode of being: it is present presence [*anwesende Anwesenheit*] itself.

So, what is procured in this making-present (that is, in the uncovering of something) is the uncoveredness or presence-now of something present; and presence is what characterizes beings themselves insofar as they are. In other words, being is understood as presence, and presence and presence-now are understood as presenting. To that extent, being can and must be determined, via truth, as presence, such that presence-now is the highest form of presence.

Plato already characterizes being as presence-now. And the word οὐσία (which gets peddled around absurdly in the history of philosophy as "substance") means nothing other than "presence" in a sense that we still have to specify. But in all this it is necessary to emphasize that, yes, the Greeks (Plato and Aristotle) do determine being as οὐσία, but they were very far from understanding what is really entailed in defining being as presence and as presence-now. Presence-now is *a characteristic of time.* To understand being as presence on the basis of presence-now means to understand being in terms of time.

The Greeks had no suspicion of this unfathomable problematic, which opens up before us once we have seen this connection [between being and time]. This connection also lets us explain for the first time the difference between presence and presence-now, as well as between presence-now and its modes. At the same time [194] it lets us understand why it is possible, especially in a preliminary state of the interpretation of being, to identity the two of them [viz., being and time]. Once we have understood the internal coherence of understanding being in terms of time, we will have a light, as it were, to shine back over the history of the problem of being (and the history of philosophy in general) so that finally it acquires some sense.

In that process we come to see that Kant is the only philosopher who even suspected that the understanding of being and its characteristics is connected with time. But his very conception of time blocked him from achieving a fundamental understanding of the problem— that is, blocked him from asking the question at all. In his *Critique of Pure Reason,* Kant did not attain the appropriate basis for synthesizing the schematism of the concepts of the understanding (where time is the really fundamental concept) with the basic function of consciousness, transcendental apperception. If this inner connection had opened up to him, he certainly would have taken an essential step beyond the whole of ontology—but on an inadequate basis, to be sure.

To take this step you need an understanding of time that breaks radically with the traditional understanding. Kant, however, held firm to the traditional concept of time. Not only that, but from the outset and throughout his entire problematic, he oriented the concept of time to knowledge and the question about the possibility of knowledge, viz. intuition. Nonetheless, his discussion of time—and above all the problem of the schematism, which Kant himself calls wholly obscure—remains something quite positive, whose fundamental significance has not been properly exploited even to this day.

The supposedly new concept of time that Bergson put forth by way of criticism of Kant is a complete misunderstanding of the positive element present in Kant.

Our task now is the following: Using our insight into the inner connection between truth—or uncoveredness as presence-now—and being as presence, we have to clarify [195] the degree to which the three conditions of the possibility of falsehood are connected among themselves, so that we can then show that there is falsehood only insofar as there is temporality.[50]

50. [Here (Moser, p. 410), at the end of part I of the course, Heidegger ends his lecture of Friday, 18 December 1925, and a three-week Christmas break begins. He opens the new year and part II of the course with his lecture of Monday, 11 January 1926.]

Part II

PART II

The radicalized question: What is truth?
(A retrieval of the analysis of falsehood
in terms of its ur-temporality)

§15. The idea of a phenomenological chronology

The conclusion that we have drawn is also an enigma.[1] In other words, the conclusion of the preceding analyses has brought us, intentionally and radically, to the central problematic of philosophy. The conclusion of the investigation up to this point is not an end but a beginning.

So what does it mean that we now take the preceding investigation and the phenomena we have articulated—statement, truth, falsehood, synthesis—and relate them all as a unity back to this phenomenal context of time? If this kind of interpreting and philosophically understanding such a trivial phenomenon as the statement really is philosophical, and if we assert it to be such, then can we appeal (if it makes any sense at all) to Kant? In his *Reflexionen,* Kant says: "The business of the philosopher is not to give out rules but to dismember the secret judgments of common sense." "The secret judgments of common sense"—that means those unspoken, unknown, and un-un-derstood comportments that underlie all the daily comportments of existence. It is the business of the philosopher to bring these secret (hidden) judgments of common sense to light, and to do so in a way that dismembers them.

For Kant, dismembering, ana-lysing, means two things. In the first place he understands analysis in a very broad, formal sense where it simply means: to separate an already given thing into its [198] elements, to divide a particular concrete concept into the component parts that go to make it up. But "analysis" and "analytic" also have a

---

1. [Heidegger opened his lecture of Monday, 11 January 1926, with a 1,450-word summary (Moser, pp. 411-417) which is omitted in GA 21.]

broader, fundamental philosophical meaning for Kant: to lead something back to its "birthplace." In that case "analytic" means the same as bringing to light the genesis of the proper sense of a phenomenon, pressing forward to the final conditions of the possibility of something already given.

But such an analytic presupposes some directives about the horizon within which the analysis is to move, so to speak, in order to find the genetic conditions of a phenomenon and of its possibility. Our thesis is that truth, being, and consequently falsehood, synthesis, and statement are, in some kind of (for the time being) obscure sense, connected with the phenomenon of time; and this already delineates the horizon for our philosophical analytic of propositions. Only an investigation that is adequate to such a philosophical analytic can be considered to be authentically philosophical.

Traditionally we put our minds at ease regarding logic by saying that a proposition is something simple and ultimate; it is synthesis and division. Finally everyone understands that thesis. But on the other hand no one understands how there could be any further questions at all regarding a determination like this and a phenomenon like the statement. The point is not just to give you closer contact with a concrete understanding of statement and truth, the phenomena that are our topic. It is much more essential for your philosophical studies and reflection for you to see that the real problem of philosophy is the "obvious"—"the secret judgments of common sense." And perhaps you notice how little of philosophy, as it has been practiced up to now, is a matter of philosophical reasoning—only in a few circles and to a limited extent—and how it is dominated much more by common sense. Philosophy can make good its claim to being a science (in fact the basic science) only if we drive common sense out of philosophical reasoning. [199]

Let us now take the dogmatic conclusion that we first arrived at and pose it once again in three theses:

1. Being means presence.
2. Truth means the now-present.
3. Presence and presence-now, as characteristics of presenting [*Präsenz*] are modes of time.[2]

The analysis of the proposition is now oriented toward time. In other words, our project will be to clarify the characteristics of time with reference to the phenomena we have been discussing—truth, falsehood, synthesis, and statement in its three different meanings. The characteristics whereby these phenomena are temporal, we call their ur-temporal

2. [Compare with the four theses at GA 21, p. 205.15–17.]

characteristics. I am intentionally employing this strange usage—
ur-temporal—because the word "temporal" [*zeitlich*] has been mostly
claimed by natural, pre-philosophical speaking where it simply means
that something runs its course, or happens, or takes place *in* time. However, when I say that a phenomenon is ur-temporal I do not mean that
this phenomenon is a process or a movement, much less that it happens
in time. Therefore, "temporal" [*zeitlich*] in the sense of running its course
in time, is not the same as "ur-temporal" [*temporale*], which means first
and foremost that something is "essentially characterized by time."

When we inquire into just how far certain phenomena are essentially characterized by time, we take as our theme their ur-temporal
structure—in a word, their ur-temporality [*Temporalität*]. The project of
investigating the ur-temporality of phenomena is one that relates the
phenomena to these very ur-temporal determinations and consequently
(if it is a philosophical investigation) relates them to [ur-]time as such.
This fundamental philosophical examination that has [ur-]time for its
subject matter we call a chronology, indeed a *phenomenological chronology*.

Natural-scientific awareness also uses the word "chronology," specifically for a discipline within history's auxiliary sciences, one that
deals with things like measuring time in history or issues dealing with
calendars, dating, and so forth. [200] The adjective "phenomenological" attached to "chronology" is meant to indicate that this "*logos*-of-
time," this study of [ur-]time, has a philosophical focus and above all
has nothing to do with the practice or theory of measuring time. The
project of a phenomenological chronology is to study the ur-temporal
determinedness of phenomena—that is, their ur-temporality—and
consequently to study [ur-]time itself.

Let us now place our analysis of the statement within the context of
tasks associated with such a chronology. At the moment we need not
further explain the idea of this chronology as one of the fundamental
areas of research in philosophical science. Least of all need we try to
relate it to the other philosophical disciplines, such as we know them,
so as to project a system of these disciplines with reference to this
chronology. We leave all that aside precisely because it could turn out
that this chronology will shake the traditional disciplines to their very
roots, and so it would have been a senseless exercise to classify things
in the traditional sense. We are interested only in the task that pertains to this chronology, quite apart from the role the other disciplines
may have in the system of philosophy.

It's true that no one until now has staked out the field of this investigation into chronology. What's more, the very idea of such an investigation—and thus of its field—has not even been opened up. The
clearest indication of that is the uncertainty that characterizes the
philosophical employment of the concepts and determinations of time.

Correlated with that is the heavy-handed, unsophisticated way people usually speak of time and of timelessness versus temporality, as if these were the simplest things in the world. As I indicated earlier, the only one who started to grope around in this darkness, but without managing to see the fundamental significance of his attempt, was Kant. However, within the very narrow chronological field that he worked in, Kant already saw [201] the obscurity of the phenomena that he met there.

One piece of evidence for that is a statement Kant makes in the *Critique of Pure Reason* in connection with his explanation of the schematism, and it serves as the rubric for the particular way the problematic of time emerges for Kant within the *Critique of Pure Reason*.

> This schematism of our understanding with regard to appearances and their mere form is a hidden art in the depths of the human soul, whose true operations we can divine from nature and lay unveiled before our eyes only with difficulty. (B 180–181)

Now, we do not want to naïvely maintain that the project Kant doubted could be carried out has in fact been carried out and surpassed. But what he called obscure and almost inaccessible, we take up as an authentic philosophical challenge—to shed light on this night and get a grip on what is there so we can understand it. In this way we will take seriously the philosopher's job of "dismembering the secret judgments of common sense." In fact, perhaps the phenomena that circle around ur-temporality and time are these secret "judgments" of human reason.

As in every field where Kant's investigations really latch onto issues, here too, in this field of the problem of time, Kant keeps the horizons open. The way he carries out his investigations shows that he is struck by the phenomena, maintains his characteristic reserve in front of them, and shows his reflective caution about hastily assaulting a phenomenon. When he reaches his limits, he leaves the problems there—which is more helpful for later research than forcefully arranging some half-baked ideas into an imposing system.

Kant's understanding of time as expressed in the doctrine of schematism remains isolated and was completely misunderstood by the Idealism that followed. An extreme example of that is Hegel, who expressed himself on the schematism in his *Lectures on the History* [202] *of Philosophy.* The point of the schematism is to show in what way the understanding, the spontaneity of reason, can be qualified to determine the forms of intuition as forms of receptivity. Or more exactly, the point was to show to what extent the categories as *a priori* determinations of the unity of reason can relate to what stands over against it [*Gegenstände*] as objects [*Objekte*]. The question of the connection between understanding and sensibility leads Kant to look for a mediation, and he finds it in time. Hegel writes in his *Lectures on the History of Philosophy*, vol. 3, p. 570:

> This connecting [of the two, sensibility and understanding,] is again one of the most beautiful pages in Kant's philosophy. Here pure sensibility and pure understanding, which were formerly expressed as being absolutely separate and opposed, become united. The outcome is a perceptual-intuitive understanding or an understanding perception. Kant, however, does not pull these thoughts together. He fails to perceive and grasp that he has brought the two elements of knowledge into a unity—the in-itself of a double sameness. Knowledge itself is in fact the unity and truth of both moments. Thought and understanding remain one particular thing and sensibility another; and here the two are bound together in an external, superficial way, as a piece of wood and a leg might be tied together by a piece of rope.[3]

That is Hegel's conception of the meaning of the schematism. He sees it as merely an extrinsic conjoining of understanding and sensibility. On the other hand he does praise Kant for having brought these two together at all, for having (in Hegel's opinion) approximated in some way the Hegelian idea of the dialectic, although in fact Kant's inquiry is totally different. To the degree that Kant does aim at mediation here, Hegel praises him. But Hegel has absolutely no understanding of the real meaning, the central problematic, that Kant hit upon in the schematism.[4]

* * *

There are two reasons that primarily and necessarily prevented Kant from understanding the idea of a chronology—or more exactly, that denied him a fundamental understanding of what he had *de facto* carried out first in the schematism and then in the Doctrine of [203] Principles. In the first place, the typically rigid separation that Kant makes between sensibility and understanding prevented him from being able to connect in any way all that falls on the side of the understanding (the transcendental apperception and all the activities of the understanding) with time. What pertains to sensibility as receptivity had to be denied to the understanding as spontaneity. Insofar as the forms of intuition, space and time, belong to sensibility, time is pushed

3. [Cf. *Lectures on the History of Philosophy*, trans. Elizabeth S. Haldane and Frances H. Simson (Bristol: Thoemmes Press, 1999; repr. from the 1895 edition), p. 441. Translation is emended here in keeping with Heidegger's lecture (Moser, p. 424).]

4. [Here (Moser, p. 427) Heidegger ends his lecture of Monday, 11 January 1926, to be followed by that of Tuesday, 12 January, which opened with a 330-word summary that is omitted in GA 21.]

completely over onto the side of sensibility. And everything that pertains to the understanding—and consequently to the transcendental
apperception, and thus to the ultimate unity of consciousness—is pre-
temporal. In the first place, therefore, it is this gaping chasm that prevents Kant from permitting (or seeing) any temporalities, any ur-temporal phenomena, in the activities of understanding.

A clear proof of this is Kant's interpretation of the principle of contradiction, where he excludes the temporal determination "at the same
time" from the formulation of this principle. He does so on the grounds
of the following argument:

> The principle of contradiction traditionally has its validity as a
> principle of formal logic, a principle of analytics.
>
> But because every temporal determination is a synthesis,
> there therefore can be no synthesis present in the fundamental
> principle of all analytic judgments.
>
> Therefore, the phrase "at the same time" must be excluded
> from the formulation of the principle of contradiction.

The second reason that prevents Kant from seeing the transcendental apperception and the understanding in their ur-temporality is
Kant's very understanding of the concept of time. Kant's grasp of the
notion of time operates within the conception that was mediated to
him by the philosophical tradition coming from Leibniz and Newton.
According to them, time (in a very general sense) is the schema for the
ordering and determination of the manifold of what is given in the
receptivity of sensibility. In other words time, taken as this schema-
for-ordering, is limited to and primarily and exclusively related to,
nature. Even Hegel understood time in this sense. [204]

To be sure, Kant's philosophical interpretation of time is different
from that of Leibniz and Newton, but only in a certain respect. Fundamentally and in its essentials, Kant's interpretation operates on the same
ground as theirs, which in general we can understand as: Time is the
schema for ordering nature. We can take this schema for the ordering of
natural processes in Newton's sense, where time as the schema-for-ordering is itself a *res,* a being, an existing actuality. Or we can understand
time as this schema-for-ordering, in Leibniz's sense, as an *ordo,* an ordering in general, the being of which is not determined any further than
that. Or we can interpret this schema-for-ordering in the Kantian sense,
as a form of intuition. But in all of these cases the concept of a schema-
for-ordering is thought to pertain to natural processes, to succession.

In other words, this is the same conception of time that Aristotle
uncovered and determined for the first time in his *Physics,* where time
is encountered and understood with regard to the experienced objective world. Seen with regard to the world, worldly processes, and the

kind of determination that pertains to them, time in the sense we just mentioned is something just there on hand, and it has the possibility of being philosophically interpreted in various ways.

But is this approach to time, i.e., with regard to the objective world and its processes, the only approach? Or is the primary and normative approach to be found in other possible approaches? These are questions that we have to ask, of necessity, in a fundamental explanation of the phenomenon of time. Otherwise we abandon the whole problematic surrounding time to an explanation that remains on the level of the accidental rather than the fundamental. And in the final analysis, the way of understanding time that first emerged with Aristotle and then influenced the entire tradition remains on that level—although, as can be shown, there are specific reasons why it does so.

As long as we cling to this concept of time, it will be impossible to interpret transcendental apperception in the way we want to—viz., chronologically, with regard to time. And the same goes for any activity of understanding, or of consciousness in the broadest sense. [205] But that's the same as saying that the chronological problematic—i.e., pointing out ur-temporality in the various comportments of existence—can be worked out only if we first get free of this traditional concept of time and show that in the final analysis this concept of time is founded on an *original* concept of time, and also show that in existence there are specific elements that make it necessary to understand time in that ur-temporal sense. If, whenever we discuss time, we remain doggedly oriented to the traditional concept of time, what little we have said about the connection of being and truth in the preceding lectures will inevitably be misunderstood, or at best not understood at all.

Our theses are:

1. Being means presence.
2. Truth means presence-now.
3. Presence is understood in terms of presence-now.
4. Presence-now is a mode of time.[5]

What does time mean? We don't want just any definition of time. Even if such a definition were possible and available, it would be of no help. Rather, everything comes down to seeing the phenomenon of time itself in an original way. That requires its own paths and preparations, its own preliminary investigations, and it cannot be attained in a single stroke. We say that time is not merely and not primarily a schema for determining how changes get ordered. Rather, properly speaking, time is existence itself. But that is still only a sentence, just as the first thesis above

5. [Compare with the three theses at GA 21, p. 199.5–6.]

is still a merely arbitrary proposition. In fact we know nothing about time, and we don't care to be told anything about it.

But let's stay focused on the subject matter and the project we have settled on: the analysis of the proposition. Let us especially stay with the question about the conditions of the possibility of truth and falsehood in propositions, i.e., the question about the essence and origin of synthesis. If we do, we will reach the theses we have posited. We are faced with two possibilities when it comes to developing our investigation and moving toward a truly philosophical understanding [206] of the traditional theme of traditional logic.

1. We first ran across the phenomenon of time in a merely dogmatic set of observations, but now we could explicitly embrace the task of pointing out and interpreting time. In the course of such a thematic investigation we would need to reach a point where we clearly see presence-now as a mode of time. That would give us the basis for proving how and why we can and must understand presence in terms of now-presence and for bringing out the connection between the two. This is the proper issue-oriented way to conduct an investigation that single-mindedly pursues any new phenomena that show up, while disregarding any other goals or any concern for a forced (and finally suspect) systematic unity. But that approach to the investigation would have to renounce the economy of a lecture course. If we adopted this approach and pursued the phenomena in the requisite way, we would never get back to the proposition, the statement, and truth—at least not this semester.

2. The second possible approach begins with the subject matter we have chosen and stays with it. However, it takes the conclusion that we arrived at dogmatically and now uses it as a guiding thread. It takes what we have already uncovered about the structure of statement and synthesis and tries to see its ur-temporal character. This approach allows the phenomenon of time to guide our study of the subject matter. But this approach also has its drawbacks. Yes, we will certainly understand, within certain limits, those ur-temporal characteristics; however, in the process; ur-temporality as such will always remain more or less hidden. To be sure, the guiding thread is determinate, but it remains obscure—a weak and flickering light with which to illumine the path of our investigation. But one can easily overcome this deficiency by getting clear on ur-temporality via an interpretation of its ur-temporal structures, [207] and thereby getting clear on time itself, not in isolation but in its ur-temporal function.

In a sense we're repeating what we said earlier, in §12, but now we have a chronological aim. We need to work out an analysis of the conditions of the possibility of propositions and of synthesis in terms of their ur-temporality. We led synthesis back to the as-structure, and that means we now have to explain the ur-temporality of the as-structure. We have characterized this as-structure as a basic hermeneutical structure of existence. We likewise showed how the "as" of this basic hermeneutical structure gets leveled down to the "as" which is used to determine things that are merely there. So, the foundational analysis of statements in the ensemble will have to show the ur-temporal character of this process of leveling down, that is, the specific ur-temporality of the process in which the means-whereby of involvement gets modified into the mere subject matter of apophantically determinative statements—in short: the ur-temporality of thematizing as such.

These analyses will allow us to clarify the phenomenon of now-presence and thus its connection with presence. All of this will make possible a relative understanding of the extent to which being equals presence and truth equals now-presence. Only in this way will we acquire the correct means for giving a definitive, philosophical interpretation of *Metaphysics* IX 10. And then we will also see the limits, imperfections, and ambiguities of the Greek inquiry into the problematic of that treatise, as well as the reasons for the obscurity of it. Only then will we finally be able to answer the questions we formulated in connection with that treatise (cf. §13-b, above): Why did the Greeks and all ages thereafter understand that truth meant intuition-truth? Why must we first and foremost understand intuition-truth as the basic form of truth? And why does traditional logic, as a consequence, operate within the specific problematic of this form of truth? [208]

§16. The conditions of the possibility of falsehood within the horizon of the analysis of existence

Let us briefly recall the three conditions:

1. The tendency to uncover, that is, the prior already-having of something;
2. The determination via "as" (the delotic[6] synthesis); and
3. The togetherness of beings (the ontic synthesis).

In our earlier investigation, our aim was set on the interconnection and unifying root of these conditions. According to what we finally said, the unity of the conditions is grounded in ur-temporality.

We establish the interconnection between the conditions not by syl-

6. [See page 157, note 47, regarding "delotic."]

logistic argument, but by insight into the phenomenon itself. We pursue
the three conditions individually in their ur-temporality. But if they are
all originally interconnected within ur-temporality, then the more our
analysis gains insight into the ur-temporality of one of them, the more
clearly we will see the others as well. Or more precisely, we will see the
whole context of being that they delimit: the comportment of existence
becomes visible.

We characterized the first condition in two ways: 1. the prior-having of something, and 2. the tendency to uncover. And we spoke of
this condition on two occasions. The first time was in our analysis of
the statement (§12), when we said that the statement is grounded in a
prior understanding. We gave the example of chalk: The prior understanding concerns the concrete act of writing as an involvement-with.
In that analysis we did not consider whether the statement that is
grounded in such a prior understanding was true or false. We took as
an example a true statement: "This chalk is white."

We also treated this same phenomenon when speaking about deception (the example of the deer). There we began with a false statement, but again we showed that, as a statement (whether it be explicitly asserted or not), it too was grounded in a prior knowledge. But in
this case our analysis went further. We pointed out the structure of
[209] this prior knowledge (GA 21, pp. 192ff.). We said that the prior
act of letting something encounter us is a comportment within which
we constantly live and in which the tendency to uncover the encountering thing can also lie as an interpretation and determination that
goes after the thing. The prior letting-encounter and the prior-having
of something ground the tendency to uncover whatever is already-had
in these ways. "Tendency" is a mode of being-disposed for the explicit
"approach" of something. And this tendency in turn grounds and supports the mode of uncovering that thing.

These phenomena—letting something encounter, the prior-having
of something, and the tendency to [uncover] something—must be
shown in their ur-temporality. But to do so we must have secured the
very horizon within which we can meet them. In other words, these
phenomena have to be brought back to the context of being where
they are what they are. But this context-of-being is one to which the
statement belongs, whose conditions of being we are now pursuing.

We said that we live constantly in this state of letting-things-
encounter-us. This, along with the already-having of something and
the tendency to [uncover] something, are comportments of ourselves,
i.e., comportments of the being [Seienden] that we are and that we
call existence. Therefore, these comportments are ways that existence can *be*, ways in which it is as it is and can be *as* existence.
Therefore, we understand the aforementioned phenomena as modes

of the being of existence, and we give them corresponding terminological determinations.

The constant letting-encounter / already-having of something is existentially and *a priori* a *being-unto* and a *being-familiar-with* something. Tendency-unto is a being-out-unto something. Clearly, then, the second condition of the possibility of falsehood—viz., the determining by way of the "as," or taking a look at, or the delotic synthesis—is also to be understood as a way that existence *is*.

The third condition concerns the entity that is to be understood, first of all by way of knowledge of the world. "World" *can* also mean existence to the extent that it is a [210] being [viz., ourselves] about which we can deceive ourselves—and often do, to a large measure in acts of *self*-deception. We don't have to be *ourselves*. There can also be (and first of all is) the being that we ourselves are not, but to which we relate and with regard to which we have a [certain mode of] being.[7] To come back to the first condition, mostly we have merely changed the terminology [e.g., being-unto, being-familiar-with, etc.]. This is not insignificant because it shows that, in clarifying the phenomena we understand by these terms, the goal must be to interpret the "being" that presses to the fore in such expressions as *being*-already-with and *being*-out-unto.[8]

*   *   *

Therefore, we will clarify the structure of existence to the extent that is especially necessary for understanding these comportments. The lack of such an analysis of existence is ultimately why ur-temporal phenomena remain in the dark and haven't been understood up until now. We thereby come face-to-face with a task. . . . No, to put it more exactly: Constantly throughout this entire course, we have been really working at an analysis of this phenomenon of existence, but without saying so explicitly. In our introductory investigations of psychologism we raised the question: When, in a concrete judgment, the real act of judgment is separated from the ideal content of judgment, how are the two related to each other? There we formulated the question in such a way that we had to ask "What then constitutes the proper connection-of-being between ideal and real being?" and more precisely, "Is it even possible to ask what constitutes the bridge?"

Now this question has become concrete for us. To be sure, we already have readily available terms for such analyses of comportments,

7. [Heidegger is referring, of course, to everyday "fallenness" and inauthenticity.]

8. [Here (Moser, p. 444) Heidegger ends his lecture of Tuesday, 12 January 1926, to be followed by that of Thursday, 14 January, which opened with a 320-word summary that is omitted in GA 21.]

taken in the broad sense of what we now call "conscious processes" or "lived experiences," and all of these terms naturally already harbor a certain conception of the structure of existence. Traditional epistemology, ethics, and so forth have done a lot for the analysis of these phenomena, but the truly crucial investigations [211] have been lacking up until now. These investigations precede every concrete analysis, and once and for all they determine, in terms of itself, the being [*Seiende*] whose comportments are especially to be studied. For the most part, when analyzing existence, philosophers work with categories that are indifferent to existence or that are drawn from contexts of being that genuinely have nothing to do with it.

Given the aim and particularly the limitation of our project, our analysis of existence now confronts us with particular and principled difficulties. One could say, of course, that this existence—which we ourselves are, each one of us—is truly and properly the closest thing to us. As Augustine has already asked in his *Confessions*, book 10, chapter 16:

> *Quid autem propinquius meipso mihi?*

> What is closer to me than myself?

And in the same chapter where he poses that question, he also says:

> *Ego certe laboro hic et laboro in meipso: factus sum mihi terra difficultatis et sudoris nimii.*

> I work hard here, I word hard on myself {when I study consciousness, the soul}, and I have become to myself a field of hard labor and immense personal struggle.

Let us keep these thoughts present to mind as we take up the analysis of existence in an effort to really see at least some of its structures. In this context it is not a matter of providing definitions or descriptions that can be understood in a very general way. It's a matter of really bringing structures out into the clear so that we can then see, within the horizon of those structures, what we have been calling ur-temporality.

With the letting-encounter and already-having of something, we have met up with the clarification of deception. In order for me to be able to be deceived, in order for something to misrepresent itself to me and to appear as something it is not, the thing that so appears has to have already encountered me. It has to appear, in some way or other, precisely «during» the misrepresentation. To put it concretely: I have to be moving in the forest, for example, or if not in the forest [212] then someplace else, if I am to be able to be deceived about things in the world and in the knowledge of the world. That need not mean that such an act of letting-encounter must have been explicitly performed before deception can occur. Rather, it means that *if* I am deceived, *if* I fall into deception, I first of all must have been *a priori* with something in the world. This fact of being *a priori* with something of the world, this being-unto and being-with a world, is not just the ground of (i.e., what makes possible) deception. Rather, it belongs to my existence itself. It's not the case that I first must bring myself into the state of letting-something-encounter-me. In fact, that's not even possible, since insofar as I am at all, I already have an ontological relation to a world, in fact to my own world, and this ontological relation belongs to the determination of the being of my "I am." Insofar as existence is its own *ek-*, its own "out there," it is in a world. The word "being" [*Sein*] in the term "being-out-there"[9] means, among other things (but not exclusively) being in the world. It is entirely wrong to think that philosophical statements deal with human beings *and* their relation to the world. Basically we'd have everything backwards if we understood this phenomenological state of affairs as if human beings first of all were beings unto themselves and then, in addition to this, also had a relation to the world. Being-in-the-world (of course we will have to determine the meaning of this better) already is the being of each human being.

This letting-the-world-encounter-us, this *a priori* having-the-world, does not engage existence only once in a while and then disappear again. Already-being familiar with a world underlies every one of existence's possibilities-of-being *qua* possibilities-of-human-existence. This already being familiar with the world bifurcates, branches out, is disseminated and dispersed into a multitude of ways of being involved with whatever is there. It directs itself to what is there, takes account of it, exploits it, uses it, transforms it, augments it, and so on and on. Even calculating and knowing the world are a mode of this involvement with the world. Mostly they remain fused with an involvement-with that is not [213] merely and not primarily cognitive. Nonetheless, they can also become free of that, so that existence engages itself in knowing the world as an autonomous way of being involved with it.

This structure of existence—being-in-the-world—is an essential one but not the only one. Its priority (its "constancy"—its *a priori* facticity) is a wholly proper priority.

For the most part statements maintain themselves primarily within a particular involvement-with, that is, they are carried out on the basis of being-in-the-world. However, with that the phenomenon of being-already-with is still not adequately understood. We have to distinguish between the structure of being-in-the-world in general and its basic comportment in which this structure, as existential, maintains

---

9. [That is, *Dasein*, in the non-technical sense.]

itself. Every particular involvement-with happens on the basis of being-in-the-world. But this constantly prior being unto and in the world
is also an *a priori* being *with* the world. This, by way of contrast to
existence as being-*in*-the-world, is a very special form in which this
structure is enacted, namely: As in-the-world, existence has *a priori*
given itself away *to* the world in using it, exploiting it, and so on. Existence not only "is" *in* the world in an essential way, but also "is" fallen
into the world. The world encounters us not as some indifferent "place-
in-which," where existence operates. Existential being unto the world
is a matter of being essentially assigned [*Angewiesensein*] to the world
and hence it is an *a priori* being-fallen into the world.

A-priori-being-with the world is neither an indifferent way of being
unto the world nor a mere dwelling in it in the sense of observing it,
staring at it. Rather, this with-the-world means being essentially assigned to it, being absorbed in it, operating in it as having been handed
over to it. Human existence's way of being with its world is never anything like the way things are with each other *qua* juxtaposed. This kind
of being-with-each-other (for example, the way the chair is there with
the door) is the way that two things, both of which belong to the world,
are next to each other. Here too, because our language is not formed
according to the rules of formal logic, [214] it is a bit inconsistent.

Imagine a walking stick leaning against the door or wall. One might
say that the one touches the other. But on closer reflection we should
not speak of "touching"—and not because we could show that there is
ultimately some space between the two. Rather, on principle the
walking-stick does not and never can touch the wall, even if there
were absolutely no distance between it and the wall. For that to happen, the wall would have to be able to encounter, and be encountered
by, the walking-stick as a thing in the world. One thing can touch
another only if it is a being that—as such, intrinsically, and of its ownmost being—has its world. Only in that way can it touch another being,
and only thus can the thing touched be uncovered in the touching
and become accessible in its being as something there. So we see that
in saying "Two things touch," we are taking existence's way of being
unto the world and transferring it to a thing that appears *within* the
world and therefore, in itself, is worldless.

On the other hand the ontological relations of worldly things and
events can also get transferred to existence. An example of that: when
we speak of the "movement" of thinking and neglect to say what
"movement" means here or could mean. Most often we mention only
this transference of world-oriented discourse to existence. Existence's
being-*with* is not, therefore, juxtaposition, i.e., a continuous or discon-
tinuous filling up of space.

Being-with is one way the structure of being-in-the-world is enacted.

It has its own specific "how," which prescribes that we must understand existence's specific being unto its world as concern for that world. This is not just any characteristic of existence, but one that is determined by existence's basic way of being. Only with reference to this basic way of being can we phenomenally understand *a-priori*-being-with in a broad enough way to bring out its ur-temporal structure.

Some might think that when we define existence in terms of the structure of being-in-the-world, we are grounding our interpretation of existence in some general biological structure. [215] This characteristic of being-in-the-world, they might say, pertains in a certain sense also to plants and animals, because to the degree that they are at all, they have their worlds, their own specific (broad or narrow) environments. This ontological determination "being-in-the-world," if understood within that horizon and applied to existence (the being of human beings) is, they will say, merely a species of the broader genus called "to have a world." It is a short step to understanding things that way. But on closer view it is clear that whereas we may have to attribute "having a world" to plants and animals, we can do so only insofar as we have first understood this structure as it pertains to our own existence as such.

We can arrive at the biological basis of human being—i.e., the basic structure of our "biological being" in the narrow sense—only if beforehand we have already understood "biological being" as a structure of existence. It does not work in reverse. We cannot derive the determination "being-in-the-world" from biology. It must be acquired philosophically. This means that even biology *qua* biology cannot see the structures of "biological being" in its specific objects, for *qua* biology it already presupposes such structures when it speaks of plants and animals. Biology can establish and determine these structures only by transgressing its own limits and becoming philosophy. And in fact more than once in the course of the development of modern biology, especially in the nineteenth century (although only in very general characterizations and vague concepts), biologists have referred to this structure and to the fact that animals above all, and plants in a certain sense, have a world. To my knowledge the first person to have run across these matters again (Aristotle had already seen them) was the biologist K. E. von Baer,[10] who referred to these structures in his various lectures, but only in passing, never really thematically. More recently his suggestions have been taken up by von Uexküll,[11] who now deals with this problem the-

10. [The Prussian-Estonian Karl Ernst von Baer (1792–1876), who, as the founder of comparative embryology, discovered the mammalian ovum and the notochord. Heidegger mentions him at *SZ*, p. 78 / tr. 84.]

11. [Jacob von Uexküll (1864–1944), best known for his *Umwelt und Innenwelt*

matically, not in a [216] philosophical sense, however, but in connection with specific investigations in biology.

I must emphasize that from these references we at first gain very little philosophically for being-in-the-world as a structure of existence. The point now is to understand the meaning of the being of this structure. The regional horizon for biology and for all of psychology (which nowadays likes to call itself anthropology) presupposes the philosophical question about the structure of existence itself. This is a philosophical question—more precisely, a categorial question—and it cannot be reached, much less answered, by a psychological or biological inquiry.

These remarks are important for contemporary philosophy, because we find philosophers (I am sure you are familiar with this) who try to attack this *Lebensphilosophie* and show that the "philosophy of life" (as it so haplessly calls itself) is biological philosophy. This kind of opposition to the philosophy of life began with Rickert and from the beginning was based on a misunderstanding. It mistakes the categorial problematic of philosophy with regard to life for a biological problematic. Rickert is correct insofar as the philosophy of life's investigations and conclusions have *de facto* not pressed forward into categorial structures, even though directed toward seeing something like that. From the very title "philosophy of life," you can see that it does not really understand what it is about. This title is a tautology, since philosophy deals with nothing but existence itself. As regards *Lebensphilosophie*, the only thing more brilliant than doubting that philosophy is always about life is to doubt that botany is always about plants. This problematic of existence must be understood from the beginning as a philosophical problematic. So we now ask: [217] On what basis and in what way does being familiar with the world get determined in its "how," namely, as concern?

We begin with a concrete example as we approach this structure of existence, in which already-being familiar with the world is taken as concern. Being-with, we said, is in the mode of being essentially assigned to the world. It will suffice to point out some things we take for granted, things that are overlooked but still remain puzzling: e.g., the fact that I stand, sit, lie somewhere, on something. These seem to be trivial phenomena, hardly worth philosophy's attention. But in the concrete, existence is always essentially assigned in a specific relation to its lived world.

Let's take ourselves, right here and now, as an example. We are es-

der Tiere (Berlin: Springer, 1909; 2d exp. edition, 1921), as well as for his *Theoretische Biologie* (Berlin: Paetel, 1920), which was translated by Doris L. Mackinnon as *Theoretical Biology* (London: K. Paul, Trench, Trubner / New York: Harcourt, Brace, 1926).]

sentially assigned to a specific lived world with a specific structure—in this case, a specific space, prepared with specific goals in mind, so that it is quiet enough and warm enough not to disturb the imparting of information, which is supposed to happen on my side, and the understanding of it, which is supposed to happen on your side. We constantly need and make use of the lived world—but without directing our attention to it. That, in fact, constitutes its taken-for-granted-ness, the peculiar kind of being of the lived world. Looking at our existence even more concretely—say, in terms of the communication that happens in the lecture—we see that during the lecture there can occur a comportment such as writing on the chalkboard. Insofar as I am living in the lecture, I am, in my very existence, essentially assigned in a certain sense to the chalkboard, to the chalk. Let us say that without paying any particular or explicit attention to it, I peel off the paper from the chalk so that I can write with it. That is a specific activity that has a solid connection with my comportment and my existence, but one does not require any special organization.

This activity is unto something and makes use of it in the lived world with which I am preoccupied. Activities like this, as well as all more developed [218] kinds of involvement with things in the lived world, I characterize as "concernful involvement." I mean this expression as a phenomenological-philosophica1[12] term, which means that I do not use it in some pre-scientific sense or as applying to an individual science. I understand it with a philosophical intent. In everyday usage, *besorgen* means to attend to something, to carry something through; or in the form, *etwas sich besorgen,* to procure or get something for oneself. We also say: "I am *concerned* he won't come," by which we mean, "I *fear* that he won't come." All of these meanings are blended into the philosophical use of the term, which correspondingly is quite broad on principle and yet need not be empty.[13] But this breadth does not exclude precision. In fact it demands it. What, then, is this broad basic sense to which we must appeal when we say that using the chalk is an act of concern?[14]

* * *

In the case of the chalkboard and chalk, we can use "concern" in one of its everyday meanings. In occupying-myself-with the chalkboard, I procure some chalk for myself. I get it, provide myself with it as immediately suitable for writing. This procuring in the sense of getting-

12. [Moser, p. 458.24.]

13. [Moser (p. 459.13–14) contradicts GA 21 (p. 218.11) on *leer,* "empty." I follow Moser here.]

14. [Here (Moser, p. 460) Heidegger ends his lecture of Thursday, 14 January 1926, to be followed by that of Friday, 15 January, which opened with a 1,240-word summary that is omitted in GA 21.]

for-myself is an act of concern—in fact, it is concern in an original and fundamental sense of the term. As being unto the world, this concern has a meaning fundamentally related to existence, a meaning that determines each of its concretions such as getting, using what has been gotten, or surrendering what has been gotten. I procure for myself some chalk—as something I can write with—for the specific act of writing. I do this writing in order to emphasize what I am saying, to facilitate your retention of it, to make it possible for you to write down what I am saying, to take notes on it. This reinforcement of what is being said is done in the service of communicating an analysis of phenomena. This communication has the function of letting you come to see the phenomena I am speaking about, of bringing you face-to-face with the subject matter. And this is being done so that from these phenomena you might form an understanding of them; and this, in turn, so that that you might understand the problematic of logic and the essence of truth.

So we have a series of comportments, [219] from a certain way of using chalk all the way up to understanding the essence of truth, all of them ordered successively in the unifying form of an *um . . . zu*, an "in-order-to." But the "in-order-to" phenomenon comes to light inadequately by our pointing out these comportments. This ordering of comportments is merely a recognition of the comportments themselves. In fact, the order of the comportments, as we listed it, would be wrong if we understood it as the order of their being. That is not at all the case. In fact, the ontological relations [of these comportments] come in the exact opposite order.

It is *from out of* my purpose of acquiring the understanding of truth and preparing it [for communication to you], and it is *in and for* this purpose that my existence arrives at the chalk within this lived world and that my being unto the world enters into concern for these things in my lived world.

There is a network of comportments that precedes the activity in question. In turn, this network of comportments is and lives by intending something. This anticipation is one of the comportments of my existence in which I live in order to execute the task that has laid hold of this existence of mine. Living in this network of comportments, I comport myself to this task.

But this task is nothing but a way my very own existence *can be*. This is not just any possibility, but one into which my own existence has been placed as a possibility of itself. This possibility "is" my very existence—not something that could be met with or found elsewhere, whether with other people or in the lived world. Existence is this possibility in such a way that existence comports itself to it as its very own being. That is, insofar as existence is the way it is, it is concerned for its very own being. And that is its fundamental kind of existence: that in its being, it is concerned for that very being.

Ultimately (but not exclusively) the network of comportments, oriented to this in-order-to, is directed to this: that existence might be in the possibility as which it has chosen itself and [220] into which it has posited itself. In its very being, existence is out unto its own being as the being with which it is concerned.

We need to understand this determination still more precisely insofar as the being of existence can be understood, in its structure, more completely as being-in-the-world. In other words, to the degree that we make basic statements about the being of existence, if these statements are to touch on the complete phenomenon, we must keep in mind the structures we have brought to light heretofore.

---

§17. Care as the being of existence. Concern-for and concern-about, authenticity and inauthenticity

As being-in-the-world—i.e., as being familiar with the world—existence is out unto its ownmost being as what it is concerned about. The basic kind of being [*Sein*] of a being which *is* in such as way that, in its being, it cares about that very being [*Sein*]—this kind of being [*Sein*] we call *care*. Care is the basic mode of the being of existence, and as such it determines every kind of being [*Seinsart*] that derives from the ontological structure of existence.

The phenomenon that we characterize by the term "care" is a very special structure of existence, and everything depends on a correct philosophical interpretation of it. The crucial point does not consist in establishing that existence is concerned about its being. The point, rather, is to interpret this phenomenon in the direction of a primordial understanding of being.

Clearly Kant had this state of affairs in mind when he said, using traditional ontological categories: Humans belong to those "things whose existence is an end in itself." Or as he once put it: "Existence is an end in itself." Or again, [human beings are those] "whose existence has an absolute value in itself." Kant provides these determinations in §2 of his *Groundwork of the Metaphysics of Morals*,[15] and for him they are the basis and the proper metaphysical (that is, ontological) condition of the possibility [221] of the fact that there can be a categorical imperative, that is, one that can be expressed categorically rather than hypothetically, as do the usual imperatives in an "if . . . then" proposition. A categorical imperative is not preceded by a prior condition regarding something

15. [*GM*, p. 428 / tr. 36–37.]

else, but is an imperative in which the condition categorically embraces the conditioned and has absolute value. And this being that exists as an end in itself is human being, that is, every rational being.

With this citation I will show three things: that Kant had this structure in mind; that he also (as is obvious) expressed this structure in traditional ontological categories such as "ends"; and that as he established and determined human being as an end in itself, he also understood the human being as having absolute value in itself. It is quite clear that what he is trying to do here is to determine more exactly the *ontological* statement that existence is an end in itself by introducing the notion of *value*. This is the clearest proof (unexpressed, obviously) that, to begin with, the determination "end-in-itself" is insufficient to clarify what is meant here. On the other hand, the structure that we understand under the rubric of "care" is oriented from the beginning not simply to characterizing this kind of being [*Seinsart*], but also to understanding it in its being [*Sein*]—something that was not even an issue for Kant.

The question now is how to understand more originally this phenomenon of care, in which all the comportments of existence originate, especially being unto the world as concern, along with all of its modes. When I say that the modes of comportment unto the world (including the modes of concern) spring from care, you must remember that care, as existence's kind of being, is co-original with existence as being in a world. Yet nonetheless we can still say that in a certain regard [222] one of them originates from the other. In any case we must reject the misunderstanding that existence first of all is or could be something that is concerned about its [own] being and then somehow, as isolated care, occasionally comes unto a world that it is concerned about. The case, rather, is that existence's entire structure belongs to the phenomenon of care because care is what characterizes existence. So, care is a determination of existence; existence is being-in-the-world; and care is at the same time *a priori* concern. Therefore the possibility of clarifying the phenomena of *a priori* letting-something-meet-us or of being *a priori* familiar with something—and in general the phenomenon of being concerned-about—depends on how far we succeed in making care itself accessible.

We have analyzed the network of comportments that (to put it extrinsically) stretches from involvement with the chalk all the way up to the goal of communicating an understanding. And we analyzed a lecture as communication and as a comportment of my own existence. In all that, we showed (granted, in a somewhat one-sided fashion) that existence's being is at stake in this comportment. But in our analysis we omitted an essential connection: that at the very same time, although in a different way, the current existence of those who are listening and understanding is likewise at stake. One might think that the care of the existence who is communicating is "concerned *for*" and "deals with" those who are listening, and that they are always there in the lived world and hence fall within the circle of its being concerned-about. But this wrongly interprets the phenomenal state of affairs.

You the listeners are not objects of a concern-about. As a form of communicating the subject matter and helping people see it in a lecture, care is never being concerned-about, because the lecture cannot really produce in you the vision of the subject matter but can only awaken it or arouse it. Therefore, that which care *qua* communication wants to communicate cannot, in its most proper essence, be an object of concern in that care. Instead, another existence, as care, takes it into its care. Accordingly the kind of being that the communicating existence has in relation to [223] the listeners is not a being-familiar-with, and it is not a being concerned-about. Rather it is a *being-with*, it is a mutual-care, or better: being concerned-for [*Mitsorge, genauer: Für-sorge*]. This expression too must be understood as a phenomenological concept.

Being concerned-for likewise has other possibilities and forms (although this is not the place to go into them). But regarding being-with-others in the basic comportment of being concerned-for, we have to make a fundamental distinction.

Concern-for can be carried out in a way that virtually takes away the other's care. In concern-for him I put myself in his place: I step in for him, which entails that he give himself up, step back, and accept ready-made the concern I show him, thereby completely freeing himself from his care. In the kind of being concerned-for where care "steps in," the person on the receiving end becomes dependent and dominated, even though the domination may be entirely unspoken and not experienced. We characterize this first kind of being concerned-for as one that "steps in" and takes the place of the other—takes away and dominates. By contrast there is a second kind of being-with-the-other that does not step into his place (his situation and project) and take it away, but instead carefully steps ahead of him, not so as to take away his care—which is himself, his very existence—but to give it back to him. Such concern-for does not dominate but liberates.[16]

* * *

The second kind of concern-for is the concern-for of authenticity, because the existence who receives it can and should return to himself and

16. [Here (Moser, p. 476) Heidegger ends his lecture of Friday, 15 January 1926, to be followed by that of Tuesday, 19 January (Heidegger did not lecture on Monday, 18 January), which opened with a 550-word summary that is omitted in GA 21.]

become his own authentic self. Here I certainly do not understand the other existence primarily in terms of the world I'm concerned about. Rather, I understand the other's existence only in terms of himself. By contrast, the first mode of being concerned-for is concerned for the other in such a way that, in his place and at his service, it procures for him a possible possession. It understands the other existence in terms of the things that he is concerned about, which are giving him difficulty. This concern-for throws the other out of his place, as it were, and engages only with what must be done [224] to restore the other to a now-guaranteed possession of that thing. This kind of being concerned-for treats the other like a nothing, as if he had nothing of existence about him. In this form of being concerned-for he is not present as his own existence but as inauthentic existence, as something merely there in the world, someone who cannot get anywhere with his life.

We have characterized two extreme modes of being concerned-for—the one authentic, the other inauthentic—because only from out of these two extremes can we shed some light on those factical concretions that we understand as "mixed forms" (for reasons that are embedded in existence itself and cannot be further explained here).

Existence's being-with-and-for-each-other, as existential, is an *a priori* being-with-and-for-each-other *in* the world and thus also a mode of *being concerned* about the world that is exercised with-and-for-each-other. The two kinds of such being-concerned-about the world are ontologically different, depending on the kind of being-concerned-for that the concern has and on the character of care itself. Likewise the lived world, or particular things within it, can be objects of concern in different ways, depending on how each existence relates to the lived world and is engaged *with* it and *for* a specific being concerned-about. In that case, being-with-each-other is determined simply by how people deal with the same thing.

The possibilities of for-each-other are confined within certain limits. For example, in being-for-each-other there can be distance and reserve, not to mention outright mistrust. However, in the opposite direction, being-with-each-other can also be determined not from the thing with and for which they are engaged but from each one's own existence that is with the other. From that bondedness with the other there can first arise the authentic issue, i.e., the correct concern about the same issue. Only from that does "communication" (as we now call it) arise. So we see a peculiar conjunction between the two phenomena: on the one hand, the being-with-each-other of being concerned-for, and on the other, being concerned about the world itself. [225]

If we hope to understand the phenomenon of being concerned-about as the kind of being with which existence is in the world—we must understand this concept in a sufficiently broad sense. That is, we have to understand it as a structural concept. It is neither created out of nor limited to specific concrete ways of comportment. Above all it is not limited to modes of comportment like acquiring or producing something, or making it available. So it is not limited to those modes of being concerned-about that we call active comportments in the narrow sense. Instead, it includes letting something be: letting a field lie fallow, putting something aside, giving it up, as well as all phenomena we can characterize as "letting go of." All such comportments are modes of being concerned-about. When I neglect something, I don't do nothing. I do something, but I do it in the mode of "not." Neglect is a very determinate concept correlative to being concerned-about, and possible only in it. There is neglect only where there is care.

The term "concern" must be understood very broadly as the name of a structure. In explaining this phenomenon I cannot now delve into the meaning of this structural concept itself or the specific methodological problems associated with it. Such a discussion would get us too involved and take us away from our real subject matter.

By way of summary we can say: Existence's basic kind of being is to be concerned for its being, and this basic kind of being is understood as care. Insofar as existence is essentially being-in-the world, care is co-originally *concern*. And insofar as existence is being-with-others, existence's basic of being is likewise concern-*for*. Being concerned-about and being concerned-for are constitutive of care, and when we abbreviate and use just the term "care" in our explanations, it must be properly meant and concretely understood as care that is concerned-about and concerned-for. "Care" in an emphasized sense means that concern-about and -for *qua* care, [226] are concerned for our being as care. This makes it clear that the basic structure of our existence, which we abbreviate as "care," encompasses a multitude of phenomena and that we have not come up a simple phenomenon with a simple structure on which the rest are built. Rather, just as being-in-the-world, being-with-others, and being-concerned-for-ourselves are all constitutive of existence, so too the ontological meaning of these comportments are co-original.

Being concerned-about and being concerned-for are co-original possibilities of existence. Therefore, we say very generally that these same structures, which indicate a multiplicity, are equally original. That wards off the notion that one of these structures is derivable from the other, that one is built upon the other. And in so doing, we certainly have not said anything about the unity of the multiplicity of concern-about, being concerned-for, and especially concern-for-oneself. Above all, nothing has been said about whether there is only one kind of unity to this multiplicity or whether "unity" is or is not the right name in this context, for certain possibilities that existence has. With regard to the question of the unity of these multiple structures, we can say negatively only that this unity is not a sum in the sense that it comes after the parts and is only the sum of them. Rather, the unity of this multiplicity is a wholeness that precedes the multiplicity and is its origin and that, as it were, first releases parts from that wholeness.

But with all of this we still have not gained much toward an adequate understanding of the issue *if* the point is to understand this unity of the multiplicity not just in a formal sense but rather as the unity of a being that has the character of existence. Clearly we must understand this unity of existence as a mode of its being. The aforementioned modes of authenticity and inauthenticity become important for clarifying this phenomenon of the unity of existence, and what's more, they intersect with the modes of genuine and non-genuine. There is a non-genuine authenticity, that is, existence may be a non-genuine [227] being-with-oneself; and there is a genuine inauthenticity, that is, a genuine losing of oneself that grows out of the concrete existence in question.

The problem of the unity of existence—or more accurately, the unity of these basic and manifold structures—is understood in the history of philosophy mostly under the rubric of the ego and the unity of the ego and of the self—where "ego" is taken primarily in the sense of the theoretical ego or, as we say, the pole of theoretical acts. This is very clear in what Kant says: "The 'I think' must be able to accompany all my acts" (*Critique of Pure Reason*, B 131). This "I think" is what constitutes the general possibility of the unity of consciousness. If we want to understand this "I think" in a very broad sense, the way Descartes understands the *cogito*, there is still a secondary meaning accompanying the first one (or maybe it is what is properly meant), namely, that at each moment the manifold of existence's current comportments can be understood by existence as its own unified experience. I mention this problem of the unity of the multiplicity only in order to indicate to you that as we continue to make progress in analyzing existence's being as care, we naturally should not remain content with a simple characterization of these manifold structures.

The term "care" itself, as well as the phenomena it includes, fundamentally refers to a structural phenomenon. It should never be understood in a pre-scientific sense as expressing an everyday experience of existence in which one could say that human life is worry and hardship. If it is understood that way, the characterization of existence would be a specific interpretation of specific experiences. It would be a specific worldview characterization that could then grow into systems of worldview interpretations of existence, such as pessimism, for example. Our interpretation of existence in terms of care has nothing to do with characterizations of that type. Rather, the basic structure [that we have worked out] is first and foremost the presupposition for the fact that perhaps, in large measure, existence [228] *may* be worry and hardship in that pre-scientific sense.

As long as existence is, it is always in a specific mode. But that means that existence is not set, once and for all, in just one specific mode that would exclude any ability to be otherwise. Properly this means that whenever existence behaves in a particular way, that way remains only one possible way of behaving. Existence can, in principle, give up that first way and enter upon a different way of behaving. Therefore, "possibility" is a determination that belongs in principle to the modes of comportment, and this possibility does not disappear when a particular comportment is *de facto* chosen and lived out.

In this more detailed interpretation of comportments we also encounter difficulties insofar as the concept of possibility has up until now gone entirely unclarified in scientific philosophy. And to the degree that it has been clarified, the explanations typically only go as far as possibility in the modal sense, where it is seen in the context of statements and of the certitude that can accrue to them. In that case, the idea of possibility is seen in connection with actuality and necessity as determinations of being, i.e., the being of nature in the broadest sense. The meaning of possibility and the kind of structures of possibility that pertain to existence as such have been entirely closed off to us until the present. Therefore the explication of existence constantly runs up against difficulties because it refuses from the start to conduct investigations into the issue by making any use of traditional concepts.

One of the basic possibilities of existence's being that we have already mentioned is that of authenticity and inauthenticity. I will go into this briefly because we will be making use of this distinction later in clarifying the difference between authentic and inauthentic truth. In looking at the phenomenon of care, we have brought out three [229] structures of existence: being-in-the-world, being-with-others, and being-concerned-about-oneself. Furthermore, as so characterized, this existence is essentially always *my* existence. In ontological statements about this being that I call existence, the personal pronoun must necessarily be also mentioned: this being [*Seiendes*] that has the character of existence is an "I am" or a "you are." The way we understand this is that existence, by its very essence, is always mine, and not in the sense of some formal generality. Rather, existence is always mine *to be* in this way or that and *to be* such and so. Existence is always mine insofar as existence has *a priori* decided the way in which it is mine—not that existence itself has necessarily made the decision, but rather in the sense that "a decision has already been made" about my existence. "Existence is always mine" means factically that existence has a self that must be appropriated in one way or in another and to one extent or another. It has a self that it must grasp and understand as its own to a greater or lesser degree. Or in the deficient mode, it has not yet grasped itself or has already lost itself. First and foremost, existence has usually not yet achieved itself or has not yet found itself (during its youth, for example). Or it has lost itself, perhaps even at the most vital point of its life. Existence can have lost itself—and not yet have found itself—only insofar as existence, in its very being, is mine, i.e., my possible authentic existence. The two modes of authenticity and inauthenticity are grounded in the fact that existence as such is mine.

What is more, the inauthenticity of existence does not refer to less being or an inferior grade of being. Rather, inauthenticity precisely can indicate existence in its full concretion—its many activities, its liveliness, its interestedness, its ability to enjoy—in all of which it concretely lives and moves. For the most part—and this is important—existence comports itself neither in the mode of authenticity nor in that of simply being lost, but instead in a remarkable indifference. That, in turn, is not nothing but something [230] positive—the averageness of existence, which we call "everydayness," and which is especially difficult to understand categorially in its structure and in the meaning of its being. I have said something about this in earlier courses and will not go into it here.

In this connection, we need to understand that the possibility of inauthenticity and its dominant role is comprehensible only in terms of the structure of existence. As we said, existence is being in the world. When we pointed out this structure we emphasized right off that it mostly takes the form of familiarity with the world. That is to say, concern loses itself in its world and gets determined primarily in terms of the world it is involved with. We must remember that this form of concern as familiarity with the world, which we can now characterize as inauthentic concern about things, is a fundamental way that existence is. We go into this phenomenon precisely because our *a-priori*-having operates chiefly in the arena of statements *about* the world. Natural, casual statements that we make fall within such statements about things we meet in the world, and these statements arise from concern about and dealings with the world. These statements are the precise focus of our reflections, or rather the ur-temporality of these statements. To that end, we said we must first acquire the horizon in which such a comportment—a specific statement—operates. Now we have clarified this horizon, at least in preliminary fashion.

Concern in the form of a concern that is involved in the world is a specific mode of care itself. The fact that we have given the name "inauthentic existence" to such involvement in the world does not mean that existence annihilates itself (so to speak) in its being when it loses itself. No, it means that existence, insofar as it is a concerned absorption in the world, is—as such and even in its state of being lost—a kind of being in which existence is concerned for itself. When we speak of [231] absorption in, or fallenness into, the world, that does not mean that existence's kind of being (viz., that its being is to be concerned about its being) is extinguished. If that were to happen, care would no longer be care and concern about things would be impossible. Rather, we understand absorption in the world, in the form of concern and loss of the self, as meaning that the being of the self is modified in some way by its absorption, but is still itself in this modification.

The modification is manifest precisely in the fact that, given such concernful world-absorption, existence understands itself only in and through such comportment. It knows itself and understands itself but only as related-to-its-world. Thus the world of my concern and the things with which I am involved ultimately determine me and my being. I now understand myself and regulate the possibilities of my being (whether primarily or in large measure) in terms of those things and their involvement. Even the extreme forms of this mode of inauthenticity still contain the primary structure. In inauthenticity, I am concerned about my existence.

Given the way we understand the being of existence, we can say that existence puts itself into one of the possibilities of its being and therefore into a specific possibility of concern, and in so doing remains with its world. Concern and its object are determined structurally in terms of care itself. We can interpret the most extreme case of manual engagement with something and show that even in complete self-forgetfulness, the orientation of care whereby existence is concerned for itself is still alive therein—except that the existence that is concerned for itself is now understood almost as a thing, something simply there, something you meet up with indirectly through whatever you happen to be working on at the time.

We must remember that inauthenticity is only a modification of the full structure of care. The concern that goes with inauthenticity we call [232] "fallen concern." In inauthentic concern, existence places itself into one of its determined possibilities of being, and places itself into its concern about things in such a way that its comportment is determined in terms of the object of that concern. In its involvement with the object of its concern, existence remains with that object. Whatever existence is concerned about and cares for, is where existence dwells. Those are the things existence has, and existence is concerned with possessing them and increasing that possession. All production and acquisition in the broadest sense (including the production and acquisition of knowledge about things), all of that already presumes a specific kind of possession, and so the one who already possesses is able to increase his possession. By contrast, if existence is to gain itself in its authenticity and not be exclusively or primarily lost in its world, existence needs to have already lost itself in order to gain itself—lost itself in the sense that it is always able to give itself over to worldly production and acquisition.

In Christianity and its interpretation of existence this particular matrix of being that obtains between existence's authentic being and fallen concern has undergone a specific conceptualization. But we should not understand this structure as if it were specific to a Christian awareness of existence. Just the reverse. Only because existence has this structure in itself *qua* care can there be a specifically Christian conception of existence. And because of that (although we can't go into it here), these structures can be worked out in complete isolation from any orientation to whatever kind of [theological] dogmatics. You can see the difference from two things: (1) What is at stake in *our* determinations is an analysis of structures and categorial determinations. (2) A concretion of the interpretation of existence need not necessarily be a Christian one. In fact, any philosophy—which, as philosophy, must stand outside [233] of faith—not only *may* not, but absolutely *cannot* be a Christian interpretation. On the other hand, we should not forget that this Christian understanding of existence (which for its part has changed multiple times in the course of history) is not a monolith at all, and has itself opened a specific area of existence for philosophical consideration and inquiry. This problematic pertains not just to the Middle Ages. All modern philosophy is incomprehensible without the doctrines of Christian dogmatics. On the other side, the doctrines of Christian dogmatics are entirely determined, both in conceptuality and scientific character, by the philosophy of its day.

Let me emphasize: these connections that we can uncover between care as authentic being and fallen concern, are contained in the very idea of care as the meaning of the being of existence. The kind of concern in which existence has lost itself in its world arises from the fact that existence itself, insofar as it is in a world, is essentially referred to this world in which it is. Existence is factically fallen into its world. Or: this fallenness into its world belongs to the facticity of existence. By "facticity" we understand a specific determination of the being of existence. The term does not have an indifferent meaning that would be the same as the factuality of something merely there. Nonetheless, it is, in a specific sense, a *factum* and we designate this specificity as facticity and will determine it more precisely later. Being essentially referred to the world already entails fallenness and fallen concern.

With this we have a determination of the structure of existence that is adequate for our purposes. We can now see the horizon within which any statement about the world, as a comportment of existence, is located. In particular we see what we established by taking our question in the first direction we took, [234] namely, the *a priori* letting-the-world-encounter and the tendency to uncover. Now we must determine the ur-temporality of these phenomena as modes of the being of existence and thus as comportments that have the ontological character of care. If ur-temporality is a—or *the*—basic determination of being itself, then probably care itself in its whole structure must have an ur-temporal character. And for their part, the comportments of the whole will be ur-temporal insofar as they are comportments of existence, the phenomena of concern and care.[17]

*　*　*

§18. The ur-temporality of care

Our goal is to secure a basic interpretation of the statement in terms of its ur-temporality. For that we have to clarify the ur-temporality of care as such. And for that we need we keep in mind the structures we have acquired up to this point.

We now understand concern about the world (and particularly fallen concern) as a matter of being already familiar with the world. We also characterized the care at the heart of concern as the form of being in which a being is concerned for its being. We need to understand the structure of care as "formally" as possible, not in the sense of emptying it out and reducing it to a mere relation of something to something else. We mean, rather, *formally indicating* a specific structure of existence. The peculiar thing we have to understand is the phenomenon that existence is always concerned about something.

We have said what existence is concerned about. We now leave aside two issues—the viewpoint whence existence grasps the being that it cares about, and the degree to which we explicitly enact that understanding, i.e., actually live in it or even care about it—in order to focus on our sole topic: the existential structure of being-concerned-about-one's-being, or having my being "at stake" for myself.

"Being at stake" entails that *what* I am concerned about is *not a solid possession*. And in fact, the "at stake" belongs to existence as such as long as existence is. Therefore, [235] the "what is at stake" is *never* a solid possession. However, *having*-something-at-stake means that existence is precisely a *being-unto* what is at stake. This being-unto is not a matter of being with something that is just there, but rather being with something that, of its ownmost being, is not yet a solid posses-

17. [Here (Moser, p. 492) Heidegger ends his lecture of Tuesday, 19 January 1926, to be followed by that of Thursday, 21 January, which opened with a 1,240-word summary that is omitted in GA 21.]

sion, and in the final analysis never can be. Care is being-unto, and what it is unto is the very being of existence, the being that existence always is not yet but can be. Thus, "at stake" entails a *being-out-for* one's own being as ability-to-be.

This ability is determined not primarily in terms of incidental data, situations, and the like that sometimes hit existence one way, sometimes another. All of that is existentially possible only because existence, as care, is constantly its own ability in the form of being-out-for this ability. The "at stake" entails that existence has been *a priori* placed in its ability, in fact, already placed *a priori* face-to-face with itself. Care means: existence is ahead of itself. Care, as such, is concern. Care has the structure of 1. being ahead-of-oneself, along with 2. being *a priori* familiar-with-the-world. In a phrase: *being a priori ahead of oneself and familiar with one's world*. With that, we have understood the ontological structure of concernful care.

In the investigation that follows we must limit ourselves to this issue alone. We intentionally do not treat being with others or care as concern. We omit them specifically because our chosen subject is only statements about the world, not statements about other people—even though (as is to be shown) the other is present in a certain way in statements about the world. Those other phenomena are essentially more difficult, and they would presuppose yet other reflections. And for our preliminary exposition of ur-temporal structures, the phenomena should not be developed in too complicated a fashion.

Let us remember that we are taking the analysis in a somewhat one-sided direction toward concernful care. But we also note that, as we have said, we cannot master the phenomena of concern-for and being-with either by simply broadening and modifying what [236] we have established about concern or by simply transferring being-unto-oneself and its structure over to being-unto-others as in that favorite argument:

1. Being-unto-others is very different from being unto a thing.
2. The other is itself also an existence.
3. In this case, therefore, we have the ontological relation of one existence to another.
4. But such a relation is already included in one's *own* existence, insofar as existence as such relates to itself.
5. Therefore, being-unto-another is, so to speak, merely a projection of the ontological relation of existence to itself.

It is easy to see, however, that in being-unto-oneself, that self is precisely not someone else. Therefore, being-unto-others is an irreducible, independent way of being, one that is co-original in existence along with being-in and being-unto-oneself. Contrary to the argument above, the other, the "thou," is nothing like a second "I" to whom I counterpose myself. We certainly cannot deny that the possibility of understanding another is to some degree co-conditioned by how I understand myself or my existence as such. But such conditionedness of the factical performance of understanding another already presupposes (and does not first create) being-unto-another as unto a thou. In interpreting the phenomenon of being-with as being-unto-another (as we must, in principle), never forget that we never experience other people as some indeterminate mental "centers," floating around in an empty "over-against-us." We experience each other person as an existence, a being-with, a being-with-one-another in a world. Even being-with-another lives first of all from a shared-being [*Mitsein*] with him in a world. Thus, the other is, in principle, uncovered for others in his very existence. So it is a mistake to interpret the other phenomenally as a second ego, and it is absurd to pose the problem of co-being with others in such a way that one posits the constructivistic presupposition that first I am given only to myself— and then how does this *solus ipse* manage to reach out to a thou? [237]

Let this suffice to characterize the most obvious problems that go with the phenomenon of being-with. Insofar as our topic is statements about the *world*, other people are not the subject matter of such statements. But on the other hand, recall that we distinguished three meanings of "statement":

1. pointing-out,
2. predication,
3. communication.

When a statement is a communication, the full phenomenal content of the statement about the world does include the other to whom we communicate what is said in the statement. That is, the reception and understanding of a communication made by the other means the same as that she shares with me her vision and understanding of, and her way of being unto, what is being spoken about.[18] In a statement that is shared and communicated in this fashion, two things happen: A thing becomes uncovered for another person; but more than that, a new shared-being with that other person in the world is generated. *This* is what progress in scientific knowledge means, and not the piling up of more and more results. But here too we can only allude to these phenomena.

I emphasize these connections that we will not be taking up because time and again one slips into the mistaken notion that what gets

18. [The *es* at GA 21, p. 237.12, is a misprint for *er*—i.e., "der Andere"; cf. Moser, p. 505.4.]

said about a subject during a lecture course within the appropriate methodological limits is the only thing that could be said. One can, in fact, discuss exclusively the fundamental issues, but what is discussed does not have to include everything. Having defined the limits of our investigation and excluded the phenomenon of concern-for, we may return to our topic.

The ontological structure of concernful care is what determines existence as: *a priori* ahead-of-oneself-and-familiar-with-one's-world. Is there anything in this ontological structure of existence that has to do with the temporal? And by the way, what is this "temporal," whose basic structures we are supposed to investigate? We have already emphasized the drawbacks of our chosen path, including the indeterminateness of the phenomenon of time itself, in reference [238] to which we use terms like "ur-temporality" and "the ur-temporal." Our lack of a specific orientation concerns not just any phenomenon, but *time.* Of course it is a commonplace to say that time is hard to understand, and there is no doubt that we lack a clear idea of what we call "time."

We will get some help by orienting ourselves to the everyday understanding of time, pursuing and critically discussing what is meant by "ur-temporal" characteristics, especially with regard to care. The everyday understanding of time is not wrong or the like. It has its own legitimacy and even an understandable necessity.[19]

*   *   *

The structure of the everyday understanding of time must be intrinsically ur-temporal, it must formally have a "relation to time." To say that something is temporally determined means that it is "earlier" or "later" than something else; it comes "before" or "after" something. Or it has "already" or "not yet" taken place. Moreover, we say something is "at the same time" as something else, or in another case that it is not at the same time but "of the same duration." "Earlier—at the same time—later" do not simply coincide with "past–present–future," since the past itself, as past, can be earlier or later or at the same time, and the same with the future. And even in the "now" there is a before and an after, and since they are found in every now, they are therefore found in every "just now" [*Soeben*] and "already-has-been," and likewise in every "right away" [*Sofort*]. Every "just now" is, in the very next now, a "just a second ago." The past constantly increases in its pastness. It becomes intrinsically ever-more past, so that ever-new nows and just-nows are produced and push the past into already-has-

19. [Here (Moser, p. 507) Heidegger ends his lecture of Thursday, 21 January 1926, to be followed by that of Friday, 22 January, which opened with a 560-word summary that is omitted in GA 21.]

been-ness. Although the past no longer "is," it continually becomes more and more past. The past "is" not simply past. It is not the one track of time, the one "arm" of time, that is not.

There is a plethora of time-characteristics: earlier, later, before, by now, already, not yet, at the same time, just now, [239] right way (in the very next second), now; past, present, future. With them we have essentially exhausted what can be established about time—I mean: not as regards the reckoning of time, but as regards the philosophical interpretation of the interconnection of these characteristics and of the "propositions about time" that are grounded in these interconnections, for example: "Different times cannot be at the same time."

In the course of the history of the problem of time, all the characteristics have been examined more or less with deep insight and with surety as regards the methodological focus of the analysis. In the process the terms were coined that are used for all research into time.

Here we have chiefly named time-characteristics that at first sight are not congruous, although they are "promiscuously" employed in the common understanding and imprecise everyday linguistic usage: earlier, later, before, after, already, not yet. And now we see that two of the characteristics we just named occur in the notion of the structure of concernful care: *already*-being-with and being-*ahead*-of-oneself. "Already" is the opposite of "not yet," as "before" [*vor*] is the opposite of "after."

The question remains whether the aforementioned structure of care is adequately understood when it is interpreted in the sense of the characteristics of "already" and "before" that we have just adduced. The "already" means an "already-having-been," a "no-longer-now." The "before" means a "not-yet-now" in contrast to a "now" or a "no-longer-now." Both characteristics refer to a being with reference to the fact that it is experienced as running its course "in time." And if something gets determined by these characteristics, then it is determined in relation to time.

But what does it mean that something is determined in relation to time in this fashion? And what is the condition of possibility for something being determined in this way? To speak of something as determined in relation to time is to speak of it with regard to its traversing a now.

Something can traverse a now only if it comes into a now, only if we encounter it in a now. In turn, we can encounter something only if it can show up—[240] and the only thing that can show up is something whose kind of being is presence-there. We say that what is present-there occurs in the world. So the kind of being that pertains to what is present-there is precisely this "occurring within the world."[20]

20. Presence-there and occurrence-within-the-world are to be sharply separated from being-in *qua* being in a world. The latter pertains to the very essence of

Why do we understand this coursing along in time as a passing through a now? Answer: because time—taken as that in relation to which something is determined as being in time—is and must be understood in terms of its now. The time "in" which something runs its course is time experienced as now-time. Insofar as concern must take time into account and reckon with it and calculate something with reference to it, time must be understood as now-time. Why is it that time is first of all experienced as now-time? And why is it that the time which is experienced in that way is interpreted in the sense that we've already indicated? These matters must be clarified in terms of time itself—but this is a task for a later time.

In the present context, the point is simply to see that the characteristics we have educed are oriented to the now, and not accidentally or in the sense of an empty possibility. Instead, the now-relation is constitutive of their being. They are what they are on the basis of that relation. The "not yet" is "not yet now"; the "already" is always an "already having been by now." Likewise, "right away" is a "right now," and "one second ago" is "one second ago now."

Say I pursue the "a second ago now" as it sinks into the past. What if I say that the "a second ago now" is currently "*two* seconds ago now." In that case, the "now" of "a second ago now" is still there in the "two seconds ago now." It has not been lost. Rather, "a second ago now" keeps its *own* now, even when it becomes "two seconds ago now." Moreover, for its part, the "second ago" of "a second ago now" *is* "a second ago" of "a second ago now" only because of an essential relation to a *new* [241] "now." And the original now of "a second ago *now*" has already become its own "second ago" in relation to that new now.

The "at the same time" (the other time-characteristic we mentioned) is also a now-phenomenon. Things are "at the same time" when they are "in the same now," or as we say, "at the same time." That latter phrase shows it is not arbitrary that we understand time as now-time, as time which is oriented in terms of the now.

According to this explanation of time, the fact that something is time-determined means that it is experienced as present-there now or is understood as something present-there or not present-there (in the form of a not-yet or a no-longer). Something that we encounter in this

existence's kind of being. A stone or a table is present within the world. It is a thing-*of*-the-world. It *is*, but it never is in-a-world in the sense of being in and being familiar with a world. By contrast a human being is, strictly speaking, never just present-there within a world. We attain this supposedly "primary" form of being only when we are dead. In fact, only at that point is a human being something [that is] just present-there—because then the human being is no longer "there" [*da*] in the sense of existence that we have explained.

way is "in" time, or as we also say, it "falls" within time, within such and such a time. Such-and-such-a-time is determined on the basis of an enumeration of nows.

Is care time-determined in this sense? Does "already"—taken as the structural moment of "already-familiar-with" [*Schon-bei*]—mean the same as "already having been"? Should we say that being-familiar-with is essentially the same as being in the now? And wouldn't that mean (since being-familiar-with and being-in-the-world are modes of existence's being) that existence, as being-*already*-with, is already no more? The result of that would be: at every now in which existence is, existence is no more—i.e., is not. Obviously we do not mean anything like that. Rather, the "already" is precisely a characteristic of existence's being. It must determine existence's being positively. It cannot express a being-no-longer.

Or does this "already" mean the same as "already beforehand"? Existence is already beforehand a being-familiar-with—but already beforehand in relation to what? The determination "already" should hold with regard to existence itself. But the "already" cannot mean: "already before *itself*." It cannot mean that existence was already with its world before it was at all, because if existence was with its world, then it *already was,* and it is impossible for existence to enter into being "later" than this "already."

Therefore the "already," as a moment in the ontological structure of "already-familiar-with," does not refer to or determine a being as regards any "having-been-earlier-than" or "having-been-later-than" either itself or anyone else. [242]

Correspondingly, the same holds for the "before" [*vor*] in the phenomenon of "being-ahead-of-oneself" [*Sich-vor-weg-sein*]. Again, this characteristic of "before" cannot mean that existence as care is "beforehand" in relation to itself, as if it were earlier than it "is," for existence precisely *is* insofar as it is ahead-of-itself.

As time-characteristics, "already" and "before" have nothing to do with any thing that occurs "in time" (that is, in its now). They do not refer to any thing that can be determined in this now according to an "earlier than" or a "later than." Therefore, although care is determined by time-characteristics, it is not time-determined in the sense that it occurs, as a being, "within time." But that does not mean it is something outside of or above time. "Extra-temporal" and "supra-temporal" are only modifications of being-in-time, and they presuppose this being-in-time as what makes them possible. Therefore, care is not time-determined in this sense.

But can it be time-determined at all? What would that mean? As we have explained, care is the being of existence. Therefore, it is not itself a being, and certainly not a being "present-there." If "already"

and "before/ahead of" were to have the sense of time-determinations—i.e., if they were to determine the "how" of being-in-time—
then care *qua* being [*Sein*] would be a time-determined being [*Seiendes*]. But to take being [*Sein*] as a being [*Seiendes*] is obviously a
contradiction, and doubly so in the present case insofar as it is truly
contradictory in the first place to take the being of a being (namely,
existence) to be a being [*Seiendes*] that is totally opposed to existence.
Care not only is not time-determined in the aforementioned sense,
but also absolutely cannot be that. And yet "already" and "before/
ahead of" are time-characteristics! Therefore, the only possibility left
is that their temporal meaning is not the one expounded up to this
point, but a different one. In what sense is it different?

From what we said earlier, insofar as care does not refer to a being, it
is not related to a "now" within which something present-there does
and can occur and through which it acquires a certain temporal determinability. The characteristics "already" and "before/ahead of" are
[243] determinations not of any being at all but of a certain kind of
being. At first it is unclear what it is supposed to mean that "already"
and "before/ahead of" are not time-determinations of a being [*Seiendes*], but time-characteristics of a kind of being [*Sein*]. But then it would
seem that we are back at square one. Nonetheless, even if we have not
acquired anything positive, we have gained something essential in the
form of a "prohibition," namely, the indication that if "already" and
"before/ahead of" are time-phenomena, the most readily available interpretation of time as now-time is of no help here. Therefore, we must
come up with a different *meaning* of time (not a different *time*). In the
process perhaps we will later see why and to what extent it is the case
that time is and must be experienced above all in the sense we have
already discussed.

What path can guide us to this different meaning of time and finally help us understand the temporal meaning of these characteristics that we designate as "ur-temporalia"? I have already mentioned
that as we walk our chosen path, we are walking and working without foundations. We did not begin by coming up with an original and
proper meaning of time from which we could philosophically deduce
these time-characteristics as such. Quite the contrary, we began with
the readily available understanding of time as "now-time" and have
been using it to grope our way toward the proper meaning of time. We
want to illumine and delineate more sharply the initially obscure
time-characteristics of "already" and "before" in contrast to the common understanding of them. For that we need to go deeper into the
everyday understanding of time (which is not *per se* wrong, but has its
own legitimacy and necessity), and we need to determine more precisely the structures we draw from it. We do so in order to make sure

that the thread guiding us in clarifying everyday time (and that is to lead us to original time) is itself securely grounded.[21] [244]

* * *

§19. Preparatory considerations toward attaining an original understanding of time. A return to the history of the philosophical interpretation of the concept of time

Our goal is an ur-temporal analysis of care. So we began by determining the time-character of those moments that first push to the fore as time-determinations in the structure of care, namely, already-familiar-with in being-ahead-of-oneself. First we drew our attention to the moments of "already" and "before/ahead of," and in so doing we remained oriented to characterizing the kind of time that is accessible in the everyday experience of time. We focused on the common concept of time because it is the only one that has been theoretically and conceptually worked out in philosophy heretofore (although only within certain limits).

Characterizing the common concept of time entails understanding time in terms of the now. The now plays a preeminent role in the common understanding of time insofar as we determine the other two time-characteristics—past and future—in relation to it, the past as the no-longer-now, and the future as the not-yet-now. So the now-relation is essential for understanding the past and the future.

As regards the understanding of time as now-time, we can determine something as temporal only insofar as its kind of being is mere presence, that is, only insofar as we understand the thing as having that kind of being. Given the very meaning of its being, only a being that has the character of mere presence has the intrinsic possibility of passing sequentially through a now.

We also say that a being falls within time, or more exactly that at any given moment it falls within a now. So we can reverse the proposition. If something's time-determination is "falling within a now," its kind of being is mere presence. The being of the merely present pertains primarily to the world, that is, to nature. World and nature are not identical. World is the categorially broader concept, rather than nature being the broader concept and [245] world a determined section of it. No, nature is the world only insofar as it is uncovered in a determinate way.

With our focus set on the common concept of time, we asked: Do the moments of care that we first came up with—"already" and "ahead

---

21. [Here (Moser, p. 520) Heidegger ends his lecture of Friday, 22 January 1926, to be followed by that of Monday, 25 January.]

of"—have the time-characteristics of ordinary time? Our analysis has shown that this is impossible. The moments of care cannot have the ordinary sense of "temporal." If they did, the very structure of care—a form of *being*—would have the character of *a being*, since we have shown that only the present-there can have the determinations of ordinary time. Care is not a being but a way of being, specifically existence's way of being, which is the opposite of mere presence and the merely present. Therefore, there is no way we can understand "ahead of" and "already" in terms of the ordinary understanding of time and its characteristics. Hence the need to ask how, if at all, the "already" and "ahead of" can be understood temporally.

For that to happen, we will have to come up with a more original (or more cautiously: a different) understanding of time that will allow us to determine the meaning of these characteristics. The methodological path we are following does not have such an understanding of time at hand. Instead we have to acquire it indirectly and in the following way: While holding firm to the characteristics of care that we have already gained, we propose the hypothesis that their time-characteristics have a different sense, so we orient ourselves in a more precise way to the usual concept of time and its structures. In highlighting those characteristics, we will soon arrive at a broader understanding of ur-time. Only then can we understand how, within the original understanding of time, ur-temporality is possible.

We want to highlight the initially unclear time-characteristics of "already" and "ahead of" as determinations of care in contrast to the ordinary concept of time. The more securely and concretely we understand the ordinary concept of time, the more confident will be our progress. [246] To that end, let us direct ourselves very briefly to the history of the development of the concept (and thus the interpretation) of time heretofore. Naturally, in doing so, we do not need to come up with an extended history of the concept of time. Instead, we will pause only at certain points in that history where the explanation of the concept of time took on a certain fundamental, ontological significance. We do so with the intention of thereby showing that right up to our own day the philosophical interpretation of time has in fact been oriented to the ordinary understanding of time; we will prove the thesis that right up to today, time has always been understood as now-time.

Some philosophers, in the course of expounding the phenomenon of time, especially recently, have made a distinction between objective and subjective time, or between transcendent and immanent time. This distinction says nothing, however, because it could well be that even the so-called "immanent" time, the time of lived experience, merely carries over into itself the characteristics of the so-called transcendent or objective time. We will see that this distinction between immanent/subjective and transcendent/objective time remains caught up in the understanding of time as now-time. If the now is the proper being of time, it would be consistent to say that to a certain degree time, taken as a whole (i.e., the unity of present, past, and future), has within itself an imbalanced kind of reality. There is the properly real, i.e., the present. In turn every now has (as Lotze puts it) two unequal arms of non-being stretching out in both directions: one into the past and the other into the future. But the two arms are different: the non-being of the past is the no-longer, and the non-being of the future [247] is the not-yet.

Lotze's image characterizes very clearly the way the real accent of temporal being falls on the now, the now-present. In our everyday experience of time we understand it as something we use for reckoning in our concern for the world, something we can use to compute the events we encounter in the world. In this way, concernful being-in-the-world places "time" within its "calculating." In so doing, everyday experience understands nothing more about what all this means, and it requires no further understanding as long as it manages to put time at its own disposal for purposes of calculation. In this sense, these events in the world fall "within time."

The theoretical study of events in the world purely as incidents of movement *qua* change of place is one example of an independent, determinately oriented elaboration of calculative concern and time-reckoning. Movement is understood this way. Such a theoretical-calculative study of the world consists in uncovering and determining *nature*. In principle, natural science embraces the foundation and horizon of all concern about the world. In determining the pure processes of nature, it uses time for its calculations, in basically the same way that pre-scientific experience does when it focuses on and takes account of things in the world as regards, e.g., the basic events of the change of day and night. For the investigation of nature—i.e., physics—time is inserted into the basic formula by which physics determines its objects: $s = c \cdot t$ [*spatium = celeritas · tempus*]. That is, the distance covered by something in motion is equal to its velocity multiplied by the number of now-points the movement runs through as long as it persists. Here as well, the processes fall "within time" in the sense that we explained.

Now if the idea of nature is not limited to material processes but includes all processes of things present, whether they be physical or mental, then in this sense mental processes as well as physical ones fall within time. Aristotle already understood explicitly this business of the "in time" taken in this broader sense. Later [248] Kant gave particular emphasis to the fact that the data of inner (and not just outer) sense—in fact, the data of outer *and* inner sense—determined time. There is no question that this is very obscure, and Kant gave only a rough exposition of the connection.

Let us give the name "world-time" to the time in which worldly data and natural processes (in the narrow sense) fall. Here we understand "world" in the philosophical sense: the "wherein" of existence's being. At this juncture we cannot go into a proper explanation of the concept and structure of "world." We are still completely in the dark about what this world-time basically is and how we are to understand it. All we know is that this time, understood as now-time, is the time wherein we encounter whatever is present.

A philosophical reflection does not fall out of the sky, nor is it an arbitrarily concocted undertaking. Like all knowledge it grows out of our factical existence and its everydayness. To the degree philosophical reflection tries to direct itself to time, it will let itself be given time in the form in which neutral world-experience knows time. That is to say, when philosophical knowledge stands in connection with science, it will understand time in the same way the phenomenon is already given in science. But on the other hand we also have to say: *If* a philosophical discussion of time has its place in the context of a philosophical reflection on nature; and *if* we treat time primarily within this context (in a controlling, perhaps even exclusive way), then philosophy will understand time basically as world-time. The same holds if the explanation of time gets connected with the question about the possibility of a scientific knowledge of nature, as is the case with Kant. The same goes if the context of the philosophical discussion of time is even more encompassing than that of an investigation focused specifically on nature; an example of this is the question about the origin of the world, or even its creation, as in Augustine and Neo-Platonism, where [249] eternity is posited over against the world understood as all beings within time.

The systematic location of the investigation of the phenomenon of time within a given philosophy is the index of the basic conception that guides the endeavor. Wherever time is seen in connection with world, nature, or created beings, it is understood as now-time, and "temporal" means: occurring and running its course "within time."

This concept of time has dominated all philosophical reflection about time ever since Aristotle first came up with it and presented it in his *Physics* Δ 10–14 with a conceptual power that has never been equaled since. From Aristotle to Hegel, and even more so in the period of post-Hegelian philosophy, this concept of time has remained the guiding thread for the question of time. Why? Basically because the time that is understood in this way is the very kind of time that primarily and persistently imposes itself upon our everyday experience.

Bergson's recent, independent investigation of time is no exception to the rule. It appears to attain to some new insights, and it seems that

Bergson wants to overcome the traditional concept and press forward to a more original concept of time. But on closer examination we see that Bergson falls into the very concept of time that he is trying to overcome—even though (and we should clearly emphasize this) Bergson is guided by a correct instinct.

Bergson's goal is to work out the difference between time and duration. Duration, however, for Bergson is nothing but lived time, and this lived time, in turn, is merely object-time or world-time, insofar as it is considered in the way it shows up in consciousness. A clear indication that Bergson failed to break through to a conception and categorial knowledge of ur-time is the fact that he understood even lived time—duration—as (in French) *"succession,"* with the sole proviso that the *succession* of lived time is, he says, not a quantitative *succession* laid out in individual now-points. Instead, this *succession* is a [250] qualitative one, in which the individual moments of time—past, present, and future—permeate each other. With that he has reached the limit, for he does not say what quantity or quality is; he provides no principled discussion of these two guiding threads, but simply presupposes them as already known. Moreover, he describes qualitative time—duration—merely in images, with not a word about working out any kind of concept. The essential point, therefore, is that Bergson certainly does try to get to authentic time by way of the phenomenon of duration, but he understands duration once again in terms of *succession*.

Only because today we still do not yet understand the proper sense of world-time can we come to believe that Bergson has understood time in a more original way. That he failed to do so is shown by the fact that he misunderstands the time which he defines as time in its proper sense and which he distinguishes from duration. He fails to understand time in its own sense, and instead identifies it with space. In this regard, we must say that even though it is not completely obvious, Bergson conducts his analysis of time in constant opposition to Aristotle's concept of time. In his early years Bergson made extensive studies of Aristotle, and in 1889, the same year his first investigation on time and duration appeared, he published a small treatise, his dissertation, *On the Concept of Place in Aristotle*. Place and time are treated by Aristotle in the same book. And it is quite clear how Bergson arrived at his concept of duration in opposition to quantitative time, namely, by misunderstanding Aristotle's definition of time as ἀριθμὸς κινήσεως, i.e., as the number— or better, the what-gets-numbered—of movement.

In his later writings Bergson has not changed the exposition of time given in his early work. On the contrary, he has maintained it up to the present day. The essential and enduring element of his philosophical work does not lie [251] in this direction at all. Rather, the things of value, for which we are grateful, are found in his text *Matière et Mé-*

moire.[22] It is a basic text for modern biology, and it contains insights that are far from exhausted yet. Today it is Scheler, above all, who is strongly influenced by it. Let this stand as a preface to our historical orientation. Since current opinion takes it as obvious that Bergson has discovered a new concept of time, we should discuss it critically and at length.

We will now take up a historical approach to the concept of time with the intention of concretely appropriating the temporal character-istics of time as the tradition experienced them.[23] At the same time we will demonstrate the predominance of a specific interpretation of time. We proceed to a further explanation of the historical development of the understanding of time and to an exposition of the concept of time, going backwards in history. Our investigation is intentionally oriented to a similar investigation that we have already conducted, namely, into the history of the concept of intuition.[24] There is an inner connection between the phenomenon of intuition, the predominance of the truth of intuition, and the specific form of the dominant understanding of time, viz., as now-time. We begin our treatment, which aims at getting a better grip on the ordinary understanding of time, with an analysis of time in Hegel.

---

§20. Hegel's interpretation of time in the *Encyclopaedia*[25]

Hegel treats time thematically in his *Encyclopaedia of the Philosophical Sciences,* part II, *The Philosophy of Nature.*[26]

---

22. [Henri Bergson, *Matière et mémoire. Essai sur la relation du corps à l'esprit* (Paris: F. Alcan, 1896); translated by Nancy Margaret Paul and W. Scott Palmer as *Matter and Memory* (New York: Zone Books, 1988).]

23. [Here the Moser transcript (p. 531) clarifies GA 21 (p. 251).]

24. [Heidegger may be referring to his course of Summer Semester 1920, "Phän-omenologie der Anschauung und des Ausdrucks," which has been published as GA 59, *Phänomenologie der Anschauung und des Ausdrucks. Theorie der philosophischen Begriffs-bildung,* ed. Claudius Strube (Frankfurt am Main: Vittorio Klosterman, 1993).]

25. [Heidegger was to make use of this section of the lecture-course in writing §82 of *Being and Time;* cf. *SZ,* pp. 566ff. / tr. 481ff.]

26. [The edition that Heidegger uses is Hegel, *Encyklopädie der philosophischen Wissenschaften im Grundrisse (1830),* ed. Gerardus J. P. J. Bolland (Leiden: A. H. Adriani, 1906), which contains the *Zusätze* (Addenda). A newer edition, also with the *Zusätze,* is *Encyklopädie der philosophischen Wissenschaften im Grundrisse (1830),* ed. Eva Moldenhauer and Karl Markus Michel (Frankfurt am Main: Suhrkamp, 1970). See also *Hegel's Philosophy of Nature,* ed. and trans. M. J. Petry (London: George Allen & Unwin / New York: Humanities Press, 1970), with *Zusätze;* and

Section One: Mechanics
  A. Space and Time
    [1. Space in general. §§254-256]
    2. Time in general. §§257-260

This thematic context allows for no misunderstanding: time is connected with space, but not the way it is in Kant and in the tradition of
the philosophy of nature generally, ever since [252] Aristotle—namely,
as "space *and also* time." Rather, Hegel's explanation tries to show
something more—that space *becomes* time:

> The truth of space is time, so that space becomes time; it is not we who,
> subjectively as it were, make the transition to time; rather, space itself
> makes the transition {into time}. In the usual representation {by which
> Hegel means: In the naïve view}, space and time are quite separate: space
> is there, and then we *also* have time. Philosophy fights against this "also."
> (§257, Addendum)[27]

By that last sentence Hegel means: philosophy sublates the difference.
In the naïve view of common sense, space and time are different,
whereas for absolute thinking no such distinction may hold: Space
becomes time. When thought in an absolute fashion, space "is" time.
Bergson has expressed the opposite thesis, not "Space is time" but
"Time is space." Both theses are untenable; but both are on the scent
of a phenomenal connection between space and time. Basically both
are referring to the same thing but without understanding what they
mean by their diametrically opposed propositions. And both Bergson
and Hegel destroy what there is of authentic content in their theses, by
sublating it not with a solid, sure truth but by a fundamental sophistry
that Hegel's dialectic lives off.
    We now go into this thesis a bit further in order to clarify how time
is experienced and understood in Hegel, namely, as the time of nows.—
"Space becomes time." That means: When it is thought in an absolute
philosophical way, space "becomes"—i.e., comes into "being" and thus
"is"—time. What does "is" mean here? Does it mean the same as in the
sentence "The chalk is a book"? In that case "is" means: "The chalk
has the whatness (and the thereness) of a book." They are both the-
very-same.
    Let us ignore for a moment the basic inadequacy of explaining a
categorial relation (e.g., between space and time) in terms of a relation
between concrete things (chalk, book). Let's use the example simply

Hegel's Philosophy of Nature, trans. A. V. Miller (Oxford: Clarendon Press, 1970),
without *Zusätze*. I use and amend both translations.]
    27. [Heidegger's glosses are recorded in Moser, p. 532.9-11.]

to clarify what Hegel means by "is" when he says "Space is time." He does not, in fact, mean that they are the-very-same, even though, in his Romantic fashion, he lets this meaning mix with his own. Yes, "space is time"—but Hegel would [253] resist someone saying, "Everything spatial is temporal," or even, "There is no such thing as space; rather, everything is only time." Naturally that is not what "is" means in the sentence, "Space is time."

The "is" in the thesis "Space is time" means that space has the being of time or that the being of space is determined by time—in fact, is determinable *only* by time. This is something Hegel does not understand, and yet he must somehow have it in mind if his thesis is to have any meaning at all. Space gets its way of being determined—i.e., the fact of its being-thought-absolutely—only from time. But something's having-been-thought-absolutely is that thing's truth. And the being of something is thought in the truth of that thing.[28] That is why Hegel says: "The truth of space {i.e., its being-thought absolutely: its being} is time." How can we understand that more precisely with regard to the phenomenon of space? Although we can't go into a long discussion of how Hegel determines the concept of space, we will discuss it just enough to let us understand phenomenally how and why Hegel can say "Space becomes time."[29]

*   *   *

According to Hegel, space is the "unmediated indifference of nature's being-outside-itself" (§254).[30] By way of clarification we can say that space is the abstract multiplicity of points that *could* be differentiated. Space itself is not broken up by these points, but neither does space first arise from them or put itself together out of them—because the points themselves are already space. And so, even though space is determined by these points which can be differentiated and which themselves are space, space itself remains without [any internal] differentiation. The differences themselves are of the same character as what they differenti-

---

28. ["Und in der Wahrheit ist das Sein von etwas gedacht" (GA 21, p. 253.11-12).]

29. [Here (Moser, p. 534) Heidegger ends his lecture of Monday, 25 January 1926, to be followed by that of Tuesday, 26 January, which opened with a 480-word summary that is omitted in GA 21.]

30. [Heidegger's words, both at GA 21, p. 253.20-21, and at Moser, p. 536.29-30, are: "Die 'vermittlungslose Gleichgültigkeit des Außersichseins der Natur' (§254)." That is a somewhat free citation of Hegel's: "Die erste oder unmittelbare Bestimmung der Natur ist die abstrakte *Allgemeinheit ihres Außersichseins,*—dessen vermittlungslose Gleichgültigkeit, *der Raum.*" In English: "The first or unmediated determination of nature is the abstract universality of nature's being-outside-itself—the unmediated indifference of that being-outside-itself—namely, *space.*"]

ate. Nonetheless, insofar as any point differentiates anything at all in space, that point is the negation of space, although in such a way that this negation itself remains *in* space (a point is, after all, space).[31] Thus the point does not raise itself up out of space as if it were something different from space. To put it in Kant's terms, points are merely limitations of space, as are all other spatial phenomena and all space that is determined, i.e., delimited by points, lines, or planes. [254] Space is the non-differentiated outside-each-other of a multiplicity of points. But space itself is not a point; rather, as Hegel says pregnantly, space is *Punktualität*, "punctiformity" (§254, Addendum). This is the basis for the principle by which Hegel thinks space in its truth, which is to say: as time.

> The negativity which relates itself, as a point, to space and which unfolds its determinations, as line and plane, within space is, however, while in that sphere of outside-itself, also and equally a *for-itself*. Negativity posits its determinations in it {i.e., in the sphere of the *for-itself*} but, at the same time, posits them as in the sphere of being-outside-itself, thereby appearing as indifferent vis-à-vis the immobile juxtaposition [which is space]. As thus posited for itself, it {namely, this negativity, the point} is *time*. (§257 Paragraph)[32]

Thus, the negativity of the point—which we explained earlier and which in a word is "punctiformity," i.e., space—is, when posited for itself, time.[33]

Our interpretation will now be directed less at Hegel's formulation than at making accessible the phenomena that are intended therein. The points along with the lines and planes that a point can become are determinations of space that delimit space and thus can constitute a specific space. These determinations or delimitations of a given space are themselves space. But understood "logically" in the sense of Hegel's logic, this means that these determinations and differences, these limits of space, insofar as they themselves are spatial and *are* space, simply remain *in* space. Such limits and differences are what they are by being different-from-something-else, i.e., by negation. A point, *qua* negation, has an indifferent subsistence in space: it arises in space and does not escape it. This indifference of its subsistence *qua* negation is precisely what characterizes space.

---

31. [Moser (p. 537.14–15), with "so, daß diese Negation (Punkt ist ja Raum) im Raum selbst bleibt," corrects GA 21 (p. 253.30–31), which has "so, daß diese Negation im Raum (Punkt ist ja Raum) im Raum selbst bleibt." The Moser text is also closer to *Being and Time;* see *SZ,* p. 567.1–2.]

32. [Heidegger's glosses are found at Moser, p. 538.2–7.]

33. [By "punctiformity" Hegel means the "dot-quality" (Edith Wyschogrod) of something, whence derive lines and planes.]

When we experience or represent space, we represent its limits in their indifferent subsistence, and thus immediately represent the negation. If space is represented in this way, space certainly appears and shows itself, but we do not understand it in its being. [255] Something is understood in its being only in thought. Only when space is understood in its being—i.e., only when it is thought—is the truth of space attained. But a thing is thought, in Hegel's sense of "thought," not when it is immediately represented, i.e., not when the determinations of the thing to be understood simply subsist (are merely there)—in the present case, not when the point, the negation, subsists in indifference. Thinking is determining, and determining (*determinatio*) means *negatio* [negation]. The point (punctiformity, negation) ought not be simply represented. It itself must be thought, determined, i.e., negated. The negation of the negative is the thought-ness of space, i.e., its being. If negation is determined or negated, then it is sublated beyond its mere simple subsistence. Then the point is no longer in its state of indifferent, unsublated subsistence. Rather, when it itself is posited for itself, it comes forth, specifically in such a way that it posits for itself a new being-outside-itself. As the posited, it is no longer this and not yet that. Insofar as it intends itself *qua* being-outside-itself, it determines the one-after-another-ness within which it itself always stands (as μέσον [the middle], to use Aristotle's word), but in so doing, it is indifferent to the immobile one-next-to-another. It asserts and extends itself; it is exclusively "now" and no other thing. In its being-for-itself it does posit the one-next-to-another but in such a way that it is indifferent to it and is exclusively "now." It has stripped off its mere simple subsistence and has been sublated to a higher level of determinateness, i.e., a higher level of being. The negation of the simple subsistence of the point, the sublatedness of punctiformity *qua* indifference, is no-longer-remaining-inert in the "paralyzed" immobility of space. It is the changing determination of every single point—"now here, now here, now here," and so on. This constant negating of the negation is time.

Hegel does not spell this out; but if his explanation is to have any sense at all that we can express, it can mean nothing else but this constant negation of the negation. That is, positing the points is in and of itself a matter of letting each single point be encounterable; and such letting-something-be encounterable is in each instance a matter of "now here, now there"—i.e., letting something encounter us [256] in a now. In every point, a now. The point has its determinateness, its being, in the now. The point is a now-point. And so Hegel says: "The point thus has its actuality in time" (§257, Addendum). And again: "The truth of space is time" (ibid.). That is, the pure thought-ness—the being—of space is time. The point is the now. Hegel determines the being of the point as that in and through which the point *qua* point is encounterable. In general, in all his categorial explanations, Hegel does not understand the being of something simply in terms of its thought-ness. Rather, he makes this being-thought be the equal of being. Because the pure thinking of the punctiformity of space thinks the now (i.e., time), for that reason space "is" time.

Through this interpretation we suddenly see that Hegel here understands time as now-time. Only on the un-understood basis of this un-understood presupposition does Hegel's explanation of time in terms of punctiformity in §256 make any sense. Time *qua* negation of the negation (the latter *qua* point) is not just any self-sublation. It is the self-sublation of punctiformity. Time, conceived in terms of space, is self-sublating punctiformity. More exactly, time is what is always necessarily co-posited—as the now—in the sublation of punctiformity. Exactly why the now is co-posited, and why it is co-posited in this way, are questions to which Hegel does not and cannot provide any further information.

Hegel determines the being of space as time. Therefore we might ask, "Doesn't being get determined here quite unambiguously in terms of time? Isn't Hegel operating clearly within the problematic of time-as-horizon?" It might seem so, but he is light-years away from those issues. We first have to remember: Hegel determines space not *in terms of* time but *as* time. It's true: he does determine one form of being in relation to time, but only the being of space. And he determines the being of space not *in terms of* time but *as* time.

By way of summary we can say:

1. Even with the one and only being that he does determine in relation to time, Hegel does not understand the ur-temporal function of time, but rather [257] misinterprets time (in keeping with his method) by making it into the being of space itself.
2. In principle Hegel does not see the function of time for interpreting being. If he did, he would have had to introduce time already into his discussion of being in general. But we find no trace of that in Hegel—in fact, quite the opposite.
3. Hegel is unable to understand the ur-temporal function of time because he conceives of time in the traditional-dogmatic way as now-time.
4. That he conceives of time in this way is documented by the fact that he puts time together with space. But space is the *ordo eorum quae sunt simul* (Leibniz),[34] "the ordering of things that are there at the same time"—of things that are present at the same time (i.e., in each

34. [Cf. "I have demonstrated, that space is nothing else but an order of the existence of things, observed as existing together; and *therefore* the fiction of a material universe, moving forward in an empty space cannot be admitted." *The*

now), simultaneously. Hegel puts time together with space in such a way that he even removes the "and" between space and time.

But we have still have not finished our investigation of Hegel's explanation of time. We now want to understand positively how Hegel understood his concept of time. As regards ur-time there is nothing we should expect from Hegel, and nothing we can learn from him. That notwithstanding, his interpretation of the time of everyday experience can indeed help bring us closer to the forms of time-determinateness of everyday experiential time. I begin with some further explicit evidence of his understanding of time as now-time: "The now has a monstrous privilege—it *is* nothing but the individual now. And yet, as soon as I pronounce it, this self-vaunting exclusivity unravels, dissolves, disperses" (§258, Addendum). Therefore, what has being is the now. The now-moment alone *is*. The now is the "concrete unity" of "the abstract moments" of past and future. (§259, Remark).

> Furthermore, in nature, where time is the *now*, there occur no *subsistent* differences between these dimensions {namely, past and future}. (§259)
> {The present moment, as now, is} the immediate disappearance of these differences {being as passing over into nothing; nothing as passing over into being} into individuality {the now}. (ibid.)
> If one considers time positively, one can say: *Only* the present moment is. The before [258] and the after are not. But the concrete present is the result of the past, and it is pregnant with the future. The true present is therefore eternity. (§259, Addendum)
> {Eternity is equal to the} absolute present. (§258, Addendum)
> Eternity neither will be nor was, but instead it *is*. (ibid.)

From this experience of the phenomenon of time we now can also understand the way Hegel understands the concept of time: "The concept of time {is} becoming" (§259, Addendum).

Recall that what appears within the priority of the present moment is the now. To a certain degree we are used to this conception of time: we grew up with it. But this priority is not understood right away. Time *is* in the now and as the now, only in order to disappear in it again. But this disappearance of the now is precisely the *being* of time. Because time properly is the now, this now-being [*Jetzt-Sein*] must be taken up in this concept. According to its concept, time is "*intuited* becoming" (§258 Paragraph), where "intuited" means experienced in its individuality, and this individuality is the now. This concept makes it clear that

Leibniz-Clarke Correspondence, ed. H. G. Alexander (Manchester: Manchester University Press, 1956), Leibniz's fifth letter, par. 29.]

time itself, understood as intuited becoming, is something-present which, as now, is there as disappearing.[35] As being there now, time is exclusive of everything else, where "everything else" means, more precisely, all other points. This present excluding—or as Hegel says, "this existent abstracting" (ibid.)—is not such an excluding "in general" but rather in relation to space. Hegel understands becoming, which makes up the concept of time, as disappearing, as the "abstraction of using up" (§258, Addendum): the pure letting-disappear which itself disappears.

Why, within this becoming which he understands as time, does Hegel emphasize passing-away, even though he holds that coming-to-be belongs just as originally to becoming? In fact he says that time is coming-to-be *and* passing-away (§258, Addendum). And yet in that same context he again equates temporality with the past and takes becoming as disappearing. Hegel cannot explain why time *qua* becoming is now more disappearing and passing-away than it is coming-to-be [259]—he cannot say why he understands it this way. When Hegel puts the emphasis on passing-away in his determination of time as becoming, he does so not on the basis of any philosophical justification of this explanation. Rather, he follows the ordinary understanding, quite naïvely and yet with good reason. In the ordinary understanding of time, we say "Time passes" but never "Time comes-to-be," even though the latter could be said formally and with equal legitimacy, especially according to Hegel. Moreover, no earlier theories of time have clarified (nor can they) even on their own grounds, why, if time is becoming, it has to be strictly disappearance. Already in Aristotle's explanation of it, time was assigned to passing-away and not to coming-to-be. Why that is so remains obscure.

Now we ask very briefly about Hegel's determination of time as intuited becoming and how time, understood in this way, relates to the things themselves and, on the other hand, to subjective consciousness. In posing the question in this way, we remain within the traditional conception of time. According to Hegel (§258, Addendum) time itself is the process of things. Because things are finite—i.e., not determined by total negativity—they are temporal. The converse does not hold: things are not finite because they are in time. "Things themselves are temporal," and thus "the process of . . . things themselves makes up time" (ibid.). On the other hand, Hegel says that time is "abstract subjectivity" (§258). So on the one hand, time is the things themselves; but at the same time, time is abstract subjectivity, pure being-in-itself. In all of this one must bear in mind that when Hegel thinks of the formal self-differentiation of one thing from another, such that in the difference something is related to its own self, he of

---

35. [Here Moser (p. 549.1–4) clarifies GA 21 (p. 258.19–20).]

course understands such self-differentiating as subject and subjectivity. That is, he introduces into the difference of one thing from another an idea that can't be found there. Then, on the basis of this sleight of hand, he can say: As a point that posits itself for itself, time is also abstract [260] subjectivity. So, time is the things themselves, time is pure self-consciousness, and time is neither of the two. Therefore, here too, in this concrete example of his explanation of time, we once again have the same surprising fact: Hegel can say everything about every single thing. And there are people who discover profound meaning in such confusion.[36]

*   *   *

What characterizes the ordinary understanding of time is its conception of time as now-time. In the last lecture, our interpretation made that clear as regards Hegel. In the course of that lecture we brought out a variety of different characterizations of time which Hegel, for his part, would not consider to be different. Instead, he would simply trot them out for us as "dialectically" one and the same—with the possible exception of the one he admittedly mentions only *en passant,* namely, that time is a passing-away. We don't need Hegel's dialectic to show that time is properly *only* passing-away. That is bound up with a topic we shall investigate later.

Let us now recall and characterize the remaining determinations:

1. Time is the negativity of punctiformity, the self-negation of the now-point, or equally the now's being-for-itself in the self-externality of succession.
2. Time is intuited becoming, i.e., it is *becoming* that is always understood in its individuality. "Understood in its individuality" means the same as the now that is immediately seen as present-there. The now is the being of the not-yet, and as such, at the same time it is likewise the no-longer of its being—it is the transition from nothing to being, and from being to nothing, which is exactly what Hegel means by "becoming." Insofar as this becoming is always concentrated in the now, it is intuited becoming.
3. The now is the negation of the negation-*qua*-punctiformity, and as this negation of the negation, it is a self-exclusion that at the same time *is* for itself [*für sich* seiendes]. Hegel now understands the formal structure of a thing's self-differentiation as a reflexive relation to itself, a self-differentiation that can be said of anything at all, regardless of what kind. Hegel understands this self-differentiating

36. [Here (Moser, p. 546) Heidegger ends his lecture of Tuesday, 26 January 1926, to be followed by that of Thursday, 28 January.]

and being-for-itself as subjectivity. [261] And therefore Hegel can say—brilliantly, but without any real basis—that to the degree that time is the negation of the negation, it is abstract subjectivity, pure for-itself-ness in being-outside-itself.

4. Time is the being of space, and consequently, as the being of the spatial, it is for Hegel the very process of things themselves.
5. Time *qua* now-time is the truth of space. The phenomenal content and legitimacy that underlies this thesis can be clarified by way of Kant's and Leibniz's conceptions of time and their explanations thereof. To anticipate: That Hegel *can* say (without understanding its proper sense) that the truth of space is time, is grounded in the ur-temporal structure as simultaneity and in the fact that punctiformity as space in general must be characterized by simultaneity. "Simultaneity" means that every point is co-present [*mitanwesend*] with every other point in every now.

When it comes to taking a critical stance on all this, we must remember two things. (We prescind here from our emphasis on the fundamental limits of Hegel's conception of time, namely, that he knows time only as now-time.)

1. Time is characterized as intuited becoming only thanks to the formal and empty schema of *being—nothing—becoming,* a schema whose many dubious characteristics we cannot discuss in the present context.
2. From within Hegel's own position, it is incomprehensible why time, as he says, is a "using up." The ordinary experience of time lives off this phenomenon directly. However, it necessarily remains a puzzle within the horizon of Hegelian dialectic.

It is clear that Hegel's interpretation of time is bound up exclusively with the now, the now-present, insofar as it is precisely the now-present that properly and exclusively *is.* This is clear from the fact that Hegel quite consistently dismisses the past and future as non-being. But since they must be something, he says: "They are necessarily only in subjective representation, in *memory* and in *fear* or *hope*" (§259, Remark). It is characteristic [262] of Hegel that he refers to this merely in passing and as something of no real importance (cf. "subjective representation"), and then moves on. It is also characteristic that he designates memory, fear, and hope as subjective representations.

Lining up the past with memory and the future with hope is a determination already familiar to the everyday experience of time. It is a determination that Aristotle (from whom Hegel obviously got it) had already grasped theoretically, although only (and typically so) as a form of naïve consciousness, without in any way seeing the inner relation of time to hope, fear, and the like. Aristotle says:

> τοῦ μὲν παρόντος αἴσθησις, τοῦ δὲ μέλλοντος ἐλπίς. τοῦ δὲ γενομένου μνήνη. (*De memoria et reminiscencia*, 449b27 ff.)

> Perception {Hegel would say "representation"} is related to the present, hope to the future, remembrance to the past.

In the same context, Aristotle says:

> εἴη δ'ἂν καὶ ἐπιστήμη τις ἐλπιστική, καθάπερ τινές φασι τὴν μαντικήν. (ibid., 449b11 ff.)

> There may also be some kind of science related to hope, which some call divining or prophesy.

Ἐλπίς, hope, which is coordinated with the future, is also connected by Hegel with fear. We find this connection as well in Aristotle's *Rhetorica* (B, 12), where he treats ἐλπίς in connection with φόβος [fear] and ἔλεος.[37] Ἔλεος does not mean "pity," which is the way one usually translates it and thereby misunderstands the whole theory of the tragic in Aristotle. Rather, ἔλεος means "being in dread for" [*Bangesein um*]—in this case, someone else.[38] It has nothing to do with pity in our sense of that term. [263]

---

§21. The influence of Aristotle on Hegel's and Bergson's interpretation of time

Before going on to a brief characterization of Bergson's thesis—which corresponds materially with Hegel's, even though it is set against it—I will make a brief aside. This morning one of my old students called my attention to Hegel's explanation of time in his *Jena Logic*. The *Jena Logic* is a manuscript that was published only a few years ago (just before the war, and for the first time).[39] Hegel prepared it for the purpose of his Privatdozent lectures in Jena. It is a first step toward what would be-

37. [GA 21, p. 262.23 and Moser, p. 550.13 (which indicates that the oversight is Heidegger's own) incorrectly have "*Rhetorica* II, 2" (which treats of ὀργή, anger) instead of II, 12 (1389a21-22), where Aristotle writes: ἐλπὶς τοῦ μελλοντός ἐστιν, ἡ δὲ μνήνη τοῦ παροιχομένου. The topic of φόβος is treated in *Rhetorica* II, 5, and ἔλεος in II, 8. Φόβος and ἔλεος are treated together in *Poetica* 14 (1453b1 ff.).]

38. [The text Heidegger apparently has in mind is ἐλεοῦσιν ἐγγὺς αὑτοῖς τοῦ δεινοῦ ὄντος at *Rhetorica* II, 8 (1386a23-24).]

39. [G. W. F. Hegel, *Hegels erstes System*, ed. Hans Ehrenberg and Herbert Link

come *The Science of Logic.* (A new edition of the *Jena Logic,* edited by Lasson, has been published in the Philosophische Bibliothek series in 1923. The earlier edition was textually inadequate.)[40] This Jena fragment contains not only a logic but also a general ontology and parts of the philosophy of nature, but it does not have the philosophy of spirit. What I am telling you about the history of the concept of time has quite a long past as regards its formulation, so I'll have to be brief and restrained in explaining the concept of time that slipped me earlier. But even a quick run-through shows it to be richly informative in many ways.

Allow me to mention something that may not interest you much but that is important to me insofar as it completely substantiates the interpretation I have been presenting. In these fragments Hegel gives an extended explanation of the phenomenon of time ("extended" in the sense that he describes the dialectical steps thoroughly, since he is not yet caught within the real straightjacket of his system, or does not give to the presentation the compressed form it has in the *Encyclopaedia*). Right from the start let us note the context within which Hegel explains time: it is in the philosophy of nature, the first part of which is titled, "The Solar System." In connection with his clarification of the phenomenon of ether [264] (today we would say "matter" in the broadest sense), Hegel first explains the concept of movement, and here the trajectory of his investigation goes from time to space—the reverse of the *Encyclopaedia,* even though the content is the same in both.

The explanation of time is dialectically more concrete. The dialectic is complete and thorough: there is more here than in *The Science of Logic.* On the other hand, Hegel's explanation does not yet possess the elaborate structure of his own dialectic itself; that is, he still lacks the proper theoretical concepts of dialectical synthesis: being, nothing, and becoming. He simply works—quite securely, to be sure—within this dialectic. "Therefore in fact there is neither present nor future but only this relation of each to the other" (p. 203). Later on he will call this relation of each to the other "becoming," which is to say that becoming is precisely a relation. I emphasize that he still lacks those distinctive dialectical concepts, and I must say: this lack works to the advantage of his explanation.

A brief delineation of the content may suffice. On the page just cited, Hegel says: The now (which, I repeat, is the proper phenomenon

(Helberg: Helberg Akademie der Wissenschaften, 1915). The text was published in the winter of 1915.]

40. [G. W. F. Hegel, *Wissenschaft der Logik,* ed. Georg Lasson (Leipzig: Meiner, 1923); this work was also published as vols. 3–4 of Hegel's *Sämtliche Werke,* and vols. 56–57 of the series, Der philosophische Bibliothek. See also *The Jena System, 1804–5: Logic and Metaphysics,* ed. and trans. John W. Burbidge and George di Giovanni (Montreal and London: McGill-Queen's University Press, 1986).]

of time) cannot resist the future. The current now will be overcome by the not-yet-now, the future as ever pressing upon it. Here too we can see that Hegel, entirely consistent and consonant with the natural understanding of time, sees time and becoming as running from the future through the present into the past, i.e., as a "passing": a future that passes into the past. So the now, as a now, is a not-yet-now (the future) that has become the present now. In this sense the present now is the future. Hegel even says so explicitly: "The future is the essence [*Wesen*] of the present" (ibid.). Here he understands *Wesen* in the Greek sense—as that-from-which-arises every now as now, viz., from out of its not-yet-now. I intentionally emphasize this thesis of Hegel—that the essence of the present is the future—because in a lecture I presented in the summer of 1924,[41] I emphasized not that the future is the essence of the present but [265] that the future is the meaning of temporality. But the meaning of the thesis I hold is diametrically opposed to what Hegel says here. We will come back to that later. What is clear is that Hegel understands time as coming from out of the future, through the present now, into the past. For Hegel, the past is real time, "time that has turned back into itself" (p. 204). But because every former or past moment is always a former *now*, time in a certain sense constantly runs back into the present, and, as Hegel says, is thus an endless "circular movement" (ibid.). As regards the reality of time, here again it becomes clear that the proper accent is on the past. This is a matter that I cannot explain now because it is much too difficult: in a very particular sense, the idea of the now-present "exceeds itself" [*übersteigert*]. That is, for Hegel the present now is not simply the present now. It also is the now-present of the past. With this thesis Hegel is as far from the proper sense of time as it is possible to get.

Even on a first reading of Hegel's exposition, it takes only a superficial knowledge of Aristotle's philosophy to see the obvious: What underlies this outline of a system and this particular piece of it is nothing less than a direct paraphrase of Aristotle's treatise on time, and this is something quite important. But you should not misunderstand me when I say this. I do not mean to say that Hegel is dependent [on Aristotle]. Quite the contrary, it is devoutly to be wished that our philosophy today were even more dependent on Greek philosophy than it is—not by simply appropriating it but by positively understanding the issues. Here again it is clear that Aristotle has helped out not only Hegel but many philosophers before Hegel and even more of them after. I say this now only as regards Hegel's treatise on time, but I take it that, in its es-

---

41. ["The Concept of Time," trans. Theodore Kisiel, in Theodore Kisiel and Thomas Sheehan, eds., *Becoming Heidegger: On the Trail of His Early Occasional Writings, 1910-1927* (Evanston: Northwestern University Press, 2007), pages 200-213.]

sentials, his entire philosophy of nature is simply a paraphrase of Aristotle in a dialectical mode. During this period Hegel was engaged in a deep study of Aristotle. But we lack a compass [266] for this terrain and have no clues about Hegel's concrete, historical relation to Aristotle.

[Hegel's treatment of time] may be a paraphrase of Aristotle, but it is nonetheless one that operates within the self-assuredness of Hegel's dialectics. It kills off the proper content of the Aristotelian interpretation [of time] and preserves instead certain formal, empty results. The following are some merely extrinsic examples that come to light at a first reading of the text.[42]

1. Hegel understands the now—Aristotle's νῦν—in the first instance as a limit; Aristotle says: ὁρίζειν, ὅρος—"to limit, a limit." Hegel takes the νῦν as a point; Aristotle says στιγμή, point.
2. Hegel determines the now as the absolute "this"; Aristotle says τόδε τι.
3. Hegel understands time as a circular movement; in the last book of the *Physics,* Aristotle connects time with the σφαῖρα, the circular movement of the heavens.

The only difference is that Hegel simply identifies and mixes up the aforementioned determinations—limit, point, absolute this—whereas Aristotle's labors properly consist in showing the founding connections between this-here, point, limit, and now. To put it in Aristotle's terms, he tries to show how these determinations, in themselves and according to their structure, follow (ἀκολουθεῖν) from one another.

Instead of all the mindless drivel that gets written about German Idealism these days, what we really need is for someone to carry though a real investigation of this factual connection of Hegelian and Greek philosophy, along with evidence of where they diverge. That way the history of philosophy might have some relevance. It's also clear from what we said that Hegel's thesis—viz., that space is time, or as he puts it in this preliminary analysis, that time is space—as well as Bergson's thesis (that time is space) both go back directly to Aristotle.

I already emphasized that Bergson carries out his treatise on time in strict connection with his close study of Aristotle. He writes in his *Essay,*

Le temps, entendu au sens d'un milieu où l'on distingue et où l'on compte, n'est que de l'espace.

Time, understood as a field [267] in which we make distinctions and count, is nothing else but space.[43]

42. [Regarding the following, cf. GA 2, p. 570 n. 14. / tr. 500 n. xxx.]
43. Henri Bergson, *Essai sur les données immédiates de la conscience* (Paris: Félix

This thesis is possible only on the condition that time is understood from the outset as now-time, on the basis of a particular context, namely, the constitution of space in simultaneity. Time is not space, any more than space is time. But time is simply the possibility wherein the being of space can be determined existentially-temporally—but not because the being of time is space, but because being in general, as the being of every being, must be conceived of in terms of time. Or at any rate, according to the state of our present philosophical possibilities, being can be singularly understood in terms of time. I do not want to be so entirely dogmatic as to say that being can be understand *only* in terms of time. It may well be that tomorrow someone will discover a new possibility. That is why we can never say that space or nature or any other being is time. Strictly speaking, we cannot even say "Being is time," but only that "The being of this being bespeaks time." Or more exactly still: "The human understanding of beings—and I emphasize *human*—is possible from out of time." I stress "human" because in philosophy we really must stop confusing ourselves with the good God—unlike Hegel, for whom that confusion is a principle.

But as I said, Bergson does not limit himself to this thesis. Rather, confronted with this concept of time, which he identifies with space, he tries to make us understand that ur-time is duration—ur-time, which he also calls "real time" or "real duration." Of course we get very little philosophical information out of him on this, because he says nothing about the meaning of "reality," and tells us nothing about the ontological nature of the life or consciousness wherein he finds real or lived time.

According to Bergson, time is space and quantitative succession, and it is distinguished from duration, which is qualitative succession. The very phenomenon of time (now-time) is shifted from the category of quantity to that of quality. Bergson [268] thinks he has located the metaphysical essence of time (therefore, authentic time) in duration, and so he takes time in its usual sense to be space. But in so doing he shows that he has not understood time. If he had, he would have had

---

Alcan, 1889), p. 69. [Heidegger's manuscript and Moser (p. 556.1) correctly reference page 69, whereas GA 21 (p. 267.3), employing a later edition, cites it as page 68. The passage cited here can also be found in Henri Bergson, *Œuvres,* Édition du centenaire (Paris: Presses Universitaires de France: 1959, 1970), p. 62.1-3. (The *marginal* pagination of this edition follows the 1939-1941 editions of Bergson's works, the last to be published before the author's death on 3 January 1941.) See also Henri Bergson, *Time and Free Will: An Essay on the Immediate Data of Consciousness,* trans. F. L. Pogson (London: George Allen & Unwin, 1910; repr. New York: Humanities, 1950), p. 91: ". . . time, understood in the sense of a medium in which we make distinctions and count, is nothing but space." Heidegger translates Bergson's *milieu* with the German *Feld.*]

to find a way of showing that the kind of time he takes to be space is not space at all, but is precisely time—however, only a specific temporal mode of time.

Bergson's path for arriving at his thesis that time is space is different from Hegel's, but in principle he coincides with Hegel. Bergson's path is grounded on an inadequate analysis and interpretation of Aristotle's definition of time as ἀριθμὸς κινήσεως: that which is counted in movement. Characteristically, Bergson prefaces his analysis of time with an analysis of number, that is to say, he orients his entire investigation to Aristotle. But Bergson himself understands number in terms of space. He says that *"toute idée claire du nombre implique une vision dans l'espace,"* that is, "every clear idea of number implies an intuition of space" (ibid., p. 60;[44] cf. also pp. 64, 172).[45] We could say: The units of numbers and the numbers themselves are distinguished on the basis of their presence in space. What exactly gets numbered or counted within movement? Movement is change of place. What gets counted within movement is the number of points that the movement has run through. They are what get counted, and they are the only things that can be the countable. However, in an act of counting, a now that is counted in this way—a now of time—could not sustain itself so as to make it connect with another now, i.e., so as to be taken collectively, along with that other now, without remaining simultaneous with that other now. That is why Bergson says it becomes space (ibid., p. 60).[46] Now we can see the inner connection with Hegel's thesis. To be sure, the only way to attain a proper understanding of this common foundation is to analyze the ur-temporal structure of measuring: the structure of the discovery of nature in general, within which measuring has a constitutive function. [269]

What Hegel carried out regarding space, Kant had already understood in a more principled and concrete way. Kant did so with explicit attention to the basic categories of nature in general. Kant sees the function of time more concretely (1) because he has a freer position on the things themselves and allows questions to arise from those things,

44. [*EDI*, p. 60 / tr. 79. Heidegger translates *idée* as *Vorstellung* ("representation" or "presentation"), and *une vision dans l'espace* as *eine Anschauung des Raumes* ("an intuition of space"). I translate Heidegger's German translation of the French. The published English edition translates the French as "every clear idea of number implies a visual image in space."]

45. [The Bergson sentence that Heidegger alludes to on page 64 could be, "l'espace est matière avec laquelle l'esprit construit le nombre" (*EDI*, p. 64) = "space is, accordingly, the material with which the mind builds up number" (tr. 84). The text that Heidegger references as "page 172" could be "et on ne mesure que de l'espace" (*EDI*, p. 175) = "the only thing we are able to measure is space" (tr. 230).]

46. [*EDI*, p. 18 / tr. 79.]

and (2) in keeping with the inner freedom of his own way of philosophizing, which admits that there are still difficulties for human philosophizing and that at every moment philosophy faces the possibility
of being up-ended. For Hegel, on the other hand, everything is clear,
and he himself is in possession of absolute truth.[47]

*   *   *

§22. A preliminary look at the meaning of time in Kant's *Critique of Pure Reason*

We have already alluded to Kant's philosophical position on time
when we first characterized the problematic of ur-temporality. That is
because in a certain sense Kant is the one who made the most progress
in this problematic despite all the limits within which the time-prob-
lematic remains even in him. Even for Kant time is the time of nature,
taking "nature" in the broad sense that includes both physical and
mental nature. But we should consider the following. When we say
that mental nature—the mental succession of ideas in the broadest
sense—is determined by time, an essential exception must be made,
one that determines Kant's entire problematic, namely that the proper
determination of subjectivity in fact falls outside time, subjectivity as
the "I think" that must be able to accompany all my ideas if the mental
is to be at all a unitary context. [The exception is] that the "I think" or
the transcendental apperception—the very unity of consciousness—
falls outside time. From the beginning and throughout, we must keep
in mind that the concept of time is oriented to nature [270] in the
broadest sense. It is oriented to nature also in the sense that in his
doctrine of the antinomies Kant explains the problem of the possible
origination of the world, the question of the creation of the world, in
connection with the problem of time.

It is typical of Kant that whenever he reaches a crucial problem-set
in his *Critique of Pure Reason,* he is forced to go back to the issue of time.
Time occupies a privileged place right from the start. Kant does not
think, as Hegel did, that there is just space, and *also* time. Rather, time
has a principled priority in the problematic of the *Critique of Pure
Reason.*

To make the point in a merely extrinsic way: Time is treated for the
first time in the Transcendental Aesthetic. But it is treated yet again in
the Transcendental Logic—in fact, in both parts of the Transcendental

47. [Here (Moser, p. 558) Heidegger ends his lecture of Thursday, 28 January
1926, to be followed by that of Friday, 29 January, which opened with a brief 100-
word summary that is omitted in GA 21.]

Logic, the Analytic as well as the Dialectic. In the Analytic it is treated under the rubric of the analogies of experience, and in the dialectic, under the rubric of the antinomies. In the Analytic it is treated in an even more particular way within the question of the schematism. But the schematism is what links together the two fundamental parts of the Analytic, namely the Analytic of Concepts and the Analytic of Principles; and so the schematism belongs to both parts. Everywhere we look—the Transcendental Aesthetic, the Analytic of Concepts, the Analytic of Principles, the Dialectic—we encounter the problem of time. So even from this quick run-through it is already clear that time plays an exceptional role in the context of the whole. And within these various areas of the philosophical explanation of time within the *Critique of Pure Reason,* time undergoes different determinations, which of course cohere among themselves. We cannot say that as of now anyone has achieved a real interpretation drawn not just from Kant's words and sentences but from an understanding of the issue, an interpretation that would bring to light, and above all demonstrate the intrinsic necessity of, this inner connection between the problematic of the *Critique* and the problem of time. This task is identical with [271] getting a real understanding of the unitary problematic of the *Critique of Pure Reason.*

This problem of the unity of the problematic of the *Critique of Pure Reason* is precisely what has occupied the attention of the Marburg School in particular. At a philosophical level, the Marburg School has far surpassed all contemporary interpretations of Kant in the one-sidedness and violence of the way they have proceeded. Cohen took transcendental apperception as the real center of Kant's problematic, and tried to interpret the entire *Critique* from there, from the Transcendental Analytic and specifically from the demonstration of the origin of the categories and principles; i.e., he tried to put the Transcendental Aesthetic aside as a domain that could stand on its own. In other words, in as much as time is determined as pure intuition in the Transcendental Aesthetic, Cohen tried to determine it in terms of logic, as a concept of the understanding. He carried this out systematically in the first volume of his system, *Logik der reinen Erkenntnis* (1902).[48] Cf. also Natorp, *Die logischen Grundlagen der exakten Wissenschaften* (1910).[49] The principle behind the Marburg Kant-interpretation is to dissolve this twofoldness of sensibility and understanding (or of being-given and being-thought) into being-thought [*Gedachtwerden*] as pure thinking—i.e., to dissolve it

48. [Hermann Cohen (1842-1918), *Logik der reinen Erkenntnis* (The Logic of Pure Knowledge) (Berlin: B. Cassirer, 1922).]

49. [Paul Natorp (1854-1924), *Die logischen Grundlagen der exakten Wissenschaften* (The Logical Foundations of the Exact Sciences) (Leipzig: Teubner, 1910; 2d edition, 1921).]

into the [Transcendental] Logic. Cohen attempted to comprehend the origin of all constitutive determinations of knowledge in general as rooted in the transcendental apperception. Therefore, this interpretation of the *Critique of Pure Reason* is designated as a *logic* of the origin. I have already mentioned the consequences this has for the understanding of time within the problematic of the *Critique*. Here time can no longer be a form of intuition or a pure intuition, as Kant interpreted it. Instead, it must be understood as a category.

On the other hand, very little is gained by trying to show that, contrary to this notion, such a deduction of time from pure thinking cannot be carried out and that it is thus impossible to dissolve the Transcendental Aesthetic into the Logic. [272] The problem of the unity of intuition and thinking remains unsolved even today and perhaps has never been posed as a real problem at all. Only an unrelenting investigation into time in terms of its temporality, will put us in a position to clarify that what Kant understood as the transcendental apperception and placed outside of time *is* the basic determination of temporality itself. Only from that position can we show that the Transcendental Aesthetic is not an accidental add-on and not (as the Marburg School thought) an unassimilated leftover in Kant's work. Instead, we can show the full-fledged necessity of the determination of time as a form of intuition. From that position, we can restore to the Transcendental Aesthetic its rights in such a way that we can bring out the unity of the problematic of the *Critique of Pure Reason* without doing violence to the work. In the present context I cannot present this broader interpretation. Instead I will limit myself simply to laying out for you Kant's delineation of time according to the various directions his questioning takes in the *Critique*.

-----

§23. The interpretation of time in the Transcendental Analytic

Kant's best-known characterization of time (and the only one that is usually cited) is the one in the Transcendental Aesthetic, where time (like space) is determined as a form of intuition or as a pure intuition. These concepts have created great difficulties for understanding Kant, and in fact still do today, so long as we merely hold on to the *verbal* concepts and especially the formal opposition of form and content. This is especially clear in the problem of space. Of course everyone says that when space is defined as a form, we should not understand it as a container into which content is then poured. [273] But this negative definition does not get us very far in understanding what is meant here in a simply formalistic way by "form." We need to see the internal structures of the context that Kant himself had in view but did not analyze. If we want to understand this definition of time as a form of intuition, the first thing we have to do is to clarify what "intuition" and "form" mean here.

a) An explanation of the notions "form" and "intuition"

As with "concept," the primary character of an intuition is presentation. A presentation, taken as a presenting [of something], means being directed to and having an object. Intuition and concept are the two modes of presenting that Kant recognizes. Intuition, as a particular kind of presenting, is characterized by the fact that intuition is related immediately to an object and that, in such being-related, the object is immediately given. In the kind of presenting called "intuition," the object has the possibility of being immediately given, and nothing more. The senses are the ways such giving-of-something occurs. Each sense has its field of givenness and provides a manifold from within that field.

Each sense (and Kant does not analyze this further) has its own distinct field. Colors can never be heard, sounds can never be seen. But colors and sounds each have their own determinate mode of access. And for its part, each sense's field of givenness embraces a distinct manifold of what can be given perceptually within that field. There is a manifold of colors, of sounds, of smells, and so on. Whatever can be given within the field of a sense must be investigated according to its relevant *a priori* structure. Kant (like all philosophy up to now) omitted that investigation. Husserl in his early Göttingen lectures was the first [274] to carry out such a specifically phenomenological investigation. He did so usually under the rubric of an *Ästhesiologie der Sinne* or theory of sense-perception, an elaboration of the relevant structure of color in general, of sound in general, and so forth—as the precondition for anything like a scientific psychology in the sense of research into actual data. Kant did not examine this area in any detailed fashion. He simply took it for granted in its rough contours, and within certain limits it was sufficient for his purposes.

Kant saw that the manifold of each sense's field of givenness has the determinate character of "one-after-another" or of "at-the-same-time." This applies to each particular sense and to sense in general. Insofar as it is a manifold, whether in the general or specific sense, it has the character of manifold-ness. To put it more generally and yet more specifically, Kant saw that the manifold of every field of sense has the determinate character of one-after-another or of at-the-same-time.[50] It does not matter whether the self-giving manifold of a sense's

---

50. [More literally: "Kant has seen that the manifold of such a field of givenness, whether of one sense or of sense in general, insofar as it is a manifold, is

field is explicitly ordered in its one-after-another-ness and shows up as delineated, differentiated, determined, ordered numerically; *or* whether it shows up as undelineated, undifferentiated, undetermined, and unordered. To begin with, it is phenomenally irrelevant whether the manifold is ordered and shows up in a specific order. Whether ordered or not, it is still a manifold. Whenever something encounters the senses, the encountering thing *qua* encountering is always presented on the grounds of a prior view of what lets a manifold meet the senses as a manifold.[51] A pre-view of a manifold as such is the precondition for anything being able to be given as a manifold.

What Kant saw was this: letting a manifold encounter the senses entails (as we now interpret it more precisely in phenomenology) a pre-viewing of something on the basis of which we can speak of an order or a lack of order at all. That pre-viewed something is the basis-on-which anything given [275] is articulated *as* ordered or unordered. "Unordered" does not mean a complete absence of order. It merely means the privation of an order, such that the unordered *could* be ordered. This means that even though unordered, it is still a manifold and thus already understood via a pre-view of a manifold. But that means that pre-viewing a manifold as such is constitutive of letting a manifold encounter the senses. This manifold-ness in terms of which

characterized by the character of manifold-ness, whether in general or in specific terms—Kant has seen that the manifold of every field of the senses is determined by the character of one-after-another or at-the-same-time."]

51. [(1) *Hinblick.* In normal German usage the noun *Hinblick* is used in the phrase *in* or *im Hinblick auf:* "in view of," or "with regard to." In the present lectures, however, Heidegger often uses *der Hinblick,* without the preposition, as the name for an antecedent pre-view (pre-understanding) of the basis-on-which a manifold is ordered. He argues, for example, that without an antecedent *Hinblick* of what circularity is, one could not recognize something as circular. When it is used in this sense, I translate *Hinblick* as "pre-view" (i.e., pre-understanding) and *Hinblickname* as the act of taking or having a pre-view, hence as "pre-viewing."

[(2) *Worauf.* As a relative adverb, *worauf* (as in *das, worauf*) can mean "[that] on which or to which" and, when the referent is an entire clause, "whereupon." Heidegger often turns the word into a noun, as in the phrase, "das Worauf eines Hinblicks." In that case, it formally means "the object of a pre-view," i.e., that toward which a pre-view is directed, that which a pre-view pre-views. However, the specific *content* of that pre-viewed object is the *principle in terms of which* or the *basis on which* something is put in order. For example, the principle "redhead-or-not" might be the principle for sorting out a group of people. When *das Worauf* is used in the formal sense (*das Worauf eines Hinblick*) I translate it as "the object of a pre-view." When the context, as is often the case, requires a focus on its specific *content* (the principle governing an order), I translate it as "the basis-on-which" (something is ordered)—which is awkward, but surely better than "the principle-in-terms-of-which of a pre-view."]

any manifold becomes intelligible, need not be comprehended thematically. The point is this: One-after-another-ness is the *pure* one-after-another. It is the basis for my understanding a one-after-another *thing* in its one-after-another-*ness*. However, it need not be thematically intuited and comprehended in the process.[52]

The essential thing in all this is that, prescinding from orderedness or unorderedness, order necessarily presupposes a pre-view of something that gives sense to an order *qua* order. The difficulty in understanding all this comes from the brevity with which Kant lays these things out, and above all in the ambiguity in his use of the notion of order. In German the word *Ordnung* ["order"] really means the same as *Ordnen* ["putting in order, ordering"]. When we say, "So-and-so is concerned with the *Ordnung* of his papers," it can mean that he is engaged in ordering them: he is actually putting them in order. But the sentence can also mean that he is preoccupied with the *order of* his papers. In that case he is looking for a principle, the basis-on-which that he must pre-view if he is to put the papers in a specific order. This pre-viewed basis-on-which is constitutive of any "order" as such. As regards any manifold that encounters the senses, it is one-after-another as such, pure succession—that is to say: *time*.

What, then, does Kant mean when he says that time is a "form of intuition"? Nothing other than: time is [276] the unthematically and antecedently (i.e., pure) presented basis on which a manifold is able to meet the senses. This is the phenomenological content of all talk about form in contrast to matter. Those terms mean nothing as long as they are used loosely, vaguely, and without a focus on the real issues they refer to—or rather, they mean "everything" insofar as every single thing can be differentiated in terms of matter and form.

Kant designates time, like space, as not just a form of intuition but as pure intuition. As with my earlier explanation of the notion of intuition, here too we see that this pure intuition is not an intuition of the same type as the *intellectus archetypus*. This *intuitus* is not *originarius* but *derivativus,* because it does not have the intuited so immediately as to create the intuited in the very act of intuiting it. Instead, it must first let the intuited be given to it (only in that way does it have its intuited), but given purely—i.e., prior to and independent of the understanding receiving any determination. When we say "prior to" such determinations, we mean that pure intuition is not founded on, not composed of

52. [More literally: "The characteristic is precisely that, in letting a manifold one-after-another encounter the senses, one-after-another as such—i.e., the pure one-after-another on the basis of which I understand at all a one-after-another-entity in the one-after-another—this pure one-after-another need not itself be comprehended and thematically intuited in the process."]

empirical intuitions, of which it would be the generalization. Rather—
and again, this is the essential issue; it is what Kant saw—pure intuition
entails that a pure manifold as such is given immediately without need
of a synthesis on the part of the understanding. On the shoals of these
phenomenal facts, the interpretation of the *Critique of Pure Reason* that
the Marburg School tried to carry out breaks apart and sinks.

Nonetheless, this characterization of space and time as pure intuitions has a very obscure element that cannot be clarified on Kantian
grounds. To put it very broadly: Someone who is [philosophically] unsophisticated might say he cannot think anything using space and time
as pure intuitions. And in fact you cannot think anything using those
pure intuitions, you cannot even show something phenomenally. All
one can do is show how Kant got to this notion by way of a specific
dogma. For example, Kant designates time as *ursprüngliche Vorstellung,*
an "original presentation" (B 48) [277]. He understands a presentation
[*Vorstellung*] as an act of present*ing,* an act of having something. But in
terms of the phenomenal facts of the matter, what he really means is
that time is what is originally present*ed.* In his use of the notion of presentation, Kant wavers between what he has seen ("phenomenologically," as we would put it today) and what he is unable see because of a
certain dogma. In Kant, *Vorstellung*—"presentation"—means *Vorstellen,*
"the present*ing* of something." But in his demonstration, Kant saw that
the one-after-another is something that is always already co-presented
prior to the presenting of something. In the Transcendental Aesthetic,
Kant himself speaks of space and time as that "within which" (B 34)
sensations are ordered. But even in Kant this "within-which" remains
undetermined. We showed it to be the pre-viewed basis-on-which. A
pre-view [of that basis] is constitutive of every instance of ordering.
This pre-viewed basis-on-which is not something that is further ordered. That would require having a pre-view of yet a further basis in
terms of which the first pre-viewed basis would be ordered. In other
words, time itself is not thought by way of a synthesis but is prior to
every synthesis, i.e., prior to anything which, like a synthesis, is a determination of the intellect: a concept. Time is a simple manifold that
is given immediately. Space and time are "original presentations,"
where "presentation" refers to an intuiting, not a concept. Thus they
are "original intuitions."

What you read over and over again in the standard Kant-literature
is that the notion of a "form of intuition" obviously and emphatically
does not mean that time is intuited. But that is a complete misunderstanding of what Kant intends. The argument goes as follows:

1. Presenting is the presenting of something. And so in this case intuiting is the intuiting of something.

2. But that "something" is an object, and objects are determined by form and content.
3. But the form is what conditions the intuited object.
4. Therefore, the form cannot itself be intuited.

Or in another form: The notion "a form of intuition" does not mean that time gets intuited, because otherwise Kant would mean that pure intuition is intuited, and nothing like that is to be found in Kant. [278] Well, certainly Kant did not mean to say that the intuiting is itself intuited. His point, rather, is that the intuited—namely, time—is intuited (unthematically) as the pre-viewed basis-on-which.

Kant says that what we pre-view as the basis for a manifold to encounter the senses—first space and then time—is subjective. But that certainly does not follow from the phenomenological meaning of a form of intuition. Kant comes to his position on the basis of a Cartesian dogmatism that he took over without further ado. This is the basic thesis of that dogmatism: What is given first, foremost, and prior to anything else—i.e., what is given *a priori*—is the *ego cogito*. But then Kant (and not just Kant, but his predecessors also) turned that thesis on its head in the following way. I have shown (and so has Kant, correctly and phenomenologically, in his treatment of space and time) that space and time are given prior to any specific spatial or temporal thing. That which is given originally in this way belongs to the *ego cogito*. But remember now: Descartes says that what is given first and before anything else is the *ego cogito*, the *cogitationes*. But it does not follow that whatever is earlier than something else has to be a *cogitatio*. But Kant in fact draws this conclusion. In directing himself to the phenomena, Kant sees that space and time are something given *antecedently* as the conditions of the possibility of understanding any manifold at all. But on the basis of Descartes's dogma this means: Because it is *a priori*, what is originally given in this way prior to something else must be subjective, must be a *cogitatio*. Therefore, what is primarily and originally intuited—that which is had in a pre-view—must be an act of the subject, an intuition in the sense of an intui*ting*. That's the sense in which Kant says that space and time are "pure intuitions." Here part of a phenomenological demonstration gets mixed up with a dogma that in a sense will later smother it. And with that, the whole problematic of [279] space and time in the Transcendental Aesthetic falls into a dark pit from which it cannot escape.[53]

53. [Here (Moser, p. 575) Heidegger ends his lecture of Friday, 29 January 1926, to be followed by that of Monday, 1 February.]

*   *   *

We are considering Kant's idea of time. At all the decisive points of
the *Critique of Pure Reason* Kant returns to time; it is the phenomenon
that gives his investigation its material continuity. This in itself already
gives a rough idea of the significance that time has within the Kantian
problematic. The way Kant treats time at each of those various points
is also instructive, especially when we consider the peculiar way he
weaves together for a good while a procedure that is phenomenological but then goes back to entirely dogmatic and constructivist arguments. Sometimes what he has seen phenomenologically is able to
determine the broader context of his questioning, but at other times
the weight of a dogmatic position simply smothers the effects of his
phenomenological insights. Therefore, a scientific study of Kant (which
I separate from a set of lectures merely aimed at a general education
and the preparation for exams) requires a positive and productive con-
trol of the phenomenological problematic as well as a philosophical
mastery of the central problem of past philosophy since the Greeks.

Kant did not explicitly see the phenomenological problematic. Instead, he moved within it, as does every authentic philosophical investigation. That is, phenomenology is not something unique or unusual,
it is not a certain direction in philosophy, nor a system of philosophy.
Rather, it is something quite obvious although at times difficult to
comprehend, namely that in philosophy one should not blather on
and on but should speak of and from the things themselves. That is
easy to demand, but hard to live up to.

Even today, when phenomenological research proceeds with sure-
ness within certain limits, there are still dogmas, second-hand issues,
obscurities, missed opportunities. There is no such thing as pure phenomenology. In fact by its very essence it is, like all human undertakings, burdened with presuppositions. Philosophically, the point is not to
eliminate these presuppositions at all costs [280] with arguments, but
rather to admit them and to orient the research positively and materially in terms of those presuppositions. Admittedly, alongside presuppositions like these there are others that no philosophical investigation
can ever get to. Behind the back of every philosophical problematic
there lies something that philosophy itself, despite its superior degree of
lucidity, does not see; in fact philosophy possesses such lucidity precisely because it is completely ignorant of that presupposition. And it is
naïve and unphilosophical for philosophy to think it has found *the* truth
for all eternity instead of realizing that philosophy exists only to open
up new areas of focused rather than random progress [toward truth].
Kant's "weaving together" that I just mentioned is, on the one hand,
due to his ignorance of the phenomenological problematic as well as in
his way of approaching history; but on the other hand it is an essential

interweaving that no philosophy (much less any particular science) can eliminate of and by itself.

In our interpretation of Kant we must make do with an expedient and put the greatest emphasis on understanding the phenomenological beginnings, and merely allude to the dogmatic problematics and theories that Kant inherited. We will especially have to forego an exposition of the actual inner connection of the two.

Our basic task will always be to phenomenologically "loosen up" the phenomena Kant has actually or presumably seen. Only within that [phenomenological] horizon will we begin to see the outline of those dogmatic theses. To use those theses as a starting point is to remain blind in principle to the exhibition of new phenomena. The best outcome such an approach can have is to notice the new opinions in contrast to the earlier ones.

Kant interprets time, like space, as a form of intuition—a form of inner intuition. The outcome of our analysis was that "form" is the unthematically and antecedently presented basis on which [281] a manifold is allowed to encounter the senses. Because the phenomenological analysis during the last lecture[54] obviously could not be carried out correctly, I will repeat it now in a more extensive way, because it is also materially important for the analysis of certain temporal phenomena.

"Form"—the pre-viewed basis-on-which—has a relation to the sense-manifold, to the appearances as the indeterminate objects of empirical intuition. The appearances are indeterminate, i.e., are not determined within thinking. In this case it means that appearances are not determined in a determinate act of scientifically thinking the manifold of appearances as a unity that is nothing other than nature itself. In this regard, the appearances are indeterminate in the first instance—but they can be determined. In place of "to determine" Kant also says "to order." Considered in relation to scientific thinking, the manifold that first encounters the senses—which is to say, the appearances—is unordered. However, in themselves the appearances in fact *are* ordered insofar as I am oriented to them in the lived natural world.

Kant certainly did not investigate the whole dimension of this first-hand order within the lived world. Rather, from the beginning his problematic is oriented to the determining and ordering that is carried out by scientific thinking, and in a sense he based himself on the appearances only insofar as they were relevant as the possible and necessary terrain of scientific characterization. One may choose to say that the manifold of appearances—insofar as it *is* a manifold—is indeterminate or unordered with regard to its determinability by scientific thinking. However, in the given appearances there is a certain articu-

54. [Friday, 29 January 1926.]

lation: they are given as not nothing, but as a manifold. So, being a "manifold" is already a certain characteristic of the given; in fact we have to say that it is already an absolutely primary order—which may be an absolute *lack* of order with respect to scientific determination.

The essential point of the phenomenological analysis of the last lecture was to show the following: If the sense-manifold [282] stands in an essential relationship to possible ordering, then the very essence of ordering necessarily requires that the manifold that encounters the senses has to encounter them on the basis of an antecedent view of something that makes it possible for a manifold (i.e., whatever is given *as* a manifold) to encounter the senses. The very idea of ordering constitutively entails pre-viewing a basis-on-which, and whatever is given as order-able gets articulated on that basis. Whenever a sense-manifold is given as susceptible of order (whether it is actually ordered or not), the very giving of that manifold entails a pre-view of [manifoldness as such] whereby that manifold is a manifold at all.

From the start Kant takes it as an established fact that a sense-manifold has an essential relation to being ordered (i.e., to being determined via the understanding). Knowledge has two stems: sensibility and understanding. Neither can substitute for the other, neither can be dissolved into the other. Right here at the beginning, the Marburg School's interpretation of Kant collapses. In positing, quite dogmatically, these two stems, Kant is backed up to a degree by a long and venerable tradition of philosophy. From early on, thinkers had distinguished (and Aristotle was the first to clarify) αἴσθησις (letting-something-be-given) and νόησις (determining something in thought). And thus the first part of Kant's interpretation of knowledge in the *Critique of Pure Reason* is called the "Aesthetic." It deals with αἴσθησις or perception. And the second part, which deals with νόησις, is really a "Noetics," or as Kant calls it, a "Logic." Only the togetherness of both, sensibility and understanding, constitutes knowledge.

As I say, Kant begins with this fact of the two stems. He does not show in any preliminary and more radical investigation how intuition and thinking, or being-given and being-thought, are, by their very nature, [283] referred to each other; nor does he show what more original ontological nexus of human existence itself might perhaps demand this togetherness and make it possible in the first place. Instead, he bases himself on tradition as if it were a certain and natural understanding that realizes as an unproblematic fact that sensibility and understanding belong to knowledge. But such a vague and general reason cannot be the basis for a profound and fundamental interpretation. Kant presupposes the two stems and then explains the ways they are related. But this whole approach is precisely the source of some essentially detrimental factors. For example, because he divides them at the outset and keeps them divided thereafter, he runs up against the problem of how to mediate these two stems and their functions, how to unify them, and what might be the underlying basis that supports the real, concrete unity of knowledge. As a result, Kant thinks he is forced in a way to dissolve one stem into the other—sensibility into understanding—or in any event to base sensibility on understanding. He likewise thinks that he is forced to introduce the phenomenon of the imagination to mediate them. Kant fails to clarify the imagination phenomenologically; above all he leaves obscure the imagination's proper and basic relations to both sensibility and understanding. Naturally there are some sentences and interpretations that delineate the relations, but not in the sense of an actual exposition of these two structures.

Kant has neglected to plow up the field, phenomenologically and categorially, where these two stems—and especially what is supposed to mediate them—might grow in the first place. The Idealism that followed Kant was bound to neglect this task even more, because it could no longer muster the sober dispassion and solidity for the job as Kant had set it out. Husserl is the first one to see and elaborate the fundamental importance and universal significance of this task [284] in his *Ideas*. People characterize that text as Kantian, but in its foundations it is essentially more radical than Kant could ever be.

b) The constitutive moments of ordering

On the premise of the intrinsic relation of being-given to being-thought, and in keeping with Kant's procedure, we now pursue the connection of the idea of order with the phenomenon of the form of intuition. We begin with a specific order within everyday experience (Kant's "empirical intuition"), above all in order to show how previewing belongs to the act of ordering.

Suppose we have a bunch of spheres of different sizes and made of different kinds of material—and suppose they are be ordered. The bunch of spheres is unordered, and the task is to sort them out and group them. But how? The assignment—"The spheres are to be ordered"—is insufficiently defined because nothing has been said about what the job entails. We know the unordered is to be ordered, but the question is: Ordered in terms of what? The job of putting something in order is adequately defined only when the basis-on-which is specified. Yes, the assignment could be presented in such a way that the "how" is not stated. But that does not mean the "basis-on-which" is not part of the task of ordering or has been forgotten or is not there because it's irrelevant. No, the "basis-on-which" has been thought through so well that it is obvious. The basis-on-which is not defined but it is still constitutive of the job of putting things in order. As always, ordering is by nature an ordering on the basis of something. So:

Whenever something is given to and encountered by the senses in some kind of order, it is given and encountered within a pre-view of the basis on which it is and can be ordered.

In the case of the spheres, the pre-viewed basis-on-which could be color. Then all the spheres of the same color, [285] regardless of their size and material quality, are grouped according to specific colors. Those colors are taken from out of the given manifold before us, because I would hardly order them in terms of green if I found no green spheres in the manifold.

Therefore: (1) A pre-viewing is constitutive for ordering. (2) In the present case, the pre-viewed basis-on-which [viz., "color"] is to be drawn from the manifold in front of me. But that is not required. For example, I could order the spheres serially in terms of the order in which they catch my eye each time I cast my glace directly at the manifold. In this case the pre-viewed basis-on-which is not a determination that belongs to the spheres themselves, but is a possible mode of a particular way of encountering them, the mode of "immediately-catches-my-eye." The fact that some specific element of their make-up is why they catch my eye does not change the fact that the pre-viewed basis-on-which is drawn not primarily from the thing itself, because I am prescinding from whatever it is that makes a sphere catch my eye. The only "norm" at work each time I cast another glance is: "whatever-catches-my-eye-first."

A basis-on-which that is drawn simply from the things themselves is distinct and different according to the ontological regions that the objects belong to. If the task is to put Bach's fugues in order, color would certainly be excluded as a possible basis-on-which, as would material quality.

Here we cannot go into the various ways a pre-view comes to be generated and achieved. Instead, let us keep this firmly in mind: In any concrete act of ordering, it doesn't matter whether or not I am explicitly aware of pre-viewing, or whether or not I'm committed to having such a view. All of that is irrelevant to whether a pre-view is present and operative in that concrete act of ordering or not. The fact that a pre-view [necessarily] belongs to an act of ordering is prior to all the ways in which one might carry through that fact or demonstrate it.

It is a given that experience is always ordered experience. Just why that is constitutive of human existence and its way of being will be shown later. [286] Underlying such experience is (antecedently and constitutively) a pre-viewing. This pre-viewing entails that, even when it is *explicitly* enacted in the process of carrying out an act of ordering, the pre-view does not thematically focus on the basis-on-which I order those things. Pre-viewing the basis-on-which I order things is constitutive for carrying out the ordering, but in the process it is equally unthematic. The basis-on-which (say, "color" or "material quality") is certainly "in view," but it is not thematically comprehended. That is, I am not thematically focused on, e.g., the content of color as such. If I were, I could never get around to ordering what's in front of me. The specific structure of all this is that the pre-viewed basis-on-which is constitutive for the ordering; but the pre-viewing itself is unthematic. Naturally it can be rendered thematic at any given moment. But when I do that, I step out of the specific conduct of ordering something, and I now take the pre-viewed basis-on-which as the primary given.

This is the analysis of the structure when we track it down in a concrete, natural process of ordering. However, the dimension of the problematic that I analyzed in a simple and direct fashion in the last lecture is something quite different. Say we prescind from the specific, material, and factual orderedness of things given within a region of experience. Say we direct our view to the given as such, regardless of its content, regardless of the specific sense-field it belongs to. If we do so, we see (and Kant put his finger on this phenomenon right from the beginning) that whatever is given is a manifold, regardless of any ordering that might be relevant. Thus, to be "manifold" is a phenomenal determination of the given, regardless of whether the given is ordered or not ordered according to whatever concretely relevant viewpoint. Take any field of sight—say, a manifold that is a wild whirlwind of colors without a trace of order to it. Even in this spread of the given— this buzzing bustle of sensation, as it is often and unclearly put,[55] [287] although one is unsure whether it is a given or just a bustling confusion that runs its course in the mind—even this whirlwind of indeterminate given objects has the character of being "manifold," and thus does have a determination and articulation that in the broadest sense (and even precisely in Kant's sense) has to be understood as an order. Kant's determinations here are so general and crude that he gives no further attention to the proper structures of the phenomena.

This primary and phenomenally first order that is given—"a manifold"—underlies every case of order or lack of order. But that articulation of the given, that primary "apartness" [*Auseinander*] of the data,[56] is a mark of some arrangement, and to that degree it entails the

55. [Given Heidegger's early allusions to William James in his 1919-1920 lecture-course, *Grundprobleme der Phänomenologie* (GA 58, p. 10.29-30) and in his 1925 course, *Prolegomena zur Geschichte des Zeitbegriffs* (GA 20, p. 28.14 / *HCT* 23.12), it is possible that the text here is an allusion to James's phrase—in writing of a newborn baby's impression of the world—"one great blooming, buzzing confusion." See William James, *Principles of Psychology* (New York: Holt, 1980), p. 462.]

56. [Heidegger's *das Auseinander* (very roughly, "the outside-one-another") is a nod to the traditional definition of extension as *partes extra partes*—parts of a whole

following: This phenomenally first arrangement of the manifold stands within a pre-view, and the object of the pre-view can only be pure manifold-ness itself—in the external sense of just a multitude characterized by a primary apartness.[57]

* * *

Everything that encounters the senses is—no matter how indeterminately and variably—a "here" and a "there." The act of fixing the "there" underlies every specific concrete order, but does so without calling attention to itself. Take, for example, the manifold of spheres. Each time I select a sphere, each time I pick up a sphere, I direct myself to that sphere as something fixed in a "there"—its very own "there"—and I do so without needing to attend explicitly to its being fixed in a "there." I simply do something with the sphere. Even chaos and confusion entail the apartness of the multitude in terms of here-and-there.

For Kant what is given in inner sense is the simple manifoldness of one-after-another. This means that the mental stuff encountered [in inner sense] is encountered as coming-one-after-another, whereas the physical elements encountered in outer sense are encountered in terms of the simple manifoldness of next-to-each-other and behind-each-other. Space and time as the simple manifoldness of next-to-each-other and one-after-another are that which I pre-view in enabling a manifold to encounter outer and inner sense respectively. First and most importantly, all experience lives with determinately ordered things, but in such a way that as it experiences them, [288] it is *not* thematically concerned with the content of the pre-view and not even with the pre-viewed basis-on-which as such. Here we will not discuss the traditional idea that what is first given are things with their "sensible" qualities. But this much is already clear: (1) I do live in a pre-view of something on the basis of which I understand whatever gets ordered in this order; and (2) the pre-viewed basis-on-which is not thematically noticed. The pure and thematic pre-viewing of a basis-on-which is not something we do every day. In the "immediacy" of experiencing and determining, the specific basis-on-which is not thematic, much less the pre-view of the pure manifold that lets the manifold encounter the senses.

Although these bases-on-which are unthematic, I do live in them; and the more they ground the originating pre-views that underlie everything, the less thematic they are. Those originating pre-views are

that are external to ("apart from") one another—a *philosophoumenon* that goes back at least to book 4, chap. 6 of Ockham's commentary on Aristotle's *Physics;* see vol. 5 of his *Opera philosophica,* p. 52.]

57. [Here (Moser, p. 590) Heidegger ends his lecture of Monday, 1 February 1926, to be followed by that of Tuesday, 2 February.]

the "taken-for-granted." They do not show up in the arena of everyday concern and observation, even though they undergird what is immediately given. They are foreign territory to the everyday view, which always looks to what is close at hand—not just foreign, but inaccessible to that view—a state of affairs that harbors and hides *the* enigma for philosophy.

In a phenomenal sense, it is not just the primary arrangements—one-next-to-another and one-after-another—that do not stand out. The pre-views that are bound up with them and the objects of those pre-views also go unnoticed. Because of the essentially unthematic character of the pre-view, its object remains completely in the background, even though, given the fact of its primacy, it is always already present. Before all others, these two bases-on-which—space and time—are antecedently in view in and for every instance of a manifold being able to encounter the senses.

The foregoing should have philosophically clarified what Kant means when he says that space and time are the "within-which" of a possible order. However, he also says that space and time are intuitions (*Anschauungen*), (original) presentations (*Vorstellungen*). [289] If we take these characterizations literally, unsustainable consequences follow immediately. Space is a presentation, but in the Kantian sense: Presenting something (*Vorstellen*) is one of the "formal conditions of sensibility that lie *a priori* in the mind" (B 122–123). Yes, but we have to ask: Insofar as we experience anything spatially localized *as* spatially determined, do we really understand it in its spatial manifoldness by a pre-view of something mental? Isn't it ordered, rather, on the basis of the apartness of sense data? It would seem that Kant's manner of speaking and interpreting collide with the obvious phenomenal content of what is actually there in the pre-view. When I put something in order, am I focused on the basis for the ordering, or am I focused on some mental state of affairs: the pre-view*ing* as such? Kant means the basis-on-which, the object of a pre-viewing, but he is compelled to interpret it as [the subject's] act of pre-viewing.

How did Kant come to take the pre-view*ed* basis-on-which as an act of pre-view*ing*, thereby understanding space and time as an act of presenting? Presenting something is obviously a characteristic of the mind, or in Descartes's terms, the *mens* or *animus*. (Kant's word *Gemüt* is simply a translation of those Latin terms.) So presenting, by its very being, belongs to the subject. But in defining space and time as the "wherein" of ordering, Kant also claims that this "wherein" must reside in the mind, ready [for sensations]. But why? Why is this "wherein" subjective?[58]

58. [For Heidegger, the *Worinnen* is likewise the *Worauf*—i.e., that "wherein" sensations can be ordered in terms of certain relations and thus put in a certain

Remember that Kant sees (although very crudely, phenomenologically speaking) that space and time have a fundamental priority in all concrete acts of experience. For him, space and time are always already co-given, not along with anything else but as what precedes, underlies, and articulates everything else. In traditional terms, space and time are *"a priori."* And there is a position that claims that anything *a priori* belongs to subjectivity. But this position (whose legitimacy has not been demonstrated) is in fact an overturning of Descartes's (equally problematic) thesis that [290] what is given antecedently to everything else is solely and properly the *ego cogito*, the *cogitationes*. The *cogitationes* are the way in which the *mens* or *animus* (or for Kant, the *Gemüt*) has its being. So when anything is shown to have the character of priority (as is the case with space and time), that means *eo ipso* that its kind of being is that of the *cogitatio* or *animus*, and in Kant's words must "lie ready [in this case, for sensations] in the mind" (B 34).

Thus, on the basis of their demonstrated *a priori* character, space and time are *cogitationes*, representations residing in the subject "subjectively." The less problematic Kant found the phenomenal demonstration of the apriority of space and time, the more he followed this dogmatically based interpretation of their apriority. And he found it unproblematic because he carried it out in such a rough and ready way. Kant did not probe the structures of ordering as such: the preview itself; having a pre-view; the pre-viewed basis-on-which; and all the rest. And the reason why Kant could not carry out such analyses was that he, like the whole tradition before him, and Descartes especially, lacked any understanding of the basic structure of all these "presentations" and behaviors—namely, intentionality. Intentionality is essential for getting a radical comprehension of the problematic, but it also makes the problematic much broader and more difficult than Kant could ever have imagined.

Once we comprehend the phenomenological content as shown here, we have to say that space is what is originally presented in the kind of pre-viewing we detailed above. Leave aside the fact that Kant, on the basis of his concept of "subject," can supply no effectual meaning to what a "subjective form of intuition" is supposed to mean. Even then, this kind of subjectivity simply does not follow from the phenomenal content. If you take "subjective" as referring to a behavior that belongs exclusively to human existence, then we might say that

form, is also that *on-the-basis-of-which* they are so ordered. Every basis-on-which (*Worauf*) sensations are ordered is pre-viewed antecedently to any actual ordering. Heidegger contests the position that the *Worinnen*—i.e., the *Worauf*—is "subjective."]

the discovery of a purely measurable space in the world around us is "subjective," and that the further elaboration of such space in a geometry is "subjective." But even that does not in the least say that space is subjective or that space has anything to do with the subject! [291] I don't see why space couldn't be "objective" and yet still *a priori*. Of course the meaning of "*a priori*" would still have to be worked out as "what-one-is-antecedently-with." Let me clarify that.

In experiencing an empirical manifold, we antecedently "have" space as the object of a pre-view. The possibility of antecedently-viewed-space can be understood only in terms of the most basic structure of human existence, which I show to be "being-in." In turn, being-in can be understood only in terms of temporality. Therefore, antecedently having space as the object of a pre-view is grounded in the prior fact of being-in-the-world, being-in-space—where "being *in*" has the character of "being given over *to*." [59] As soon as we see the problematic in terms of this original basis, then we can give a phenomenally grounded meaning to the statement that space is "subjectively given" (i.e., "already resides in the mind"). "Subjectively given" now means: given with the subject, which now means: given with human existence, and specifically human existence as being-in-the-world.

The interpretation of these structures presumes a radically different basis from the one Kant was able to have on the basis of Cartesian dogmatism. Last semester[60] I treated these matters in detail—the specific foundation of possibility of the givenness of space, its foundation in human existence itself and particularly in the structure of being-in; and I stressed that, to the degree it is founded on a Cartesian problematic, the Kantian problematic loses its meaning.

The basic defect underlying this whole problematic reaches much further back. It is connected with the fact that in the first place one does not take the phenomena the way they are encountered, but instead uses certain dogmas to construct "states of affairs." One resists understanding the structure of human existence itself as a specific way of being-spatial, or more precisely of being-in-a-space. One resists seeing that an essential structure of the human way of being is to be in the world, to be in space—but in a way that is entirely different [292] from how other things are in space. (I spelled out earlier how that way is different.) And one resists this primary determination of the subject as spatial because of an old dogma that still dominates philosophy—the doctrine (whether we admit it or not) of the immor-

59. [*Sein auf* does not mean being-"unto" or "toward," as if there were some point prior to the unto-ness or toward-ness. *Sein auf* is another term for *Geworfensein*: being *a priori* immersed in and familiar with "the world," i.e., the human realm of sense.]

60. [That is, in Summer Semester 1925; see GA 20 and *HCT*.]

tality and the so-called "spirituality" of human being. Some say that in their real, true being, humans cannot be in space; otherwise they would not be immortal. That is, they prejudge the case from the beginning by claiming that human beings are or must be immortal. In other words, they ground a specific thesis about the ontological structure of human being on what they believe.

To me, however, it seems that for scientific philosophy the road should run in the opposite direction, and that the only possible road is first of all to look at the facts about human existence's structure and to make this determination of being-in-space part of the original starting point, and in this way to begin with what we know, not with what we believe. None of this says that what we believe is impossible. But making a clean start at questioning clearly means tracking down all such dogmas that underlie these determinations of person, spirit, and the like—and getting rid of them. And so we see that underlying an apparently bland and uncontroversial problem like the being of space there are theses like the immortality and spirituality of human being; and that these theses implicitly or explicitly prevent us from seeing things the way they are. We begin with an ego that is not spatial and then use some kind of hocus-pocus to work our way into space.

Kant's position goes back to Descartes as regards this peculiar conception of the *a priori* as an entity in the sense of a *cogitatio*. Kant never got beyond Descartes's position, nor did he ever question its foundations. One might object that in a noteworthy section of his *Critique of Pure Reason*, which is titled [293] "Refutation of Idealism" (B 274–275), Kant did try to overcome the Cartesian position. But this objection is mistaken. In that section Kant tries to demonstrate the existence of things in space; i.e., he thinks it necessary that the being of the outer world (as we would put it) has to be proven, and he declares it an outright scandal that philosophy has no such proof. But insofar as Kant thinks the outer world *must* be proven he presupposes the Cartesian position, namely, that at the start I do not yet securely possess this curious outer world, but rather have to *prove* it in the strict philosophical sense of that word. This refutation of idealism is a refutation only of material idealism, as Kant puts it; and it is precisely a proof for the Cartesian position within the Kantian problematic. The reason I mention this peculiar refutation of idealism (which should be compared with the valuable remark in the Preface to the second edition of the *Critique*, see B xxxix), is that we will need to come back to these interpretations in another context—because they are in fact of momentous significance and, given his position, are the most radical thing Kant could say about the being of the world in relation to human existence or the subject. They are even more significant insofar as time is the guiding thread of the argument. And this is the place where Kant makes the greatest advance into the problematic of ur-temporality, although without breaking through to it. Once again it is clear, especially in the note later added to that Preface, how Kant was never sure (in a good sense!) about his position but was always starting over in an effort to check his theses against the facts. From this constant effort of Kant's were born the insights that more or less clearly underlie these arguments. [294]

c) Form of intuition and formal intuition

In the whole problematic of space, Kant never takes up the more original question about how pure geometric space could be discovered by starting from the space of the lived world. That is because he does not thematize the whole phenomenal realm of the lived world but instead, from beginning to end, sticks with his question about measurable space. Within that realm he distinguishes, of course, between space as a form of intuition—an original presenting of this pure manifold as next-to-each-other—and "formal intuition" (Transcendental Deduction §26, note; B 160–161).

What is meant by space as a form of intuition as distinct from a formal intuition? First, a very general remark. In and through the formal intuition, space is first determined as the object of a science: the object of geometry. A form of intuition is the *pure* manifold, the pure manifold as such. That is, it is the pre-viewed basis-on-which, and as such it is unthematic. This basis-on-which can itself be made thematic and can be comprehended and determined. But determining is a synthesis, and a synthesis is an act of bringing-together into a unity. The formal intuition, Kant now says, is what *gives* unity: it attains a determinate spatial something. Every determinate spatial something—everything determined in that formal intuition—is for Kant a limiting of the whole of space. So we could interpret formal intuition as the intuited and thematized object of a pre-view insofar as it is determined in the pure synthesis "which does not belong to the senses" (as Kant says in that note). This thematized object of a pre-view, this basis-on-which [appearances are ordered]—in other words, the form of sensible intuition, the form that gets determined in formal intuition—is possible only insofar as the form [of intuition] underlies formal intuition, that is, only insofar as the form already contains the object of the pre-view as a pure manifold of the corresponding relations.[61] [295]

Thus formal intuition is founded on the form of intuition. Insofar as this is the case (and Kant never understood this in his interpretation),

---

61. [That is, the pure form antecedently has (as the content of a pre-view) space and time as pure manifolds, but always and only in terms of the relations that give them their form.]

formal intuition belongs to space and not to the understanding. Nonetheless, one could say: If pure manifoldness (space as the form of intuition) is determined by synthesis, and if synthesis, precisely as *pure*
synthesis, is the act of the understanding, then space, insofar as it is
determined by the synthesis of understanding, no longer belongs to
sensibility. But in his note, Kant says the exact opposite. Why must he
say that? Because the unity that always underlies this pure synthesis,
this bringing-together, is not a unity in the sense of a concept of understanding (a category). Rather, the unity in and through which I
bring together spatial constructions and determinations, is itself a kind
of space. That is, the limitations of space—points, lines, surfaces, and
such—are themselves space.

Kant saw that there is in this case an entirely original synthesis—a
very peculiar "synthesis"—that necessarily belongs to space precisely
because its unity (the unity correlative to it) itself has a spatial character. In the last sentence of his note, Kant says:

> For since through it {i.e., the synthesis} (as the understanding determines
> the sensibility) space or time are first *given* as intuitions {i.e., first properly
> as determined intuitions}, the unity of this *a priori* intuition belongs to
> space and time, and not the concept of the understanding. (B 161)

Many have taken exception to the words "are given" and have sug-
gested that Kant changed his way of speaking here because elsewhere
he says that something is thought by way of synthesis and is given by
way of intuition, whereas here he says that something—namely, this
unity—is given by way of synthesis. Kant has to speak this way because
the unity itself has a spatial character. And we need not invoke some
change in terminology or identify an allegedly vague use of language.
Rather, we should see that he had to say "given" in this case, even
though the [296] synthesis cannot be given in itself. But in this case it
can be given, because what the synthesis gives—the unity—is space: a
spatial determination in the form of a limiting of space. What is more,
Kant wrote the word "given" in italics—so we should presume that, in
employing the term, he gave some thought to it and, given the difficulty
of the analysis here, did not use some vague form of talking.

Kant's remark above has played an enormous role in the literature on
Kant. The Marburg School, for example, has interpreted it in a way diametrically opposed to the way that I just did. Because Kant says here
that space is a formal intuition—a synthesis—the Marburg School con-
cluded that in the final analysis space in Kant is therefore something
that has to do with the understanding—synthesis—and therefore we
must try to deduce space from the pure activity of the understanding.
But the exact opposite is the case, and it is precisely this note that shows

how Kant emphasized, and always maintained, the autonomy of pure intuition over against the activity of the understanding. A. J. Dietrich has made most headway in interpreting this passage, in his *Kants Begriff des Ganzen in seiner Raum-Zeitlehre und das Verhältnis zu Leibniz* (1916).[62] But I must say that in the final analysis not even Dietrich has understood the proper sense of this passage, because he tries to explain this word "given" in the note as a vague use of language instead of showing the opposite: this word is demanded by the issue itself.

So the formal intuition that Kant discusses is founded on the form of intuition. This distinction makes it clear what Kant means (on my interpretation): This possible pre-viewed basis-on-which, which is constantly unthematic in ordinary experience, can be thematized; and when it is thematic, it is a delimited field of objects proper to a specific science, namely, geometry. Now, insofar as geometry is a constitutive moment in mathematical physics and in the mathematical sciences of nature themselves, [297] this distinction will naturally have essential significance for understanding the epistemological structure of mathematical-physical knowledge.[63]

* * *

To return to the question of time, we must say that, as regards the philosophical understanding of time, the dogmatic argument about the *a priori* status of time has gained us nothing as regards the subjectivity of time. For even if we were to grant that, in distinction to space, time is in fact "subjective," it still has not been shown how and why time as time — and not just as a form of intuition — can be the "wherein" of the ordering of all appearances in inner sense. There is nothing that explains that such time is subjective. One simply asserts that it is, using the same dogmatic arguments as with space. And above all it is not shown that time is *only* a form of intuition of inner and outer sense. And to go in the opposite direction, it is not even shown to what degree and in what way subjective time can at all be objective, and what this objectivity means. Only in demonstrating that do we show that a general determination of time is possible and, on that basis, an empirical determination of time.

So much for the understanding of the relevant content of the con-

62. [Albert Johannes Dietrich, *Kants Begriff des Ganzen in seiner Raum-Zeitlehre und das Verhältnis zu Leibniz* (Halle: Max Niemeyer, 1916). The text was the author's *Habilitationsschrift* at the University of Berlin, and was issued as no. 50 in the series, Abhandlungen zur Philosophie und ihrer Geschichte; the first edition has been reprinted (Hildesheim and New York: Olms, 1975).]

63. [Here (Moser, p. 606) Heidegger ends his lecture of Tuesday, 2 February 1926, to be followed by that of Thursday, 4 February, which opened with a 500-word summary that is omitted in GA 21.]

ception of time in general as a form of intuition. To repeat: In my interpretation, time is the unthematically presented basis-on-which, one that accompanies every act of letting a manifold be encountered as such, insofar as that manifold becomes accessible through inner sense. In his *Anthropology* §4, Kant says that inner sense "sees the relations of its modification [i.e., of whatever determines it] only in time, and therefore in flux, where the stability of observation that is necessary for experience is lacking."[64] The inner sense is nothing other than empirical apperception, i.e., the empirical self-consciousness in which self-consciousness, the self or I, is encountered simply as an object, not a subject. [298]

d) Space and time as given infinite magnitudes; *quantum* and *quantitas* in Kant's interpretation

According to Kant, space and time are forms of intuition, not objects that are intuited. And yet in the same context in which he explains space and time (in the Transcendental Aesthetic), Kant also gives another characterization of space and time, in terms of their content. Although he says that space and time are forms of intuition and thus *cogitationes,* he also says: "Space is presented as a given infinite magnitude" (B 39).

In this second case space is obviously not understood as a form of intuition, but is understood from the point of view of content, i.e., as an "object," although, as we will soon see, certainly not in the Kantian sense of that word, namely, an objectivity that is *thought* through synthesis. Concerning time, Kant therefore says: "The original presentation *'time'* {Kant means: time as present*ed*} must be given as unlimited" (B 48). So even though space and time are not objects, they are nonetheless presented, they are a "presented." They are what is previewed in a pre-view. In fact, here space and time are understood to be prior to all determinations, i.e., not as formal intuitions but as forms of intuition.

To illustrate this first determination of the content of space and time that we recognize—namely, as an infinite given magnitude—we have to go back to our analyses of the phenomena of ordering and preview. In interpreting the determination of space and time that we now have before us, we will stick with the formulation in the first edition, where Kant says much more clearly: "Space is presented as an infinite given magnitude" (A 25). If you recall my earlier analyses of the given-

---

64. *Akademie-Ausgabe,* vol. 7, p. 134. [In translation as Immanuel Kant, *Anthropology from a Pragmatic Point of View,* trans. Mary J. Gregor (The Hague: Martinus Nijhoff, 1974), p. 15. I gloss Gregor's "its modifications" (*seiner Bestimmungen*) above.]

ness of a manifold, you will remember that I demonstrated the following: A manifold that is given *as* a manifold—i.e., in the character of manifold-ness, and specifically in the character of spatially one-out-side-another and one-next-to-another [299]—that manifold, insofar as it is given and given *as* a manifold with the above characteristics, can be understood only by way of a pre-view or pre-understanding of manifoldness as such, in this case, of apartness as such. Without such a pre-understanding of apartness as such, it would be utterly impossible for anything spatial to be given. We need not have a concept—a specific categorial consciousness—of a manifold *qua* apartness. The unthematic pre-view suffices. And according to Kant this pure manifold—space—is something that, by its very way of being, has to be *given*. Space is a given-and-presented [*Raum ist Gegeben-Vorgestellt*].

To make that clearer: "Given" is distinct from "thought." So "given" means: not thought, neither produced nor producible by the understanding and its basic activity of combining. This manifold is encountered in the field of the outer senses; and we will not take it only as a spatial one-outside-another. That manifold is not articulated simply in such a way that, within the manifold, one thing is distinguished from another, and that other from yet another, etc., so that, within this given manifold, this would not be that, and that would not be this. In other words, what we encounter is not a simply *multitudo*, as the Scholastics would put it, something "just-different-in-general." The character of manifoldness in this manifold that we encounter is not a simple empty otherness. No, we encounter the manifold in terms of its manifoldness. This manifoldness must itself be given in its own particular way, because the articulations made on the basis of this manifoldness are relevant to the issue in this sense: This is not simply different from that, but is *next to* that, and that is *behind* this; and yet another is *under* or *over* that. These specific characters—next to, behind, in front of, under—are ones that, even if I had all the time in the world, I could never conjure up by pure thought out of the mere distinction of one thing from another. [300] Next to, behind, in front of, under—these have to be given—which means that, of their essence, they are the pre-viewed that is given in a pre-view. And as what is essentially given—i.e., given as this determinate manifoldness as such—they are the condition that makes possible a determining comprehension of a specific "next to" or "over" or "under."

Therefore, these features—next to, over, under, in front of, behind—that make up the pure manifoldness of space in general, are conditions of possibility of every possible determinate spatial relation. That means that "next to," "over," and "under" are not determinate kinds of relations—they are not species of the genus "relation-in-general"—any more than intuition is a species of concept. "Relation-in-general" simply cannot be determined to a particular species called "Next to" or "Under," because relation-in-general is not the underlying basis of the "next to" and the "under" and the "over" in the sense of making them possible—as if first there had to be "relation" in order that there could be a "next to." It's the other way around. Only because the next-to is intrinsically what it is, can it, *qua* next-to, be understood as a relation. If I determine the "next-to" or the "under" as relations, I say nothing about them *as a* "next-to" or *as* an "under." "Relation" is also a feature of phrases like "more boring than" or "more stupid than." As regards their content, "more boring than" and "next to one another" have nothing to do with each other. They are completely disparate, and yet I can determine both of them as relations. So, in calling both of them "relations," I am saying nothing. That is, "relation" says nothing about the content that belongs to the essence of "next-to" or "under."

In keeping with its essential content, this pure manifoldness—space—has to be given. And it underlies all particular spaces, which themselves are specific limitations of space. We also say that spaces are "this or that large" according to certain ways of measuring them. But space itself, the pure manifold, is not [301] "this or that large," but is what makes it possible for anything to be "this or that large." So when Kant says that space and time are infinite given magnitudes, he does not mean they are something "infinitely large." I will delay for a bit my interpretation of the word "infinite," but the word "magnitude" in this context means the same as "quantity," or as Kant puts it, *quantum.* The way Kant uses Latin terms here is the exact opposite of German usage, and this has easily led (and continues to lead) to a misunderstanding. When Kant wants to indicate that "magnitude" refers to quantity, he uses the word *quantum.* But when he wants to indicate that it refers to *this* or *that* "*quantum*"—i.e., a specific amount—he uses *quantitas.*[65] In German we put it the other way around. We call a ration of beer a *quantum,* and what we mean is: *this much* beer as regards quantity. So we use *quantum* for "this much" or "that much," and we use "quantity" for much-*ness.* Kant uses the words in the opposite sense, and he has his own good reasons for doing so. He cannot use the word "quantity" to indicate that

---

65. [To belabor the point: (1) In general usage, the Latin *quantum* (from the adjective *quantus*) has to do with a concrete, specific amount of this or that. (Question: "How much iron?" Answer: "That much iron."—*Quaestio: "Quantum ferrum?" Responsio: "Tantum ferrum.")* (2) The Latin *quantitas* is an abstract noun that indicates not a specific "this much" or "that much," but the general "how-much-*ness*" of this or that. But Kant inverts these two meanings, as if he were translating *Quantitas non est qualitas* (Quantity is not quality) by *Quantum non est quale.* That is: to indicate *Größe* ("magnitude") in the abstract sense of *Großheit,* Kant uses *quantum* rather than *quantitas;* to indicate *Größe* in the sense of a concrete, specific *so und so groß,* he uses *quantitas.*]

space is a magnitude, because "quantity" for Kant is a determination that belongs to the understanding—it is a category—and Kant wants to insist that space is something given and that this condition of givenness is of the very essence of space.

This, then, is how we should understand the meaning of *Größe* or magnitude: as quantity. Now, what does it mean when Kant says that space (as well as time) is an *infinite* magnitude? "Infinite" is a determination of quantity; that is, according to its idea, it has to do with the question of how-much. Regardless of whether we can determine the how-much makes no difference to the meaning of "infinite"—it still refers to a certain quantity: an endless quantity—or as one says, a quantity that I can go on determining *ad infinitum* without ever reaching a limit. But the ability to be endlessly determined (in the sense of "never reaching an end") is not and cannot be the meaning of "infinite" in this context, at least so long as "magnitude" means the same as "quantity." "Quantity"—the essence of every determined *quantum*—can never have this or that size. And that means: by its very essence, it can never be subjected to endless determination. [302] Rather, magnitude in the sense of quantity—as an endlessly ongoing determining—is the finitely infinite condition of possibility of *being-quantitative*, which is what underlies everything that has this-or-that *quantum*.

But then what is meant by an "infinite" magnitude? From what I said about "endlessness," it is clear that "infinite" does not refer to something in the field of continuity but rather something that underlies continuity itself and that Kant expresses in this way: Space and time are infinite magnitudes. This means that insofar as space and time get determined, they are always in relation to what is determined as the whole is in relation to the part. The character of wholeness is essentially different from the character of the part, or more exactly, the character of part-ness. If I begin with something that is, by essence, a part and that is unable to exist except as a part (as is the case with any specific space as contrasted with space as such)—if I begin with what is essentially a part, I will never get to the whole. Every part—in this case, every specific space, even if we can think of it as determinable *ad infinitum*—and therefore even an infinite space, a space that can be determined *ad infinitum*—always presupposes space as a whole. Therefore, this infinity in the sense of the unlimitedness of proceeding, is possible only on the basis of the infinity that Kant now understands as "the whole." Kant never investigates and determines the concepts of "infinite" and "finite" in a univocal sense (the terms have various meanings in Kant). Nonetheless it is clear that in the present context he is using the words "infinite" and "infinity" in Descartes's sense of *infinitudo*. Descartes himself, however, did not determine *infinitudo* in a positive sense. Speaking of it in his *Meditations*, he said that every finite thing (*finitum*) is infinitely different from the infinite (*infinitum*). That means there is no bridge between the two—or more exactly, the very notion of bridging them by moving forward into the infinite is itself a finite notion.

"Space as an infinitely given magnitude" means to say that space is always the whole within which all spaces are merely parts, and that all these parts are themselves space. The word "infinite" in the above determination [303] of space and time has nothing to do with determinability—i.e., has nothing to do with limits and lack of limits—because determinability entails synthesis; and as Kant says, every synthesis, even if it goes on *ad infinitum,* is finite—precisely *as* a synthesis, i.e., as a form of determining. Earlier I stressed that Kant does not use the words "infinite" and "finite" in a univocal sense, any more than he does so with "magnitude." The reason is, in part, that throughout their history these concepts have played an important role and have undergone continual modification.

We have tried to give a phenomenological interpretation of what Kant means by his simple and lapidary propositions about space and time as infinite given magnitudes, and from what we have said, it should now be clear where the difficulties lie regarding a more precise determination of these phenomena: they lie in understanding how wholeness relates to part-ness, and in seeing which categorial modifications are possible here. As of today, even the most elementary structures of these basic concepts still elude us despite all efforts to work them out. Once again it is Husserl who has made the only independent and productive advances, in *Logical Investigations,* volume 2, Third Investigation, "On the Theory of Wholes and Parts."[66]

Later we will show the intrinsic consistency of these determinations that Kant gives to space and time: infinite, magnitudes, given, presented. In a different formulation, Kant says in one place that "all the parts of space, even unto infinity, are simultaneous" (B 40). This phrase "simultaneous, even unto infinity" points to the primary givenness of space as a whole. And in his *Reflexionen,* no. 4046, he says: "As regards potential simultaneity, time is infinite. Thus we present space as *actualiter* infinite."[67]

This means that in every "now" the unlimited pure manifoldness of space is present. In the "now" as such—and therefore, in time—there are no limits and boundaries by which we might determine how much [304] space could be present in a "now." Rather, in every "now" the entirety of space can be presented. You can see that, even as we bring

---

66. *Logical Investigations,* vol. 2, pp. 433–489.

67. *Reflexionen zur Metaphysik,* in *Akademie-Ausgabe,* vol. 17, p. 397. [*Actualiter:* "in actuality" or "actually."]

a robust phenomenological interpretation, Kant in these passages has already penetrated deep into the structures of space, structures that later became, for Hegel above all, the bases for his interpretation of the "punctuality" of space in terms of the "now."[68]

To a certain degree we have now delineated the object of the pre-view, i.e., the form of intuition, as regards its content. As an infinite given magnitude, time is the condition of the possibility of experiencing and determining a specific delimited one-after-another. If we want to say that time is taken "quantitatively" here, we need to understand that in a philosophical, categorial way. It does not mean that time is "quantified." It means, rather, that time is understood as the object of a pre-view concerned with order, and as such it is what makes it possible to order a quantity of one-after-another.

On the basis of his conception—his *double* conception—of space and time as (1) forms of intuition and (2) infinite given manifolds, Kant is now able to determine them directly as "sources of knowledge" (B 55). That is, in every act of experiential ordering and determining, space and time are the sources from which we can and must draw. Time is a source of knowledge—that is the fundamental interpretation of time, and it underlies and supports everything else that Kant has to say about time.

Even if this interpretation is not unambiguous, nonetheless, by following this guiding thread, Kant manages to provide a series of fresh conclusions about the function of time, even though it is still undecided whether they can be sustained in the form in which they are presented. Up to this point we have gained the following determinations about time:

1. Time is the form of inner intuition.
2. Time is an intuition.
3. Time is an infinite given magnitude.
4. Time is a source of knowledge.

(In this hardly clear list, we are immediately struck by the difference in character between the first, second, and fourth determinations [305] and the third one.) Using these determinations we have to make two things clear: how it was possible for Kant to assign time a preeminent role (even higher than space) in the interpretation and knowledge of nature; and how Kant, in clarifying this fundamental role of time, entered the arena of the problematic which we designate as ur-temporality and which we are trying to approach, indirectly, by tak-

68. [Heidegger later refers to this same issue in *Being and Time*, §82(a), with reference to Hegel's *Encyclopedia of the Sciences*, §257 (Addendum) and §254 (Addendum).]

ing our clues from Kant. We will have to come back to these determinations so as to use them to show why the problematic of the ur-temporal remained hidden from Kant.[69]

*   *   *

---

§24. The function of time in the Transcendental Logic. A characterization of the problematic

First we tried to orient ourselves concretely regarding the general way Kant comes at time, and in so doing we have intentionally left unexplained Kant's specific formulation of the problem that drives these considerations. Our interpretation took us back to the context that Kant for his part never researched or even envisioned. Kant's basic aim (to which these considerations in the Transcendental Analytic belong and which they help to realize) is different from a thematic analysis of knowledge or consciousness as such. Our task now is to understand that basic aim more precisely, so as to fundamentally clarify (1) the problem-context within which the phenomenon of time, as we have characterized it, operates, and (2) the way of treating the phenomenon of time which the basic problem-context prescribes. If it turns out to be no accident that time shows up in all the decisive parts of the *Critique of Pure Reason,* then in the final analysis we will have to formulate the problematic of the *Critique* [306] in such way that the question of time stands at the center of that problematic.

I now want to spell out this central problematic, which is not explicit in Kant, and clarify it, starting with what we have already explained. From our encounters so far with Kant's determinations of space and time, what guidelines for our research have emerged? Within empirical intuition Kant finds pure intuition. In the empirical intuition of the outer world he finds space; in the empirical intuition of one's own self he finds time; and indeed, space and time are the conditions of the possibility of the givenness of the manifold of their respective areas. But what form of research led Kant to find anything like conditions of the possibility of givenness? He investigates empirical intuition and looks for conditions of possibility in that intuition. That is, he looks for what it is in empirical intuition—or more exactly: in what is *intuited* in empirical intuition—that is already prior to empirical intuition. And why precisely in empirical intuition? Because empirical intuition is the primary form in which knowledge is carried

69. [Here (Moser, p. 619) Heidegger ends his lecture of Thursday, 4 February 1926, to be followed by that of Friday, 5 February, which opened with a 750-word summary that is omitted in GA 21.]

out. Kant investigates knowledge—and more precisely, scientific knowledge—in terms of the conditions of its possibility. And why is it that he investigates scientific, theoretical knowledge in terms of the conditions of its possibility? What motivated this investigation? Answer: Kant's concerns for a scientific metaphysics, i.e., scientific knowledge of three specific entities: God, the soul, and the world.

Kant asks: What elements constitute scientific knowledge of entities? And he investigates scientific knowledge not in order to demolish metaphysics but in order to find a scientific metaphysics. He is looking for a touchstone that would tell him whether what has been put forward up to now as scientific knowledge of God, the soul, and the world can be and is scientific knowledge at all. [307] Kant's aim was not set on the limits of knowledge but on the positive possibility of knowledge. The fact that he came up against limits was a trick that the issues played on him. The fact that he respected these issues shows that he understood how to philosophize.

As we said, there are two stems constitutive of knowledge: sensibility and understanding. If we want to assert something about an entity and to determine it in its being by such a statement, the entity first of all has to be given *to* the act of determining. So we have to ask about both the conditions of the possibility of the giving of the entity, and the conditions of the possibility of the scientific determining of the entity that has been given. This means that in the second question we ask about the conditions of the possibility of the connection between the conditions of the possibility of one stem and that of another. Only when we show the conditions of the possibility of the *connection* of those two sets of conditions have we philosophically conceptualized knowledge, as regards its possibility, from out of the unity of the two stems. Which means: The fundamental task is to interpret the being of this very unity; and in turn: we can meaningfully ask and answer that question only if we first achieve an understanding of being as such.

But this formulation of the question—as a question about the conditions of the possibility of the connection of the conditions of sensibility and understanding—is still too empty and formalistic, and it hardly corresponds to the concrete focus that Kant's investigation had in view. The question is further trivialized if it is posed as an inquiry into form and content, or if one goes even further and asks how the unity of form and content manages to agree with the object. In those cases one is asking questions that never crossed Kant's mind. When Kant talks about form and content, these concepts have a completely concrete meaning that has arisen from actual investigation. [308] They are not the uprooted and groundless concepts that are so much in use today.

In his investigation, Kant presses ahead and inquires about the prior element in scientific knowledge as such. What is already given beforehand in everything that is given empirically? What is already thought beforehand in everything that is understood as given-and-thought? The latter question asks what makes possible the "determinedness" (the thought-ness) of the given. Now, to determine and to think mean to combine a manifold that has been given. Hence the question: What makes possible the combining of the given? That question is not simply identical with: "What makes possible the unification of understanding and sensibility?" Rather, the first question ("What makes possible the combining of the given?") prepares for the second one; or more exactly, it shows that the second question cannot be posed in that fashion.

The relevant question in the investigation is about what must *a priori* underlie the combinability of a given manifold. Combining is an act of the understanding. Therefore, what gets combined is what is given to the understanding. But the understanding is *cogitatio*. Therefore, for Kant (given his Cartesian orientation) the only thing that can be given to and combined with the understanding ("internally," he says) is what itself has the character of a *cogitatio*. Which means: presentations are what get combined. However, the presentations that are to be combined are given as a manifold of inner sense. And the manifold of this manifold of inner sense has the character of next-to-each-other and one-after-another—in other words, the character of time. Therefore, the presentations that are combinable by the understanding are in fact combinable [only] by way of a pre-view of time. So now we understand the question in more precise terms: What makes possible the combinability of the pure manifold, i.e., the combinability of time? To combine is always to determine. And so: What makes possible the determinability of time?

This is the central question that Kant did not ask but that nonetheless [309] underlies the question he *does* ask about the general determination of time as such. The question about the general determination of time as such is *the* question toward which the Transcendental Logic's positive investigation of the Analytic of Principles and finally the Analogies [of Experience] flows. To go to the heart of the matter: This question is the principle guiding question toward which everything else converges. But this question about a general determination of time contains the more radical question about the conditions of the possibility of the determinability of time as such.

What is to be determined is time as a pure manifold. Or to put it more precisely: What is to be determined is the manifold that has the character of time *thanks to* a pre-view of this manifoldness, "time." Thus, determining this manifold requires a pre-viewed unity on the basis of which a particular "combined" is a specific unified something.[70]

70. [Cf. Moser transcript, p. 627.30–32.]

Let us anticipate the problematic and delineate it in a general way. Kant says: The unity of all combining—and thus the possibility of combinability at all—is grounded in the transcendental apperception, the "I think." So now we confront the question: What is the condition of the possibility of the determinability of time as such in an "I think"? Or even more precisely: What is the condition of the possibility that time as such and an "I think" be together? Let me stress: I am radicalizing the problematic of Kant's *Critique* in terms of *this* question. If you say that this question cannot be found in the *Critique*, I readily admit you are right. But we must ask whether *this* is not the question that first makes the entire problematic of the *Critique* intelligible.

In his Cartesian way, Kant thinks that everything that can be demonstrated as prior (*a priori*) in what is known in an act of knowing must belong to the subject. This means that time, as an intuition, is something that already operates in the mind; and it means that the "I think" is an act of spontaneity of the mind. Thus the question becomes that of the connection between time *qua* intuition and the "I think"—both as determinations of the mind. It becomes the question about the basic context of [310] subjectivity, or as I would say: of human existence. It is quite clear in Kant's research that he unquestionably had in mind this horizon that I have just been explaining. Both in his doctrine of schematism (B 180–181), where he deals with the action of time, as well as in the Transcendental Deduction, where he deals with the "I think" and synthesis, Kant says that the state of affairs is veiled and obscure. But he lets these contexts remain in their hiddenness.

Let me repeat once more: This is about the conditions of the possibility of a conjunction between time as such and the "I think" as such. On the one hand time is the form of the manifold that underlies all acts of thinking *qua* determining; and on the other hand the "I think" is what must be presupposed as providing a possible unity to every act of combining in thought. The two fundamental elements—pure manifold as such and pure unity as such, both of them as the *a priori* of a determinability as such—this is the problem that underlies the real issue in Kant's investigation. Only if we pose the question in this way, i.e., about the conditions of the possibility of the ontological connection between both determinations of the mind (namely, time as pure intuition and the "I think" as an act of the mind's spontaneity), do we comprehend the question philosophically. But at the same time that entails something else, namely: Yes, interpreting this ontological connection between time and the "I think" is the basic task; but on the other hand, I can put this task in motion only if, in asking about the being of this ontological connection, I have a clear notion of what being in general means.

Post-Kantian Idealism also attempted to solve the problem of the unity of sensibility and understanding. However, in trying to do so, it

did not pursue (much less see) the relevant presuppositions that Kant
had left undeveloped. Instead, it continued to pursue the question in
the Kantian (more exactly, [311] in the Cartesian) fashion, by putting
the emphasis from the beginning on the "I think," on the I, so as to
understand knowledge from the I as starting point and from a still
more original determination of the activity of the I as the pure-fact-of-
activity, a *Tathandlung*. In Hegel, the problem appears to be directed
entirely toward the objective; but he holds fast to the same problem,
and in fact his whole philosophy cannot be understood at all unless
we keep it within the horizon of this question. The only thing is that
the question gets displaced in Hegel and becomes more obscure due to
fact that his solution to the problem is extremely Kantian, but at the
same time he has recourse to Greek ontology in its objective orientation. He thus gives the false impression of actually solving the problem, whereas in fact all he does is completely obfuscate it. What I
mean is that, in trying to solve Kant's problem, Hegel utilized every
possible means generated by the history of philosophy theretofore.
The intrinsic need to do so comes from Hegel's impulse toward dialectics, and the intrinsic consequence was that he understood his philosophical position as the absolute completion of all philosophy up until
then.

And so, as we ask about the possibility of the being of a connection
between time as such and the "I think" as such, we must pose the
question more radically, and that means not orienting ourselves toward any determinate theses. It is not a matter of championing a new
standpoint, as the Romantic Idealists did, but rather of getting in our
sights the unresolved issues in Kant's position. And philosophers must
have patience, regardless of whether they do or do not find the truth.
Kant works with and within this connection of time and the "I
think"—with and within, yes; but without ever asking about the connection itself. But as Kant works within his concrete investigation into
this connection—an investigation that is the most exciting that can be
found in scientific philosophical literature—he reaches the limits of
what can possibly be asserted about time. And these are limits that
were posed to him by his whole approach to the question. [312]

What we want to understand now is (1) the meaning behind Kant's
way of treating time in this context, and (2) what positive features of
time emerge from that treatment—so that, beginning from a "negative
example" (so to speak), we might understand the problem of ur-
temporality. To do that, we need at least a rough understanding of
Kant's problematic, but one that is concrete enough to prevent us from
reducing Kant's problem to an empty formula; but, by rearticulating
that problematic, to promote our effort to get to the issues and phenomena. So first of all we need an adequate understanding of Kant's

problematic: Why did he assign this basic role to time? And how did he justify that basic role of time?

We said that, for Kant, scientific knowledge has to be studied within the horizon of the question of the possibility of a scientific metaphysics. And the best guide in investigating knowledge is scientific knowledge. But for Kant, scientific knowledge means mathematics, and specifically mathematical natural science. A science is scientific only insofar as it contains a mathematics. But we must understand correctly. Kant assigns this preeminent role not to mathematics as such but to mathematics as an *a priori* discipline. Thus he understands mathematics more as Descartes and Leibniz do: as *mathesis.* Kant certainly does not think that if a scientific metaphysics (a scientific knowledge of God) is to be possible, it will have to be "mathematical" in the usual sense. As Kant understands the word, in order to be "mathematical" a science must be demonstrable and universally valid in its *a priori* foundations. The same meaning of the word is found in Spinoza's determination of "geometric" in the phrase *more geometrico* ["in geometric fashion," in the title of the *Ethica*]. Kant's question is about the possibility of a scientific metaphysics—the possibility of [313] a scientific knowledge of certain entities: God, the world, and human being—*not* a scientific knowledge of numbers or of geometrical figures. That is why Kant has to orient his question about the conditions of the possibility of scientific knowledge in terms of the scientific knowledge of the entities of nature.

Like the preceding interpretation, the one that follows is phenomenological, i.e., we will push through to what Kant implicitly had to have in mind. In any philosophy that offers possibilities leading to the issue, this is the path we have to take—the only philosophical path. That is: we have to confront the philosopher in a communicative dialogue and help him be born aright. This is no novelty. It is Socrates' ancient method of maieutics. In confronting him, we also run the risk of finding (as is now not the case with Kant) that everything will end up in complete confusion and obscurity. The question that is relevant right now is: What is known *a priori* in mathematical natural-scientific knowledge? More precisely: What determinations reside within what-is-known by this knowledge as such? The fact that we can pose the question this precisely has been made possible by Husserl's clear (or relatively clear) elaboration of this problematic in his *Ideas for a Pure Phenomenology.* The question is: What resides within the whole of the what-is-known in mathematical physics? And what are the essential determinations of this what-is-known that characterize it as what it is, namely, nature?[71]

71. [Here (Moser, p. 634) Heidegger ends his lecture of Friday, 5 February 1926, to be followed by that of Monday, 8 February, which opened with a 315-word summary that is omitted in GA 21.]

§25. The question of the unity of nature

We first ask the question in a way that Kant himself in fact did, namely: What resides in what-is-known in mathematical natural-scientific knowledge? What belongs to [314] the known as such? This question is not asking about the totality of the results these sciences produce but rather about the thought-content of any and every result *qua result* of mathematical physics. To put it more precisely: not the thought-content but rather what *has* to be thought, i.e., what belongs to the known *as-such* in any mathematical natural science. In the most general terms this known-as-such is nature.

Phenomenologically understood, nature is an entity which can be discovered within the world and of which it can be said that it underlies all worldly things and all worldly ontological connections insofar as they are determined by materiality—in short, nature can be found in everything of the world. Now, as such an entity, nature is accessible in various ways. In one instance, for example: we come to an understanding of nature by way of the things-of-use that are most immediately given in our lived world. For example, when I lift up a chair and let it fall, I can observe "falling" in that chair—because certainly the chair falls not because it is a chair but because it is consists of wood. Insofar as I understand it as nature, I have to first of all prescind from . . .—I prescind from it insofar as it is a chair. As regards this "falling" as a way of being, there is no difference between this chair and that walking stick or hat, or any other thing-of-use. That, then, is one way that nature becomes accessible: by way of an understanding that prescinds from the primary character of things.

We can also experience nature pre-scientifically in the direct way, as when I speak of a waterfall out there in nature, or of fir cones that fall from trees out there in nature, or of a chunk of stone that cracked off from a boulder and fell. So, I have nature in the sense of "nature out there" just as originally as I have chairs, tables, and hats. And this "nature outside" is the nature of physics and biology, although not yet as discovered in its specific way of being natural. When it is understood by natural science, this entity "nature" has to be understood as [315] an entity that is always there on hand and that, as something ever-there, goes through changes always in such and such a way.

So in our original natural experience we see, within the same context of being, *both* things-of-use that humans have produced out of natural materials *and* things-of-nature that humans have not produced but that have emerged either by growing or by some other process. And the whole field that includes both these types of things has the character of extension and localization. What is more, each of these things exists either now, or at some time, or usually, or always. And so we encounter them directly in time. Kant, who did not primarily orient his analysis in this fashion, failed to see that time determines the things of the environment just as originally as space does. In his theory, time determines things out there in the environment only mediately, and it determines them immediately only as the givens of inner sense (parallel to the way space determines them immediately only as the things of the environment). This thesis of Kant's is phenomenologically wrong—it collides with what is immediately found in the given. And Kant has to accept this state of affairs, despite his theory, even if he does so after the fact, as when he says that time is the universal form of the encountered manifold both of outer and of inner sense. Therefore, from the beginning, spatial and temporal determinateness reside in the known of natural-scientific knowledge, regardless of what the content of that known may be.

But what is known by natural science—namely, nature—is, insofar as it is known, something expressed, something determined in propositions. Whatever this entity nature may be, every statement of this science already posits and presupposes determinate propositions that are the basis of (and that are explicitly or implicitly co-asserted in) every natural-scientific judgment. These propositions are the fundamental principles that express what underlies every determinate change within nature *as* a change within nature. Laws of nature do not regulate just this or that specific process in nature. They determine nature in general as nature. Those propositions are the Analogies of Experience:

> [First Analogy:] Principle of the persistence of substance: In all changes of appearances, substance persists, and its [316] *quantum* is neither increased nor diminished in nature. (B 224)
>
> [Second Analogy:] Principle of temporal sequence according to the law of causality: All alterations occur in accordance with the law of the connection of cause and effect. (B 232)
>
> [Third Analogy:] Principle of simultaneity, according to the law of interaction, or community: All substances, insofar as they can be perceived in space as simultaneous, are in thoroughgoing interaction. (B 256)

(I will not go into the question of why Kant calls these principles "analogies.")[72]

These principles contain determinate basic concepts. For example, in the Second Analogy—the principle of temporal sequence according to the law of causality—we find concepts like "cause" and "effect," or more

72. [See Kant, *Reflexionen*, no. 4675.]

precisely (and in phenomenological terms), "consequence." These principles express something about nature *qua* nature, about what goes to make up nature. They express what is co-thought in every concrete act of determining nature whenever it is determined. These principles express something about the basic lawfulness that constitutes nature in general. Therefore, we cannot arrive at these propositions by way of experiencing specific processes of nature; rather, all experience of nature already presupposes these propositions, and only on the basis of these propositions is experience of nature possible in the first place.

That is the reason why Kant (and basically Hume before him) realized in a very acute way the absurdity of trying to get these propositions from outer experience or (as Kant would say) from experience at all. Within the known of natural science as such, there reside not only spatial and temporal determinations but also: (1) other prior determinations that are expressed in propositions *qua* principles of the type just mentioned; and (2) propositions and concepts that intend and express some content-factor of nature; and content-issues that are co-intended when I deal with specific laws of nature—specific physical, chemical, magnetic, or acoustic laws. [317] Whenever we think of nature, whether within pre-scientific experience or any other kind of experience, nature must always already have such content and structure about it—if phrases like "thinking about nature" and "understanding nature" are to make any sense at all. These elements that belong to the essential content of nature are more or less explicitly thought in our actual experience of nature. And in science itself these principles are more or less clearly and completely known—which is a far cry from saying that they have already been [explicitly] recognized. In every concrete attempt at ordering something, these principles are already antecedently co-expressed, whether explicitly or not.

What is prior in this sense is the *a priori* of nature or of the knowledge of nature. But what is *a priori* must already be operative in the mind. Now according to Kant, whatever is expressed in the principles is not given. It is not even given in the way a pure manifoldness in general (space and time) is given—any more than the concepts of these principles (e.g., cause and consequence) could be given the way space and time are. Therefore, as *a priori* they must be already operative in the mind, but without being *a priori* intuitions. The only remaining possibility is that these propositions and concepts belong to the other stem—to the understanding.

It is clear that this should be so. Judgments and concepts have always been taken as activities specific to the understanding. But how are such propositions about nature in general supposed to be already operative in the understanding? The understanding is the faculty of judgment, the faculty that presents the presented by way of relating and combining.

But how is that understanding supposed to create, as if *ex nihilo*, concepts and principles that, by what they name and say, intend not an empty "something" but a very specific entity, namely nature? The venue of explanation in the present case is not the Aesthetic but the Logic, the science of the understanding and its activities. Formal logic has to do simply with thinking about something in general regardless of its content. It can tell us absolutely nothing about the origin of the concepts that are necessarily co-thought in the what-is-known of knowledge—concepts like "cause," "consequence," [318] reciprocal action, substance. These are *a priori* concepts, and yet they have a content. The same with the principles (they express something about the content-field of nature). So the question becomes: How are content-oriented statements about entities possible, when what is expressed in those statements does not and cannot come from experience and is not taken from the givens of experience? How can content-oriented statements come from the pure understanding? How can a statement express something about a specific entity not by drawing what it expresses from the entity but by remaining a pure act of understanding, one that does not admit of being given anything and yet remains object-oriented? That is the meaning of the question: How are synthetic *a priori* judgments possible?—i.e., propositions of the understanding which, without being measured beforehand against things, are nonetheless in accord with them, i.e., "are true" (according to B 296). In this way we pose the problem of an explanation of the understanding, one that investigates it in terms of how a pure action of the understanding can be true, which is the problem of a "logic of truth" (B 87).

The problem is: How can thinking remain in and with itself in its action and, in so doing, also be related to objects, i.e., express something about content in its concepts and propositions? There is no problem in seeing how Descartes's position shines through the problematic, viz., where in the first instance it is shown that within the known of natural-scientific knowledge there is some content with the character of being prior: basic concepts and principles. But according to the theory, this "prior," the *a priori* content, resides first of all and fundamentally within the subject—which means that the *a priori* is understood as first of all and fundamentally subjective. And then one asks how in the final analysis this subjective feature of the understanding nonetheless can and does relate to objects. Here too we can see (although at a much higher level of the problematic) how Kant remained imprisoned in this way of posing the question: How does the subject in its knowledge get out to the object? Kant no longer asks the question [319] so primitively, but basically it is the same problematic.

So basic principles and basic concepts are already intended and expressed beforehand in the known. This gives rise to the first task: ascertaining what these basic principles and concepts are. But Kant does not stop there. For him there is the second task, the truly important one of demonstrating the legitimacy of these basic principles and concepts as activities of the understanding, i.e., as originally present only in the subject. That means, as Kant puts it, providing them with their "birth certificate" (B 119) on the basis of which they have objective validity, i.e., do in fact determine nature as an object.

The first task of demonstration, which consists in ascertaining the ensemble of basic principles and concepts, is the task of the metaphysical deduction of the categories. Here Kant shows the following: These basic concepts arise from the understanding and are concepts of possible unities that pertain to the ways the understanding can judge. As an act of combining, every act of judging is a function of unity; and how many concepts of unities I can produce depends on how many functions of unity I can demonstrate. These concepts of the forms of unity that are possible in the judgment are the pure concepts of the understanding, or the categories. The second task—that of the transcendental deduction— is the task of proving that these concepts of the understanding are the conditions of possibility whereby alone we can think something as an object and as a natural object. Kant's explanation of the understanding and its action is quite analogous to the transcendental explanation of the senses, where of course Kant explains space and time both metaphysically (i.e., dogmatically) and transcendentally.

In the known of mathematical-physical knowledge—in the entities that it intends—reside space-time determinations, plus the rules that are articulated in the principles, plus determinations that express the basic concepts themselves. Does that exhaust all that always already resides beforehand in what this knowledge intends? [320] We have set out everything as regards the given except the decisive thing: that which is intended in all the principles and categories. The spatio-temporally determined is understood beforehand as the unity of nature itself. In thinking nature itself we have already priorly thought its unity, from which every statement about nature is drawn and to which it returns, whether that statement is a principle or an empirical proposition. This unity—nature—is the most prior of all that resides in the known as such. The primary *a priori* of unity—as the underlying ground that supports a possible togetherness of the manifold, and as the matrix within which any manifold must be together—must be concretely determinable as: nature.

Such a unity "constitutes what is essential in any knowledge of the objects [*Objekte*] of the senses, i.e., of experience (not merely of the intuition or sensation of the senses)" (B 218-19). "An *object*, however, is that in the concept of which the manifold of a given intuition is *united*" (B 137). In Kant's language, that refers to a prior condition of possibility which, because it is *a priori* in the most original sense, must obviously, already, and most originally reside in the mind. Knowledge, as we have seen, is comprised of the two stems (sensibility and understanding). But the understanding is the faculty of judging—i.e., the faculty of the function of unity. *Ergo*, the understanding is what we were looking for as this condition of the possibility of the unity of the given manifold. This is an extrinsic way of arguing the point.

Kant looks more precisely into the structure of the understanding itself. The understanding is certainly the "source of combining," because a combination could never come about through the senses and also could never be contained even in the form of intuition. "All combining is . . . an action of the understanding" (B 130). Combining (synthesizing) entails a manifold, but not only that. Combining or relating requires a pre-view of the basis-on-which this can be combined with that. This "with" requires a "together," the σύν requires a ἕν. Combining combines by way of a pre-view of unity. To combine is to unite, and in [321] all uniting, *unity* is already antecedently presented. Transcendental unity "alone is objectively valid" (B 140).

I call your attention to the connection of these observations with our earlier ones about Aristotle's position on σύν and ἕν in relation to ὄν. We have now reached an area where the same issue is in play. Insofar as this unity in general makes possible combining and unification, it is a constitutive presupposition of every action of the understanding. Here again we meet the phenomenon of the pre-view, but we have to distinguish it from what we set out in the analysis of order. There it was a question of the pre-view of manifoldness as such, on the basis of which a given manifold gets understood. Here it is a question of a pre-view of a unity on the basis of which a manifold is to be combined as this *specific* manifold.

As regards its structure, combining is the presenting of a unity (*qua* basis-on-which) that enables the manifold be thought as a "one thing." This synthesis-enabling unity is what Kant, in a striking turn of phrase, calls a "synthetic unity" (B 130).

> The presentation of this unity cannot, therefore, arise from the combination. Rather, by being added to the presentation of the manifold, it makes the notion of combination possible in the first place. (B 131)

Therefore, it is not the understanding *as combining* that constitutes that unity. Rather, the understanding [*qua* combining] has need of that unity. This unity must be able to be given as such if there is to be any understanding [*qua* combining] at all. Therefore Kant says that this unity "itself contains the basis . . . of the possibility of the understanding, even in its logical use" (B 131) of pure combining, where it is not a matter of combining a concrete, determinate thing.[73] The very notion of combining, in the essence of combination itself, already necessarily entails a pre-viewing of unity.

The next question now is: What is this unity that makes possible combination as such and therefore the understanding itself? [322] By answering that question we will arrive at the originary *a priori* of all combining, i.e., of all determining. With that we will arrive at the ultimate *a priori* of the possibility of determining a manifold as such. And since a manifold as such is determined by the form of time, we will arrive at the most originary possibility—that of determining time as such.[74]

*   *   *

§26. The original *a priori* of all combining— the transcendental unity of apperception

If we are to demonstrate this unity philosophically as the most original, this means we have to demonstrate a "transcendental unity" (Transcendental Deduction, §16, B 132), i.e., one that is the *a priori* condition of the possibility of the knowledge of nature in general. To comprehend unity as *a priori*, i.e., to comprehend it in terms of the understanding and its action, means understanding it as a unification. To say unity is prior within the known is correspondingly to say that it is also prior in the subject. That is, unification is the most original action of the understanding—the ur-action of the subject—i.e., as the unifying and combining that makes possible every concrete act of unifying. Combining entails both a manifold as combinable and the pre-viewing of a unity on the basis of which the manifold can be together, i.e., be in a unification.

---

73. [The complete sentence in the *Critique of Pure Reason* reads: "We must therefore seek this unity (as qualitative §12) someplace higher, namely in that which itself contains the basis of the unity of different concepts in judgments, and hence [contains the basis] of the possibility of the understanding, even in its logical use." In §12, Kant had discussed the traditional *transcendentalia* (*unum, verum, bonum*, etc.) not as supra-categorial predicates of *things* but as logical requisites for the *cognition* of things (B 113–114). He therefore reads *unum* as the necessary unity not of the thing out-there but of the *concept* of the thing out-there. He calls this transcendental unity "qualitative unity," in contrast to the quantitative category "unity" in the Table of Categories (B 95). That transcendental, qualitative unity lies in the "higher place" that is the transcendental unity of apperception.]

74. [Here (Moser, p. 648) Heidegger ends his lecture of Monday, 8 February 1926, to be followed by that of Wednesday, 10 February (Heidegger did not lecture on Tuesday), which opened with a 660-word summary that is omitted in GA 21.]

As the ur-action of the understanding, combining presupposes the [prior] presenting of a unity. Therefore, this presenting of a unity is even more original than any given act of combining. The question now is: How are we to understand this unity—or better, this most original presenting of unity—as *a priori*, i.e., as a *cogitatio*?

We must remember that what is given first of all is the manifold of the presentations given in inner sense. In these presentations (which are intuitions) something is presented, i.e., given. In order for there to be anything known at all [323] in knowledge—i.e., for anything to be a given—it must be given to me and must be, in some sense, an object "for me." The presentation therefore cannot simply flow on, one after the other. Rather (according to Kant), this presenting (of something) must be given to me. That is, the present*ing* must be present*able* to me myself (and this must be a permanent possibility) *if* what is given in these presented-to-me presentations is to be accessible to me at all. Knowledge—or the possibility of something being known—necessarily entails the possibility of the belongs-to-me-ness of whatever is presented. A knowing entity—in the broadest sense: presenting entities, thinking the given—must, in its essence, be a presenting *of* this presenting. Or more precisely, [knowing entities must be] a presenting of the fact that I am currently presenting something as in-being—not as a bare *cogitare* ["thinking"], but rather as *cogito me cogitare* ["I think myself thinking"], as Descartes says in his Second Meditation. Kant says as much, almost word-for-word, in his *Logic:* "Consciousness {as *res cogitans*} is really a presentation that another presentation is in me."[75]

He does not know just some presenting-of-something. Rather, this presenting is such that, in carrying it out, I think myself—i.e., "I think *sum cogitans*" ["I think the I-am-the-one-who-is-thinking"]. Every intuition and presentation must be able to be accompanied by this "I think" (*cogito me rem cogitantem* ["I think myself as a thing-that-is-thinking"]), because only in this way is something-given possible at all as given-for. . . . Every intuition (in the sense of *what* can be intuited) is necessarily referred to a possible "I think." Whatever can be given is referred to a "for." This phenomenon of the "for"—for me, for us—is something we should always keep in mind. Kant calls it the

---

75. Kant, *Akademie-Ausgabe*, vol. 9, p. 33. [Heidegger's interpolation is taken from the Moser transcript (p. 651.30). The text is from "The Jäsche Logic," published with Kant's permission in 1800 by Gottlob Benjamin Jäsche (1762–1842) as *Immanuel Kants Logik. Ein Handbuch zu Vorlesungen* (Königsberg: Friedrich Nicolovius, 1800). This is published in English as Immanuel Kant, *Lectures on Logic*, trans. and ed. J. Michael Young (Cambridge: Cambridge University Press, 1992). The text Heidegger cites is at page 544.31–32 (introduction to chap. 5); Young remarks in his introduction that "a great deal of the text is attributable to Jäsche" (p. xvii).]

being-of-something-"in-me" (B 131).⁷⁶ Everything that can be given, that can be intuited (in Kant's language: every intuition), even the pure intuition, time—all that is referred to a "for" and only in such a "for" can it be given at all.

In the first place, this "I think" in which is grounded the belongs-to-me-ness of presentations, cannot be derived from anything else. It is an original act of spontaneity. The grasping of oneself in the *cogitare*, this act of apprehending the "I am the one who is thinking"—this "I think" does not mean that my thinking is [324] an activity that just occurs. Rather, it is an expression of the thought which is the "I am thinking," the *sum cogitans*. In the second place, this "I think" is one and the same in all consciousness. Only through this relation to the I that thinks, to the "I am thinking" (i.e., the "I have this presented in this act of presenting"), can the manifold that is given in such a presenting have a unity. The *a priori* unity is grounded in this *cogito me cogitare*. Kant takes his orientation basically in the direction of Descartes's position, and maintains that position, but he does not stand firm on that ground. Instead, he tries to go beyond that position by asking what it is that makes possible this very belonging-to-me-ness: "In the same subject in which the manifold is encountered, this manifold has a necessary relation to the 'I think'" (B 132).⁷⁷ That means: The subjective, which for Kant is that which is given first, must be able to be present together with the I (which is the basis of my subjectivity) in which something is given. In order for this something to be referable to the I, this I must itself be comprehended, and that means: In having-present the I, the thinking, I also have present, together with it, that which is given to this thinking, that which is thought by this thinking. And the given *can* be given only in such a "having-the-ego-present *qua* having-the-given-co-present."

Therefore, the belonging-to-me-ness of anything is grounded in this original ability of something to be related to the I, to an I that must always think of something. This original synthesis within which alone the given is giveable, combines the given with the I as that which is comprehendible at every moment in the self-identity of its existence. This constant self-identity of the I with which the given as such is [*a priori*] combined—or this combining wherein the constant self-identity

76. [Also "mir angehören" (B 132-133).]

77. [While retaining the sense of Kant's sentence, Heidegger drops *Also* („therefore"), substitutes *dieses* („this") for *alles* („all"), and inverts the word order from „Also hat alles Mannigfaltige der Anschauung eine notwendige Beziehung auf das ‚Ich denke' in demselben Subjekt, darin dieses Mannigfaltige angetroffen wird," to „In demselben Subjekt, darin das Mannigfaltige angetroffen wird, hat dieses Mannigfaltige eine notwendige Beziehung auf das: Ich denke."]

of the I is something that is [*a priori*] "related-to"—*that* is what makes up the original unity of the *cogito*. This is the original unity present in the synthesis of the manifold as such with the I that exists insofar as it is a *cogitatio*, i.e., *a priori*—but a unity as pure apperception: a "transcendental unity." [325]

When we read Kant's explanation of the pure apperception, we see clearly how much he struggles to make this issue understandable: this ultimate structure of the ur-action of understanding *qua* synthesis. Nothing might seem be more obvious than that consciousness of something is at the same time self-consciousness. It might seem that nothing more could be made of it. But for Kant a further question arises: What is the *ground* of the belonging-to-me-ness of the given?

I can only place the manifold presentations next to one other, and only further unify the unifications themselves (i.e., present an ensemble of the manifold of presentations) in such a way that, in doing so, I comprehend myself in each case as the same combining I. But [this is possible] only on the assumption that there is already given beforehand the possible togetherness of the given manifold as such as a whole with the I that thinks a determined manifold. This is the "ground of the identity of apperception" (B 134). This togetherness of the given as such with the I is already given beforehand in a prior synthesis in which this original "unity [is] antecedently thought," "thought beforehand" (B 133–134, note).

> And thus the synthetic unity of apperception is the highest point to which one must affix all use of the understanding, even the whole of logic and, after it, transcendental philosophy; indeed this faculty is the understanding itself. (B 134, note)

Therefore, it is the understanding as combining that constitutes the most original *a priori*, as we discovered in our general reflection at the beginning of this treatment, when we called this argumentation "extrinsic." How is Kant's explanation different from that?

Kant says that combination entails unity, a unity that is already presupposed as object of a pre-view. But in the analysis that we just finished, we saw the exact opposite: It is the original synthesis that makes up the unity.

The original synthetic unity of self consciousness is: [326] (1) the originary synthesis which makes unity possible, and (2) the originary unity which makes synthesis possible. The second is constitutively contained in the first. Synthesis entails the self-positing-in-its-identity on the part of the I, in fact of the I that thinks, that presents something. As *a priori*, unity is a consistent, ever-present character of the *cogitatio*. It is the constant self-identity of combining *in* every act of combining.

Kant calls this unity "qualitative," in contrast to (cf. B 131) the category of unity as the category of quantity. Here "quantity" means "particularity" and "singularity" which, in the mode of particularity, pertains to the forms of pure intuition insofar as there is but a single space and a single time. Kant determines qualitative unity in connection with an interpretation of the *unum transcendens* [the "transcendental one" of Scholastic thought], according to which we say that *omne ens est unum* ["whatever is, is one"]. Such a "unity of the comprehension of the manifold of knowledge" is [simply a] "logical requisite and criterion of the knowledge of things" (B 114).[78] This requirement of unity is a "logical rule of the agreement of knowledge with itself" (B 116).[79] Kant says "logical"—and that means: it resides in the very structure of understanding as a *cogito me cogitare*.

Of its very essence, the understanding is a combining, but not only or primarily any specific act of combining. Rather, the understanding is always an "I combine." In other words, the combining of a specific manifold of presentations is possible only as based upon an underlying "always already having combined the to-be-combined manifold of presentations with me *qua* I-combine."[80] And this "already-have-combined-whatever-will-be-given" (whether the given-in-general or the given in a specific act of combining) is what constitutes the "for[-me-ness]" that belongs to the very being of the "I." The original synthesis that carries out, and posits itself *as* carrying out, any particular synthesis—*that* is a unity, a μόνας, a monad.

The basic question that concerns us is about the connection between time and the "I think," and the possibility of that connection. Our critical discussion with Kant, from which we hope to gain a posi-

---

78. [Kant asserts that, "These supposedly transcendental predicates of things [the *unum, verum, bonum* of medieval philosophy] are nothing other than logical requisites and criteria of all knowledge of things in general. . . . In all knowledge of an object [*Objekt*] there is, namely, *unity of the concept*, which we may call *qualitative unity* insofar as, by means of it, we think only the unity of our comprehension of the manifold of our knowledge." Heidegger, because he is referring to only one of the scholastic transcendentals, changes Kant's two plurals ("Erfordernisse und Kriterien") to singulars ("Erfordernis und Kriterium").]

79. [Here again, Heidegger changes a plural (*Regeln*) to a singular (*Regel*).]

80. ["Always already having (done this or that)" is Heidegger's way of speaking of what Aristotle calls τὸ τί ἦν εἶναι, the essence of a thing, understood as "what that thing is *a priori*" or "what that thing *always already* is, insofar as it is." Both in Aristotle's Greek and in Heidegger's German, that notion is (not unproblematically) expressed as "what the thing already *has been* insofar as it is," not in a chronological but in an ontological sense. Here Heidegger is saying that any specific act of combining is grounded in the essence of the understanding (in what the understanding always already is—"has been"—insofar as it is). That essence is to combine the to-be-combined with the self as *a priori* combining.]

tive insight into ur-temporality, concerns time, [327] the "I think," and their connection. To get on the right footing for explaining the "I think" (and to avoid wrestling a ghost) it is important to get clearer on the meaning of this original act of spontaneity.

If our goal were a detailed interpretation of Kant, we would have to discuss how the Neo-Kantians interpret apperception. We can leave that aside here. But just to give you an overview, I might underline the fact that regarding all the adumbrations of a so-called epistemological or logical subject (and of consciousness in general), Neo-Kantianism says that it is a matter of something logical, a mere concept. Of late they have tried to carry out this epistemological interpretation (which is pure construction) by connecting it with Scheler's doctrine of the person. But putting the two together only increases the confusion and makes it less possible to understand the simple meaning of transcendental apperception. We should note above all that Kant never dreamed of determining this I of transcendental apperception, this consciousness in general, as a mere concept.

Kant distinguishes between an empirical and a transcendental apperception (self-apprehension). Empirical apperception is the intuiting, via inner sense, of the manifoldness of presentations as one-after-another. In empirical intuition *qua* empirical there are given appearances and objects (although as scientifically undetermined) as something mental that is articulated one way or another: as sensation, as striving, as a pleasing or displeasing impression—that is, a comprehension of an objective something-or-other that can be determined as regards the whatness of its content. But on the other hand, transcendental apperception is, as the name suggests, a self-apprehending, understood with an eye to the possibility of an *a priori* knowledge. In other words, transcendental apperception is itself the most original *a priori* of knowledge.

The "I think" is the expressed content of a "merely intellectual presentation of the self-activity of a thinking subject" (B 278). It is the expression of a direct comprehension of my self: *sum cogitans*, I am thinking. [328]

"I think, *therefore* I am" is no inference. (*Opus postumum*, Akademie vol. 22, p. 79).[81]

---

81. [Editor's note: Kant, *Akademie-Ausgabe,* vol. 22, p. 79.] [Translator's note: The edition Heidegger cited was *Kants Opus postumum,* ed. Erich Adickes (Berlin: Reuther & Reichard, 1920). GA 21 cites *Opus postumum* according to the *Akademie-Ausgabe,* vols. 21–22, which was published only in 1936. For an English edition see Immanuel Kant, *Opus Postumum,* ed. Eckart Förster, trans. Eckart Förster and Michael Rosen (Cambridge: Cambridge University Press, 1993), 187.]

This act of apperception (*sum cogitans*) is not yet a judgment about an object. (ibid., p. 89).[82]

Of course, the presentation *I am*, which expresses the consciousness that can accompany all thinking, is that which immediately includes the existence of a subject in itself, but not yet any *knowledge* of it, thus not empirical knowledge, i.e., experience. (B 277)

In this context, Kant's note in §25 becomes clear:

The "I think" expresses the act of determining my existence. The existence is thereby already given, but the way in which I am to determine it, i.e., the manifold that I am to posit in myself as belonging to it, is not yet thereby given. (B 157)

What is presented is "only the spontaneity of the act of determining"— which is the reason "that I call myself an intelligence." Therefore, in this apperception my existence *qua* existence is simply given, but it is not determined as an object.

The *cogito* as something expressed, means: ". . . *me cogitare; me esse; sum cogitans*" [(I think) "myself as thinking, myself as being, myself as the one who is thinking"].[83] In this self-comprehension, nothing can be made out as regards its what-content. As original *a priori*, it always has the function of giving what it is related to as constant identical unity, namely: the whole given, determined manifold of knowledge. Logical consciousness knows no what-content; rather, it knows only "that I am" (B 157). This comprehension of the self, when seen in terms of the determination of the mental, is without content, empty. It says nothing about how, or as what, I appear to myself, nor does it say what I am as a thing-in-itself. Even less so does this act provide any knowledge of my self (B 158), but only of the fact that I am here: existence in the sense of being-there-ness. My "existence" is "thereby" given. Thus Kant says in the *Opus postumum*:

The consciousness of my self is a logical act . . . (*Akademie*, vol. 22, p. 69).[84]

This is merely a logical act, an act of thought . . . through which no object is yet given by me. (ibid., p. 79)[85]

---

82. [This text is not included among the selections translated in the Förster and Rosen edition of the *Opus postumum*.]

83. ["Das *cogito* als Gesagtes sagt: *me cogitare—me esse—sum cogitans*."]

84. [This text is not included among the selections translated in the Förster and Rosen edition of the *Opus postumum*.]

85. [*Opus postumum*, trans. Förster and Rosen, p. 187.14–15.]

In using the word "logical," Kant means to say: The entity is not intuited nor given in its "what," but is posited and comprehended in its existence merely as data.[86] [329] And this *cogito me cogitare* is an act of spontaneity, constantly repeatable in self-identity, such that I identify myself as existing, as in existence, and only to that extent. To say that this act is "logical" certainly does *not* mean, "Thinking thinks something that is thought," whence one might try to infer the following: "If what it thinks is a mere thought, something merely logical, then it is a concept; and therefore the epistemological subject is a mere concept"—as if Kant would ever have let himself imagine that the highest point to which all philosophy can be attached—indeed, all transcendental philosophy—is a mere concept.

This self-positing I, this I that gives itself in its being-present, is the "logical personality" (*Reflexionen*, no. 5049).[87] But in no way does that mean that it is "logical" in the sense of something merely thought, and even further in the sense of a concept. In its self-positing, the I gives itself as existing. It expresses no "what," i.e., it attributes no predicate to itself. Rather, this I is the subject of a predicate-less pro-position, the subject of a positing.[88] That is, the I is a "subject" and only a subject.[89] This subject underlies every proposition and every expression—every *cogitare* is a *me cogitare:*

> But for that reason, it is only a subject to which no predicate is attached, (1) because no subject is thought in regard to it; (2) because it is presupposition and substratum of other subjects. (*Reflexionen*, no. 5297)

In this passage we note how Kant gives the concept "subject" a peculiar twofold meaning. In the first sense, the subject is a "grammatical subject" as distinct from a "predicate." That is what Kant means when he says the I is a predicate-less subject. However, this predicate-less subject *qua* I is also a "subject" as contrasted with an "object." The original synthesis of unity is grounded in this subject and directly constitutes its being. [330] So the subject is the condition of the possibility of comprehending any entity insofar as any comprehending of an entity presumes the co-comprehending of that entity as *one*.

That is why Kant calls this I that can be comprehended in pure ap-

---

86. [„. . . nur als Befund," i.e., merely as findings.]

87. Kant, *Akademie-Ausgabe*, vol. 18, p. 72.

88. [Heidegger is playing on the connection of *Satz* (proposition) with *Setzung* (positing).]

89. Ich—*sum*, und zwar Ich—*cogitans;* Ich, der Verbindende des Verbindens; mein Mitvorhandenes ein jederzeit in allem Verbinden. [Perhaps: "*Sum cogitans:* I—precisely *as* I—am thinking. The I, the one who is the (*a priori*) combiner in all acts of combining. My being (is) ever present with and in every act of combining."]

perception, simply in its constant and self-identical presence, the "logical personality." He calls it a "personality" insofar as it is understood in terms of its original activity, that of the understanding *qua* combining as such, the combining of the given with the understanding itself. We will now explain more precisely how Kant is *not* (as one might allege) moving in a circle in his analysis of the transcendental unity of apperception; and we will do so in order then to ask: What is this original synthesis of the given as such with the I?[90]

                              *   *   *

First of all we need to get rid of a misunderstanding. One might say: Kant explicitly emphasizes that combining presupposes unity. But when we ask what the unity underlying this combining might be, the answer is: synthesis. And what about this synthesis? In any synthesis, as an act of combining, a unity is antecedently presented. So the synthesis is referred back to a unity. But that unity, in turn, is referred back to yet another synthesis—and so on *ad infinitum*. Proceeding that way, we never get to firm ground; in fact we arrive at the opposite of what Kant was looking for, viz., the original, the "one" to which everything else is to be referred.

That objection, however, overlooks an important fact. The synthesis that Kant calls "original," the synthesis in which he saw fit to ground the unity that makes every synthesis possible—and to ground even this foundational synthesis itself—this original synthesis is not just any synthesis but a quite exceptional one.

What makes it so exceptional is the fact that one of the things it combines is the I; and the I means: "I think." I am that "for" which something can be given. Insofar as I am, I am that very "for."[91] The I is the "for-whom-it-is-given" of whatever can be given and thus whatever can be determined. The "for-whom-it-is-given" (which is I myself) is likewise the that-which-determines. To combine something with the I—i.e., to let it *be with* this I[92]—means that the "something" has the possibility of being-given-for. . . . [331] This act of combining requires no further

90. [Here (Moser, p. 662) Heidegger ends his lecture of Wednesday, 10 February 1926, to be followed by that of Thursday, 11 February, which opened with a 670-word summary that is omitted in GA 21.]

91. ["Ich bin das seiende Für selbst." The *selbst* here is emphatic ("that very 'for' . . ."), and not reflexive ("the for-itself").]

92. [This point anticipates what Heidegger will write a few months later in the manuscript of *Being and Time;* cf. *SZ*, p. 201.12–14 / tr. 192.35–37: „Wenn innerweltliches Seiendes mit dem Sein des Daseins entdeckt, das heißt zu Verständnis gekommen ist, sagen wir, es hat *Sinn.*" What can be meaningful or meaningless? Cf. ibid., p. 201 / tr. 193: Only Dasein's „eigenes Sein und das mit diesem erschlossene Seiende." And cf. also *SZ*, p. 429.35 / tr. 371.35–36: „Wenn wir sagen: Seien-

pre-view of anything on the basis of which the "combineds" might be combined into one. Rather, the pre-viewed unity is itself one of the "combineds." As [antecedently] brought together with the I as "I think" (the *cogito*, the I-place-before-myself in the broadest sense), the pre-viewed unity requires no further unity. Rather, the "togetherness" that goes with the act of combining is the very givenness-for-an-"*I*."[93]

At the same time, pre-viewing the "I am the one who thinks" (the *ego sum cogitans*) is the synthesis, because I *as such* means "I think," i.e., "I relate myself to the given." To comprehend the I in its presentness (as a comprehension of the "I think") is a co-apprehension of what is thought in the I's thinking. That is why Kant insists so emphatically that the I cannot be given as an object [*Objekt*] in the sense of an object [*Gegenstand*]; it is not something that I could stay with awhile and say something about. Instead, comprehending the "I think" means comprehending the for-whom or for-what. It is to comprehend the "give-able-for. . ." Comprehending the I means that the comprehending I carries out the "I think," carries out the thinking—i.e., the determining, i.e., the combining of the manifold. For the I to be given in its pure presentness *qua* I means for it to "be" the "for," i.e., it means for the I to make possible the very give-ability of the given for me.

What makes it difficult to understand these phenomena is the inadequacy of the means that Kant had for his effort of understanding them. For example, the formal structure of the act of combining had to suffice for determining an entity (the I) that has an entirely unique kind of being; and then, throughout the entire treatment, the meaning of the being of this entity is left undetermined—or, what more disastrous, he understands that being in the simple and direct sense of mere presence.

---

des ‚hat Sinn', dann bedeutet das, es ist *in seinem Sein* [which is correlative to ‚das Sein des Daseins'] zugänglich geworden."]

93. [The argument seems to be: (1) "I think" means "I combine something with the I that does the combining," i.e., with the "I-combine." (2) But "to combine" means "to bring into unity," i.e., to bring about the togetherness-in-unity of what is to be combined. (3) Such bringing-into-unity is *unification* and as such requires a unity as the basis on which (or the prior norm whereby) the to-be-combineds are unified. (4) That unity is not perfect one-ness. Rather, as the prior norm for unifying, that unity means: "unified-with-me-the-unifier," the one who is, and cannot exist without, the unification-of-something-with-me. (5) In that sense, the antecedent normative unity is a "must-be-a-unity-such-as-I-am," and thus indicates not an absolutely perfect unity but a combined or synthetic unity as is the I *qua* "I-combine" or "I-synthesize."(6) When the to-be-unified is *a priori* brought together with the "I-synthesize," the synthetic unity prescribed by the pre-viewed "unified-the-way-the-I-is-unified" is *a priori* effected, and no further unity is required. (7) "Unified" means *Zusammensein*—having-been-brought-together-in-unity. As regards what gets unified, its "being-*together-with*-the-I-unify" is its "being-given-*for*-the-I-unify." (8) Therefore, whatever is combined is *ipso facto* given-for-the-I.]

Not only does Kant take over Descartes's position on the *cogito sum* with its influence on the meaning of the *a priori*, but he likewise takes over, as beyond question, the ontological conception of being as the *esse* of *esse creatum:* as mere being-present, mere happening-to-be. (Right now I can't show in detail that Descartes in fact understood the *sum* in his *cogito sum* in this way. [332] I demonstrated that in some earlier lectures by way of a thoroughgoing interpretation of the *Meditations.*)[94]

In the final analysis Kant interprets these structures of the I and the "I think" in terms of the co-presence of something-present and an "I." However, he likewise interprets the I as something that *has . . .* , as that for which some thing is present. He interprets the I as the constantly self-identical, to whose very presence thinking *qua* "I think" can come back at every moment in which a being-present-*with* is possible. To put it briefly: Kant tries to interpret the "I think something"— or in general, the "I have something given"—with ontological determinations that pertain to the "something" that can be given but that do not pertain to the "I think" and the being of the "I." He thinks he can understand the "logical personality" within the formal structures taken from a form of being that in Kant's sense is simply the ontological opposite of the "I." He determines the I—which in fact he sees and understands as the most original and the absolutely unique—by means of empty, formal ontological determinations.

The original synthesis is characterized by the fact that (1) it is itself the I's act of relating-to-something, and this relating-to is always an "I have"; and likewise that (2) by its nature it is the pre-viewing of unity, an act that is *a priori* constitutive of the I *qua* combining. This I—or as Kant constantly says, the pure apperception—is this original synthesis; or the [pre-viewed] "unity" is a synthetic unity of the pure apperception.

The original synthesis, which we have interpreted as the phenomenon of self-apprehension, is the most original in yet another sense: because it is the basis of every concrete act of combining, each of which, for its part, requires its own specific pre-viewing or presenting of a unity. These unities that pertain to the various possible actions of the understanding as unifications are what we must discover if we are to show, in the basic statements, what is *a priori* known in the knowledge of nature (i.e., what is thought beforehand in the principles). These unities are the pre-viewed bases-on-which [333] of every act of judgment. Kant finds them (or believes he finds them) by establishing the possible

94. [*Einführung in die phänomenologische Forschung,* Heidegger's first lecture-course at Marburg, Winter Semester 1923–1924, was published under that title as GA 17, ed. Friedrich-Wilhelm von Herrmann (Frankfurt am Main: Vittorio Klostermann, 1994; 2d edition, 2006); published in English as Martin Heidegger, *Introduction to Phenomenological Research,* trans. Daniel O. Dahlstrom (Bloomington: Indiana University Press, 2005).]

ways of unifying—a "Table of Judgments"—as the possible forms of combining. He thinks that this Table provides the totality of possible forms of unity, the possible forms of pre-viewing for these specific ways of combining. These unities, conceptually grasped as the various possible pre-viewed bases-on-which of combining, are the categories. With that, the transcendental, *a priori* structure of the second stem of knowledge—the understanding—is laid out. The structure of the first stem—sensibility—was delineated as the forms of intuition, space and time.

Givenness as such is possible only in a "for" that is constituted by an original synthesis that is expressed as the "I think." This synthesis is the condition of the possibility of every concrete act of combining; and (*a priori*) transcendentally it is the condition of the possibility of the primary function of unity, namely, judging as a pure action of the understanding. These pure concepts of unity, which pertain to all its ways of functioning, are supposed to be endowed with *a priori* content. (They are, after all, determinations of the content of nature's being.) Where does this *a priori* content come from since, as transcendental, it cannot be drawn from experience? How can these pure concepts of understanding, as unities constitutive of merely empty actions of understanding, have any relation to objects [*Objekte*], to content-determined objects [*Gegenstände*]? What is given as essentially *a priori,* and what is given universally?—specifically, given in such a way that (1) it is something given in general for every action of the understanding that is supposed to determine something in the object [*Objekt*]; and so that (2) this universal given determines every empirical given in its being-given?

This *a priori* given, which *a priori* and universally lies "in front of" the understanding and which, at the same time, determines everything that can be given to sensibility, is, according to Kant, time. Because it is a form of the givenness [334] of inner sense, it is a form of the givenness of that to which an action of the understanding, as an action of the subject, can first and only direct itself. (The understanding remains "in the subject.") But then it is not a form of outer sense, much less a form of those appearances that natural knowledge is supposed to determine. Therefore we must first show how time, which is primarily and properly the form of inner sense, can also be the form of outer sense and its givenness, and consequently has to be the *a priori* to which, first of all and without exception, every action of the understanding, as a combining of the given, must be referred.

§27. Time as the universal *a priori* form of all appearances

To what degree is time, as pure intuition, the universal form of all givens? How does Kant show that time, although primarily and properly the form only of inner sense, is also the form of outer sense?

We must keep in mind two propositions: "Time cannot be a determination of outer appearances" (B 49), and "On the contrary, time determines the relation of presentations in our inner state" (B 50). So time is unequivocally denied of outer appearances and attributed to inner appearances alone. And yet in the second sentence Kant shows quite precisely that the first sentence holds only in a relative sense. He says: "Time is an *a priori* condition of all appearances in general" (B 50); time is "the formal condition . . . of the connection of all presentations" (B 177). But space, on the other hand, is "limited merely to outer intuitions" (B 50). Kant demolishes the limitations that he previously and explicitly expressed in the first sentence. How so?

Time is first of all the form of inner sense, i.e., of the presentations that show up for this sense. As determinations of the mind, these belong to our "inner state." They are *cogitationes*. [335] The mind is a region that we "fill up" with *cogitationes*, with presentations. He says that "the presentations of *outer sense* make up the proper material with which we occupy our mind" (B 67).[95] But insofar as we fill our mind with these presentations—i.e., have them given to us in inner sense—they stand in the form of time. Even the presenting of the outer sense, as a mental occurrence, is something that is given in the inner sense; "presentations in themselves" are inner states, whatever they happen to be presenting. Insofar as the presentations of the outer senses, as presenting something, are mental states, they are "in time," one-after-another—and they are so "in themselves." As presenting, they place something before [us]; and they are presentations in the sense of that-which-is-presented. Insofar as Kant uses "presentation" in this twofold sense of the "presenting" and the "presented," he can understand the being-in-time of the presenting in the same way that he understands the being-in-time of the presented. Therefore, the outer appearances, as they come to be the kind of presentations that, according to Kant, are given to inner sense, are themselves determined as one-after-another: they are determined in time.

> Because all presentations, whether or not they have outer things as their object, nevertheless as determinations of the mind themselves belong to the inner state, while this inner state belongs under the formal condition of inner intuition, and thus of time, so time is an *a priori* condition of all appearance in general, and indeed the immediate condition of the inner intuition . . . and thereby also the mediate condition of outer appearances. If I can say *a priori* [that is, from out of the subject] that all outer appearances are in space and are determined *a priori* according to the relations of

95. [The German "das Gemüt besetzen" can have the stronger sense of "to fill up the mind," as well as the weaker sense of "to engage the mind."]

space, so from the principle [*Princip*] of inner sense I can say entirely generally: all appearances in general, i.e., all objects of the senses [all entities that are encountered], are in time, and necessarily stand in relations of time. (B 50–51)[96]

This is the inferential reason Kant uses to show that time is the universal form of the givenness of whatever can be determined. [336] As a consequence, time becomes the first and the only possible *a priori* object of acts of pure *a priori* determining, i.e., of the pure actions of the understanding. This is why, for Kant, time becomes in a certain sense the ground from out of which he draws the objectivity of the pure forms and the empty forms of the unity of the actions of the understanding.[97]

*   *   *

From the being-in-time of the mental (the presenting) Kant reasons inferentially to the being-in-time of the presented. Why does he make this inference at all? What requires that a time-determination be attributed as well to the appearances of our outer perceptions, i.e., to outer appearances? Answer: our natural experience, namely, that they certainly are time-determined. According to Kant's theory they cannot be in an *immediate* way; and therefore he has to show that they are so "mediately," by way of inner sense, insofar as they are states of inner sense. But this way of arguing (1) is phenomenologically unnecessary (there is no need of it), and (2) is not even conclusive, because from the fact that the mental occurs in time there follows absolutely nothing about what is presented mentally. On the contrary, if this way of arguing were legitimate, it would have to follow that even numbers are "in time," as well as the objects of geometry (which surely have nothing to do with natural processes)—and in fact the same with everything that is thought or presented in any action of the mind: the categories, the pure concepts of understanding to the degree they are thought by transcendental philosophy—because this thinking, this presenting, these "presentations-in-themselves" are themselves also states of mind. But Kant denies anything of the sort—for example, just

96. [In citing Kant's text, Heidegger omits two phrases from the text: (1) the *Dagegen* ("On the contrary") that begins the sentence and that indicates the contrast between the limitation of space, as pure form, to outer intuition, and the more general application to time, as pure form, to all appearances; and (2) Kant's parenthesized phrase, *unserer Seelen*—i.e., "(of our souls)"—the omission of which is indicated by the ellipsis above.]

97. [Here (Moser, p. 675) Heidegger ends his lecture of Thursday, 11 February 1926, to be followed by that of Friday, 12 February, which opened with a 650-word summary that is omitted in GA 21.]

think of how he crossed out the word *zugleich*—"at the same *time*"—in his interpretation of the principle of contradiction. Or are the acts of spontaneity exempted from the being-in-time of *cogitationes*? Are there, therefore, some *cogitationes* that are outside of time and some that are in time? And further, some whose presented content is also in time, and some whose presented content is not? [337]

Kant never demonstrates that or why this state of affairs is this way; he simply presupposes it as a fact. But the basis for his argumentation is the Cartesian presupposition that what is given first and above all is the act of presenting, and that the only way, the necessary way, to get to what-is-presented begins with and passes through this act of presenting. This presupposition also hinders Kant from seeing (1) that the world, the lived world, is given just as immediately as—no, even *more* immediately than—what is given in inner sense, and (2) that we have an equally immediate experience of the one-after-another and the at-the-same-time in our experience of the lived world. We first experience the one-after-another in the change of day into night, in the movement of the sun, in the way things around us change place, and so on. We use the sun to determine time, and so, the sun is time. Time is the sun, the heavens. These statements are not poetic fabrications; they express what one sees first of all—as Plato says: Time is the heavens. From this you can clearly see that we encounter time first of all precisely in the things given to our outer senses and that it requires a very artificial attitude in order to see time the way Kant wants to: as something that is found, from the beginning, purely and exclusively in the one-after-another of presentations. This position—that time can be experienced even when it is dark, i.e., when I see nothing in the world but am referred purely to myself and to the course of my thinking—this was underlined for the first time by Aristotle in his treatise on time: time as experienced in the κίνησις of the soul's νοεῖν ["in the movement of the soul's apprehending"].[98]

Kant's proof of the universality of time cannot be sustained in its motivation, its presuppositions, or its procedure—but nonetheless its outcome is incontestable. However, the fact that Kant in the first place requires and makes use of this proof uncovers the presuppositions behind his position. We must understand and remember how and as what Kant determines time in the light of this presupposition.

We now understand that time is characterized in two ways. (1) Time is pure intuition, where the act of intuiting is a determination carried out by the mind.

> Time is simply a subjective condition of our (human) intuition . . . [338] and outside the subject it is nothing. (B 51)

98. [On sensing time in the dark, see *Physics* Δ, 11, 219a4–6.]

[Time] adheres not to the objects themselves but only to the subject that intuits . . . {the objects? or time?} (B 54)[99]

Space and time . . . are only in the senses and outside of them have no reality. (B 148)

These remarks, as well as the beginning of §6 of the Transcendental Aesthetic, make it clear how (as we have already shown) Kant transforms both Newton's notion of time as a *res*, and Leibniz's as an *ordo rerum*, into a *cogito*—a determination of the mind.

(2) We have also encountered a second delineation of time as the pre-viewed basis-on-which of a specific type of pre-viewing. In this case, time is given-and-presented as an infinite magnitude. In this second characterization, time is an infinite whole of the pure manifold of the one-after-another—or, as Kant puts it: time is a *quantum*.

Our task now is to gather up these new gains and push ahead to a radical interpretation that will clarify the connection between these two characterizations.

§28. Time as original pure self-affection

The pure act of intuiting—time[100]—was interpreted as an antecedent, unthematic viewing of the pure manifold as such "within which there is nothing but relations of one-after-another." This antecedent viewing is a way the mind *is*. It has this pre-viewing from out of its own self, for the very essence of its kind of being is to have such a pre-view. But we showed that the object of the pre-view is the very condition

99. [In Kant's German, the object of "intuits" is *sie*, which here can mean either "them" (the objects) or "it" (time). The Guyer and Wood translation (like the earlier Norman Kemp Smith translation) opts for the former; Heidegger, after the word *sie*, inserts in brackets: "die Gegenstände? Zeit?"]

100. [In this section, Heidegger's own understanding of time (which he will soon spell out more clearly in *Being and Time*) begins to make its appearance. No longer a mere natural-cosmic measure of movement, *Zeit* is now designated as the self's most fundamental *a priori* / ontological "act," so fundamental that it is the very being of the self. This antecedent ontological "act" has the reflexive sense of the self's "acting upon and affecting itself." In *Being and Time*, time will be presented as the self's self-generating (*sich zeitigend*) "temporality," i.e., human existence's finite (and indirectly self-referential) way of being. That being consists in (1) being open for any encounter (*gegenwärtig*) by (2) living into its own apriority (*gewesende*), which is (3) being the ontological basis on which the self can be encountered at all, a possibilizing basis-on-which that ever "recedes" (i.e., on principle can never be exhausted, only ended by death) while ever "arriving" (*zukommende; Zu-kunft*) precisely by making encounter possible.]

whereby anything can be encountered at all. So here time is the condition that makes it possible for anything given to be given in the articulated form of one-after-another. The object of the pre-view, then,
is a purely given whole of one-after-another-ness.

By antecedently seeing that object, the mind or self, of itself, provides itself with the fundamental possibility of being encountered by
[339] anything out there. This pre-viewing, this antecedent, if unthematic, act of having the basis-on-which [something can be received],
is the *a priori* act of letting something encounter the self. This is the
fundamental way the self *is*. It is the self's basic kind of being, whereby
the self, in and of itself, lets itself be encountered by, concerned by, or
in Kant's terms be affectively modified (*sich affizieren*) by another, viz.,
the basis-on-which.

This unthematic pre-viewing is the mind's originary act of affecting
itself—its self-affection. In it the mind relates itself to an infinite given
magnitude: *time*. Time is the way in which the mind lets itself be given
anything at all. It is the most original, universal form of how-some-
thing-can-be-given; it is the mind's original, universal self-affection.
As the self's way of letting itself be concerned about anything, it is the
ontological condition of the possibility of meeting up with anything.

But since this being-affected [*Affektion*] does not rest on sensation,
i.e., is not a character of any empirical intuition, it must be designated
"pure" self-affection. Intuition as pure intuition (time) is certainly not
an *intuitus originarius* [originating intuition] in the sense of the *intellectus archetypus* [the intellect that is the archetype of things], because
the subject does not first create time.[101] It is an *intuitus derivativus*—that
is, an *intuitus originarius* that befits a created entity. In this case the
existing subject, as created, has the possibility, arising from itself, to
affect itself with itself and in an entirely original sense. That is why I
say: according to Kant, time is original, universal, pure self-affection.
Up until now, Kant-scholarship has completely overlooked this proper
sense of time—although in one passage Kant does expressly comprehend the phenomenon of time in this way.

The upshot of this phenomenological analysis is that time is original pure self-affection. And that is no different from what Kant says.
What we have been calling "the act of pre-viewing the basis-on-which"
is what, Kant writes,

101. [Kant defines God's *intuitus originarius* as an intuition "through which the
existence of the object [*Objekt*] of intuition is itself given" (*CPR*, B 72; cf. B 135,
138–139). Kant contrasts the divine *intellectus archetypus* and the human *intellectus
ectypus* in *Critique of Judgment*, §77 (*Akademie-Ausgabe*, vol. 5, p. 408). See *Critique
of the Power of Judgment*, ed. Paul Geyer, trans. Paul Guyer and Eric Matthews
(Cambridge and New York: Cambridge University Press, 2000), p. 277.34.]

[can] be nothing else than the way the mind is affected by its own activity—viz., by this positing of its presentation [*ihrer Vorstellung*]—and hence affected by itself, which means that as regards its form, it is an inner sense. (B 67–68)

The original printing of the B edition has the text as above: [the mind is affected by] "this positing of *ihrer Vorstellung*," where *Vorstellung* ["presentation"] means *Vorstellen* [the mind's act of presenting]. [340] But later editions emended the text to read "the positing of *seiner Vorstellung*," a change that is completely unnecessary and robs the sentence of its rich meaning.[102] We have to say (1) that the spontaneity of the self consists in the modes of its act of presenting;[103] (2) that the pre-viewing that we have characterized—namely, time—belongs fundamentally to that spontaneity; and (3) consequently that, just as fundamentally, spontaneity *qua* self-affection is receptivity.

Time, understood as this most fundamental self-affection, is "antecedently letting a pre-viewed basis-on-which be given." This "antecedent letting" is the condition of the possibility of the mind being occupied with presentations as manifolds antecedently given for combination and determination by the understanding. In self-affection, time posits for itself the very self as the one who, on the grounds of this self-concern, can be encountered by something. ("Time gives what can be determined" [B 158, note]; this giving is, as such, the *actus* of my activity.) This positing comes about not through being-affected. Rather, self-affection—time—is the condition of the possibility of any and all ability to be affected. In phenomenological terms: it is the condition of the possibility of being unto an other that we may encounter.

For Kant, it is the subject and its presentations that are given first of all; and by passing through them, as it were, we then apprehend and

102. [In his edition, *Kritik der reinen Vernuft. Text der Ausgabe 1781 mit Beifügung sämmtlicher Abweichungen der Ausgabe 1787* (Leipzig: Reclam, 1878), Karl Kehrbach (1846–1905) replaced *ihrer* with *seiner*. All current German editions of the first *Critique* use *ihrer*.

Heidegger clarifies this passage in a footnote to *Kant and the Problem of Metaphysics*, 5th ed., trans. Richard Taft (Bloomington: Indiana University Press, 1997), p. 133 n. 266: "The proposed change of 'their presentation' to 'its presentation' (*des 'ihrer Vorstellung' in 'seiner'*) removes from the text precisely what is essential. The 'their' is not supposed to express that the presentation is a presentation by the mind, but rather that the presenting that is posited by the mind presents the 'pure relations' of the succession of the now-sequence as such and allows them to come toward receptivity" (translation slightly revised).]

103. [More literally: ". . . the spontaneity of the self is what it is in the modes of its act of presenting."]

determine the outer world. The sense of this problematic entails that this manifold of presentations must itself be given—i.e., we must be able to be given something. What we said earlier about time as self-affection must be understood within these limits ("limits" in a Kantian sense). Because Kant unjustifiably restricts time, as a form of intuition, to the inner sense; and because his analysis fails to probe the structural connections between the prior view, the in-view-of, and the issue of letting oneself be encountered by a manifold; for these reasons, even the structural connection that we have laid out—time as original, universal, pure self-affection—could not come out in the straightforward, decisive way that its fundamental significance deserves. [341]

In this way the double determination of time becomes intelligible: first of all, as pure intuition and then as an infinite whole of the manifoldness of the one-after-another. The prior letting-oneself-be-given is, in an unthematic way, time. Likewise *what* that prior letting lets itself be given is time—which is to say that the subject affects itself with itself. Here alone, in this interpretation of time as original and pure self-affection, can we get to the authentic whole of the phenomenon of time. The first determinations of time in the Transcendental Aesthetic (which people usually just rattle off without understanding the context) are only partial determinations of the whole (viz., time as self-affection). Time is what lets the pure intuitable be given—and thereby is the very thing that gets intuited. Thus it is not some object that is present.

Kant penetrated no further into this dimension of the phenomenon of time. But *de facto* he makes the most of this sense of time when he studies the connection of time and the "I think." And we must stress that this fundamental determination of time recedes completely into the background even while it materially underlies his explanations, most notably in the major chapters of his treatment of time in the analogies and the schematism—which is the reason why the commentators can't help misunderstanding them. Instead, a different concept of self-affection emerges in Kant: the understanding as the determining of the given, and as the very spontaneity of the synthesis. The imagination

exercises an action on the *passive* subject, whose *faculty* it {the understanding itself} is. Therefore we rightly say that the inner sense is affected thereby. (B 153–154)[104]

104. [Heidegger may misread this passage slightly. (1) The subject of the sentence is not the imagination but the understanding (*der Verstand*, B 153). (2) The synthesis that the understanding performs is the unity of the action (*die Einheit der Handlung*) that the understanding itself performs *through* the imagination's

[T]he inner sense is affected by ourselves. Every act of *attention* can provide an example of this. (B 156, note)

According to these passages the understanding determines inner sense as inner intuition. Put otherwise, that which is first given to me in the synthesis is determined by the understanding as an object. Here "self-affection" means [342] concern with oneself, i.e., thinking is concerned with the given. Kant points out (at B 152) that the idea of self-affection necessarily has something paradoxical about it, since being-affected is different from functioning. The senses are affected whereas the understanding functions. The understanding is spontaneity, whereas sensibility is receptivity. But now spontaneity itself is supposed to be receptivity, especially so and exclusively so in this phenomenon of self-affection. The self, in its very being, is supposed to be the condition of the possibility of letting something encounter it.

By interpreting time as the original, universal, pure self-affection, we have led the heretofore disparate features of time back to an essential phenomenon. But with this phenomenon we have also entered an area that we had previously started to explore while analyzing the transcendental apperception—which, as it turned out, was also the condition of possibility of the "existence" [Kant's word, *Dasein*] of objects: entities as objectively determinable. And this transcendental apperception was itself also an act of spontaneity. This spontaneity of the I (the self) is thus equiprimordially pure apperception and pure self-affection, pure "I think" and time. So we are back to the context of our basic question. Earlier (p. 255) I said: "It is a matter of the conditions of the possibility of a conjunction of time and the 'I think'," and, "Only if we pose the question in this way, i.e., about the conditions of the possibility of the ontological connection between both determinations of the mind (namely, time as pure intuition and the 'I think' as an act of the mind's spontaneity), do we comprehend the question philosophically." The interpretation of time that we have gained so far clarifies the connection between time and the I, between self-affection and transcendental apperception. Or to put it more prudently: It puts us face to face with the real difficulty. [343]

For Kant there are two self-positings in spontaneity. Kant got to this dimension by pursuing his inquiries, but he never made it primary in

transcendental synthesis. (3) By way of that action (cf. *durch die [d.h. die Synthesis] er (der Verstand)*), the understanding *qua* active, is able to determine itself *qua* passive-receptive inner sense, since the inner sense is in fact a faculty of the understanding. Thus (4) "The understanding, under the title of a *transcendental synthesis of the imagination,* exercises that action [of synthesis] on the *passive* subject, which is itself a faculty of the understanding. Thus we can rightly say that inner sense is affected by that action."]

his research in a thematic way. Instead, as is his wont, he pursues these determinations only in a reductive fashion: they remain for him simply determinations of the mind, *cogitationes* of the *res cogitans,* determinations that now pertain to both stems of knowledge: sensibility, αἴσθησις, and the understanding, νόησις. According to Kant, this characterization of the *res cogitans* in terms of spontaneity and receptivity is the metaphysical or ontological characterization of the subject, whereas the determination of sensibility and understanding as, respectively, the faculty of intuition and the faculty of concepts, is the logical characterization of the subject. Kant makes this distinction in the introduction to his *Logic,* §5.[105] Thus, when taken as ontological characteristics, receptivity and spontaneity determine the subject's kind of being, whereas when taken as logical determinates, the faculty of intuiting and the faculty of combining determine the subject's comportment. But from the start, their connection remains unclear. We have to ask: How are these comportments—intuiting and combining—grounded in the determinate being of spontaneity and receptivity? The possibility of both of these kinds of being of the subject (spontaneity and receptivity) must be determined in terms of this entity's basic kind of being.[106]

*   *   *

§29. The question about the connection between time as original self-affection and the "I think"

Our question now is about the connection between "I think" and time.[107] We are looking for the answer via the path we have charted:

105. [The "Jäsche logic" in Kant, *Akademie-Ausgabe,* vol. 9, p. 36 / tr. 546.]

106. [Here (Moser, p. 690) Heidegger ends his lecture of Friday, 12 February 1926, to be followed by that of Monday, 15 February, which opened with a 330-word summary that is given in part in n. 107.]

107. We are trying to bring together the characteristics of time, trying to make time comprehensible as a unified phenomenon by way of its diverse and seemingly disparate determinations. Only from that can we comprehend how the phenomenon of time comes to have such a central role in the *Critique of Pure Reason.*

Time is the original, universal, pure self-affection by, or being affected by, itself—*original* because it comes forth from oneself; *universal and transcendental* because it is the letting-oneself-be-affected-by . . . that antecedently underlies every specific act of being-affected-by-this-or-that; *pure* because time is not determined empirically-experientially by isolating its component parts, but as a whole—which likewise means: unthematically, not by way of an objectifying comprehension. It cannot be comprehended by any objective apprehension. From out of my own self I let myself be constantly affected by myself and in such a way that what affects me is not itself observed.

Time is a pure pre-viewing-of . . . Time is what is pre-viewed in the pre-view-what role time plays in the fundamental task [345] of Kant's transcendental investigation. The theme of Kant's investigation is to clarify what is *a priori* known in our knowledge of nature, where "*a priori*" means: from out of the original actions of the subject. The mind's actions and positings belong to the two stems of knowledge: sensibility and understanding. Understanding determines sensibility. Our question is: In what sense is the universal *a priori* of sensibility, namely time, the to-be-determined for the *a priori* of understanding, namely the synthetic unity of apperception? How does it look, this *a priori*, transcendental, general time-determination that supposedly makes possible the antecedent concrete scientific experience and study of nature in general? How do we understand "time" in this case? and what do we mean by a "determination of time"?

At the same time, we need to get a more precise view of such questions by seeing them within the horizon of the phenomena we brought out in our phenomenological interpretation of Kant's problematic. Time is the condition of the possibility of encountering something at all. As such a condition, time has the character of an antecedent, unthematic pre-viewing of the infinite whole, the pure manifoldness of one-after-another. And this pre-viewing, in turn, has the structure of the subject's being-affected-by-itself. Such pre-viewing is the basic form of [346] "letting something encounter oneself," a "letting" that is generated *by* the pre-viewing itself. From the other side: The "I think" is the condition of the possibility of the "for whom" the encountered thing can encounter. As such a condition of possibility, the "I think" has the character of the most basic pre-viewing, the one that pre-views the constant presence of the self-identical I that something might encounter. As pre-viewing that constant presence, the pre-viewing is the most basic synthesis, and its structure is the very structure of the subject's being. That being is: "from-out-of-itself-and-unto-itself letting-something-be-present-with itself, the subject, as the constant for-whom."

Both of them, time and the I, are what is pre-viewed in a pre-viewing, and both are unthematic. Time is not perceivable as an empirical object, and the I is not an object that can be determined by way of predicates. Instead, both time and the I are the prior, unavoidable pre-viewed of the unthematic pre-view that goes with any concrete act of knowledge. Both are originary modes of being of the subject. In this phenomenological characterization, time and the "I think" lose their

---

ing. Time *qua* time is given so unthematically that, precisely by being so given, time is the condition of the possibility of relating to entities.

In a certain way Kant sees this character of time; but time nonetheless remains basically undetermined and not valorized—something that is bound up with the undetermined-ness of spontaneity's kind of being.

"disparate" character that they have at first glance and that they have had for Kant and the tradition both before and after him. Instead, the possibility of showing the phenomenological connection between the two grows more promising.

But how are we to understand the connection? Is time a mode of the "I think"? Or is the "I think" a mode of time? Or are both of them modes of an even more original connection? Our final position on Kant's conception of time will necessarily lie in our answer to this question. We should not present our response as simply a counter-thesis to Kant's conception of time. Instead we must show, on the basis of the interpretation we have carried out thus far, that the radical conception of the relevant connection of the phenomena that Kant treats requires the answer that we give.

Can we, using Kant's work itself, get an understanding of how Kant determines this relation between transcendental apperception and time? He determines this relation—certainly not by [347] expressly asking about and searching for an answer, but nonetheless he does make use of it. And how does he make use of it? Once in his doctrine of the *schematism* of the pure concepts of understanding, and then again in his proof of the *analogies* of experience. From the way Kant makes use of the relation of time and transcendental apperception in these texts, we should be able to gather how he understands time. Only by pursuing these considerations and demonstrations with the intention of seeing how time is thereby understood, will we have the opportunity to complete our understanding of how Kant characterizes time. Only in this way, can we ask and answer the critical phenomenological question about the relation of time and the "I." But that will mean nothing less than a concrete characterization of the problematic of ur-temporality in contradistinction to Kant's interpretation of time. And it will be the interpretation of that same ur-temporality within the task of a clarification of the scientific knowledge of entities.

§30. Interpretation of the First Analogy of Experience in the light of our interpretation of time

We begin with a phenomenological treatment of the analogies of experience, and in fact we limit ourselves to the discussion of the First Analogy. Kant says in a general way: The analogies

> exhibit the unity of nature in the combination of all appearances under certain exponents, which express nothing other than the relation of time (insofar as it comprehends all existence in itself) to the unity of appercep-

tion, which can obtain only in a synthesis in accordance with rules. (B 263)[108]

Every determination of nature, as a synthesis, is grounded in the original synthesis of apperception. But insofar as it is a determination of appearances that are encountered in time, every determination of nature is a determination of the being-in-time of nature, [348] and thus a determination of time. If it is to determine objects, the synthesis is bound to a view of time in general. The rules of the synthesis are co-determined in terms of time. A synthesis is essentially a determination of time; and, as a synthesis of the scientific knowledge of nature, it is a determination of the objective being-in-time.

But what does it mean to "determine time"? We first ask: What does an empirical determination of time require? And secondly: What does an objective-scientific determination of time require? We shall take the explanation only as far as is necessary to interpret the First Analogy and the schematism.

Time (that is, the time wherein the data appear) is to be determined empirically. We start with the way in which time is first given in Kant's sense, and then analyze these modes of the givenness of time. We are not saying that this mode of time-givenness is the primary mode within natural experience. It is primary only on the basis of Kant's starting point. For Kant, what is first given is the manifold of presentations in inner sense. If I behave purely passively—i.e., if I just let that manifold be given to me—then one can see that the "presentations" are given in [the form of] *pure change:* There is the beginning of something and the end of it: this, that, and the next thing. What is present only for a while changes, and in its place comes something else—now this, now that, a pure perception of what is present. There is only change (never a one-after-the-other succession) as long as I abandon myself simply and directly to whatever is present—in which case I let myself be simply taken prisoner by what is present, without following it toward its disappearance or looking at what might come after it. I cannot determine this pure change temporally; or more exactly: as given over to this pure change, I do not comport myself in a time-determining way.

I do that only when I consider the time-character of what is currently present and changing, and say "now." But even when I do that, I could just say "now, now." Only when I take hold of the time-character of the [349] self-repeating changing things, only then is there ever a now. But if I also try somehow to determine this "now" and

108. [*CPR*, p. 320.]

understand it as this "now," then I say: "Now, when this and that is present," or "Now, when this and that appear." Every determination of "now" says, in no matter how vague a way: "Now, when this or that happens." In every "now" I determine that "now" with regard to some thing that is there, some thing that is also and always already on hand. "Now, when *this* or *that* exists"—the "this or that" which I regard as there in my determination of time, is a something just-there that is surely accessible to me—to me in this now and not to some other I in another now. If I want to communicate this determinate "now" in its content—this "now" as I have determined it purely for and from out of myself—this now-determination would not be a now-determination for someone else. Now, right when the knife falls off the table, I feel pain. But when communicated, this now-determination ("now that the knife is falling") is, in the event (for we must maintain Kant's hypothesis of the isolated subject), a time-determination that says nothing to someone else, because even if he had until doomsday, he could never figure out the "when" of when-the-knife-fell. In fact, in a strict sense this "when" says nothing even for me once I recall that I am simply maintaining the attitude of pure perception that was characterized above. The now-determination says something simply and only about the current "now." But suppose that this now-determination ("now, when the knife falls from the table") should encounter in the pure change of presentations, so that it were something that, in my abandonment to change, I have and understand as given to me. In that case this "now, when the knife falls" would not be a "now" at all, because the "now" is perhaps "now, when the clock strikes the hour."

Every time I say "now," I am always already directed to something on hand—that is a necessary condition for every time-determination, but not a sufficient condition for an objective time-determination. In order for an objective time-determination to be possible, that to which I must always come back as already on hand, must itself be something to which I can constantly come back as being the same [350] and, what is more, as something to which everyone can come back at any time. The thing on hand must itself be ever on hand. In our social co-existence, a time-indication that goes back to something present ("Now, when the knife is falling from the table") can indeed mean something for whatever entities are right there with me in the same lived world, but it says nothing to other people who aren't. On the contrary, "Now, when the sun is at its zenith, the knife falls from the table"—*that*, within certain limits, is an objective determination.

Even with this, to be sure, the "now" has not yet been sufficiently determined. The important thing is only this: At all times and in every "now," I and the others for whom time is to be determined must be able to come back to that "now." This means: The "now"—which the I always says, and which is to be objectively determinable—is essentially a "now" for which the current concretion of the I is irrelevant. The now is essentially a possible now-there-for-any-I—but which concrete I, as well as which specific "now," is indifferent.

Consequently, that which I must be able to come back to is characterized as "any-now-at-all" and "any-I-at-all." The only thing that is necessary is the unity of the original synthesis "at every time" (B 220). The "now" is somehow an I-related "now." But again, if an objective time-determination is to be possible, for this "now" and every "now" there must always and ever be something underlying, for all intents and purposes a *substratum* or a *subjectum*, "the everlasting existence of the proper subject in the appearances" (B 228).[109] This *subjectum* that already underlies every "now"—and underlies even more so every [pure] manifold of nows and every one-after-another and every at-the-same-time—this *subjectum* is time itself. (Compare: Every determinate time is part of all time.)

- "All appearances are in time, in which alone, as substratum (as persistent form of inner intuition), both *simultaneity* as well as *succession* can be presented. The time, therefore, in which all change of appearances is to be thought, lasts and does not change." (B 224–225)
- "For change does not affect time itself, [351] but only the appearances in time." (B 226)
- "Time itself does not elapse, but the existence of that which is changeable elapses in it . . .
- [Time] is itself unchangeable and lasting." (B 183)

Time as a whole is what I must come back to as everlasting persistence—except that I cannot come back to it, because:

- "Time itself cannot be perceived." (B 219)
- "Time cannot be perceived for itself." (B 225)
- "Time cannot be perceived in itself." (B 226)
- "For an empty time that would precede is not an object of perception." (B 231)
- "Time [is] not an object . . . by means of which {as if it were itself an appearance,} appearances could be held together {in a synthesis}." (B 262)[110]

109. [Heidegger changes Kant's genitive ("the principle . . . of the everlasting existence") into a nominative.]
110. [Without Heidegger's ellipsis or bracketed additions: "absolute time is not an object of perception by means of which appearances could be held together."]

In other words: Time is not something present out-there. It is not something that can be empirically intuited. But that means that time in itself is not determinable. I cannot determine any "now" in an absolute way by way of the pure pre-view of the whole of time, because any determinate "now" always already bespeaks a "now, when . . ." Every now-determination is essentially relative to some present thing; and only to the degree that this present thing (with regard to which time is determinable at all) can be fixed, is a determination of time possible.

By the way, Einstein arrived at this same framework for determining time by pursuing some quite specific, concrete problems in physics. The principle of the theory of relativity—that all time is the time of a certain place—is a principle that is grounded in the very essence of time, insofar as what is present in the sense of being present in nature can be determined only place-wise—i.e., only in terms *of* a place and relative *to* a place. There is no absolute perception of time. In a certain sense, as regards something present in nature, I can never simply and directly fix its "now" as given absolutely. Instead, the now is always a "now, when . . ."

Time itself as a whole cannot be perceived, i.e., is not empirically intuitable as something present. Nonetheless time does show up as something given, and in such a way that what gives it [352] remains hidden. Then how is a time-determination of time to be possible if every determining of time, every saying of "now," is a matter of coming back to something present—while that present something is not itself accessible in any absolute way? Kant now says: *If* time as such is to be determinable, and *if* in that process time as a whole cannot be comprehended as that to which I come back and from out of which I somehow determine an absolute now-position—*then* in the appearances themselves one must be able to find antecedently a substratum that presents time. There must be something *"that always exists,* i.e., something *lasting* and *persisting"* (B 225). And what exists in this way is substance. Time is presented—it is rendered sensible—in substance as persistence. As we will show later, time is the schema of substance: time *qua* persistence presents a rule for determining natural entities as substances. (Substance cannot be intuited any more than time can. Persistence is the rule for rendering something sensible.) The intuition *time* is the pre-viewed basis-on-which of pure intuition, and as so previewed, time cannot be determined, i.e., cannot be directly comprehended in any synthesis. But to the degree that it is determined, it is determined through a synthesis that, as such, undergirds a rule. Therefore, even though a direct determination of time is intrinsically necessary but essentially impossible, there is a path that we can take via a rule of the understanding—one that, as a rule of the understanding, is antecedently indicated by the "I think" and its original unity.

This is the way time as the persistent is presented in the principle of the First Analogy: "In all change of appearances substance persists" (B 224).

If a time-determination is to be possible at all, this principle is the *a priori* condition that rules and renders determinable all time-relations. It is born of the necessity of rendering a determination of time *a priori* possible as regards the unity of the transcendental apperception, since time itself is *a priori* not perceivable. This principle stands "at the head of the pure and completely *a priori* laws of [353] nature" (B 227). It is the principle that expresses the conditions of the possibility of the objectively determinable being-in-time of nature. It establishes *a priori* how any entity-that-is-in-time must be at each moment *if* it is to be determinable, in accordance with its objective being-in-time, *as* this entity that is in time at every moment. As the principle of "existence in time," it expresses a general time-determination, i.e., a rule of time-relations as such. In this case it expresses the fact that something which persists must underlie all one-after-another and at-the-same-time. Only by way of this permanent something is existence endowed, in the various parts of time, with a magnitude, in the sense of *quantitas*, a magnitude that we call "duration." As Kant says, duration is the "magnitude of existence" (B 262), the magnitude of presence—i.e., the measure of "how long," from when to when. And every "when" is determinable by a "then," and this "then" is a "now." The determination of the now, of the how-long, and of duration are possibly only on the basis of this something-persistent.

If an objective knowledge of nature is to be possible, the unity of the transcendental apperception requires that there be something that persists. You see that, given this observation, new determinations of time emerge. Likewise it already becomes clear how time functions in a specific way (to put it roughly) in the transcendental apperception's movement toward or transcending to the world. For Kant's original Cartesian position itself requires that the *a priori* necessary conditions of this movement must be exhibited; and this movement itself, in its necessity, is nothing else that the whole of the presuppositions that underlie every empirical time-determination and time-reckoning. In every indication of time there reside the principles formulated in the analogies, and primarily the principle of the First Analogy, "In all change of appearances substance persists"—a principle that is not gotten from, but rather underlies, all empirical experience.[111]

---

111. [Here (Moser, p. 705) Heidegger ends his lecture of Monday, 15 February 1926, to be followed by that of Tuesday, 16 February, which opened with a 700-word summary that is omitted in GA 21.]

Why—i.e., with what legitimacy [354] and necessity—is this principle required for the being of nature such as it confronts us?

As we derive this principle of persistence in connection with the necessity of an inter-subjective time-determination, a new and essential feature of time emerges: time is persistence. As Kant says, "Persistence gives general expression to time as the constant correlate of all existence of appearances, all change and all accompaniment" (B 300).[112] Persistence is the condition of the possibility of one-after-another and of at-the-same-time. If the time-relation is determined as at-the-same-time, then time is understood as a sum-total. When taken in the relation of one-after-another, time is understood as a series. If I determine time (the time-relation) primarily as duration, then time is understood as a magnitude. Magnitude, series, and sum-total are the essential viewpoints within which time necessarily must be able to be placed in every time-determination as a time-reckoning. And from this necessity, in turn, the three analogies are then derived, corresponding to the viewpoints of magnitude, of series, and of sum-total, respectively.

I have already explained that in this derivation of the analogies nothing is said directly about the connection of time with the "I think." Nonetheless, we can see here a trait in common between time and the "I think." Even though it cannot be perceived, time as the persistent is, as such, the underlying—i.e., it is the *subjectum* in the strict sense in which Kant himself uses the concept *subjectum*, ὑποκείμενον. But Kant has also already characterized the "I think"—which can be constantly identified as the self-same—as *subjectum* in this sense. The I is the *subjectum* not so much in the sense of the "subjectivity" of the I in the sense of an ego. Rather, it is the *subjectum* in the sense of "the underlying" that has no predicate.

Accordingly, time is the subject's "persistent" self-affection; it is that which originally and constantly affects; and it is that to which every [355] time-determination as a synthesis of the "I think" must come back, but to which it *cannot* come back [fully], so that the subject, as necessary and persistent, determines the substance of nature itself—in fact antecedently—with regard to time and in relation to apperception. This *a priori* determination is a principle. Given the constant self-identity of the I itself, the relation to the time-determining "I think" must be a constant relation in the sense that it constantly comes back to the same *subjectum*. This particular connection between the persistence of time and the necessity of a rule for determining time is something that Kant makes a remarkable use

112. [The Guyer and Wood footnote to this passage comments that "accompaniment" (*Begleitung*) connotes "the accompaniment of one state of affairs by another, i.e., what Kant is here otherwise calling 'simultaneity' or coexistence" (*CPR*, p. 300).]

of in the brief section that bears the title "Refutation of Idealism" (B 274–275), to which, in the preface to the B edition, he added a correction (B xxxix–xli). Kant says: I am empirically aware of my presence, namely in the first place in the sense of the flow of presentations. My presence is a being-present in time. But the one-after-another of presentations is possible, as one-after-another, only on the basis of something permanent that is independent of this one-after-another. Insofar as this one-after-another is the *inner* one-after-another of my presentations; and granted the necessity that there be something permanent that is independent of the one-after-another—on these conditions, it is also necessary that there be given the presence of a [realm of] outer being: something permanent outside of me. The presence of this something-permanent—the world—is necessarily included in the determination of my own existence as within-time, and forms a single experience with it. This experience of myself, Kant says, as the pure one-after-another of presentations, would not really take place unless there were at the same time something external, something permanent. Indeed, he says:

> The "How?" of this {connection} can no more be explained than we can explain further how we think at all of what abides in time, whose simultaneity [356] with what changes gives rise to the concept of change. (B xli)

This reflection, which constitutes the kernel of the "Refutation of Idealism" in Kant's sense, gives expression to the aforementioned connection of time and permanence. The function of time becomes clear here: What is present first of all is an empirically given existence; this something-present presupposes within itself as pure change and one-after-another, that there is something present that is permanent, something that abides and does not change in time: the world of things, or nature in the broad sense. Or if we begin from the side of nature and the world: In nature, taken as something that abides, within its whole field, there is a region of happenings—viz., the pure one-after-another of my presentations—that likewise have the peculiar feature of being accessible to me, from which we can conclude that there must be present something permanent as the ontological condition of the one-after-another. With this, Kant claims to have carried out, from out of and by way of the concept of time, a strict and necessary proof of the presence of the outside world. We must keep clearly in mind the point of departure of this proof—which is the pure presence of a one-after-another whose kind of being is not different from the kind of being of the what-is-permanent, which consequently is shown to be the world as what-is-permanent.

Therefore, time is the phenomenon with relation to which the presence of nature is demonstrated to be co-present with the empirical I.

Here time is used for a fundamental statement about the presence of the
world and of the empirical I—or more precisely, for a statement about
the necessary co-presence of the one with the other. Stated as a principle: Time co-functions in the clarification of how something present is
able to be determined. It is the "constant correlate of all existence {i.e.,
presence} of appearances." Thanks to time's *a priori* relation to the unity
of apperception, Kant now arrives at these fundamental principles: the
analogies [357] that he says have a regulative character. This means
that they *a priori* regulate the various ways of determining—the various
syntheses of the relations of—whatever exists in time.

The understanding is the faculty that brings about comprehension.
The fact that we comprehend anything at all is due to the understanding as a combining. But the determinateness of everything determinable is the determinateness of the *a priori* form of everything determinable—i.e., of everything given—and that *a priori* form is time. Therefore,
time co-functions in constituting the understanding of anything at all;
that is, it co-functions in the constitution of meaning. Time co-functions in and for constituting the possibility of pure concepts of the understanding relating to the given objects and, in this relating, intending
some meaningful content, intending *some thing*—that is, the possibility
of the pure concepts having present a *meaning*, a sense.

From the fact that time co-functions to constitute understanding in
general, in connection with the determining of the determinable, we
come to what *seems* to be a new structural connection between time
and the "I think," but which in fact is the same connection we already
discovered in the First Analogy. How time is connected with and functions in the formation of an understanding in general is what Kant
discusses under the rubric, "The Schematism of the Pure Concepts of
the Understanding."

---

§31. The schematism of the pure concepts
of the understanding

In the *Critique of Pure Reason,* the section of the investigation that bears
the title "On the Schematism of the Pure Concepts of Understanding"
is the one in which the function of time and its connection with the "I
think" are thematized in a properly concrete way, but in the same way
that we have already pointed out: by making use of some kind of connection while leaving it entirely undetermined.

This chapter [358] on the schematism is the real center of the *Critique
of Pure Reason.* The whole structure of the book stands or falls with the
doctrine of the schematism of the pure concepts of the understanding
and with the sustainability of this doctrine. However, current Kant-

scholarship is of the opposite opinion. It has simply passed over this chapter on schematism as baroque and obscure, thinking that one can get on with an interpretation of the *Critique of Pure Reason* without this truly central item. Even [Erick] Adickes, a scholar who has earned great esteem for his scholarly interpretation, remarks in his edition of the *Critique:* "In my view, we should not attribute any scientific value to the section on schematism, since it was inserted quite late in the 'brief outline' for systematic reasons" (1889, p. 171 n.).[113] But even if one emphasizes the fundamental significance that the schematism has for the *Critique of Pure Reason,* nothing is gained by such a blind, dogmatic insistence on the importance of the schematism. Instead, we must gain an understanding of the phenomena that Kant hit upon under this rubric but that he in no way mastered.

By clarifying what Kant means by this schematism we will get, retrospectively, a clearer understanding of the context that he presupposed in the analogies. The "I think" of the original synthesis antecedently thinks "unity." Every possible *a priori* unity of combinability in accordance with the pure forms of combining, *qua* unity, is what guides the determinability of a manifold of the given, and therefore is necessarily related to time as the form of the given as such. Accordingly, time is that wherein the *a priori* actions of the understanding can be *a priori* rendered sensible—or as Kant once put it: can be given a "sense," i.e., be related to objects and thereby be determined to a certain content.

The question is: How can a pure concept of the understanding, which in and of itself merely expresses the pure condition of an act [359] of the understanding as such, be related to appearances—i.e., to something that, on its side, is given from out of itself to the understanding? How can it be related to appearances in such a way that it asserts something about the appearance—i.e., something regarding its content, something that belongs to its content not just occasionally but necessarily? The issue is not about how it happens that, now and again, given the right occasion, I apply the correct category and form to some stuff that is given. That is, it is not about how, when confronted with a manifold of sensations, I am able to choose the fitting and right category with which to clothe the given stuff. Kant quite correctly never posed such a question. Instead, what he asks about is something that is fundamental to his Cartesian position: How is it at all possible for pure understanding, from out of itself, to determine something that must necessarily be *given* to it? In demonstrating this *a priori* possibility, one proves *a priori* the possibility that the pure con-

113. [Guyer and Wood provide historical and textual clarification of this point (*CPR,* p. 728 n. 51).]

cepts of the understanding can relate to appearances—one proves the possibility of their objective validity.

The general condition of a possible applicability of a category to objects consists in the fact that the category as such and in general must contain in itself, *a priori,* something sensible. But this something-sensible, insofar as it is *a priori* necessary for the objectivity of the category, is at the same time that which restricts the applicability of the category to sensibility, to appearances in general. This condition—the something-sensible that a category must be able to have—is what Kant calls the schema of the categories, the schema of the pure concepts of the understanding.

To understand that, let us first ask: What does a "schema of a concept" mean in general? And even before that: What does "schema" mean? Kant distinguishes (although not always or in all respects rigorously) between "schema" and "image." In this context, let us ask more concretely about the difference between the two, and about the difference between "image," "depiction," and "schema" (or "schematizing"). [360] As regards this present consideration and the earlier ones, let me say: I am lecturing not about Kant but about *logic.* And just as the earlier phenomenological interpretations of synthesis clarified the basic structures of the possibility of the *judgment,* so now, our explanation of the schematism will discuss phenomenologically the basic structures of the possibility of *concepts in general.*

But how can we bring together image and schema, depiction and schematizing, for the purpose of working out their differences? How do they differ from each other, and how do they belong together?

Image and schema are intuitables [*Anschauliches*] that can be produced in such a way that, as intuitable, they portray something they themselves are not. They let the thing be seen or understood in different ways according to the case: depictions in intuitables; and sensibilizations.[114] Sensibilizations differ from acts of intuition [*Anschauungen*], and portrayals [*Darstellendes*] differ from intuitables [*Auschaunbarem*] insofar as the intuitable can be *directly* grasped, that is, it gets intuited *only as itself.* Grasping and understanding a depiction (i.e., what's grasped: the portrayal or image of something) must necessarily, primarily, and thematically grasp, comprehend, and (in the broadest sense) understand *what is getting depicted.*

We said, "to be seen or to be understood." We made this distinction with a view to whether the depiction itself is sensibly intuitable or whether what is to be depicted *qua* sensibilized is, of its essence, not sensibly intuitable. (Kant calls the latter case the sensibilization of *concepts.*) This distinction between the [sensible] portrayal of a [sensibly]

---

114. [That is, they make something be "related-to-the-sensible."]

intuited and the sensible portrayal of something that essentially cannot be depicted, seems to be clear, but on closer inspection it is inadequate. Nonetheless, we will begin with this distinction and will explain, in order, four different modes of sensibilization:

1. Sensibilization of *appearances,* [361] i.e., of empirically intuitable objects.
2. Sensibilization of *sensible* concepts, i.e., empirical concepts.
3. Sensibilization of *pure* sensible concepts.
4. Sensibilization of the *pure concepts of the understanding.*

In the fourth sensibilization, the theme of our interpretation is nothing other than the transcendental schematization, the transcendental schema that Kant understands as time, or better, as the transcendental determination of time (B 178).[115]

a) Sensibilization of appearances

The sensibilization of appearances happens as the simple depiction, in an image, of some specific object of experience. This is an image-as-copy [*Abbild*] of something in the strong sense of the term: a facsimile, a reproduction of a specific thing-out-there in an image that is painted, drawn, or produced in some other way, such as in a photograph, which is a simple copy of something that is visible in [natural] light or under illumination. The photograph is accessible through intuition: it shows me a specific—and in fact only one specific—visible object: this house, this dog, this tree. I can never photograph either "house in general," i.e., the whole of what belongs to a house, or the way "house in general" belongs to this particular house. I always photograph only hous*es.* The image, as Kant correctly says, has "as its aim . . . [an] individual intuition" (B 179),[116] i.e., it always depicts an individual this-here.

An example of one specific kind of image-as-copy is a death-mask. (I will not go into the mask in general as a phenomenon of depiction.) The image-as-copy—the death-mask—can itself be further copied, drawn, or photographed. In the photograph of the image-as-copy [i.e.,

115. [The text Heidegger alludes to is presumably, "an application of the category to appearances becomes possible by means of the transcendental time-determination." (*CPR,* p. 272).]

116. [Kant's sentence at B 179 focuses on the schema as a product of the *imagination,* in contrast to just any sense-image. Heidegger's citation, however, takes from that sentence only what applies, by implication, to a sense-image. Cf. *CPR,* p. 273: "The schema is, in itself, always and only a product of the imagination. But in this case the aim of the imagination's synthesis is not an individual intuition but only unity in the determination of sensibility. Thus a schema is to be distinguished from an image."]

the death-mask] I can directly see the thing that is primarily intended and depicted: the countenance of the dead person and thus the dead person himself. The countenance being depicted is directly visible in this [photographic] image-as-copy. And what is depicted, the depicted content [namely, the countenance], the content that appears in the photograph of the death-mask, leads us back (as we say) directly and exclusively to [362] what is being depicted, which is always a [single] this-here.

However, the specific thing being [photographically] depicted, that which I see in the [photographic] image—namely, this death-mask—could also be used as a determinate depiction of a *concept.* In that case the image, the [photographed] death-mask, now shows how a death-mask *as such* looks. That is, the photographic copy is used as an exemplary illustration of the sensible concept "death-mask." In this case, it is the concept "death-mask" that gets depicted. The "aim" of the depiction is now "the unity in the determination of sensibility" (B 179), i.e., to show how this one determinate "whatness" (namely, "death-mask") "looks" in distinction to every other thing.

That notwithstanding, the *genuine* meaning of a photographic image is not "illustrative example [of a concept]" and never can be.[117] What the photographic depiction depicts, is the face of a specific dead person—Pascal, for example—and not one particular case of "Pascal" as an illustrative example of the concept "Pascal-ness." Nonetheless, what we find emerging here is a notion of "image" that differs from the notion of image-as-copy and yet goes together with it as an "image-of." How that is so, we shall see in what follows.[118]

* * *

b) Sensibilization of empirical sensible concepts

We have named the second kind of sensibilization as "the sensibilization of an empirical sensible concept." To some degree we have already characterized this kind of image in what we have just said, namely: The goal of the depicted now aims at the general essence "mask" or "photograph" or the general essence of any other sensible thing ("house," "dog," "table," and so on). But the depicted is always and necessarily an individual "this." When I depict the concept "house" in a sensible form, I must necessarily draw or paint a specific house. I

117. [That is, the sense of a photographic copy as a depiction-of-something is usually and properly a depiction of a *particular thing* rather than an illustrative example of a sensible concept.]

118. [Here (Moser, p. 720) Heidegger ends his lecture of Tuesday, 16 February 1926, to be followed by that of Thursday, 18 February, which opened with a 760-word summary that is omitted in GA 21.]

cannot draw "house in general"—only a house of this specific size, these specific colors, this specific set of materials, and so on.

The constitutive features of "house in general" can vary widely over a broad field [363] and across different viewpoints (size, color, materials). Moreover, each one of these multiple variations can join with another determinate variation to depict a specific house. Every intuitable depiction of the empirical concept "house" has antecedently decided on a specific set of determinate variations as regards the essential features of what is to be depicted, viz., the essence "house."

What is to be depicted in this case is itself empirically intuitable. (I can always directly see a specific house.) Nonetheless, by its very concept it is much harder to reach through the depiction (the imaged house) than *pure* sensible concepts are reachable by way of sensibilization. I mean "pure sensible concepts" in the sense of geometrical concepts.

In the sensibilization of concepts, the thing to be sensibly depicted— viz., the concept—functions as a rule governing a general "antecedent sketch" [*Vorzeichnung*] that is not to be restricted to only what the sketch depicts, i.e., renders visible. That which is to be depicted in the sensibilization, therefore, functions as what shows up in the rule governing the sensible depiction. Or more precisely: The concept that is to be depicted sensibly is the basis governing the rule that governs the depiction. That which does the depicting [of the sensible concept]—i.e., a drawing of a specific house—does not make a copy of the essence "house" the way a photograph of this tree reproduces only this specific tree. Rather, the drawing sensibilizes the essence "house" in such a way that the essence "house" prescribes the kind of sensibilization and the kind of possible sensibilization. And this rule which governs the intuitive depiction of a concept and which is prescribed by the content of the concept itself, and which governs the procedure of the sensibilization—this is what Kant calls a *schema.*

Between the depiction of sensible appearances (in the sense of a pure image) and the sensibilization of an empirical concept, there is something else that is neither a depiction nor a schematizing in the Kantian sense (and I will allude to it only in passing). That is the [364] depiction of an image in a work of art. A photograph, an image of a dog in a handbook of zoology, and a painting called "The Dog"—each depicts something different, and in a different way. The deer in the forest—those, for example, that Franz Mark has painted—are not *these* in *this* specific forest, but simply "A Deer in the Woods."[119] We can also call this kind of depiction in the artistic sense a "schematizing," the

---

119. [Franz Mark (1880-1916), the Munich-born German Expressionist who died in World War I. See, for example, the reproduction at http://www.artchive.com/artchive/M/marc/deerwood.jpg.html.]

sensibilization of a concept, as long as we do not understand "concept" as a theoretical concept—the zoological concept of "deer"—but rather as the concept of an entity that appears along with me in my world and that, just like me, has its lived world within the world we share in common—the deer that, so to speak, is a "forest-dweller," as contrasted with the anatomical-zoological concept "deer."

So long as we heed this distinction between two types of concepts, and so long as we attend to the different kinds and consequences of understanding that go with these two kinds of concepts, we can certainly say that concepts are depicted in art. But by this I mean only that this sensibilization within artistic depiction is essentially different from both a mere "picture of" or a theoretical schematizing for, say, zoological purposes. In an artistic depiction, there is depicted a concept that, in the example we have been using, depicts the understanding of an existent—or better, the understanding of an entity as with me in my lived world, the understanding of an entity within the world and of its being within the world. That which is depicted is the deer's being-in-the-forest, along with the form and manner of its being-in-the-forest. We designate this concept of the deer, and this concept of its being, as a "hermeneutical concept," in contrast to a pure thing-concept. [365]

c) Sensibilization of pure sensible concepts

Once again we separate out the sensibilization of pure sensible concepts from the schematizing of sensible concepts. A pure sensible concept is not a thing-concept. The triangle that is drawn is never an image of the triangle in the sense of a copy but rather, in its essence, something schematized: a schema-image, a schema. One might want to say that the triangle as drawn would still be, if anything, a copy of the concept "triangle." And in fact, in the sensibilization of pure sensible concepts— geometric concepts—the multiplicity of varieties of perspective is limited. Color, magnitude, material and the like are simply irrelevant, and moreover, the one thing that can vary—figure as such—is easier to sensibilize directly. The sensible [in this case] is, as sensible, closer to the limit [of sensibility], even though in its essence it remains fundamentally different from sensibility. Here too there is no "copy," even though this expression is employed in a mathematical sense. That is, the drawing of the triangle is not a copy of the essence "triangle"—even less than the drawing of a dog is a copy of "dog-as-such."

Every sensibilized triangle is a "one"—this one here—and for fundamental reasons, it never attains the generality of a concept. Moreover, as the individual triangle that it necessarily is, it is not, and never will be, a triangle within the science of geometry, whereas that specific dog in the painting could very well exist on its own as "this-dog-here." The sides and lines [in this drawing of a triangle] are undeniably surfaces; they have an extension, which the sides of a geometric triangle, according to its concept, does not. The schema of this concept "triangle" is the presentation of the thinkable procedure for the intuitive depiction of the pure form ["triangle"] in the space of our lived world. The procedure—or, the rule of the procedure—is dictated by the concept. In a certain way the concept dictates a specific mode of its own sensibilization and thus its own "entry," as it were, into the space of the lived world, so that it is thereby illustrated in what is depicted in the depiction that produces it. [366]

d) Image and schema

In the fourth place we mentioned (and this is the real problem) the sensibilization of the pure concepts of the understanding: the sensibilization of the categories. This is not just any schema. It is, as Kant says, the transcendental schema. In order to get any further, we need a much sharper understanding of the difference between an image and a schema than we've had heretofore, and we need to nail down the notion of image that Kant has been simply using from the beginning, but that can be properly understood only by first analyzing the phenomenon of image-as-copy. We will carry out our analysis of the difference between an image (now understood in a new way) and a schema by using Kant's example of "an image of the number five" (B 179–180).

This image of the number five, which Kant adduces as five dots (• • • • •), must be distinguished from the schema of number. The reason we chose this specific example of the image of the number five in contrast to the schema of number is that later on, when we properly discuss the transcendental schematism, the question of number will surface again. However, scholars have not paid much attention to this distinction, if they go into it at all. The image of a number is one thing, and the *schema* of number is another. Most importantly, number *as* a schema is something entirely different from the previous two. Therefore, before we explain the kind of sensibilization that we put in the fourth place—indeed, in preparation for that—we shall discuss

1. "image" [*Bild*] as distinct from image-as-a-copy [*Abbild*];
2. "image" (in the new sense of no. 1) in its connection with "schema";
3. the way schematization is enacted, and the faculty of this enactment;
4. and finally, the notion of a rule that governs this enactment of schematization.

Kant writes:

This presentation of a procedure of the imagination for providing an image for a concept is what I call the schema for that concept. (B 179–80).[120]

And:

The schema is to be distinguished from an image. (B 179).[121]

Then comes the surprising sentence:

The schema of a pure concept of the understanding cannot be brought to an image at all. (B 181)

The first consequence of this [367] is that the idea of the schematism that was to be evinced precisely for the pure concepts and categories of the understanding has been overcome.

To a schema—the sensibilization of a concept—there belongs an image. In fact, it is the very purpose of the sensibilization, or schematization, to provide an image for a concept. The question is: What do we mean by "image"? To start, Kant calls these five dots (• • • • •) an image of the number five, without explaining, here or anywhere else, what the phenomenon of an image is. Is it possible at all for a number to have an image in the sense of a copy? Obviously not, since the number five does not look anything like these five dots. In fact, the number five has no "look" at all. Therefore, these five dots are in no way an image in the sense of a copy. And likewise, "schema" cannot mean "image" in this case, precisely because later on Kant will separate this image of the number five from the schema of a number.

In order to pursue this idea of an image of the number five and a possible copy of it and to briefly illustrate Kant's way of presenting it, let us try to clarify to what degree there is such a thing as the sensibilization of number. We will stick with the example of the number five.

This "5" and "V" here on the chalkboard are even less an image of the number five than these five dots are. We call these things here ["5" and "V"] numeric *signs*. But on the other hand, the five dots are more than a "sign" of the number. They have a very definite relation to "five"— although not to "five" in the sense of this thing ["5" or "V"] here on the

120. [Heidegger omits the word *allgemeinen* before *Verfahren*, i.e., "general" before "procedure."]

121. [Heidegger omits *doch* before *Schema* (while Guyer and Wood do not translate it). The use of *doch* ("certainly") in this sentence is to emphasize the difference between *Bild*, an image that is a copy of a specific thing, and *Schema* as the rule governing the sensibilization of a concept. Whereas an image-*qua*-copy-of-something "aims at an individual intuition" ("einzelne Anschauung . . . zur Absicht hat"), a schema has as its aim "the unity in the determination of sensibility" (B 179).]

chalkboard. These two things [the five dots and the two numeric signs][122] have absolutely nothing to do with each other. The most they have in common is that both have been written with chalk on the chalkboard. But these five dots certainly do have to do with "5," that is, with the concept that this numeric sign means. That is: these five dots are able to be counted by means of the concept "five," and when it comes to their "how-many," they can be determined as *this* many thanks to the concept "five." So, even though these five dots, taken in their pure thing-ness, have nothing to do with the [368] concept "five," they still do have a specific connection with the number "five" insofar as they are what-gets-counted, or what-can-be-counted, with this number.

In a certain sense, these five dots have a closer relation to the concept "five" than they do when I (as we say) "enumerate" them as "table, chair, pen, book, ashtray." Those things are also "five" as long as I abstract from their content and see each of them as just a "one-something," and then see each "one-something" as determinable in another possible "one" and as addable as this set of "ones." In a certain sense, the five dots have a closer relation to the number insofar as (1) they are not different in their content the way the five objects I mentioned are and (2) the viewpoint of "how many?" is more immediate. In addition, (3) this spatial ordering of the five dots likewise demonstrates the series-character of a numeric manifold, much more than when I depict the five dots in the form of ∴—although on the other hand one can and must say that, when it comes to indicating numbers in the natural and pre-theoretical order, very specific constellations (and not just dots-in-a-row) are employed.

Therefore, on the basis of their more limited content and greater lack of differentiation, these five dots somehow have a closer relation to the concept "five." But what we saw earlier regarding the sensible depiction of geometric figures holds here as well, only in a different form. These five dots are just as essentially different from the concept "five" as any five specific objects, regardless of their content, that one might choose. Therefore we have to keep separate:

• the numeric signs;

122. [The referent of the German "diese beiden Dinge" is ambiguous. It *could* refer to the two numeric signs—the 5 and the V—that Heidegger has just written on the chalkboard. It is also possible that "these two things" refers, on the one hand, to the five dots, and on the other hand, to the 5 and V taken together. In that case, Heidegger would have earlier drawn the five dots with chalk on the chalkboard. And it would seem he did. Twice in this paragraph he speaks of "these five dots," thereby giving the impression that they too, like the 5 and the V, were up on the chalkboard.]

- the intuitive depiction of a "so many" in a manifold of visible, countable things;
- the fact that I can sensibly depict the number five in yet another and very different way (which I will not go into further), namely as 8 − 3, or 4 + 1, or 167 − 162, and so on *ad infinitum.*

Therefore I can depict the number five within the act of counting.

In contrast to the second form of sense-depiction (namely, sensibilization by way of those five dots), Kant now distinguishes [369] the schema of number. And in establishing the distinction he begins with the fact that "only with difficulty [can we] get a comprehensive view" (B 179) of an image for larger numbers—i.e., a bunch of things, given to intuition, that would add up to such a large number. We can't rely on a direct comprehension of all the countable dots—we can't hold them together in a unity—that would add up to this specific number, say, "5,768." Instead, we need a specific procedure, if only for drawing the dots, a procedure that has to follow a specific rule and come to an end at a specific point. There is no direct sensibilization for such large numbers as there is for, say, the number five. Instead, to understand those large numbers we rely on the presentation of a method of their possible intuitive depiction. That means understanding the possible way of numbering something given to intuition as a succession of dots. Therefore, it is a procedure for sensibilizing a number, according to a rule regarding countable things, namely dots. The presentation of such a procedure for the sensibilization of a concept—or that which such a procedure can present—is what Kant calls the schema.[123]

* * *

An "image of the number five" simply means: something that is intuitable in some way and is meant to indicate that number. Here "image" simply means "that which appears directly to intuition." In German we speak of *Landschaftsbildern,* and the word can have two senses. It can mean "landscapes" in the sense of paintings that depict natural scenery. But it can also refer to "landscape scenery," actual landscapes that we see. In the latter case, when I see a *Landschaftsbild,* I actually see an actual landscape, not a depiction of it. The question is: How is this meaning of "image" [*Bild*] connected with the meaning of what we earlier called an *Abbild,* an "image-as-copy"?

In an *Abbild,* an image as a copy, we distinguish between the *Abbildende* and the *Abgebildete,* i.e., the painting itself that depicts something

123. [Here (Moser, p. 741) Heidegger ends his lecture of Thursday, 18 February 1926, to be followed by that of Friday, 19 February, which opened with a 580-word summary that is omitted in GA 21.]

(or: the depiction) and that which is depicted in it. That which does the depicting is this picture here, painted with oils on canvas. But we can also turn this painting [370] into an object of discussion and study it in its own right, say, in terms of its degree of preservation. Is it well preserved or not? Has it been damaged? Was it subsequently restored? When I consider the painting in this fashion, I am looking at it primarily as a "painted thing" (that happens to depict something). I treat it as an image-thing while prescinding from whatever is depicted in it.

However, what is depicted in the painting—say, the sunflowers Van Gogh painted—does not get damaged if the picture should happen to suffer damage. Consider the case of an artist who sets out to depict sunflowers that are wilted and spoiled.[124] He will succeed at the task not by producing a spoiled picture but by producing a picture so perfectly *un*spoiled that it depicts what it is meant to: the wilted flowers. And it is what is depicted that we see if we approach and understand the picture naturally. That is what we see first of all: the thing depicted. It shows up directly—whereas it takes a mental somersault to understand the picture as a "painted thing."

The *Abgebildete*—the thing insofar as it has been copied and depicted in an image—is what we can simply intuit [in the painting]. It is what simply shows up and can been seen: the *Bild* or image. It has the same meaning here as when we speak of a *Bild* or image of a landscape. Here a *Bild* no longer means [as in the case of a death-mask] some image that, as a copy of something, refers us to that something. Here, rather, a *Bild* or image is that which, *qua* depiction, shows *itself.* It is what is intuitively visible in and through the depiction. More precisely, "image" means the "looks," the "visible aspect" the thing offers of itself. It is the *species*, what is seeable and seen, what is given to an act of intuiting. We refer, for example, to the "image" that someone can give of himself, as in the phrase, "He presented a remarkable image of himself in that situation." In this case "image" simply means what is visible in itself.

This is the sense of the word "image" that Kant uses in his exposition of the schematism. Concepts cannot be copied in an image [*abgebildet*] but they must be furnished with an image [*Bild*]. That is, they must somehow be able to offer a visible aspect of themselves in something intuitable, something which can be depicted in a procedure whose rules are dictated by the very concept that is to be depicted. [371] Therefore, visible aspects of concepts must, in principle, be able to be produced. These images—or quite simply, visible, intuitable aspects—that arise from a depiction regulated by the concepts themselves indicate the schema, i.e., they indicate the rule governing their own depictability; and by way of this rule they indicate what dictates

---

124. [See, for example, van Gogh's *Two Cut Sunflowers* and *Four Cut Sunflowers*.]

the rule itself, namely the concept. And yet these images "are never fully congruent with the concepts," as Kant says (B 181).

The schema is the rule for carrying out sensibilization, and sensibilization means the production of a visible aspect for a concept, i.e., something that shows itself and by showing itself somehow makes the concept visible, but not in any sense of copying it in an image. This production of a visible aspect is not simply a direct act of intuiting a given, because that would be a matter of simply *finding* a visible aspect already there, whereas the visible aspect has to be *produced*. It is a matter of producing a visible aspect, an image, and providing it to oneself. And this production of an image [*Bild*] is itself, we might say, an act of forming [*Bilden*]. In fact we use the word "to form" in the direct sense of "to produce." But "to produce" is an action; and the basic form of all actions, of all acts of "forming" on the part of the subject—for example, the formation of concepts—is an act of combining, a synthesis. I mean synthesis in the sense of forming and producing a possible visible aspect, a *species*. That is what Kant calls the *synthesis speciosa* or "figurative synthesis" [B 151].

This synthesis, the *synthesis speciosa*, is distinguished from the *synthesis intellectualis*, combining as an action of the pure understanding, which *qua* understanding cannot give anything. The production of a visible aspect, a *synthesis speciosa*, is therefore neither a pure action of the understanding—because the understanding *lets* nothing be seen, it gives no *species*—nor is it a pure achievement of sensibility, because sensibility only *allows* things to be given to itself, it only intuits what is given. It never, from out of itself, gives itself an image (cf. B 151). This synthesis as *synthesis speciosa* is neither [372] just understanding nor just sensibility, neither just spontaneity nor just receptivity. But neither is it both of them together. The *synthesis speciosa* or figurative synthesis must therefore belong to a faculty that is spontaneous receptivity or receptive spontaneity. And this faculty, as its conceptual form already indicates, stands between sensibility and understanding, and it is what Kant calls the imagination [*Einbildungskraft*]. He says,

> A synthesis in general is, as we shall subsequently see, the mere effect of the imagination, of a blind though indispensable function of the soul, without which we would have no cognition at all, but of which we are seldom even conscious. (B 103)

Sensibilization, as the formation of a visible aspect, is carried out in the *synthesis speciosa*, and it is an act of the imagination. Kant divides the imagination into the empirical (or reproductive) imagination and the productive imagination. In the reproductive imagination receptivity is, so to speak, dominant. Here, the having of an image is predominantly a matter of *letting* itself be given an image. It is a matter of the imagination letting itself be carried along by the syntheses (i.e., connections) as association offers them. In the productive imagination, on the other hand, spontaneity is what guides matters. And the *synthesis speciosa,* as it functions in the schematism, belongs to the productive imagination.

Sensibilization as enacted by the imagination must be kept strictly separate from sensible intuition itself. In phenomenological terms, the distinction emerges still more sharply when we contrast the phenomenal character of the corresponding objects of the imagination and of sensible, empirical intuition respectively. The indeterminate object of an empirical intuition is what Kant calls "appearance." Intuition is empirical insofar as it relates to its object by way of sensation (B 34). According to Kant, however, sensations are "presentations . . . [that] are effectuated by the *Gegenwart* {*Anwesenheit,* presence} of some thing" (*Reflexionen,* Akademie-Ausgabe [373], vol. 15, no. 619). Sensations are "presented modifications of the status of the subject through the *Gegenwart* {*Anwesenheit,* presence} of the object" (ibid., no. 619). Therefore, a sensation is a presented modification, i.e., a conscious modification given as present in inner sense, which is effected by the presence-now [*Gegenwart*] (as Kant says) of the object.

But here again Kant is basically unclear. We don't know whether he means "object" in the intentional sense or simply in the causal sense of being-present-with, i.e., the simultaneous occurrence of two events, the effecting and the being modified. The way Kant fundamentally understands the mutual presence of the outer and inner world compels us to understand presence-now [*Gegenwart*] in this passage not in the intentional but in the causal sense. That is: a sensation's being in consciousness is effected by the presence of something that stimulates and produces an effect. Of course, Kant was also aware of the intentional sense of the presence of what produces the effect, but basically he never makes use of it. This muddled concept of experience goes back to Democritus, who understood sensations primarily as a matter of touch, and who reinterpreted the intentional presence of the touchable into the mere there-ness of one thing (an atom) with another atom (the one touched). Democritus thereby changed an intentional relation—that of the intentional presence of something *for* an act of touching that reaches out to it—into the mere thereness-with-each-other of whatever produces the cause and whatever experiences its influence. This muddle in the concept of experience has held on right up to today. It is really only in the research and work of phenomenology that the concept has been cleared up and employed in a precise sense.

In order to occur, empirical intuition requires the presence of an object. Moreover, what is intuited in empirical intuition must be intuited in the intuition itself as something present on hand.

In contrast to that, Kant says of the imagination, "*Imagination* is the faculty [374] for presenting an object even *without the object being present-now* in intuition" (B 151). Here again, in the phrase "without the object being present-now," we find the same fundamental lack of clarity. Does Kant mean "without the presence of the influence [*Einwirkung*] of the object"? Or is it "without the object being seen and intended in its bodily presence"? (For good reasons, we necessarily interpret it in the second sense, even though Kant presumably thought it in the first and opposite sense.) So the *imaginatio* shows something, it provides an image ("image" in the sense our interpretation has finally established) — not in the sense of going out to something already there, but in the sense of *Ein-bildung*, forming-an-image.[125] In conceptual, structural terms, the *imaginatio* provides a specific mode of [intentional] presence for something that is not there. The image of the "five dots" is, as Kant says, a product of the empirical faculty of imagination. As I *think* the number "five," I can always "bring visually to mind" the five dots; I can, freely and from out of myself, bring into a specific kind of [intentional] presence, something that is not there.

By contrast, "the *schema* of sensible concepts (such as figures in space) is a product and as it were a monogram of pure *a priori* imagination" (B 181). The schema is a product of the imagination. With the concept "schema" Kant again oscillates, as he does with the concepts of depiction, intuition, sensation, and so on.[126] "Schema" means both the image that springs from schematization and at the same time the schematization itself, or the rule of schematization, the rule governing the procedure of the *synthesis speciosa*.

Because our intuition is in principle sensible (B 151), the provision of an image, as it can be freely carried out in the imagination, is always referred to sensibility. But even the freest and least constrained imagination can serve up only visible aspects whose possibilities are somehow prescribed by the qualities of appearances in general. Therefore, that wherein the imagination's image is formed is limited by what can possibly be given in sensibility in general.

A schema is the mode of the general procedure governing figurative synthesis. It is the provision of an image according to a rule, and the rule is prescribed by the concept that is to be sensibly depicted. [375] The rule says: The free, intuitive visualization [of the concept] must proceed in such a way that the intuitive aspect that is to be formed ren-

---

125. [The German word for "imagination" is *Einbildungskraft*, literally "the power of imagining something," creating fantasies, etc. Heidegger interprets the term as the power of forming or giving an image.]

126. [The following paragraphs have profited from a comparison of GA 21 with Moser, pp. 751ff.]

ders visible, in some way, what the content of the rule prescribes. The rule entails having a pre-view of both the concept that prescribes the rule and simultaneously of that wherein the something is to be sensibly depicted according to the rule. Through the rule and its constitutive previews, the depicted and what does the depicting are connected. In the rule (i.e., in the schema) I think the concept not simply as such, but in such a way that I understand it as what prescribes the *synthesis speciosa* of the imagination. Therefore, in the rule (the schema), the concept is understood in its prescribing function: it prescribes the manner and mode of the synthesis, of the forming-into-an image. Consequently the concept, in its prescriptive function for the actual forming of the image, is at the same time the visible aspect that can be seen in the image that gets formed. Therefore, the schema, as the rule of the *synthesis speciosa*, contains both the prescribing concept (the prescription itself) and that in which the prescribed formation of the image is to be carried out and given. To put it in objective terms: The rule combines the concept that is to be sensibly depicted with the image that is to make the concept visible. That lies in the very structure of the rule, which Kant did not analyze any further. So the notion of the schema in general is to be understood as follows. The schema is the rule governing the imagination's figurative synthesis, a rule which is prescribed by a concept and which itself prescribes the sensible depiction of the concept.

e) Sensibilization of the pure concepts of understanding

With the above we are sufficiently prepared to understand the fourth point: the sensibilization of the pure concepts of understanding. In this case it is a matter of a transcendental schema, and when we clarify that, we will understand what is meant by the schema*tism* of the pure concepts of the understanding, viz., as a procedure of the spontaneity of the understanding with regard to schemata. We will understand the schematism as the way the spontaneity of the understanding is enacted in the form of the spontaneity of the productive imagination as figurative synthesis. [376]

What pertains to a transcendental or pure schema? The concept of schema was explained earlier. The question now is:

- Can *a priori* concepts have an *a priori* depiction in something that is *a priori* given?
- Can there be a rule governing this depiction?
- Is there something that can show up *a priori* in such a way that something can be *a priori* depicted in it?
- Is there an *a priori* image for *a priori* concepts?

But Kant says that "the schema of a pure concept of the understanding is something that can never be brought to an image" (B 180). To say that there is no image for pure concepts means that, insofar as they are concepts, they cannot be by way of a copy [*abgebildet*]. "No image" means no *empirical* image, i.e., no directly accessible empirical schema-image like the five dots. Nonetheless, if the talk about the schema of a category is to have any meaning at all, there must be an image in the sense of a schema-image. The category must be able to be sensibly depicted. And the way in which it can and must be depicted is precisely what should be shown by the explanation of the schematism of the pure categories of understanding.

Why then did Kant deny so abruptly the possibility of a pure schema having an image? That is his way of saying that a pure schema must have an *a priori* image because the depiction of the pure concepts of the understanding must be *a priori* necessary and possible. The *a priori* concept must be able to be sensibilized and to show up in and as something that can show up *a priori*. But the one thing that antecedently and *a priori* shows up and in every appearances that shows up—is *time*. Time is the *a priori* of sensibility and the *a priori* of any possible *a priori* sensibilization.

However, as Kant constantly emphasizes (in the demonstrations of the Analogies: cf. the passages cited above), time is something that cannot be perceived, something that does not directly show up to any empirical view as, and only as, itself. Therefore, the sentence above, in which Kant says that a pure schema cannot have an image, can only mean: The pure understanding cannot have a *sensible* image. Rather, [377] the only possible image it can have is the *a priori* condition of sensibility itself, namely time, that which is unthematically pre-viewed in the pre-view that is antecedent in all intuiting. This pre-viewed [viz., time], which shows up constantly but unthematically in the pre-view— this peculiar sight that is seen in the unthematic pre-view—*this* is a particular and pre-eminent "self-showing": it is a *species,* an image. And therefore, even though Kant denies that a pure schema can have an image, he can still speak of time as an image. Time is a pre-eminent *a priori* image, a "pure image": "The pure image . . . for all objects of the senses in general is time" (B 182).[127]

*   *   *

We say that the pure schema of the categories cannot be brought into any image at all; that means it can be brought only into a *"pure image."* This means that there is only one thing in which the pure concepts of the understanding can and must be depicted, only one thing in which they must show themselves as what they are—and that is a single pos-

---

127. [Here (Moser, p. 756) Heidegger ends his lecture of Friday, 19 February 1926, to be followed by that of Monday, 22 February, which opened with a 450-word summary that is omitted in GA 21.]

sible visible aspect, namely, what is pre-viewed in the pre-view: time. Time is that which is first determined and then schematized in the *synthesis speciosa* (which itself is ruled by the categories), so that, as an image—a specific form of pure self-showing—it shows something, makes it visible. Time does so precisely because it has been itself determined according to the transcendental determination of time, which in each case belongs to the pure schema and constitutes time. Likewise, time—or more precisely the transcendental determination of time—is the schema, "the sensible condition under which alone pure concepts of the understanding can be employed" (B 175). The schema, as the rule governing the figurative synthesis of time, presents time itself, or more precisely: it presents the category in the image of time. A schema is a transcendental time-determination.

To get a full, rich sense of the phenomenon of "pure schema," let us define the notion of the pure schema in Latin:

> *Schema purum dicit: regula syntheseos speciosae temporis secundum unum synthesin puram intellectualem constituens sive secundum categoriam.*

> The pure schema [378] is the rule governing the figurative synthesis of time according to the unity constituting the pure synthesis of the understanding, or in other words according to the category.

The schema is the *regula syntheseos temporis* [rule governing the synthesis of time]. Or again, briefly, the schema is the *synthesis speciosa secundum categoriam* [figurative synthesis in keeping with the category]. Or as Kant puts it in even shorter form (but I will expand his words): the schema is the *categoria phaenomenon* [category *qua* phenomenon]: the schema is the category as it shows itself, the *phaenomenon*. That is the abbreviated way of saying: "the rule of the self-manifestation of the category in the image of time," the *schema categoriae per speciem temporis* [schema of the category in or through the image of time].

Of this procedure regulated in this fashion Kant says:

> This schematism of our understanding with regard to appearances and their mere form is a hidden art in the depths of the human soul, whose true operations we can divine from nature and lay unveiled before our eyes only with difficulty. (B 181-182)

In point of fact Kant looks into an abyss here, but only so as to withdraw his view immediately and to forego actually discovering this basic structure. Perhaps as well, equipped with his methodic means for interpreting "the human soul" (i.e., the structure of our human existence), he found himself confronting a barrier. He even tries to excuse himself for backing off from a radical explanation of this structure:

> Rather than pausing now for a dry and boring analysis of what is required
> for transcendental schemata of pure concepts of the understanding in gen-
> eral, we would rather present them according to the order of the categories
> and in connection with these. (B 181)

This second way of proceeding is certainly just as necessary as the first
way of explaining the pure schema in general, and it is the only practical
method for explaining individual schemata concretely. In fact, Kant
makes a good start at giving a detailed interpretation of the individual
schemata, but basically he explains only three of the twelve in any detail [379]—and characteristically, they are the schemata of quantity,
reality, and substance, in other words the categories in which existent
nature first appears as an entity that is to be comprehended in the determinate measurements of physics. Twelve schemata would have to be
developed in accordance with the twelve categories, which themselves
correspond to the twelve forms of judgment taken as concepts of the
unities constitutive of these ways of combining. (1) These twelve schemata would have to be explained in their order of succession as well as
in their inner connection. Moreover, such an investigation [would also
have to provide] (2) the rigorously demonstrated derivation of the categories from the Table of Judgments (as regards their possibility and intrinsic necessity), as well as (3) their derivation from the "I think." However, these three elements of a truly fundamental investigation of the
possible groundwork of the *Critique of Pure Reason* are lacking. So, from
the start, Kant's explanation of the schemata remains on a terrain that
is both uncertain and undeveloped. Nonetheless, we must try to shed
some light on his explanation of the schemata of quantity, reality, and
substance. And we will try to do that with an eye to our guiding question: How is time understood—or how must it be understood—in these
schemata as rules governing the transcendental determination of time?
    Staying with our already elaborated problematic of ur-temporality
is the only way to get a substantive understanding of Kant's explanation and to see how close to the problematic he was pushed as well as
why he necessarily could not get access to it. Our inquiry will ask
about the three categories of quantity, reality, and substance:

1. What does the figurative synthesis regulated by these categories
   show in the pure image of time?
2. How is this sensible appearance of time understood? That is: How is
   it that what gets determined in the *synthesis speciosa* is always time?
   What kind of determination of time is operative here?
3. In each of the three cases [quality, reality, and substance], does
   "time" mean the same thing? or something different in each case?
   and if so, why? [380]

To the three categories of quantity, reality, and substance there correspond three schemata. The schema of quantity is number, *numerus*. The schema of reality is sensation, *sensatio*. The schema of substantiality is perdurance, the *perdurabile*.

§32. Number as the schema of quantity

We should note that we have already dealt with number in our earlier discussions regarding schematism, and there the issue was a possible sensibilization—schematization—of number itself: it was a matter of discovering the schema for a number. But now, by way of contrast, it is a question of the sensibilization of the category "quantity," whose pure image is number itself. Number is primarily nothing else but the pure image of quantity. As regards its conceptual character, this pure image of quantity is a pure sensible concept; and as a pure sensible concept, number in turn requires sensibilization, a new schematization. Kant did not provide any further discussion of these various schematisms—the schematism of quantity as number; the schematism of number itself is some kind of spatial form—nor did he show their inner connection.

The schema of quantity is number, *numerus*. That means: The *synthesis speciosa temporis* is regulated by "quantity" or "plurality," and what it makes visible in the image is number. This first has to be explained in phenomenological terms, and to do that we have to come up with some answers:

- In what way does time underlie the *synthesis speciosa* in this schema, "number"?
- What kind of time-determination shows up there?
- And what does the "determination of time" mean in the schema "number"?

Kant's answer to all of this is: In the schema "number," the determination of time is the *production* of time.

In the explanation that follows you must try to really see the things at stake. The rule for rendering visible the pure category of quantity in the image of time is number. This rule [381] itself is a transcendental determination of time with regard to plurality. The mode of carrying out this determination of time is the *synthesis speciosa,* which has the pure time-manifold in view and which, as a productive giving of the image (giving it from out of itself and to itself), has to render this time-manifold visible.

Rendering the pure time-manifold visible simply means highlighting the pure one-after-another, the now-sequence, that is, the nows them-

selves: "now and now and now and now." In this, each now is of the
same kind as every other now: each now is a now. But at the same time,
each now *qua* now is different from every other one. Every now is of the
same kind as every other now—and every now is a "this," a "thus-and-
so." The "now" articulates a "this," a this which is of the same kind as
every other "this," to each of which there always corresponds another
"now." The multiplicity of "nows," which is a multiplicity of "now-this-
now-that," thus renders something visible—namely, the "this-nesses" as
such. But the highlighting of the nows whereby a "this" is rendered visible, that is, the highlighting of the nows in the *synthesis speciosa*, is performed from out of a pre-view of plurality; and this unity-providing
pre-view determines this particular "now-this" more exactly. The phrase
"now-this" means "now-this-many."[128] Moreover, the synthesis gov-
erned by the pre-view of plurality does not signify merely "now-this-
much, now-that-much." Rather, prior to the highlighting and isolating
[of the nows] that is carried out in the synthesis, the synthesis itself is
primarily a "now-this-much *plus* now-that-much." Thanks to the pre-
view of plurality, the combination via the formal "and" becomes a
"plus." Hence "one this, and another this" becomes "this 'one,' plus that
'one,' plus that 'one'"—i.e., three.[129] The "nows" are not counted in this
synthesis speciosa, because the result of the synthesis is not number but
the "how-many-nows" in the time that elapsed. Even apart from the
fact that number itself is already presupposed in any "how-many-nows"
of elapsed time, the result would still be a certain number of "nows"
that were counted. Instead of all that, the number *itself* is what is to be
constituted as a schema. Therefore, what gets combined [382] is not the
"nows." Rather, it is the pure "this-nesses" of any and all "nows," the
pure "this-nesses" that are co-given when the nows are brought into
relief on the basis of the pure image of time as a now-sequence. To repeat once more: The process of constituting the true and proper provision of an image goes as follows:

• Now-this, then another now-this—a manifold of this's, if you will.
• But this manifold is already and antecedently present in the pre-
  view of quantity, i.e., of "how much."
• Therefore, in the synthesis a "this" is already antecedently understood as a "one."

128. [In German the play is between *Jetzt-So* and *Jetzt-Soviel,* literally "now-so"
and "now-so-many."]
129. [The German changes from "ein Dieses und ein Dieses" to "dieses Eins plus
dieses Eins," etc. In English, the German *ein* can mean both the indefinite article
"a" and the numerical adjective "one." The German *Eins* is "one" as a number.]

- Moreover, the "and" of the synthesis is already understood to be characterized by quantity: one and one and one, etc.

Thus what shows up in the *synthesis speciosa temporis secundum quantitatem* [synthesis that produces an image of time corresponding to quantity or magnitude[130]] is the pure "numerical amount" [*das Gezählte*]. But we must distinguish between this "pure numerical amount" and some *thing* that gets counted up [*das Abgezählte*]. The pure numerical amount is always the particular amount as such. This amount (and every other amount as such) is what every specific number numbers-as-an-amount (and does nothing else but that). Any number [say, five] does not count up and determine something *else* [say, five *dots*]. No, the number itself is that amount. A number *is* a number only as the numbering-of-an-amount [*Zählen*]. And as this kind of numbering, the number co-numbers (if I may put it that way) along with the other numbers. To say it "co-numbers" means nothing else than that it belongs with the other numbers.

This numbering-of-an-amount, as co-numbering along with the other numbers, is the very being of number. Therefore, this numbering-of-an-amount that the number carries out "forms" [*bildet*], of and by itself, the series of numbers. By contrast, a thing that has been counted up is something that is not itself a number—or, at any rate, need not be a number. Rather, it is first of all something that we can declare to be of such and such an amount *with regard to* a number. Any manifold at all can be counted up. Numbers too can be counted up—I can say: "12, 73, 84, 51, and 67 *are five numbers.*" In this case a manifold of numbers its itself counted, but counted with *regard* to a number. The fact that *numbers* are counted up in this case does not change the fact that a *counting up* is going on. And this process, as a counting-up of numbers, is in no way identical with the pure numbering-of-an-amount.

So what is really numbered in the pure numbering-of-an-amount? Whatever the case may be, pure numbering-of-an-amount cannot number-the-amount of anything in the sense of "counting it up," because "number-of-an-amount" would already be presupposed in such counting. Rather, here it is a matter of a numbering in which the number itself and as such *is*. Such [383] numbering is the numbering-of-a-certain-amount on the part of the number itself, which is the very being of number.[131] As itself the numbering-of-an-amount, number is the rule

---

130. [For this translation of *quantitas* as "magnitude" (*die Bloße Größe*), see B 745.]

131. [In this sentence, *Sichselbstzählen* surely should not be "the number's numbering of itself." The faux reflexive is at least a passive, and more likely a tautology: "The being of a number is to be the number-of-a-certain amount," or with an

governing the possibility of rendering visible and determining any *quantum*. In this *synthesis speciosa temporis* in which number is constituted, time itself is perceived, but not thematically (since that is *a priori* impossible). Rather, time—which has been brought into relief as "now," and in fact as a "now-this"—provides, in these this's, something that can be numbered as regards an amount. This manifold of "now-this's" is not what gets numbered or counted up; rather, that manifold is the condition of the possibility of numbers themselves. Every number is, *a priori*, a determinate possibility of pure numbering-of-an-amount; that is, it is a rule. The function of time in this *synthesis speciosa* consists in providing an image—i.e., rendering visible—not itself *qua* time, but the *this's* that correspond to every now and that are of the same kind even though each "this" is different. So the this's are the condition of the possibility of numbering-an-amount. For every concrete act of counting up is possible only if I comprehend a multiplicity (however various its content may be) in such a way that I bring it into a pure multiplicity of mere "somethings." Only then can I count them up. Otherwise I could never count a pear, an apple, a stone, or any other objects.

We must remember that what is counted is not the nows. That means: the word "time" in the phrase *synthesis speciosa temporis* is not be understood as a *genitivus objectivus* [objective genitive],[132] as if time were the thematic object of the synthesis. Yet on the other hand, time certainly is the primary object that the *synthesis speciosa* relates to, such that in and through the synthesis, time appears-along-with. In this process of appearing-along-with and being unthematically brought into relief, time articulates pure ability to number-an-amount. Neither is time itself the numbered amount, nor will Kant say that counting necessarily needs time in the sense that it has to elapse in time. People usually interpret Kant this way, and then refute him by showing that

1. other behaviors also necessarily occur [384] over time; therefore time is not a distinctive feature of counting; and
2. Kant confuses counting and number; and numbers are not in time at all.

is-*qua*-copula: "The number itself *is* nothing but the numbering-of-a-certain-amount."]

132. [An objective genitive is one in which the person or thing named by the modifying genitive is the passive object or recipient of what is named in the noun it modifies. A subjective genitive is one in which the person or thing named by the modifying genitive is the subject that actively possesses or is the source of what is named in the noun it modifies. "Napoleon's defeat" expresses a *subjective* genitive if it refers to Napoleon's defeat of the Prussians on 14 October 1806; it expresses an *objective* genitive if it refers to the defeat Napoleon suffered at Waterloo on 18 June 1815.]

Kant's analysis of the pure schema "number" is quite rough, and gives occasion for such misunderstanding. But he never had in mind anything as trivial as that counting takes place over time. What he wanted to do was clarify number itself in its own proper constitution. And the decisive thing is that he discovered (to put it roughly) that time is embedded in number itself, quite apart from whether counting occurs over time or not, and regardless of whether numbers themselves are in time or not. Precisely because numbers are not *in* time, they have, as their very being, a constitutive relation *to* time itself. To be sure, this relation remains obscure in Kant, but I have tried to bring it out in my interpretation so as to determine the specific content of what Kant was after.

Insofar as Kant brings number and time together in the way we explained above, that bringing-together does *not* mean that "counting elapses over time." But at the same time it does mean that, in bringing them together, Kant has to have understood time as different from the kind of time that we mean in saying that something elapses *in* time. This latter is the time that Kant understands primarily as world-time and the time of nature. But in this transcendental determination of time, time shows up in a very different and much more original way. It appears in this way for Kant as well, even though, as our analysis has already shown, he had to hold on to the idea of time as now-time. So now we will have to ask:

- How is time understood in this transcendental time-determination of the schema "number"?
- Does this analysis of the transcendental time-determination of the schema "number," of the schema of reality, and of the schema of substance let us experience something fundamental about what time itself is?[133]

*   *   *

Our analyses of the schematism of number have prepared us for the answer to the above questions. [385] In answering them, we will have to draw out [*herausholen*] of those analyses something that Kant may have surmised, even though it remained inaccessible to him. In fact, to the degree that Kant did surmise this issue, he expressed it (and had to express it) in inadequate concepts and characterizations.

In the *synthesis speciosa temporis*, what happens is a looking-away from the now—in and through the now—and simply a synthesizing of

---

133. [Here (Moser, p. 770) Heidegger ends his lecture of 22 February 1926, to be followed by that of Tuesday, 23 February, which opened with a 430-word summary that is omitted in GA 21.]

a this with the manifold of this's with regard to "how much." So time does not show itself in the *synthesis speciosa;* rather, it shows something else without showing itself, which is to say: Time is a pure image. Bringing the sequence of nows into relief provides the pure manifold of what-is-of-the-same-kind—i.e., the pure manifold of this's—as absolutely necessary if any number is to be able to be counted at all. The being of this manifold of what-is-of-the-same-kind (i.e., of all this's) is the pure "there is given . . ." [*»es gibt«*]. *What* is given is the very being of the "that" in the phrase "*That* is given" [*es gibt* es]. But "who" does the giving? "Who" is the *es* that gives? The answer is: the now.

Kant says: The schema "number" is "the production of time itself" (B 184).[134] In this case "production" cannot mean first and foremost the bringing-forth or creating of a time. Rather, if this schematism is to have any sense at all, it means: the unthematic highlighting of the now, such that this "now" provides a "this." With regard to "much-ness," the "this" is a "so much." The character of the transcendental time-determination in the schema "number" is time-production in the sense that we have explained. It does not mean that time is first created by counting. Time is produced in the only way it can be in the present context: it is brought forth [*her-gestellt*], in such a way that it can give something. Time functions as an image that does not show itself in itself as a whole, but that nonetheless shows something else. And the *synthesis speciosa,* as providing images, gives *this* image—so much so that this image, as a now-sequence itself, always gives a this.

Kant does not explain this peculiar function of time at all. Nonetheless, he calls time a "pure image." And in the passage where he speaks of the "production of time," he speaks of "the production of time itself *in the successive apprehension* of an [386] object" (B 184).[135] That is the same as saying: producing time does not mean relating thematically to time itself; rather, it is the production of time *in* the apprehension.[136] On the other hand, this conception of the schema "number" and its relation to time provides a strong occasion for the usual misunderstandings, as if Kant were saying: "In comprehending, one-after-another, objects in the broadest sense, time is used and this counting runs its course over time."

But we can also understand "object" [*Gegenstand*] in a quite broad sense, and in this case as "the 'this' that shows up in the now." And we can take "apprehension" as "pure apprehension" (cf. A 100) of a mani-

---

134. [Heidegger omits the word *synthesis:* „. . . die Erzeugung, (Synthesis) der Zeit selbst."]

135. [Again Heidegger omits "(Synthesis)" after "production." The italics are mine.]

136. [Here following Moser, p. 775.9–10.]

fold. The "successive apprehension" would then be the pure number-ing on the part of the number itself, which certainly does not take place over time. And therefore all the more fundamentally does the successive apprehension require time, since time always provides, *a priori*, the very entity that can be counted.[137]

The Kantian explanation of number as a schema remains incomplete and lacking in clarity, but one thing is clear: An ur-temporal determination of time—in this case, the ur-temporal production of time—does *not* understand time as time that is itself measured.

Pure number numbers-an-amount—it "numbers-an-amount" along with other numbers, which do the same thing. This pure numbering that number is, is in itself a highlighting of the now. Time is embedded in number as such; this pure numbering that number itself is, is a rule for counting off the countable. Number is a condition of the possibility for the countability of something, i.e., for the fact that entities can be quantitatively determined. That is, number—the schema, the ur-temporal time-determination that we have characterized—is the condition of the possibility for the fact that the pure category of quantity can be related to appearances, i.e., that there can be something like the measurability[138] of objects, or objective measuring in general. Along with that, there pertains to the schema of quantity the constitution of the countability of whatever encounters through time. Time provides to the pure concept of the understanding a possible relation to objects. *Numerus est quantitas phaenomenon, sc., per speciem temporis:* Number is quantity as it shows itself in the image of time. It [387] is the concept of the understanding that shows up in this way and sensibilizes itself in this way. Or, to express the same thing from the standpoint of what shows up as a concrete thing, i.e., from the standpoint of the appearances: Number is the condition of the possibility of a determinability of the given by way of an *a priori* concept—in this case, the concept of quantity.

§33. Sensation as the schema of reality

The second schema, which Kant interprets with a certain thoroughness, is the schema of reality. ("Reality" is the first category within the second set of categories, which Kant designates as "quality." With that, we see the direct connection of these concepts and the source of Hegel's way of expressing himself, where reality and quality and existence are equally united.)

---

137. [Moser (p. 776.27-28) has "Sich-zählen-könnende," instead of GA 21's "das sich zählende Seiende."]

138. [Moser (p.776.21) has *Meßbarkeit* instead of *Messung*.]

The schema of reality is sensation, *sensatio*. In this schema—i.e., in this *synthesis speciosa temporis*—what is pre-viewed in the pre-view is reality. So we have a *synthesis speciosa temporis secundum realitatem* [synthesis that forms an image of time corresponding to reality]. And here again, the schema is nothing but a rule for a real thing being able to appear in and through the image of time: *per speciem temporis*.

But what is meant by reality as a pure concept of understanding, prior to sensibilization? Kant says that reality is "what corresponds to a sensation in general" (B 182). Reality "indicates" something present "in time." Something present, as present in time, is present for a while. The question, "For how long a while?" or more precisely, "How long a while is the time [of its presence]?" or "Is that 'while' determined?"—all are, *a priori*, a matter of indifference. This present thing (which has a "while" of this or that length) is related to its "while" (however long or short it may be) by filling up a period of time. It is the present, real something, that fills up that period of time. And that something which, as a present "what," fills up a certain length of time is what Kant calls a *res*, a "something," a "thing" in the broadest sense. The essence of this *res*, this thing—i.e., its reality, or as Kant says, [388] "thing-ness" [*Sachheit*]— consists in the fact that it is a filler-of-time. The question now is how time functions as a pure image in the schema of reality (and thus in sensation), or: how time sensibilizes the concept of the understanding called "reality."

Time again is to be taken preliminarily as the pure multiplicity of the now-sequence. However, in the *synthesis speciosa secundum realitatem* [synthesis that provides an image corresponding to reality], this pure multiplicity of the now-sequence is to be taken in another perspective. Every now is *of the same kind* as every other now, while, at the same time, being *this* now. But also, every now is essentially now-something, now-something-else,[139] prescinding from what the "something" or "something-else" is and even from that the fact that this something is a "this." (Just to briefly note this in passing: You can already see that the first schematism, the now-this, in a certain sense presupposes—or in any case, is co-original with—this second schematism, i.e., this now-structure where every now is a now-something.) In the present case it is a matter of highlighting the now insofar as the now is understood as a now-something. But even a now-nothing is a now-something—that is, the now-nothing is a privation of a now-something. A now-nothing is possible only on the basis of the now in general, which is, in its essence, a now-something.

---

139. [The German *Jetzt-Das* might be rendered as "now-this," however, that would confuse *Jetzt-Das* and *Jetzt-Dieses*; hence, I render *Jetzt-Das* as "now-something" and (when it is repeated) "now-something-else."]

For Kant this *res* or "something" that shows up in every now is the sensation, because sensation in general is the first-thing-given—in the Kantian-Cartesian sense of first-thing-given for inner sense. This *res*— this "something," this "whatever-is-given," this "present-first-of-all"— this is what Kant also calls "transcendental matter." The fact that the schema of reality is sensation—which at first blush astounds us, and might seem completely unintelligible—is connected with the specific position of Descartes and with the specific conception of what is given first of all.

But every sensation, as Kant says, has a magnitude. That is, every "something," every *res*, is something-present-now—now, and again now, and again now, and then no more. Every something that shows every now-moment is only for a while, for a certain sequence of nows. A certain period of time belongs to the *res*. [389] A "while" belongs to a *res*, and with that a determinate quantity—a this-much, i.e., a *quantum* of nows—belongs to the determination of reality itself. Accordingly, a certain highlighting of the nows underlies the act of sensation, so that the nows are understood, more or less explicitly, as countable and counted nows. But these highlighted, countable nows are thereby understood primarily as now-something, i.e., as a now that as such shows a "what" and a "something." But what is primary in the time-determination of this particular schema—i.e., in sensation—is not the counting-off of the nows. Rather, it is the highlighting of the nows as now-somethings—i.e., a highlighting of the nows which counts the nows as a group, a highlighting in which the "something" of these nows maintains itself throughout, i.e., *perdures*.

In the counted-through nows, which are always now-somethings, the present thing, as something that perdures, is able to meet the senses. Here the time-determination *qua* highlighting-of-the-nows, is carried out *secundum realitatem* [in accordance with reality]. It is not a production of time, as in the case with number; rather, as Kant says, in this case the time-determination is the filling-up of time. Time-filling means nothing but letting something encounter us in a counted-through now-sequence. The counting need not be explicit. It can also remain undetermined. This *synthesis speciosa* that is the schema of quality, is, as Kant says, "the synthesis of sensation (perception) with the presentation of time" (B 184).

As you see, that is once again a very rough and easily misunderstood expression of the synthesis we are talking about. But our previous interpretation of the structure can clarify this expression in its proper sense. The now, if it is essentially a now-something, must be highlighted in order for there to be anything like sensing and a sensible at all. *Sensatio* as the schema of reality is a matter of letting something be present—a letting that simultaneously highlights time and counts through it. It is the condition for the possibility of there being anything present at all.

The function of the now in time-filling is different from its function in time-production (number). Moreover, in the schema of reality— namely, filling-up-a-certain-period-of-time—the now is also something quantitatively determined and determinable. Therefore the schema [390] of reality likewise entails the possible countability of the nows[140] and, with that, the presupposition of number and, with that, the schema of quantity. This connection is intrinsically plain and clear, if one considers that

1. the schematism is indeed centered on the question of how the concepts of the understanding can have relations to appearances through the elapsing of time;
2. the appearances present nature; and therefore
3. the entities to which the concepts of the understanding are related, are understood from the start in terms of a measuring and determining in scientific knowledge, i.e., physics.

Thus we see a remarkable linking of the schema of reality with the schema of quantity. Kant did not express himself any further on the point. That would not have been possible for him because of the fact that he strung together the categories and, correspondingly, the schemata as well, in an artificially construed table that necessarily had to cover-over the inner, material connection of the categories as well as the schemata. On a closer look there is not a founding connection in the sense that the schema of reality would be founded in that of quantity. Instead it is the other way around. Or more precisely, both are co-original—and both are founded in the schema that Kant puts in third place: the schema of substance, i.e., of purdurance.

The characterization of these two schematisms already shows that the now and the pure sequence of nows can be seen in the *synthesis speciosa temporis* in various ways, and therefore that the now-structure is richer than one has generally believed up until now and than Kant himself explicitly saw. The various modes of the *synthesis speciosa temporis* are differentiated precisely by the fact that they prescind in various ways from the full now-structure, and make use only of a specific structural moment of the now. [391]

---

140. [Literally: ". . . and so in the schema of reality there likewise lies the character of the possible countability of nows . . ."]

§34. Persistence as the schema of substance

The third schema that Kant discusses is the schema of substance, and he formulates it as persistence, or more precisely, as the persistent, the *perdurabile.* The persistent is that in which substance shows up: the persistent is the temporal image of this category. This schema is the rule governing the showing-up of a persistent real thing. This rule is, once again, a transcendental time-determination; and so it is a high-lighting of the now-sequence with regard to substance as the under-lying. But here again, time itself is not thematic. Instead, what stands in view here in the categorial pre-view of substance is, as before, the sequence of nows, which, according to its essence, is "now-something," now-something-else . . . That means:

- this "something" that shows up in the pure image of the sequence of nows with regard to the "under-lying" [sub-stance],
- this "something," as that which under-lies in every now, or more exactly, as that which under-lies every particular "something" that can be intended in any now,
- this pre-eminent "something" as the under-lying in and for every now, *is,* in every now, the ever-continuing, persistent under-lying.[141]

This permanent something that is and shows up as the "there" [*das Da*] in every now is, for that very reason, always already "there" [*da*] for every now that comes along. It is the unchangeable, the constantly already-present. It is that in terms of which every determinable "this" of a determinate now is *a priori* determined. The phrase, "Now, when this or that specific thing happens . . ." means exactly the same as: "Now, when nature itself is always already present as that wherein the specific event is occurring."

Kant's explanation of this schema is noticeably briefer than his ex-planations of the previous two schemata. Besides, the proper features of this schema, both as a schema and as a rule, remain undetermined. That is, it does not emerge how we are to understand the *synthesis spe-ciosa temporis* that is proper to this schema. He does not tell us what corresponds to this schema the way time-production and time-fulfill-ing correspond, respectively, to the previous two schemata. We look in vain for a delineation of the time-feature corresponding to substance. In his summarizing characterization of the schemata, [392] Kant merely says that this schema would present "the relations of percep-tions among themselves at all time (i.e., in accordance with a rule of

141. [Following Moser, p. 783.22–25: "ausgezeichnete; ist."]

time-determination)" (B 184). From that it is easy to gather that the
synthesis speciosa temporis of substance is related to time in the sense of
the whole of time.

We must remember that the same connection was mentioned in the
demonstration of the First Analogy. There it was a question of the production of the *a priori* condition of possibility of an empirical time-
determination. But these *a priori* conditions for an empirical time-
determination—i.e., the three Analogies—are, for their part, possible
only if their own possibility is already demonstrated—i.e., only if it is
shown beforehand and in general that, as an action of the understanding, determining *qua* determining can relate to appearances. The condition of possibility for principles of empirical time-determination is
the schematism of the understanding itself.

These connections between (1) empirical time-determination, (2)
the principles, i.e., the Analogies as the principles of the pure determination of time, and (3) the schematism, which alone is supposed to
make possible this pure time-determination, are obscured in Kant by
the fact that he uses the term "time-determination" in various senses.
The expression and what it means have their origin in the *empirical*
time-determination, which we understand as time-reckoning—i.e., as a
measuring and determining of an appearance's being-in-time. That is to
be distinguished from the *a priori* time-determination; but even this latter term has many meanings. In one case it means the relation of the
synthesis speciosa temporis to time; and just as there are various categories,
so there are various time-determinations, as *synthesis speciosa,* that correspond to them. These time-determinations of the *synthesis speciosa* are
what we characterize as the specifically *schematic* time-determinations.
They belong to the schema—i.e., the *figurative* time-determinations.
Among these, there is a time-determination that belongs to substance;
that is the one whose conception we are striving for, although Kant left
it undetermined. However, from the demonstration of the First [393]
Analogy, we could gather that this specific figurative time-determination
is the presupposition for what Kant, in the First Analogy, formulates as
a *principle,* and which he once again calls a time-determination. This
one is also *a priori,* but in the *a priori* ordering of the *figurative* time-
determinations it is given a subordinate rank. Time-determination in
this third and last sense is an *a priori* principle that underlies every empirical[142] time-measurement; but as such, an *a priori* principle is itself
possible only on the basis of a referability of the concepts of the understanding to appearances in general.

In terms of their content, the three Analogies belong with the schemata of the three categories of relation—i.e., of the three categories of

142. [Following Moser, p. 786.13–14.]

substance, causality, and reciprocal action [between agent and patient] —
which Kant treats very briefly, as in fact he does with the three categories of modality and their schemata. The fact that the Analogies and the
concepts are treated separately (and in general, the very conception of
the problem of schematism) is dictated simply by the architectonics of
the book. Kant first discusses his doctrine of the concept, then his doctrine of the proposition and conclusion. But the result is that here (as in
other parts of the *Critique of Pure Reason*) there emerge substantive issues
that lack any support.—For our present treatment, we must always remember: The term "time-determination" has many meanings, and the
individual meanings are themselves insufficiently determined, which
in turn contributes to their ambiguity.[143]

* * *

It is unclear how we should understand the structure of the figurative
time-determination of substance. At any rate, Kant furnishes no indication in that regard. That is all the more serious insofar as the figurative time-determination of substance is, as one can show, the most
fundamental one—an insight that is not only covered-over in Kant
but also kept out of the picture by the extraneous architectonics of the
Table of Judgments and the Table of the Categories.

We must try to get clear about the central and substantive meaning
of this schema and of the time-determination that belongs to it. So,
what kind of feature does this *synthesis speciosa temporis secundum substantiam* have? What is it in this category that corresponds to the mode
of the figurative time-determination? What corresponds to time-production and time-filling? In the passage we already referred to (B
184–185), Kant says: the *a priori,* rule-governed time-determination
[394] that belongs to substance concerns the order of time; that of
time-production concerns the *time-series* [i.e., quantity]; that of time-
filling concerns the *content* of time [i.e., quality]; and that of the category of modality, concerns the *ensemble* of time. From this as well, little
can be gathered, especially since Kant does not say how the time-series and the order of time differ from each other. But clearly by "the
order of time" Kant means the reckoning of the order of time, i.e.,
empirical time-reckoning.

This schema of substance also includes a special relation to time
insofar as, in it, the figurative time-determination is supposed to make
possible not the ability to be sensed and counted, but the ability to
reckon time itself: empirical time-determinability. This schema is sup-

143. [Here Heidegger ends his lecture of Tuesday, 23 February 1926, to be followed
by his lecture of Thursday, 25 February, which opened with a 400-word summary
(clarifying the four kinds of time-determination) which is omitted in GA 21.]

posed to make possible an appearance in a way that makes the appearance be objectively determinable in a temporal way. In other words, it makes possible counting-up the amount of nows of the duration of a specific real thing. Its job is to make possible the objective determination of the nows of a real thing's duration in terms of its "how much." That necessarily requires, as we showed earlier, the ability to return to something that is already constantly there. That means always already having constant access to whatever is there. The *synthesis speciosa temporis secundum substantiam* is nothing but the rule for *a priori* already and constantly having access to something unchangeable. In other words, it is the rule for letting a self-same something encounter us in every something that is now already present. Accordingly, this schema includes a certain time-filling, a certain time-determination for the category "reality." But this time-filling is not for a determinate duration, throughout a determinate number of nows. Rather, this is time-filling in the form of letting-something-encounter-us in *every* now—which entails: for every time-filling in the sense of the category of reality, for all of the prior, constant letting-the-unchangeable-encounter. In a certain way, by means of this time-filling we can help with the determining-feature of the *synthesis speciosa temporis secundum substantiam* that is lacking in Kant. We comprehend it as a preeminent [form of] time-filling, viz., ever-prior time-filling as the rule of every specific possible real [395] time-measurement, i.e., of every reckoning and determining of the magnitude of a real thing.

But now we see anew a connection between the three categories or, if you will, their schemata. It is obvious that with the schema of substance we have arrived at what really sustains the other two that we mentioned before.

The fact that Kant did not see the fundamental meaning of the schema of substance—indeed that (as we have shown) he left this time-determination remarkably obscure—is the clearest indication that for him the structure of ur-temporality in general remains hidden in principle. But on the other hand, highlighting ur-temporality, as over against Kant's doctrine of schematism and time in general, will make it clear that ur-temporality is not something invented or contrived but a field of work in which fundamental distinctions are made.

The rest of the schemata are treated only in brief fashion. This is not the place to show how Kant would have understood each individual *synthesis speciosa temporis,* or even how he would have spelled out the connection of these various syntheses according to their own structure rather than in the extraneous way he lists them in his artificially constructed Table. As regards the connection of the schemata of relation (substance, causality, reciprocal action) with those of modality (possibility, actuality, necessity) there are insuperable difficulties, because here Kant allows the borders between the two to completely hemorrhage into each other. He says that the schema of modality expresses the relation to "time itself as the correlate of the determination of . . . an object" (B 184). By contrast, he also says: "Persistence {and therefore the schema of substance} gives general expression to time, as the constant correlate of all existence of appearances" (B 266). Thus the same time-relation is claimed for the schema of modality as for the schema of a specific category of relation, that of substance. The root of these inadequacies lies not only in [396] the schematism, but in the division and derivation of the categories themselves and in their source—the Table of Judgments—whose artificial and incidental nature is shown in a remarkable way within an investigation that constantly asks for the final conditions of possibility.

We shall not go any further into the chapter on schematism itself. As regards its literary character, it is not well unified. The first sections (B 176-179) provide an insufficiently researched interpretation of schematism in the form of a popular-philosophical explanation of what should be explained throughout the whole of the Transcendental Logic. In fact, Kant carries out this rather pedantic explanation by following out the idea of subsumption, which of course is of fundamental importance for the architectonic of the *Critique of Pure Reason* (and therefore also for its dubious explanations).

It is no accident that Kant hit upon subsumption in this propaedeutic explanation of the schematism, since for Kant subsumption coheres in an essential way with the structure of the synthesis and of judgment. In general, judgment is only subsumption. To be sure, he did not clarify the structure of subsumption as regards its inner connection with the structure of the *synthesis speciosa temporis*. The usefulness of the idea of subsumption for Kant was abetted by the fact that he conceives of the *a priori* in a Cartesian sense.

The first one to show this duality in the composition of the chapter on schematism was Robert Curtius in his essay on "Das Schematismuskapitel in der *Kritik der reinen Vernunft. Philologische Untersuchung*" [The Chapter on Schematism in the *Critique of Pure Reason*. A Philological Investigation], in *Kant-Studien* 19 (1914), pp. 338-366. The subtitle indicates his goal: not a philosophical interpretation, but a clarification of its literary character. Curtius distinguishes in Kant a synthesis of subsumption and a synthesis of the schematism.[144] Only the schematism of synthesis has any substantive meaning, and it coheres with the problematic of the *Critique of Pure Reason*, especially with the time-

---

144. [Moser (p. 793.17-18) records Heidegger saying, "the subsumption-schematism and the synthesis-schematism," and two sentences later: "The schematism, as the synthesis-schematism, is the presupposition for . . ."]

based deduction of the categories. [397] But we need to say more. The schematism-synthesis is the presupposition for the ur-temporal deduction of the categories, a presupposition which Kant obviously clarified only much later and which he never understood radically as a presupposition. Further, we have to emphasize what Curtius did not adequately valorize: that for Kant subsumption and synthesis in general are equally essential, in keeping with the theory of judgment and concept that Kant took over from the tradition.[145]

However, that belongs in a thematic interpretation of Kant. We are asking about the phenomenon of time itself and, after that, about how time is understood in the doctrine of the schematism. We now ask: By what right did we say at the beginning of our interpretation of Kant's conception of time, that he held fast—indeed, in principle—to the traditional concept of time (viz., time as now-time), and that he nonetheless pushed out beyond it toward a philosophical understanding of time, thereby touching a boundary but never getting beyond it into the open?

----

§35. The time-determination of the *synthesis speciosa*

We must keep in mind this fundamental fact: Even in a very advanced philosophical understanding of time, time is always understood in terms of the now. Therefore the following consideration, which is meant to lead us into the dimension of ur-temporality, must remain oriented to the phenomenon of the now.

1. In the previous determinations of time (production of time, time-filling, and ever-prior time-filling), time and therefore the now are not thematically comprehended. Therefore, they also are not determined in some way like being counted up and measured in answer to the question, "How much time has gone by?" Therefore, here time is not the time of the appearances. Rather, it is time in relation to the I-think itself—the spontaneous synthesis of the imagination.[146] For the first time in philosophy, time is taken in its transcendental function within the *a priori* constitution of the whole of transcendental [398] truth, i.e., of that which positively determines the possibility of appearance.

----

145. [Moser (p. 793.29–794.5) records Heidegger adding: "Insofar as, for Kant, the idea of subsumption is tightly [*eng*] connected with the idea of synthesis, in keeping with his theory of judgment, we cannot easily set the two schematisms over against each other, despite the poor shape Kant left them in. Rather, we have to try to point out the inner connection between the two."]

146. [This last phrase is from Moser, p. 794.32–795.1.]

2. What is the positive characterization of time and of the now that we should take from the figurative time-determinations? First of all, it must be made clear that the way the now has been characterized heretofore—as something between the not-yet and the no-longer—in no way touches the decisive aspect. But in the modes of synthesis, a feature of time is highlighted that was never seen in the usual characterization of time but that nonetheless was constantly made use of: The now is a "now-something." The now speaks, as it were, "away from itself"; it points toward . . . "now that this-or-that . . . ," or simply, "now that . . ." Insofar as one says "now," no matter how undetermined and empty it might be, the now is, in its essence, a "now that this . . . ," a "now that this or that is encountered," or "now that this or that happens," or "now that I behave in this or that way." "Now" is essentially "now that this . . ." Even a completely isolated "Now!" that one might shout to start a footrace is a "now that . . . ," and in fact this case shows the phenomenally primary feature of the now: "from this point on." We look at a certain point on the clock, and when the secondhand gets there we shout "Now!" or "Go!"—meaning, "Now that this [second has been reached]!" And it need not be a chronometer: any event at all that the group has agreed on can serve this function.

So when we speak, as we usually do, of an individual "now" in the sense of a now-point in a series of nows, we don't really talk about a "now" but rather use some other expression, like "this thing now" which stands within a sequence and about which we have to say: "it's moving, it's flowing." At most, one still has a now-fragment to which no phenomenological sense pertains. The phenomenon of the now has already been deprived of its essential structure. And out of a multiplicity of such cut-up nows, we construct for ourselves the idea of time. Time, then, is something that is somehow "just there"—something which is given, but whose being we do not determine because we cannot. Every question about the being of time has [399] already misunderstood time. The difficulties that Augustine landed in when he asked this question (*Confessions*, book XI) are classic.

This character of "toward something" or "pointing to something" belongs to the essence of the now. Only by bringing out this character of the now can we make sense of the *synthesis speciosa temporis*. To this end, we have understood the basic structure of the *synthesis temporis*—the thesis that this synthesis is about self-referral (in the broadest sense) to a now; we have understood it as the highlighting of the now in such a way that the synthesis follows the now-phenomenon. Or better, it follows its indication, its "direction-toward." More precisely yet, the synthesis follows the now's "that-toward-which": its "something," its "this." The primary and genuine highlighting of the now is unthematic: it pursues the now in terms of what the now is in itself, i.e., in terms of the fact that the now points away from itself. The high-lighting is not a matter of contemplating this structure, but of follow-ing it as it points away from itself; and that is where the unthematic becomes thematic. Thus the various modes of the *synthesis speciosa tem-poris* are grounded in the way the unthematic pre-view of the now and the now-sequence is carried out. Insofar as these syntheses have a transcendental *a priori* character, they are antecedent. The syntheses are modes of the antecedent, unthematic pre-viewing of the pure now-sequence.

Earlier, however, we used this phenomenon of a prior, unthematic pre-view to interpret what Kant calls the form of pure intuition. From this point on, let us try to further clarify the schema of substance in its character as synthesizing. That wherein substance is sensibly de-picted is persistence. But according to Kant (B 225–226), persistence represents time itself. In this synthesis, there occurs a highlighting of the whole sequence of nows. In other words, the "something" to which every now points is understood as the "something" in every now, "at all times." Here the *synthesis speciosa* relates antecedently and unthe-matically to the whole of time; and so here the pure image of time shows up most purely. This corresponds to the fact that, since antiq-uity, substance has been understood as *the* basic category. The schema of substance is therefore the most original and most pure in its [400] pre-viewing of the whole of time with regard to its pure character of referring to the "something" as the same at all times, that is, for the whole of time. Therefore, the mode of this most original *synthesis spe-ciosa* is the prior and constant allowing of the same to encounter us. This preeminent, prior, unthematic taking-a-look is the primary *a priori* constitution of what Kant calls the form of intuition.[147] Thus that which shows up in the Transcendental Aesthetic seemingly formally and generally as a characterization of time is now uncovered as the fundamental and first *synthesis speciosa temporis*.

----

§36. The now-structure that we have attained: its character of referral and of making present. The phenomenal demonstrability and limits of Kant's interpretation of time

According to Kant, to intuit this form, this pure pre-viewing of the sequence of nows (which is to be understood in the phenomenologi-cally clarified sense of the now), is time itself. Time as this pre-view-ing is related (unthematically) to time as the pure sequence of nows,

147. [Reading "mit Form der Anschauung" (Moser, p. 799.13), instead of "mit Form anzuschauen."]

to such a degree that time itself—the antecedent, constant letting-something-encounter—is itself given, although unthematically. Because it is an unthematic relation to itself, time as the antecedent-constant letting-something-encounter-us lets the "something" be encountered as the self-same at all times.

Only when one holds fast to the genuine now-structure and observes that the primary taking-a-look at time is unthematic, does one understand what it means to say: time is an original pure and general self-affection. What *does* the affecting—namely, the now-sequence whose nows the taking-a-look pursues unthematically—is not something just-there, thematically comprehended and comprehensible. Rather, the now-sequence affects in such a way that it lets something be seen—but unthematically, as if the now-sequence itself were constantly retreating and disappearing in its constant referring-to. [401] This affecting is thus something like a constant putting-itself-aside and a liberating letting-something-be-seen. And the unthematic act of affecting on the part of that which affects is enacted by the very one affected. In other words, this constant, prior letting-something-encounter, this unthematic highlighting of the now as we characterized it above, is the pure act of rendering something present [*Gegenwärtigen*]. The now is a now-present [*Gegenwart*]. It is a referring to . . . , whereby it lets something encounter us and whereby it awaits something that can encounter. And the now is a now-present in such a way that it remains unthematic. Likewise, the pre-view of the now is unthematic. It is a letting-something-encounter-us—i.e., a making-present—that passes through the now. The now is neither a fragment nor a chopped-up now-point that is "merely-present," but rather a pointing-toward-something, a letting-something-be-seen. It is neither a fragment nor generally something merely-there, but rather the basic structure of the very act of relating in the Kantian context of the knowledge of nature.

More precisely: Making-present is first of all a condition of the possibility that a "now" can become explicit as "now something" and "now something else." Knowledge of nature (for example) is a specifically articulated way of making-present, and making-present characterizes human existence in its being-in-the-world. Only for those reasons can this human existence say "now this, now that," when it speaks about the world and about nature (although always, as it does so, co-expressing itself, its ownmost being unto the world). Above all, on the basis of this essential expressibility of the "now-something" can the "now something, now something else" be highlighted as a pure sequence—indeed as a pure sequence of blind nows, the pure multiplicity of which is the primary understanding of time in the tradition, as well as in Kant. When we say "now," what we are talking about with that "now" is not something just-there, as if I were talking

about the now as if it were like a chair or table. When I say "now," I'll
never find anything in the range of the merely-present that corresponds to what the now itself is. Likewise, in saying "now," I am not
talking about something "inner," like an act of will or a state of mind
or anything at all that occurs in the soul. [402] By the word "now" I
neither name nor speak of anything at all that is just-there. Rather,
with that "now" human existence expresses *itself*, not as something
just-there but itself in its being unto the world, i.e., in the basic form
of this being unto the world: the act of making-present.

Now we must try to bring out this connection between the now and
the (now-)present in order to see:

- how the "I think" comes to an original connection with time;
- how the basic function of the "I think" (namely, the "I combine") is
  thereby unveiled in its primary time-character;
- and how the temporality of the basic structure of the statement—
  speaking of something as something—is demonstrated in its ur-
  temporal meaning.[148]

*   *   *

What gets expressed in the now is the present [*Gegenwart*]. The present,
which is a matter of letting-something-encounter-us, is not itself present
[*anwesend*], it is not something just-there. The present is only a making-
present [*Gegenwart ist nur gegenwärtig*], making-present as a comportment. Making-present primarily expresses the being of human existence as being-unto-the-world. This being unto the world is not a mode
of being to which there can be *added* the property of making-present;
rather, the present [*Gegenwart*] is primarily the condition of the possibility of a being-familiar-with-the-world [*eines Seins bei der Welt*]. Making-
present is (primarily) a factical present*ing* [*Gegenwart*], which, in this
active and transitive sense, is a concept that pertains to the very structure of human existence and in fact expresses the meaning of the being
[of human existence] and primarily of its being in the world. We designate the ever-temporal [*jeweilige*], authentic ontological possibility of
factical human existence (however that possibility be chosen and determined) as *Existenz*. All the structures and interpretations of the being of
human existence take their orientation from *Existenz*. Likewise, all the
specific structural concepts that express the being of human existence

148. [Here (Moser, p. 803) Heidegger ends his lecture of Thursday, 25 February
1926, to be followed by his final lecture, that of Friday, 26 February, which opened
with a 35-word introduction that is omitted in GA 21. Soon after this date, Heidegger left Marburg for his cabin in Todtnauberg to finish the final draft of *Sein
und Zeit*.]

we call "existentials." Making-present, as a structural concept of human existence, is an existential.

In ordinary usage the word *Gegenwart* has many meanings. First and foremost it means: the present-now, i.e., the present moment, "now"; but also the [403] current epoch, "today." This meaning can then be formalized so as to mean "the pure now," as in the theoretical explanations of time in Hegel and others. In that case, however, "the present" means not just "now" or "today" in a concrete sense, but rather, presence [*Anwesenheit*]. When we say, "He didn't want to speak in the *Gegenwart* of others," the phrase "in the *Gegenwart*" means the same as "in the *Anwesenheit* of others."

But "in the presence of" means something more here. It does not simply mean: "When so-and-so was simply *there* with some other people, this or that happened." To better understand the meaning of *Gegenwart*, consider how the word is used in this example: "In my *Gegenwart* [usually: 'in my presence'] she didn't dare say that." It doesn't mean, "When I was just there like the furniture and someone else was just there like a wallflower . . ." No, clearly it means, "in my being present to her and in her being present to me"—i.e., in our reciprocal making-the-other-present, in our co-sharing the same world. But the phrase "in my *Gegenwart*" likewise has the sense of "in my *Anwesenheit*," i.e., in my shared existence-with-someone in the same place and at the same spot. These various meanings of *Gegenwart*—i.e., the various phenomena the word designates—are to be interpreted and conceptually understood exclusively as a concept pertaining to the structure of human existence: its primary orientation to *Gegenwart* in the sense of making-present.

But that entails the following: If *Gegenwart* constitutes a mode of time and, as a mode of time, determines the meaning of the being of human existence (insofar as human existence is being at home with the world), then time itself must be understood as the basic existential of human existence. In that case, time is no longer the name for the pure multiplicity of the now-sequence; rather, this multiplicity of the now-sequence is a derivative phenomenon, and it must be possible to derive it from time as the basic existential, although the reverse is not possible. This proof of the derivation of time as a [404] multiplicity of nows from original time as the ontological structure of human existence must likewise let us justify the legitimacy of the basic structure of time as an existential.

With regard to the being-structure of being in the world or being unto the world, making-present is the meaning of the being of human existence. The traditional conception and determination of time as now-time is an interpretation of time drawn from making-present without the latter being understood as an existential. What is authentic and progressive in Kant's interpretation consists in the fact that it does not simply attribute time to the subject as the subject's way of intuiting, but in addition makes this phenomenon—the act of making-present—the basis for Kant's interpretation of knowledge. With regard to "making-present" as an existential, we can explain the positive and the detrimental aspects of Kant's problematic, as well as its limits.

Let us not forget: The primary emphasis on present*ing* as a mode of time, still derives from a dependence on the notion of time as the time of nows. But what we need to show is that present*ing is* emphatically *not* the primary mode of time. There are two senses in which the traditional notion of time—i.e., understood in terms of the now—is not original:

- It does not touch at all on the sense of time as an existential.
- Moreover, the concept of time as now-time has its source in the foundational existential mode of time as making-present.

Taking our orientation from time as present*ing* and from making-present as the very being of human existence *qua* being unto its world, we will now try to discuss briefly the question we formulated earlier about the relation between time as original pure self-affection and the "I think" as the spontaneity of apperception.

In formulating the question, we emphasized that time *is* letting-ourselves-be-encountered by something present. Time is the pre-viewing that we characterized, and the pre-viewing is self-affection. The "I think" is letting something be co-present with the "I think," i.e., with the I itself understood as the constant "for-which" that something present can be present unto. [405] Both of these—time and the "I think"—are unthematic, both are antecedent (*a priori*), both are modes of being of the subject. The question remains: Is time a mode of the "I think"? Or is the "I think" a mode of time? Or are both of them modes of a still more original connection?

The question is not advanced by postulating that the "I think" runs its course "within time," because then we could ask: If the "I think" is itself "*in* time," how is it supposed to "bring forth" time? (Cf. *Über eine Entdeckung*, vol. 8, p. 221.)[149] How can something that is "in time" "bring forth" time? In addition to being within time, is the self, *as* this

---

149. [*Über eine Entdeckung, nach der alle neue Kritik der reinen Vernunft durch eine ältere entbehrlich gemacht werden soll,* in Kant, *Akademie-Ausgabe*, vol. 8, p. 221. Heidegger is referring to Kant's statement that our faculty of knowledge "bringt sie aus sich selbst *a priori* zu Stande," where *sie* refers both to the form of things in space and time and to the synthetic unity of the manifold in concepts. The English translators render this as "it brings them out of itself *a priori*"; see "On a Discovery According to which Any New Critique of Pure Reason Has Been Made Superfluous by an Earlier One," in *The Kant-Eberhard Controversy*, ed. and trans. Henry E. Allison (Baltimore and London: Johns Hopkins University Press, 1973), p. 135.]

temporal "I think," also supposed to affect itself and thereby bring forth time? But on the other hand, for Kant it is equally impossible to reduce the "I think" to time. So within the self as such, there remains this aporia of the connection (or lack thereof) between the a-temporal spontaneity of the "I think" and the spontaneity of self-affection, which is time itself.

The difficulty is resolved with one blow once we take seriously time as making-present. The "I think" is not *in* time (Kant is completely right to reject that) but *is* time itself, or more exactly, one mode of time—that of pure making-present. As pure making-present, human existence itself is the "for-which" of whatever it might happen to encounter; and making-present is human existence's way of letting-something-encounter-it. In making-present (taken in its proper sense), human existence lets whatever it encounters come toward human existence in such a way that neither the I becomes an object [*Objekt*] nor does time (i.e., present*ing*, taken as an existential) become an object [*Gegenstand*]. Here again Kant is entirely in the right, phenomenally speaking, when he underlines the non-objectivity [*Nichtobjektivität und Nichtgegenständlichkeit*] of the "I think" and of time. When turned into a positive statement, this is understandable only if time itself is pure making-present, pure letting-something-encounter. In making-present, human existence places itself, as it were, purely into presence-unto-whatever, and it is purely and totally absorbed by the presence-of [*Anwesenheit*] and its present*ing*-of [*Gegenwart*]. [406] So much is this the case, that time goes unseen in existence's absorption in time and in present*ing*. Rather, existence simply "sets free" whatever can encounter it in an act of present*ing* and become intelligible as something present [*Anwesendes*] in the present*ing*.

The "I think" as the "for which" of the letting-encounter is time itself *qua* pure present*ing*. Certainly this interpretation essentially goes beyond Kant (indeed, back behind him), but not so radically as to abandon the path of the phenomenal contexts that Kant himself had in mind. This claim is documented by a characterization that Kant, in one passage, gives of the I: "For this constant and enduring I (of pure apperception) constitutes the correlate of all our presentations" (A 123). But this determination of the I is almost a word-for-word definition of time, which, according to Kant, absolutely stands and persists and is the correlate of all appearances in general. When Kant really tries to investigate the phenomena, he brings time and the "I think" as close together as possible, so much so that the definitions of both phenomena are, as it were, co-extensive. Nonetheless, on the basis of a dogma that guides him, he wrenches time and the "I think" apart and keeps them absolutely separate from each other, so much so that he is *a priori* certain that they simply cannot be brought together at all.

If we understand the "I think" as a mode of pure making-present, and if we understand making-present as the very way-of-being of human existence *qua* being-in-the-world, then Kant's point of departure is fundamentally modified—in other words, the dogmatic starting-point of the Cartesian position is avoided from the very start. It is not the case that an "I think" is first given as the purest *a priori,* and then some "time" is added as the mediating point for the [I think] to come out to a world. Rather, the very being of the subject *qua* human existence is being-in-the-world, and human existence's being-in-the-world is possible only because the basic structure of its being is time itself, specifically here in the mode of making-present. [407]

Further: The "I think" (i.e., the pure formal combining of the pure understanding) is, for its part, simply a free and emptied-out mode of making-something-present—but not that the "I think" is the primary element that must first relate itself to time, and in this relating constitute a being unto the world.

The pure, unconstrained making-present—the "I combine"—is the autonomous but derivative [*abkünftige*] mode of an original making-present on the part of factical existence itself. As pure and free making-present, it is accordingly a mode of time—or more precisely, a mode of human existence's temporality—wherein time empties itself into the pure, free making-present of whatever-there-is. But insofar as present*ing* is still a mode of time, it is time in the full sense. The genesis of pure and unconstrained making-present from out of everyday being unto the world is what we have characterized as absorption in the world. It is nothing but the structure of the modification of the being of human existence in which human existence forms within itself the ontological mode of free, theoretical observation which, for its part, can be formalized into a mere "intending-something" in an "I-relate-to." The ontological transition *from* the *pre*-theoretical relation to the world, *to* a pure [theoretical] making-present, is itself a mode of temporality—and it would be absolutely impossible if human existence were not itself time.

By contrast, Kant attempts to go from the empty "I combine" to what we comprehend, as follows: As being-in-the-world, we have opened up the world and are with entities that encounter us in the environment and that we know as nature. This "we know nature" is the phenomenal starting point of the problematic of the *Critique of Pure Reason,* and Kant's problem is the possibility of this "we know nature" (even though he precisely overlooks the problem of the inter-subjectivity of the "we know nature"). The highest point from which Kant will seek to understand this possibility is the "I think"; but this highest point is questionable in the highest degree. It becomes possible as his starting-point only because of the fact that Kant orients himself dogmatically in terms of Descartes, and at the same time in terms of the idea of [408] of a certain preeminence of formal logic—of the "I combine" and its possible modes.

Certainly, Kant does not simply deduce the "we know nature" from the empty "I combine"; rather, here he must slip in, as it were, the *a priori* of time as an essential factor. Time (understood as the autonomous multiplicity of a now-sequence) has to function as that which is given *a priori*. And so, even though Kant attributes time to the subject, time in a certain sense comes to the subject enigmatically from outside. It is there as something already given, a blind *factum* pre-given for the spontaneity of thinking, which itself stands outside time. Let us prescind from Kant's dogmatic motivations: the major thing that prevented him from seeing the time-character of the "I think" is found in his inadequate interpretation of time itself. Although he makes use of the more original structures of the now in his schematism, in his theory Kant always takes the now and the now-sequence in the sense of the traditional conception of time. "In his theory" means: in the inadequately clarified theoretical orientation of the connection between time as intuition and the spontaneity of the "I think" in the conception of the ontological wholeness of the self.

Kant could interpret the knowledge of nature only in such a way that he discovered time within the very structure of cognition itself. Time is not just the form within which the act of cognition runs its course. No, it belongs to the very act of cognition. But on the other hand, the predominance of the traditional concept of time—time as that within which something runs its course—hinders Kant from seeing the structure of time (which he makes use of in the schematism) in its fundamental significance as the structure of human existence itself. [409]

---

§37. Time as an existential of human existence— temporality and the structure of care. The statement as a making-present

Our construal of Kant's conception and interpretation of time should have made it concretely clear that time functions in the being of human existence (and, in the present case, first of all in knowledge) *structurally* and not *marginally*. With that, however, we have also demonstrated the possibility of a different understanding of time, and we have already sketched out its most proximate positive determinations. And taking that as our starting point, we are finally in a position to answer our initial question—the question about the time-character of any statement concerning "world." We understand "statement" as a comportment of human existence unto the world. It[150] conceals within itself the fundamental question: the question about the ur-temporality of human existence itself as being unto the world.

We have characterized being unto the world as concern [*Besorgen*]; and the essential structure of concern is care [*Sorge*]. We established that care is the being-structure of human existence as such, and in turn we explained this structure of care as being-already-ahead-of-oneself-as-being-already-familiar-with-the-world [*Sich-selbst-vorweg-schon-sein-bei-der-Welt*]. We have previously discussed the character of "ahead" and of "already" with regard to their possible time-sense; the result was simply negative. These time-features cannot mean anything like being-in-time—a determinate form of the mere thereness of something that is merely-there: (1) because they themselves are features of a structure that has nothing to do with the mere-thereness that characterizes the world and nature; and in addition (2) because this structure is the ontological structure of that entity the meaning of whose being has absolutely nothing to do with something merely-present. And yet, on the other hand, the features of human existence that are in question here—the "ahead" and the "already"—obviously do have time-features.

In what sense is the being-structure of human existence—care—characterized by time? It is not the case that these structures—over and above what they are in themselves—are "*also*" in time and in some kind of relation to time. Rather, care is determined "by" time in such a way that care itself *is* time. Care is the very facticity of time. [410]

Temporality is the ground of the possibility of these structures of care itself. The "ahead-of-itself" is a mode of time, but not in the sense of mere presence within time. Thus time is not the kind of being that befits some entity that is merely-present.[151] It simply "is" not; its being is not a determinate kind of being, it is not the being of some entity. Rather, it is the condition of possibility of the fact that there is being (not entities). Time does not have the kind of being of any other thing; rather, time [constantly] unfolds [*zeitigt*].[152] And this unfolding constitutes the temporality of time. The "ahead-of-itself" is a mode in which time unfolds.

When we make statements such as "Time *is* that or that" and "Time *is* temporal," the word "is" has the sense of a specifically phenomenological-categorial positing which, insofar as it states anything, must

150. [The word "it" (*sie*) could refer to any of three elements of the previous sentence—namely, "the fundamental question about the time-character," or any "statement about 'world'," or "world" itself. Moser (p. 812.23-24) shows that "it" refers to "a comportment of human existence toward the world."]

151. [Moser, p. 813.26-28.]

152. [For Heidegger the verb *zeitigen* connotes unfolding from out of itself (φύσις).]

have the structure of a statement about the world. But its primary sense *qua* statement is not a matter of pointing out something that is merely-present, but rather, is a matter of letting human existence be understood. All statements about the being of human existence, all propositions about time, all propositions within the problematic of the essence of ur-temporality have, as expressed propositions, the character of indication. But they indicate only human existence, even though, as expressed propositions, they nonetheless first refer to something merely-present.[153] They indicate human existence and the structures of human existence and of time. They indicate the possible understanding of the structure of human existence, and, to the degree that it is available in such understanding, the possible conceptualizability of that structure. (Insofar as these propositions are indicative of a ἑρμηνεύειν, they have the character of hermeneutic indication.) [411] By their very meaning, statements about time are never statements about the world; but first and foremost, we do operate within the orientation and mind-set [*Verstehenstendenz*] of statements about the world. And to that extent, when statements deal with time, time is rendered inaccessible in its proper temporality. What gets formed is a concept of time by which temporality is not so much determined or even just indicated, but rather is covered-over, so much so that even the possibility of understanding time differently is disavowed. The abiding example of this orientation in interpreting time is the first philosophical interpretation of time that we have: that of Aristotle.

But the difficulty in apprehending time goes hand-in-hand with the peculiar temporality of time itself: the fact that first and foremost time conceals itself and gets recognized only in and as the non-authentic forms it takes. We look at the world and find that time is that within which all processes run their course. Whenever we try to un-

153. A worldly statement about something present, even when it is performed as a simple naming, can refer directly to the said. On the other hand, a statement about human existence as well as every statement about being (every statement about the categorial), in order to be intelligible, requires an overhaul and reorganization of the understanding in terms of what the statement is pointing out. In the aforementioned cases, what is being pointed out is, by its very essence, never something present.

The difference between a statement about the categorial and a statement about things that are present in the world remained hidden for the Greeks—for Plato as well as Aristotle—and *all* statements were understood as statements directly about the world. For that reason it has happened that being itself, insofar as it came into view, was conceived of as an entity. The hiddenness of this difference [between the two kinds of statement] and the hiddenness of the corresponding ways of talking about and interpreting [the two kinds of statements] is one of the roots of the split between Aristotelian metaphysics as a pure formal ontology and as a theology of νοῦς.

derstand time more originally, it is time conceived in this way—"world-time"—that guides all further explanations. In this way, we either do not see time at all or we see time only as a mode of what is just out-there, namely, the world or nature.

Because this understanding of time is close at hand and dominant, from the very beginning all the essential modes of time—present, past, future—get their temporal meanings fixed in terms of this understand-ing of time. As a result, these modes, in their everyday meaning, are not only unusable but also misleading. Thus "future" means: the time that is coming, the nows that are not yet here on hand but that are on their way. Let us consider those [future] nows in whose still-coming time something "is." When it comes to an entity that "is" at that time which is still to come, we say, "It *will* be." But this future—a now that is not yet present—is simply not the authentic future in terms of which time is properly temporal, any more than the isolated and delimited now that *is* present here is the real present*ing* in the sense of making-present, as we explicated it above. [In the dominant understanding,] the now is the present moment, and [412] from Aristotle to Hegel the now was understood as that which is directly present in a privileged way.

Correspondingly, "future" means: the coming presence [*Anwesen-heit*] of the now, a possible present moment in the sense just indicated. In this view, the now is understood as something within time, conse-quently something that the temporality of time cannot explain. But in fact, the future is *not* a determination of the possible presence of the now. Presence is possible only in and through the making-present of something that is first articulable through a present*ing*. And in the same way, the future, understood as something present-*qua*-coming, is possible only in an expecting [*Gewärtigen*]. Such expecting, under-stood as "letting something come toward oneself," first makes possible something arriving—a possible now that is arriving.[154]

Expecting, like making-present, is a mode of the being of human existence. And every form of expecting understands whatever it (*qua* expectation) relates to as something that possibly can be present. It un-derstands its expecting as the expecting of a [future] making-present of

154. [Moser (p. 816.25–817.6) records Heidegger saying here, and in place of the next paragraph: "Only in expecting is something futural [*Zukünftiges*]—or to be more precise, is the future of the futural—possible. Expecting, like making-pres-ent, is a mode of the being of human existence. All expecting relates itself at the same time to . . . , or more precisely, is understood as an expecting that intends a making-present. Expecting *qua* 'letting something come toward oneself' means letting it come toward *oneself* as a possible making-present of something. To ex-pect something that is coming means to understand the coming something as something that can be present. And so expecting includes an intrinsic relation to a possible making-something-present."]

something. Expecting is letting something come toward *oneself* as a possible making-present. All expecting of a [future] making-present is also
the expectation (in addition, but just as originally) of some*thing.*

Expecting, as the expecting of a making-present, is referred (the way
that making-present is) to the life-world of one's practical concerns.[155]
From the start, human existence is held in an encountering concern for
what can be produced, used, and procured—in the broadest sense, for
what it can be concerned with. But concern, as absorption in the world
of one's concerns, is always and essentially (as we showed earlier) a
shared-concern of human existence itself. In each of its concerns,
human existence itself, as regards its ability, is not the *Besorgte* but the
Gesorgte—i.e., it is not some "object" of the concern, but rather, the one
concerned. Human existence's expecting comes from its making-present: its ordering-up, making-available, taking-possession-of, holding-
on-to. And in its expecting, human existence *qua* ability is itself that to
which human existence primarily relates, albeit implicitly. In expecting, human existence is always already in the mode of being unto its
ownmost ability. As being unto this ability [413] of its own self, human
existence is "ahead of itself." And the condition of the possibility of this
being-ahead-of-itself (care),[156] i.e., the fundamental structure of this
very mode of being, is expecting. Care is possible as what it is only insofar as its being is time itself, as an expecting-*qua*-making-present. But
making-present is the ur-temporal meaning of familiarity with the
world. Ahead-of-oneself in familiarity-with [*bei*]—that is expecting-
qua-making-present, a determinate temporality of the time that constitutes the being of human existence.[157]

Since human existence's ability is never something that could be
"just there" like a thing; and since, therefore, it is not a merely-present
thing that can arrive: the word "future" is an inappropriate expression
for the *original* "futurity" of human existence. The command, "Become what you are!"—understood ontically—is possible only if, taken
ontologically, *I am* what I am becoming, i.e., only if the very being of
my ability—namely, my being-ahead-of-myself—has the structure of
expecting.

Expecting is not only expecting a making-present, and it is not only
for such a making-present. Instead, it is for a making-present as *retaining*
something in the sense of a care for retaining, a not-letting-slip-away.
Concern that is factically referred to the world, like losing oneself in the

155. [Moser (p. 817.8–9) records "die vorhandene besorgte Umwelt," whereas
GA 21 (p. 412.22) has "die zuhandene besorgte Umwelt." I follow the latter, and
render *zuhandene* as "practical."]

156. [Moser (p. 817.28) has *der Sorge.*]

157. [The subordinate clause could modify either *Zeitlichkeit* or *Zeit.*]

world of one's concerns, is a constant inability-to-hold-on-to as well as a having-to-let-go-of the worldly things of one's concerns as things that essentially change. In turn, holding-on-to has various modes, such as being deprived of; being unable to hold on to; letting slip away; no longer being concerned with something useful; forgetting; renouncing. These are modes of human existence's being—modes of its being unto its ownmost having-been. And to that having-been there also belong the objects of one's concern, insofar as human existence first and foremost understands itself in terms of them, even as things that have gotten away from it. In these modes of time that belong to making-present and expecting, *qua* retaining, as likewise with the future, we lack a corresponding term. "The past," [414] on the contrary, means a now that is no longer there, the already [gone], the no-longer-present-ness of something that could be there.

The term "ahead" indicates expecting; "familiarity-with" indicates making-present and holding-on-to. But what about the "already" [*das Schon*]? That is an ur-temporal determination that pertains to all of human existence's time and its ontological facticity. The "already" is the indication of the *a priori* of facticity. That means: The structures of human existence—temporality itself—are not at all like an ever-available framework for something that can be merely-present. Rather, in keeping with their most proper sense, these structures are possibilities for human existence to be, and only that.

And every human existence *qua* human has already personally decided, one way or the other, regarding this ability: either authentically, i.e., from out of oneself; or [inauthentically], by renouncing this possibility; or by just not yet being up to such a decision. Human existence is handed over to itself in its having-to-be [*Zu-sein*]. "Handed over"—that means: *already* in, *already* ahead-of-itself, *already* familiar with the world, *never* something just-there but always already a possibility that has been decided one way or the other. *Such* human existence is always already *prior* to what it *de facto* is at any given moment. But prior to every possible "prior" is time itself, which makes it possible that human existence can be the very possibility of its self.

To make a statement—to talk about something as something and thereby to let it be seen as something—that is a determinate possibility of pure making-present. It is letting an entity be present, and therefore is the uncovering of the presence of something that is there. That is the basic function of λόγος as ἀποφαίνεσθαι. The presence of something present, a presence that is discoverable only in a present*ing*, means nothing but the being of entities. Every statement that uncovers—i.e., makes-present—thereby says "is." It makes no difference whether this "is" is expressed verbally or not, or how it is expressed. The "is" does not have the function of a copula, but is the index of the basic function of a statement—namely, its making-present as a pure making-present, a pure letting-be-seen of the presence of entities, or of entities *in* their presence. The expressed statement, insofar as it is true, preserves in itself the [415] uncoveredness of the entity. Preserving uncoveredness means the same as being able to make something present at any time. Accordingly, uncoveredness is a preeminent form of possible present*ing:* it is the present*ing* of the entity we are talking about in its being and in its being-this-way-or-that.

The uncoveredness or truth that is had in a world-related statement bespeaks "present*ing.*"[158] And "being" bespeaks "presence." That is, the meaning of being is grasped from out of present*ing.* Only in such present*ing* is presence possible. Being simply cannot be understood in any other way. Then what is meant by "understanding"? It means: to determine something as something. An entity is understood or grasped in its in-itself-ness when it is understood in its pure being-for-itself. In other words, it is understood in and from human existence's pure present*ing* of its world.[159] Present*ing* is absolutely not subjective or subjectivistic or idealistic in the usual, epistemological meaning of those words. Rather, it is simply being unto the world, wherein the world can show itself in its in-itself-ness in terms of its various levels of approximation and determination.

Statements, insofar as they are statements about what is present, are grounded in making-present. Logic is the most imperfect of all philosophical disciplines, and it can be moved forward only if it reflects on the basic structures of its thematic phenomena, on the primary ontological structures of the logical as a comportment of human existence, and on the temporality of human existence itself. But the unexpressed basis of traditional logic is a specific temporality which is oriented primarily to making-present, which is expressed in an extreme form in the formulation of the Greek concept of knowledge as θεωρία, pure intuiting. All the truth of such a logic is the truth of intuition, where intuition is understood as making-present.

But should more radical temporal possibilities be found in the temporality of human existence, these would necessarily set an essential limit to traditional logic and ontology. Whether philosophical research can be intense enough and firm enough to make this limit a lived fact is a question that concerns the very fate of philosophy.

---

158. [Moser (p. 821.7-10) records the word *mögliche* (possible) before a hyphenated *Gegen-wart:* "But uncoveredness or truth means the same as human existence's possible present*ing* [rendering-present] its world."]

159. [". . . aus der puren Gegenwart des Daseins zu seiner Welt" (GA 21, p. 415.12-13).]

Editor's Afterword

Martin Heidegger held his four-hour-per-week lecture course on logic in the Winter Semester of 1925–26 in Marburg am Lahn. The original plan (cf. §5) was changed as the course was worked out. In contrast to traditional logic, Heidegger poses a philosophizing logic that inquires into λόγος: a logic of truth.

In the prologue he investigates the situation of present-day logic, using as an example *the* logic that comes closest to a philosophizing logic, Husserl's *Logical Investigations*. Heidegger explains Husserl's struggle against psychologism and sets forth the dimension in which that struggle unfolds.

In part I, Heidegger goes back to Aristotle's interpretation of truth. At the center of that stands the interpretation of Metaphysics Θ 10, which has presented interpreters with so many difficulties.

Part II develops the question of truth within the horizon of the analysis of *Dasein*, at the center of which lies the theme of time. An interpretation of the *Critique of Pure Reason* reveals the meaning that the problematic of time had for Kant. Here we have the core of Heidegger's later text, *Kant and the Problem of Metaphysics,* and here the individual analyses are worked out in more detailed fashion than they are in that later work.

The present edition is based on Heidegger's original manuscript, on Fritz Heidegger's typed copy of that, and on Simon Moser's shorthand transcript of the lectures. Because in those days Heidegger frequently departed from his original notes during the lectures, the comments recorded in Moser's transcript were able to be taken into account for purposes of clarification. Throughout the semester Heidegger regularly went over Moser's transcript. We find marginal notes in the transcript, as well as page-references to the transcript in Heidegger's original manuscript.

Up to §12, the section titles come from Heidegger.

For collaboration on this text I must thank Dr. Hüni, Dr. Schultze, as well as my wife [Marly Biemel]. She helped me check and proof a large part of the text and also undertook one final review of the finished text. Dr. Hüni and Dr. Schultze, as well as she, also helped in reading the page proofs.

Aachen, June 1975
Walter Biemel

Glossaries

German-English

Abbild	image; image-as-copy
abbilden	to depict; portray [see *darstellen*]
Abbildung	image; image-as-copy
das Abgebildete	what gets reproduced / copied
Abgezälte	something that is counted up
Abschreibung	a copy
abzählen	to count up
Anblick; Aussehen	visible aspect of; the looks of
angewiesen	assigned
anschaubar	intuitable
anschaulich	intuitional
Anschauung	intuition; act of intuition
anwesend	present [adj.]; something present [n.]
Anwesenheit	presence; being-present
Anzahl	the number-of-an-amount
aufdecken	uncover
Auffassung	conception; notion
aufweisen	to prove; [occasionally] to show as
aufzeigen	to indicate (apophantically)
Aussage	statement
Aussehen; Anblick	visible aspect of; the looks of
Ausser einander	outside-each-other
Bedeutung	meaning; signification
begegnen	encounter; meet
begegnenlassen	let [something] encounter / meet [us]
begreifen	to grasp; apprehend; understand
Begriff	concept; notion

347

bereitliegen	already be operative
Besorgen	concern-about
besorgend	concernful; concerned
bestimmen	determine; specify; define
bestimmt	determinate; specific
Bestimmung	determination; definition
Bild	image
darstellen	portray, depict [see *abbilden*]
Darstellung	portrayal; depiction
Dasein	human existence; [occasionally just] existence
eigenst	ownmost; one's very own; most proper
Einwirkung	influence; effect
entdecken	uncover; un-cover
entscheidend	crucial; decisive; [occasionally] essential
erfassen; ergreifen	grasp; apprehend; comprehend
erzeugen	to produce
Erzeugung	production
es gehen um	to be concerned about
etwa wie	[often not translated]
fassen	grasp; apprehend; comprehend
fundamental	basic; fundamental
Fürsorge	concern-for
Gegenwart	presenting; [occasionally] making-present [see *Präsenz*]; the present moment; the now-present; now-presence—all according to the context
gegenwärtigen	to render present; make present
gewärtigen	to expect
Gewärtigen	(the act of) expecting
Gewesenheit	alreadiness; having-been
greifen	to grasp; apprehend; comprehend
Handlung	action; act; operation
heben	to bring into relief; to highlight
Hebung	the highlighting of
Hinblick	pre-view of
das Worauf des Hinblicks	what is pre-viewed of/in a pre-view
Hinblicknahme	taking or having a pre-view of

immer schon	always already (in the sense of *a priori*)
je	currently; in each case; at each moment; [occasionally] always
Jetzt-Dieses	now-this; now this
Jetztfolge	now-sequence; sequence of nows
Man	one; people
mannigfaltig	multiple; manifold [adj.]
Mannigfaltige	multitude; manifold [n.]
Manningfaltigkeit	multiplicity; manifoldness
Mensch	human beings; [occasionally] human being; people
Nacheinander	one-after-another
Präsenz	the making / rendering present of something [see *Gegenwart*]
sachhaltig	regarding content
sachlich	relevant; pertinent; substantive; issue-oriented; objective
sachmässig	issue-oriented
Scheidung	separation
Schemabild	schema-image
Seiendes	a being; beings; entity [or when the word has no specific ontological connotation] things
Sein	being
Sein-bei	familiarity with; being at home with / in; being-with
Seinkönnen	ability-to; ability; know-how
Sein zur Welt	being unto the world
selbstverständlich	obvious; self-explanatory; goes without saying
Sinn geben	to make sense of
Solong [n.]	a "while"
Sorge	care
Soviel [n.]	amount; so-much
temporal	ur-temporal
Temporalität	ur-temporality
Umwelt	lived world; life-world
nächste Umwelt	firsthand lived world
Unterschied	difference; distinction; separation

ursprünglich	original; basic; fundamental; originary
verbinden	to combine
verdecken	to cover-over
Verhaltung	comportment
Versinnlichung	sensibilization
vorgängig	prior; antecedent
vorhanden	present; present-out-there; just-there; merely there; on hand
Vorhandenheit	thereness; out-there-ness; presence
vorstellen	to present something
Vorstellung	[mostly] presentation; [occasionally] representation
Wiedergabe	a copy
Wirklichkeit	reality; [sometimes] actuality
Worauf des Hinblicks	what is pre-viewed in a pre-view
Zahl	number
zählen	to count; to number; to number-an-amount
Zählen	numbering; numbering-of-an-amount
zukommen	come toward [us]
zukommend	arriving; coming toward us
Zukunft	future
zukünftig	futural
zunächst und zumeist	first and foremost
Zusammenhang	connection; context; [occasionally] matrix; network

English–German

ability-to; ability	*Seinkönnen*
act	*Handlung*
action	*Handlung*
actual	*wirklich*
alreadiness	*Gewesenheit*
already be operative	*bereitliegen*
always	*immer;* [occasionally] *je*
always already	*immer schon* (in the sense of *a priori*)
amount [n.]	*Soviel*
antecedent	*vorgängig*
apprehend	*greifen; begreifen; fassen; erfassen*
a priori	*immer schon; a priori*
arrive	*zukommen*

assigned	*angewiesen*
(visible) aspect of	*Aussehen; Anblick*
basic	*fundamental;* [occasionally]
	ursprünglich
be concerned about	*es gehen um*
being	*Sein*
a / the being	*das Seiende*
being at home with	*Sein bei*
being familiar with	*Sein bei*
beings	*das Seiende*
being unto the world	*Sein zur Welt*
bring into relief	*heben*
care	*Sorge*
care about [v.]	*besorgen*
care about [n.]	*Besorgen*
combine	*verbinden*
come toward [us]	*zukommen*
comportment	*Verhaltung*
comprehend	*erfassen; fassen; begreifen; greifen*
concept	*Begriff*
conception	*Auffassung*
concern about something	*Besorgen*
concerned; concernful	*besorgend*
concern for someone	*Fürsorge*
connection	*Zusammenhang*
context	*Zusammenhang*
copy [n.]	*Wiedergabe; Abschreibung*
copy-as-image	*Bild*
count up	*abzählen*
cover-over	*verdecken*
crucial	*entscheidend*
current; currently	*je*
decisive	*entscheidend*
define	*bestimmen*
definition	*Bestimmung*
depict	*darstellen*
depiction	*Darstellung*
determinate	*bestimmt*
determination	*Bestimmung*
determine	*bestimmen*
determined	*bestimmt*
difference	*Unterschied*

effect [n.]	*Einwirkung* [see "influence (n.)"]
effect [v.]	*einwirken*
encounter	*begegnen*
enumerate	*zählen*
equally original	*gleichurspünglich*
existence	*Dasein*
expecting	*Gewärtigen*
familiarity with	*Sein bei*
first and foremost	*zunächst und zumeist*
firsthand lived world	*nächste Umwelt*
fundamental	*fundamental; urspünglich*
futural	*zukünftig*
future	*Zukunft*
goes without saying	*selbstverständlich*
grasp	*griefen; fassen; begreifen; erfassen*
having a pre-view of	*Hinblicknahme*
highlight [v.]	*heben*
highlighting [n.]	*Hebung*
human beings	*Mensch*
human existence	*Dasein*
image	*Bild; Abgebildetes*
image-as-copy	*Abbild; Abbildung*
indicate (apophantically)	*aufzeigen*
in each case	*je*
influence [n.]	*Einwirkung* [see "effect (n.)"]
intuitable	*anschaubar;* [occasionally] *anschaulich*
intuition	*Anschauung*
intuitional	*anschaulich*
issue-oriented	*sachlich; sachmässig*
just there	*vorhanden*
know-how	*Seinkönnen*
let [something] encounter / meet [us]	*begegnenlassen*
lived world	*Umwelt*
looks of	*Aussehen; Anblick*
make sense of	*Sinn geben*
manifold [adj.]	*mannigfaltig*
manifold [n.]	*das Mannigfaltige*
manifoldness	*Manningfaltigkeit*
matrix	*Zusammenhang*

meaning	*Bedeutung*
meet	*begegnen*
most proper	*eigenst*
multiple	*mannigfaltig*
multipleness	*Manningfaltigkeit*
multiplicity	*das Mannigfaltige*
next-to-each-other	*Nebeneinander*
notion	*Begriff; Auffassung*
now	*Gegenwart*
now-presence	*Gegenwart*
now-sequence	*Jetztfolge*
now-this; now this	*Jetzt-Dieses*
number [n.]	*Zahl*
number [v.]	*zählen*
number-of-an-amount	*Anzahl*
objective	[occasionally] *sachlich*
obvious	*selbstverständlich*
one	*Man*
one-after-another	*Nacheinander*
one's very own	*eigenst*
operation	*Handlung*
original	*ursprünglich*
originary	*ursprünglich*
outside-each-other	*Ausser einander*
out-there	*vorhanden*
out-there-ness	*Vorhandenheit*
ownmost	*eigenst*
people	*Man; Mensch*
pertinent	*sachlich*
portray	*darstellen*
portrayal	*Darstellung*
presence	*Vorhandenheit*
presence; being-present	*Anwesenheit*
presence-now	*Gegenwart*
present	*vorhanden; anwesend*—according to the context
presentation	*Vorstellung*
the presenting of something	*Gegenwart; Präsenz*
the present now	*Gegenwart*
to present something	*gegenwärtigen; vorstellen*
present there	*vorhanden*
pre-view of	*Hinblick*
the pre-viewed of a pre-view	*Worauf des Hinblicks*

primordial	*urspünglich*
prior	*vorgängig*
to produce	*erzeugen*
production	*Erzeugung*
prove	*aufweisen*
reality	*Wirklichkeit*
regarding content	*sachhaltig*
relevant	*sachlich*
to render present	*gegenwärtigen*
representation	*Vorstellung*
schema-image	*Schemabild*
self-explanatory	*selbstverständlich*
sensibilization	*Versinnlichung*
separation	*Scheidung*
sequence of nows	*Jetztfolge*
show as	*aufweisen*
signification	*Bedeutung*
so-much [n.]	*Soviel*
specific	*bestimmt*
specify	*spezifizieren; bestimmen*
statement	*Aussage*
taking a pre-view of	*Hinblicknahme*
temporality	*Zeitlichkeit*
thereness	*Vorhandenheit*
thing	*Ding;* [or when the word has no specific ontological connotation] *Seiendes*
uncover	*aufdecken; entdecken*
understand	*verstehen; begreifen; erfassen; greifen; fassen*
ur-temporal	*temporal*
ur-temporality	*Temporalität*
visible aspect of	*Aussehen; Anblick*
what gets reproduced / copied	*das Abgebildete*
what is present	*das Vorhandene; Anwesende*—according to the context
what is there	*Vorhanden*
a "while" [n.]	*Solong*

Abbreviations

Akademie-Ausgabe	Immanuel Kant, *Kants gesammelte Schriften,* 29 vols. (Preüßische Akademie der Wissenschaften, 1902–1911; repr. 1968, Berlin and Leipzig: Walter de Gruyter)
CPR	Immanuel Kant, *Critique of Pure Reason,* tr. and ed. Paul Guyer and Alan W. Wood (Cambridge and New York: Cambridge University Press, 1998)
CW	John Stuart Mill, *Collected Writings,* 33 vols., ed. John M. Robson (Toronto: University of Toronto Press / London: Routledge & Kegan Paul, 1981–1991)
EDI	Henri Bergson, *Essai sur les données immédiates de la conscience* (Paris: Félix Alcan, 1889) *Time and Free Will: An Essay on the Immediate Data of Consciousness,* trans. F. L. Pogson (London: George Allen & Unwin, 1910; repr. New York: Humanities, 1950)
GA	Martin Heidegger, *Gesamtausgabe,* 102 vols., ed. Friedrich-Wilhelm von Herrmann (Frankfurt am Main: Vittorio Klostermann, 1975–)
GM	Immanuel Kant, *Grundlegung zur Metaphysik der Sitten,* ed. Paul Menzer (*Akademie-Ausgabe,* vol. 4) *Groundwork for the Metaphysics of Morals,* ed. and trans. Mary Gregor (Cambridge: Cambridge University Press, 1997)
HCT	Martin Heidegger, *History of the Concept of Time: Prolegomena,* trans. Theodore Kisiel (Bloomington: Indiana University Press, 1985)
Ideen	Edmund Husserl, *Ideen zu einer reinen Phänomenologie und phänomenologischen Philosophie, I. Buch: Allgemeine Einführung in die reine Phänomenologie* (Halle: Max Niemeyer, 1913) *Ideas Pertaining to a Pure Phenomenology and to a Phenomenological Philosophy. First Book: General Introduction to a Pure Phenomenology,* trans. Fred Kersten (The Hague: Martinus Nijhoff, 1982)

LU   Edmund Husserl, *Logische Untersuchungen. Erster Theil: Prolegomena zur reinen Logik* and *Zweiter Theil: Untersuchungen zur Phänomenologie und Theorie der Erkenntnis* (Halle: Max Niemeyer, 1900–1901)
          Logical Investigations, 2 vols., trans. J. N. Findlay (London: Routledge & Kegan Paul / New York: Humanities Press, 1970)

SE   *Sextus Empiricus*, 4 vols., trans. R. G. Bury (London: William Heinemann / Cambridge, Mass.: Harvard University Press, 1933–1949)

SZ   Martin Heidegger, *Sein und Zeit* (1927) (GA 2), ed. Friedrich-Wilhelm von Herrmann (Frankfurt am Main: Vittorio Klostermann, 1977)
          Being and Time, trans. John Macquarrie and Edward Robinson (Oxford: Basil Blackwell, 1962)